P9-BYO-046

CHILD ABUSE AND DOMESTIC VIOLENCE

ISSN 1935-1216

CHILD ABUSE AND DOMESTIC VIOLENCE

Stephen Meyer

INFORMATION PLUS® REFERENCE SERIES
Formerly Published by Information Plus, Wylie, Texas

GALE
CENGAGE Learning·

Farmington Hills, Mich • San Francisco • New York • Waterville, Maine
Meriden, Conn • Mason, Ohio • Chicago

Child Abuse and Domestic Violence

Stephen Meyer

Kepos Media, Inc.: Steven Long and Janice Jorgensen, Series Editors

Project Editor: Laura Avery

Rights Acquisition and Management:
Ashley M. Maynard, Carissa Poweleit

Composition: Evi Abou-El-Seoud,
Mary Beth Trimper

Manufacturing: Rita Wimberley

TABLE OF CONTENTS

PREFACE

Child Abuse and Domestic Violence is part of the *Information Plus Reference Series*. The purpose of each volume of the series is to present the latest facts on a topic of pressing concern in modern American life. These topics include the most controversial and studied social issues of the 21st century: abortion, capital punishment, care for the elderly, crime, energy, the environment, health care, immigration, national security, social welfare, women, youth, and many more. Although this series is written especially for high school and undergraduate students, it is an excellent resource for anyone in need of factual information on current affairs.

By presenting the facts, it is the intention of Gale, Cengage Learning, to provide its readers with everything they need to reach an informed opinion on current issues. To that end, there is a particular emphasis in this series on the presentation of scientific studies, surveys, and statistics. These data are generally presented in the form of tables, charts, and other graphics placed within the text of each book. Every graphic is directly referred to and carefully explained in the text. The source of each graphic is presented within the graphic itself. The data used in these graphics are drawn from the most reputable and reliable sources, such as from the various branches of the U.S. government and from private organizations and associations. Every effort was made to secure the most recent information available. Readers should bear in mind that many major studies take years to conduct and that additional years often pass before the data from these studies are made available to the public. Therefore, in many cases the most recent information available in 2017 is dated from 2014 or 2015. Older statistics are sometimes presented as well, if they are landmark studies or of particular interest and no more-recent information exists.

Although statistics are a major focus of the *Information Plus Reference Series*, they are by no means its only content. Each book also presents the widely held positions and important ideas that shape how the book's subject is discussed in the United States. These positions are explained in detail and, where possible, in the words of their proponents. Some of the other material to be found in these books includes historical background, descriptions of major events related to the subject, relevant laws and court cases, and examples of how these issues play out in American life. Some books also feature primary documents or have pro and con debate sections that provide the words and opinions of prominent Americans on both sides of a controversial topic. All material is presented in an evenhanded and unbiased manner; readers will never be encouraged to accept one view of an issue over another.

HOW TO USE THIS BOOK

Every year millions of American adults are subjected to physical, sexual, verbal, or emotional abuse by their intimate partners or family members. Perhaps even more disturbingly, millions of children suffer from such abuse at the hands of the people who are supposed to care for them. Many more have their basic needs neglected. This volume provides the best information available on the prevalence, causes, and devastating consequences of family violence. The challenges that domestic violence and child abuse pose to the legal system are also covered in detail.

Child Abuse and Domestic Violence consists of nine chapters and three appendixes. Each chapter covers an aspect of the problems of child abuse and domestic violence in the United States. For a summary of the information that is covered in each chapter, please see the synopses that are provided in the Table of Contents. Chapters generally begin with an overview of the basic facts and background information on the chapter's topic, then proceed to examine subtopics of particular interest. For example, Chapter 7: Causes, Effects, and Prevention of Domestic Violence begins by outlining several theories exploring the underlying causes of domestic violence. The chapter proceeds to analyze diverse risk factors associated with domestic violence, examining various racial, ethnic, and socioeconomic characteristics of both victims and perpetrators. The physical and psychological impacts of domestic violence receive consideration, with a focus on women and children who have developed post-traumatic stress disorder as a result of their victimizations. Efforts to prevent domestic violence, through educational and public information campaigns and through victim services programs, are discussed. The chapter concludes with an in-depth discussion of the psychological and emotional influences that prevent women from leaving violent relationships, coupled with an overview of several landmark studies examining why some women stay in abusive situations. Readers can find their way through a chapter by looking for the section and subsection headings, which are clearly set off from the text. They can also refer to the book's extensive Index, if they already know what they are looking for.

Statistical Information

The tables and figures featured throughout *Child Abuse and Domestic Violence* will be of particular use to readers in learning about these issues. These tables and figures represent an extensive collection of the most recent and important statistics on child abuse and domestic violence. For example, graphics include statistics on the prevalence of child maltreatment, sexual abuse, and neglect. They also cover the link between caregiver alcohol abuse and child maltreatment, rape by intimate partners and nonintimates, and the relationship between stalkers and their victims. Gale, Cengage Learning, believes that making this information available to readers is the most important way to fulfill the goal of this book: to help readers understand the issues and controversies surrounding child abuse and domestic violence in the United States and reach their own conclusions about them.

Each table or figure has a unique identifier appearing above it, for ease of identification and reference. Titles for the tables and figures explain their purpose. At the end of each table or figure, the original source of the data is provided.

To help readers understand these often complicated statistics, all tables and figures are explained in the text. References in the text direct readers to the relevant statistics. Furthermore, the contents of all tables and figures are fully indexed. Please see the opening section of the Index at the back of this volume for a description of how to find tables and figures within it.

Appendixes

Besides the main body text and images, *Child Abuse and Domestic Violence* has three appendixes. The first is the Important Names and Addresses directory. Here, readers will find contact information for a number of organizations that study child abuse and domestic violence, fight these crimes, or advocate influential positions on these issues. The second appendix is the Resources section, which is provided to assist readers in conducting their own research. In this section, the author and editors of *Child Abuse and Domestic Violence* describe some of the sources that were most useful during the compilation of this book. The final appendix is the Index. It has been greatly expanded from previous editions and should make it even easier to find specific topics in this book.

COMMENTS AND SUGGESTIONS

The editors of the *Information Plus Reference Series* welcome your feedback on *Child Abuse and Domestic Violence*. Please direct all correspondence to:

Editors
Information Plus Reference Series
27500 Drake Rd.
Farmington Hills, MI 48331-3535

CHAPTER 1
DEFINING CHILD ABUSE AND DOMESTIC VIOLENCE

Child abuse and domestic violence are crimes in which the victims suffer harm that is inflicted by people who are personally close to them. There is no one legal definition of either crime. In general, child abuse involves cases in which a child is harmed by a parent, other family member, or caregiver. As is explained in later chapters, child abuse often includes physical violence and sexual abuse, as would be expected, but it also includes psychological abuse and neglect, such as failure to provide for a child's basic needs for food, shelter, medical care, and so forth. Domestic violence is a broad term that refers to violence that is committed by adults against adults with whom they are relationally bound by family ties, by marriage, or by some kind of romantic or sexual involvement. Some definitions of domestic violence focus only on intimate partners, which are current and former spouses, boyfriends, and girlfriends. Domestic violence takes many forms. Although most definitions include physical and sexual assaults, other definitions also consider behaviors that are psychologically abusive, coercive, or threatening in nature. Child abuse and domestic violence are not only crimes but also social and public health problems. Researchers are increasingly focusing on the prevalence of violent environments in the United States and their negative consequences, particularly on children.

CHANGING FAMILY STRUCTURES

Child abuse and domestic violence are linked by the close personal nature of the victim-offender relationship. These problems occur within families and are sometimes collectively called family violence. During the 20th century the notion of what constitutes a family began to change dramatically. Traditionally, a "family" was considered to be a nuclear family, which Merriam-Webster (2016, http://www.merriam-webster.com/dictionary/nuclear%20 family) defines as "the part of a family that includes only the father, mother, and children." However, nuclear families are increasingly giving way to other arrangements in which adults live together and/or engage in romantic and/or sexual relationships without getting married. This social change has led to fundamental changes in the definition of family violence.

In the past domestic violence was known as spousal abuse, or more commonly wife beating, because the vast majority of intimate partners were married to each other. In addition, wives were assumed to be the only victims of spousal violence. Changing social conditions and greater awareness that women sometimes engage in violence against their intimate partners have made the broader term of domestic violence more popular. The growth in nontraditional families means that children increasingly live in households with adults who are not their biological parents. In addition, as women have joined the workforce in larger numbers, children are often looked after by someone other than their mother, including their mother's intimate partners, relatives, and hired caregivers. Thus, society has expanded its definition of child abusers beyond biological parents to other people who are entrusted with child caregiving responsibilities.

The chapters that follow describe studies that have examined the prevalence of child abuse and domestic violence in the United States. Many of the researchers assessed demographic factors, such as household composition, during their analyses to compare prevalence rates between different population subsets. Thus, it is informative to understand how household composition has changed over time.

In *Parenting in America: Outlook, Worries, Aspirations Are Strongly Linked to Financial Situation* (December 17, 2015, http://www.pewsocialtrends.org/files/2015/ 12/2015-12-17_parenting-in-america_FINAL.pdf), Kim Parker, Juliana Menasce Horowitz, and Molly Rohal of the Pew Research Center examine shifts in household compositions between 1960 and 2014. In 1960 nearly three-quarters (73%) of all U.S. children lived in households with two parents from a first marriage; by 2014 the proportion of children living with both parents from a first marriage fell to less than half (46%). Meanwhile, over this span the percentage of children living in single-parent households nearly tripled, from 9% in 1960 to 26% in 2014. In addition, 7% of all U.S. children lived with two unmarried parents in 2014.

As Table 1.1 shows, birth rates among girls between the ages of 15 to 19 years rose from 53 births per 1,000 girls in 1980 to 59.9 per 1,000 girls in 1990. Beginning in the early 1990s, however, the rate of teenage pregnancies fell dramatically in the United States. Figure 1.1 shows the decline in birth rates among adolescent girls between 1991 and 2014, by race and ethnicity. In 1991 there were more than 60 births per 1,000 girls between the ages of

TABLE 1.1

Birth rates for adolescent females, by age, race, and Hispanic origin, selected years 1980–2013

[Live births per 1,000 females in specified age group]

Characteristic	1980	1985	1990	1995	2000	2005	2007	2010	2011	2012	2013
All races											
Ages 10–14	1.1	1.2	1.4	1.3	0.9	0.6	0.6	0.4	0.4	0.4	0.3
Ages 15–17	32.5	31.0	37.5	35.5	26.9	21.1	21.7	17.3	15.4	14.1	12.3
Ages 18–19	82.1	79.6	88.6	87.7	78.1	68.4	71.7	58.2	54.1	51.4	47.1
Ages 15–19	53.0	51.0	59.9	56.0	47.7	39.7	41.5	34.2	31.3	29.4	26.5
White, total											
Ages 10–14	0.6	0.6	0.7	0.8	0.6	0.5	0.5	0.3	0.3	0.3	0.2
Ages 15–17	25.5	24.4	29.5	29.6	23.3	18.8	19.5	15.8	14.1	13.0	11.3
Ages 18–19	73.2	70.4	78.0	80.2	72.3	64.0	67.2	54.8	50.8	48.3	44.7
Ages 15–19	45.4	43.3	50.8	49.5	43.2	36.7	38.4	31.9	29.1	27.4	24.9
White, non-Hispanic											
Ages 10–14	0.4	—	0.5	0.4	0.3	0.2	0.2	0.2	0.2	0.2	0.1
Ages 15–17	22.4	—	23.2	22.0	15.8	11.5	11.9	10.0	9.0	8.4	7.4
Ages 18–19	67.7	—	66.6	66.2	57.5	48.0	50.4	42.5	39.9	37.9	35.0
Ages 15–19	41.2	—	42.5	39.3	32.6	26.0	27.2	23.5	21.7	20.5	18.6
Black, total											
Ages 10–14	4.3	4.5	4.9	4.1	2.3	1.6	1.4	1.0	0.9	0.8	0.7
Ages 15–17	72.5	69.3	82.3	68.5	49.0	34.5	34.6	27.3	24.7	22.0	19.0
Ages 18–19	135.1	132.4	152.9	135.0	118.8	101.1	105.2	84.8	78.8	74.4	67.3
Ages 15–19	97.8	95.4	112.8	94.4	77.4	60.1	62.0	51.1	47.3	44.0	39.1
Black, non-Hispanic											
Ages 10–14	4.6	—	5.0	4.2	2.4	1.6	1.4	1.0	0.9	0.8	0.7
Ages 15–17	77.2	—	84.9	70.4	50.1	34.1	34.6	27.4	24.6	21.9	18.9
Ages 18–19	146.5	—	157.5	139.2	121.9	100.2	105.2	85.6	78.8	74.1	67.0
Ages 15–19	105.1	—	116.2	97.2	79.2	59.4	62.0	51.5	47.3	43.9	39.0
American Indian or Alaska Native											
Ages 10–14	1.9	1.7	1.6	1.6	1.1	0.8	0.7	0.5	0.5	0.5	0.4
Ages 15–17	51.5	47.7	48.5	44.6	34.1	26.3	26.1	20.1	18.2	17.0	15.9
Ages 18–19	129.5	124.1	129.3	122.2	97.1	78.0	86.3	66.1	61.6	60.5	53.3
Ages 15–19	82.2	79.2	81.1	72.9	58.3	46.0	49.3	38.7	36.1	34.9	31.1
Asian or Pacific Islander											
Ages 10–14	0.3	0.4	0.7	0.7	0.3	0.2	0.2	0.1	0.1	0.1	0.1
Ages 15–17	12.0	12.5	16.0	15.6	11.6	7.7	7.4	5.1	4.6	4.1	3.7
Ages 18–19	46.2	40.8	40.2	40.1	32.6	26.4	24.9	18.7	18.1	17.7	16.1
Ages 15–19	26.2	23.8	26.4	25.5	20.5	15.4	14.8	10.9	10.2	9.7	8.7
Hispanic*											
Ages 10–14	1.7	—	2.4	2.6	1.7	1.3	1.2	0.8	0.7	0.6	0.5
Ages 15–17	52.1	—	65.9	68.3	55.5	45.8	44.4	32.3	28.0	25.5	22.0
Ages 18–19	126.9	—	147.7	145.4	132.6	124.4	124.7	90.7	81.5	77.2	70.8
Ages 15–19	82.2	—	100.3	99.3	87.3	76.5	75.3	55.7	49.6	46.3	41.7

— Not available.

aThe 1997 Office of Management and Budget (OMB) Standards for Data on Race and Ethnicity were used to classify persons into one of the following four racial groups: white, black, American Indian or Alaskan Native, or Asian or Pacific Islander. The revised OMB standards issued in 1997 permitted the option of selecting more than one race. Multiple-race data were reported by 19 states in 2005, 27 states in 2007, 38 states and the District of Columbia in 2010, 40 states and the District of Columbia in 2011, 41 states and the District of Columbia in 2012, and 44 states and the District of Columbia in 2013. The multiple-race data for these states were bridged to the single-race categories of the 1977 OMB standards for comparability with other states. Note that data on race and Hispanic origin are collect and reported separately.
bPersons of Hispanic origin may be of any race. Trends for Hispanic women are affected by expansion of the reporting area in which an item on Hispanic origin is included on the birth certificate as well as immigration. These two factors affect numbers of events, composition of the Hispanic population, and maternal and infant health characteristics. The number of states in the reporting area increased from 22 in 1980 to 48 and the District of Columbia (DC) in 1990, and 50 and DC starting in 1993. Rates in 1985 were not calculated for Hispanics, non-Hispanic blacks, and non-Hispanic whites because estimates for these populations were not available.

SOURCE: "Table FAM6. Adolescent Births: Birth Rates by Race and Hispanic Origin and Mother's Age, Selected Years 1980–2013," in *America's Children: Key National Indicators of Well-Being, 2015*, Federal Interagency Forum on Child and Family Statistics, July 2015, http://www.childstats.gov/pdf/ac2015/ac_15.pdf (accessed June 9, 2016)

FIGURE 1.1

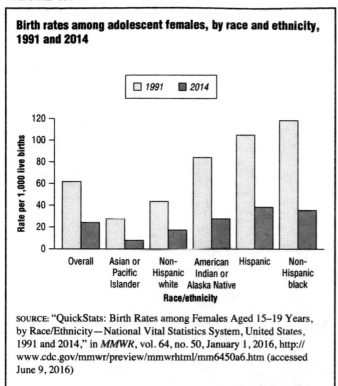

Birth rates among adolescent females, by race and ethnicity, 1991 and 2014

SOURCE: "QuickStats: Birth Rates among Females Aged 15–19 Years, by Race/Ethnicity—National Vital Statistics System, United States, 1991 and 2014," in *MMWR*, vol. 64, no. 50, January 1, 2016, http://www.cdc.gov/mmwr/preview/mmwrhtml/mm6450a6.htm (accessed June 9, 2016)

15 and 19 years overall; by 2014 this figure had been cut by more than half, dropping to approximately 25 births per 1,000 girls aged 15 to 19 years. The most dramatic decrease in teenage births during this span occurred among African American girls, from 120 births per 1,000 girls in 1991 to fewer than 40 births per 1,000 girls in 2014.

According to the U.S. Census Bureau, there were approximately 73.6 million children under the age of 18 years living in the United States in 2015. (See Table 1.2.) Of these, just under 51 million, or 69.2%, lived in households with both parents; 47.7 million children lived with both parents who were married to each other, and 3.3 million children lived with both parents who were not married to each other. Of children under the age of 18 years living in single-parent households in 2015, 17 million lived with their mothers only, and 2.8 million lived with their fathers only. Another 2.9 million American children lived in households where neither parent was present in 2015.

LEGAL ISSUES

As is explained in later chapters, child abuse and domestic violence incidents that are reported to authorities are often handled by criminal courts (courts that deal with offenders who are accused of committing criminal offenses) and/or civil courts (courts that deal with non-criminal matters). The jurisdiction of the courts over child abuse and domestic violence cases is spelled out

in the laws that have been passed by the federal and state governments. This jurisdiction has been slow in coming because historically these offenses were considered to be a private matter to be settled within families. Authorities were reluctant to get involved, except in the most egregious cases. During the late 20th and early 21st centuries victim advocates and other actors for social change successfully increased public awareness about family violence and spurred calls for greater involvement of the legal system.

Child Abuse Legislation

It is important to understand that child abuse laws pertain only to people who abuse or neglect children under their care. The abusers can be parents, stepparents, foster parents, other relatives, or other caretakers as spelled out in the law of each jurisdiction. People who victimize children who are not under their care are not considered to have committed child abuse, but they can be prosecuted for other crimes, such as assault. In addition, child abuse laws cover victims younger than 18 years old. Thus, teenagers within this age group, a population subset that is not typically considered to be "children" in other contexts, are covered.

FEDERAL LEGISLATION. At the federal level Congress has passed laws that provide funding and facilitate operation of the nation's child protection system. This legislation dates back to the passage of the Social Security Act of 1935. The act authorized funding at the federal level for grants to states for "the protection and care of homeless, dependent, and neglected children and children in danger of becoming delinquent." The Social Security Amendment Act of 1961 required each state to make child welfare services available to all children. The law further required states to provide coordination between child welfare services and social services, which served families on welfare. The law also revised the definition of child welfare services to include the prevention and remedy of child abuse. Since then the law has been amended to provide for additional funding for state foster care programs and child abuse prevention and treatment services. The funding programs are administered by the U.S. Department of Health and Human Services, which operates the Children's Bureau, a federal agency created in 1912 that is devoted to issues related to children.

The Children's Bureau notes in *Major Federal Legislation Concerned with Child Protection, Child Welfare, and Adoption* (2016, https://www.childwelfare.gov/pubpdfs/majorfedlegis.pdf) that the programs authorized under the Social Security Act are "the largest federally funded programs that support State and Tribal efforts for child welfare, foster care, and adoption activities." The programs are commonly identified by the sections of the act that authorize them and include the following:

TABLE 1.2

Living arrangements of children under age 18, by sex, age, race and Hispanic origin, marital status of parents, and other characteristics, 2015

[Numbers in thousands]

		Living with both parents		Living with mother only					Living with father only					Living with neither parent
	Total	Married to each other	Not married to each other	Married spouse absent	Widowed	Divorced	Separated	Never married	Married spouse absent	Widowed	Divorced	Separated	Never married	No parent present
All children	**73,623**	**47,670**	**3,297**	**914**	**605**	**4,829**	**2,355**	**8,303**	**139**	**165**	**1,254**	**351**	**842**	**2,900**
Male	37,629	24,320	1,703	503	326	2,466	1,179	4,213	60	71	702	186	442	1,458
Female	35,995	23,350	1,594	411	279	2,363	1,176	4,091	79	93	553	166	400	1,441
Both sexes														
Total	**73,623**	**47,670**	**3,297**	**914**	**605**	**4,829**	**2,355**	**8,303**	**139**	**165**	**1,254**	**351**	**842**	**2,900**
Age of child														
Under 1 year	3,873	2,455	467	33	7	53	63	624	—	—	8	9	57	95
1–2 years	7,979	5,212	711	91	14	174	181	1,160	5	—	25	19	126	262
3–5 years	12,038	7,709	745	149	55	496	353	1,748	32	16	114	35	168	418
6–8 years	12,339	8,007	553	174	53	723	437	1,557	20	21	164	56	142	432
9–11 years	12,358	8,176	374	155	102	950	457	1,192	15	25	240	62	124	484
12–14 years	12,385	8,062	242	154	147	1,177	441	1,015	35	44	310	85	108	565
15–17 years	12,652	8,048	207	157	227	1,255	422	1,007	32	58	394	85	116	643
Race														
White alone	53,621	37,929	2,246	595	422	3,555	1,575	3,596	88	121	1,005	264	522	1,703
Black alone	11,091	3,768	519	183	127	846	558	3,764	34	23	141	62	205	858
Asian alone	3,736	3,087	115	87	17	105	40	146	14	13	32	11	6	64
All remaining single races and all race combinations	5,175	2,885	417	48	39	323	182	797	3	8	76	14	109	274
Hispanic*	17,981	10,750	1,302	356	109	947	919	2,329	32	31	152	123	201	729
Presence of siblings														
None	15,052	7,134	800	191	130	1,158	362	2,391	39	42	448	101	432	1,825
One sibling	28,474	19,670	1,147	283	216	1,999	816	2,856	63	59	504	117	216	528
Two siblings	17,928	12,639	833	191	131	1,023	706	1,620	15	54	195	67	140	315
Three siblings	7,676	5,245	308	141	84	473	298	869	15	5	72	32	22	112
Four siblings	2,672	1,743	113	40	20	122	117	348	7	4	32	17	30	78
Five or more siblings	1,821	1,239	96	68	25	54	57	219	—	1	4	16	3	41
Presence of parent's unmarried partner														
Child's parent does not have opposite sex partner	68,140	47,670	253	882	527	4,097	2,178	7,489	125	158	994	323	545	2,900
Child's parent has opposite sex partner	5,483	X	3,044	32	78	732	177	814	14	6	261	28	297	X
Partner is also other parent	3,044	X	3,044	X	X	X	X	X	X	X	X	X	X	X
Partner is not other parent	2,439	X	X	32	78	732	177	814	14	6	261	28	297	X
Highest education of either parent														
No parents present	2,900	X	X	X	X	X	X	X	X	X	X	X	X	2,900
Less than 9th grade	2,367	1,395	171	93	43	110	129	334	10	1	22	13	47	X
9th to 12th grade, no diploma	4,785	2,086	286	120	53	303	330	1,336	6	8	76	57	124	X
High school graduate	14,956	7,461	1,141	288	161	1,242	752	2,963	71	79	363	109	326	X
Some college or AA degree	20,326	12,075	1,287	241	217	2,009	772	2,887	36	41	405	112	243	X
Bachelor's degree	15,767	13,179	322	88	91	830	243	603	8	25	243	53	82	X
Prof or graduate degree	12,523	11,474	90	83	40	335	129	182	7	11	145	6	20	X
Presence of adults other than parents														
Other relatives only	18,318	9,301	595	415	232	1,306	797	2,800	40	66	206	113	228	2,218
Non relatives only	3,500	239	151	68	76	708	228	948	16	4	256	36	301	469
Both relatives and non relatives	1,044	213	39	4	11	165	56	244	5	3	38	4	51	211
No other relatives or non relatives	50,762	37,917	2,511	426	285	2,650	1,274	4,311	77	92	755	199	262	1

TABLE 1.2

Living arrangements of children under age 18, by sex, age, race and Hispanic origin, marital status of parents, and other characteristics, 2015 [CONTINUED]

[Numbers in thousands]

	Total	Living with both parents — Married to each other	Living with both parents — Not married to each other	Living with mother only — Married spouse absent	Living with mother only — Widowed	Living with mother only — Divorced	Living with mother only — Separated	Living with mother only — Never married	Living with father only — Married spouse absent	Living with father only — Widowed	Living with father only — Divorced	Living with father only — Separated	Living with father only — Never married	Living with neither parent — No parent present
Child support receipt—mom														
Parent not present	5,651	X	X	X	X	X	X	X	139	165	1,254	351	842	2,900
Does not receive child support	61,785	46,076	3,054	844	554	2,784	1,838	6,635	X	X	X	X	X	X
Receives child support	6,188	1,593	243	70	51	2,045	517	1,668	X	X	X	X	X	X
Child support receipt—dad														
Parent not present	19,906	X	X	914	605	4,829	2,355	8,303	X	X	X	X	X	2,900
Does not receive child support	53,335	47,514	3,276	X	X	X	X	X	136	165	1,132	311	800	X
Receives child support	383	155	21	X	X	X	X	X	3	—	122	40	42	X
Stay-at-home married mom														
Child 15 or over, or not with two parents	34,002	8,048	3,297	914	605	4,829	2,355	8,303	139	165	1,254	351	842	2,900
Parent in labor force (LF) 1 or more weeks last year	25,920	25,920	X	X	X	X	X	X	X	X	X	X	X	X
Parent not in LF (NILF) 52wks lst yr caring for family, spouse in LF 52wks	10,758	10,758	X	X	X	X	X	X	X	X	X	X	X	X
Parent NILF 52wks lst yr caring for family, spouse NILF 1 or more wks	1,448	1,448	X	X	X	X	X	X	X	X	X	X	X	X
Parent NILF 52wks lst yr for other reason	1,496	1,496	X	X	X	X	X	X	X	X	X	X	X	X
Stay-at-home married dad														
Child 15 or over, or not with two parents	34,002	8,048	3,297	914	605	4,829	2,355	8,303	139	165	1,254	351	842	2,900
Parent in labor force (LF) 1 or more weeks last year	37,434	37,434	X	X	X	X	X	X	X	X	X	X	X	X
Parent not in LF (NILF) 52wks lst yr caring for family, spouse in LF 52wks	368	368	X	X	X	X	X	X	X	X	X	X	X	X
Parent NILF 52wks lst yr caring for family, spouse NILF 1 or more wks	157	157	X	X	X	X	X	X	X	X	X	X	X	X
Parent NILF 52wks lst yr for other reason	1,662	1,662	X	X	X	X	X	X	X	X	X	X	X	X
Parents labor force status														
Father in labor force, mother not present	2,291	X	X	X	X	X	X	X	132	120	1,088	289	662	X
Father not in labor force, mother not present	461	X	X	X	X	X	X	X	7	45	167	62	180	X
Mother in labor force, father not present	12,618	X	X	626	419	3,909	1,742	5,922	X	X	X	X	X	X
Mother not in labor force, father not present	4,388	X	X	287	186	920	613	2,381	X	X	X	X	X	X
Mother and father in labor force	30,443	28,639	1,804	X	X	X	X	X	X	X	X	X	X	X
Father in labor force, mother not in labor force	16,428	15,339	1,089	X	X	X	X	X	X	X	X	X	X	X
Mother in labor force, father not in labor force	2,446	2,184	262	X	X	X	X	X	X	X	X	X	X	X
Father not in labor force, mother not in labor force	1,650	1,508	142	X	X	X	X	X	X	X	X	X	X	X
No parents present	2,900	X	X	X	X	X	X	X	X	X	X	X	X	2,900
Family income														
Under $2,500	2,862	377	498	100	37	202	167	819	3	4	64	10	58	523
$2,500 to $4,999	799	96	124	28	3	99	89	259	—	5	30	16	5	46
$5,000 to $7,499	1,163	208	139	29	8	134	87	469	7	4	11	4	13	49
$7,500 to $9,999	1,094	170	102	28	20	111	108	461	—	—	16	4	19	54
$10,000 to $12,499	1,510	377	144	39	19	165	97	475	1	7	38	3	25	121
$12,500 to $14,999	1,363	313	110	50	22	182	113	419	1	5	12	6	38	91
$15,000 to $19,999	3,199	960	279	107	39	401	269	831	4	13	45	12	78	162
$20,000 to $24,999	3,640	1,397	348	79	49	407	200	820	19	5	79	30	47	160
$25,000 to $29,999	3,487	1,539	221	74	74	358	211	624	8	13	44	31	53	189
$30,000 to $39,999	6,197	3,265	394	86	87	636	285	864	21	9	154	39	99	260

TABLE 1.2

Living arrangements of children under age 18, by sex, age, race and Hispanic origin, marital status of parents, and other characteristics, 2015 [CONTINUED]

[Numbers in thousands]

	Total	Living with both parents		Living with mother only					Living with father only					Living with neither parent
		Married to each other	Not married to each other	Married spouse absent	Widowed	Divorced	Separated	Never married	Married spouse absent	Widowed	Divorced	Separated	Never married	No parent present
$40,000 to $49,999	5,697	3,505	281	52	49	498	181	666	14	21	131	43	69	186
$50,000 to $74,999	11,778	8,321	313	114	87	876	281	788	25	22	260	50	178	463
$75,000 to $99,999	9,074	7,422	163	60	55	374	91	317	24	24	151	64	78	250
$100,00 and over	21,760	19,670	181	66	57	388	178	492	11	32	219	38	82	346
Health insurance coverage														
Covered by health insurance	69,196	45,153	3,036	825	559	4,582	2,157	7,796	120	145	1,200	296	786	2,540
Not covered by health insurance	4,427	2,516	261	89	45	247	198	507	19	20	54	56	56	359
Poverty status														
Below 100% of poverty	15,822	5,068	1,575	471	195	1,447	1,071	4,138	23	39	243	88	241	1,223
100% to 199% of poverty	15,938	8,852	916	243	179	1,380	690	2,364	43	29	240	89	226	686
200% of poverty and above	41,863	33,749	805	199	231	2,002	594	1,801	73	97	772	175	375	991
Household food stamp receipt														
No	57,692	42,475	2,075	530	455	3,200	1,317	3,548	117	141	1,041	254	613	1,925
Yes	15,931	5,194	1,222	383	149	1,629	1,038	4,756	22	23	214	97	229	975
Household public asst. receipt														
No	70,887	47,036	3,069	849	586	4,614	2,178	7,355	137	156	1,223	344	792	2,547
Yes	2,737	634	228	65	19	215	177	948	1	9	32	7	50	352
Household tenure														
Own/Buying	43,992	33,821	1,132	349	358	2,237	800	2,122	63	133	769	140	389	1,679
Rent	28,771	13,429	2,088	552	245	2,536	1,474	6,067	76	32	469	190	441	1,173
No cash rent	861	419	77	12	2	57	82	114	—	—	17	21	13	47

LF = labor force.
NILF: not in labor force.
X = not applicable.
Dash "—" represents or rounds to zero.
*Hispanics may be of any race.

SOURCE: Adapted from "C3. Living Arrangements of Children under 18 Years and Marital Status of Parents, by Age, Sex, Race, and Hispanic Origin and Selected Characteristics of the Child for All Children: 2015," in "America's Families and Living Arrangements: 2015: Children (C Table Series)," *Families and Living Arrangements*, U.S. Census Bureau, November 2015, http://www.census.gov/hhes/families/files/cps2015/tabC3-all .xls (accessed June 9, 2016)

- Title IV-B Child Welfare Services and Promoting Safe and Stable Families (formerly known as Family Preservation) programs

- Title IV-E Foster Care Program

- Title IV-E Adoption Assistance Program

- Title IV-E Chafee Foster Care Independence Program

- Title XX Block Grants to States for Social Services, which is more commonly known as the Social Services Block Grant Program

Another key piece of federal legislation is the Child Abuse Prevention and Treatment Act (CAPTA), which was originally passed in 1974 and has been substantially amended since then. The Children's Bureau describes in *Major Federal Legislation Concerned with Child Protection, Child Welfare, and Adoption* the original CAPTA and its subsequent amendments as well as dozens of other related federal laws that concern child protection, child welfare, and adoption. The agency notes that the original CAPTA created the National Center on Child Abuse and Neglect to undertake the following tasks:

- Administer grant programs

- Identify issues and areas needing special focus for new research and demonstration project activities

- Serve as the focal point for the collection of information, improvement of programs, dissemination of materials, and information on best practices to States and localities

In "About CAPTA: A Legislative History" (July 2011, http://www.childwelfare.gov/pubs/factsheets/about.pdf), the Children's Bureau lists the functions of CAPTA:

- Provides federal funding to states to support prevention, assessment, investigation, prosecution, and treatment activities

- Provides federal grants to public agencies and nonprofit organizations, including Native American tribes and tribal organizations, for demonstration programs and projects

- Identifies the federal role in supporting research, evaluation, technical assistance, and data collection activities

- Mandates operation of the Child Welfare Information Gateway (https://www.childwelfare.gov), a clearinghouse for data and information related to child abuse and the child protection system

- Sets forth a minimum definition of child abuse and neglect

CAPTA was most recently reauthorized in December 2010 through the CAPTA Reauthorization Act, which extended the legislation through 2015. The Children's Bureau notes in *Definitions of Child Abuse and Neglect* (2014, https://www.childwelfare.gov/pubPDFs/define .pdf) that the CAPTA Reauthorization Act of 2010 defines

child abuse and neglect as "any recent act or failure to act on the part of a parent or caretaker, which results in death, serious physical or emotional harm, sexual abuse, or exploitation, or an act or failure to act which presents an imminent risk of serious harm."

Figure 1.2 presents a timeline of major federal child welfare legislation passed between 1974 and 2015. CAPTA expired in September 2015. Although the law had still not been reauthorized by Congress as of September 2016, the federal government continued to fund state efforts to comply with the law's basic policies. James Greenwood and Cathleen Palm note in "Family First Needed to Stop Child Deaths" (ChronicleofSocialChange.org, September 28, 2016) that during fiscal year 2016 Congress allocated $26 million toward state CAPTA programs.

STATE LEGISLATION. The Children's Bureau states in "Definitions of Child Abuse and Neglect in Federal Law" (2016, https://www.childwelfare.gov/can/defining/federal.cfm) that "while Federal legislation sets minimum standards for States that accept CAPTA funding, each State provides its own definitions of maltreatment within civil and criminal statutes."

Local child protective services agencies operate under local or state jurisdiction. As is explained in Chapter 2, the agencies receive and investigate reports of child maltreatment and refer families for treatment services as appropriate. In some cases child maltreatment offenses rise to the level of criminal acts, and in these situations the agencies refer the cases to local law enforcement for prosecution. District attorneys (or prosecutors) prosecute people who are accused of committing criminal acts. The National District Attorneys Association oversees the National Center for Prosecution of Child Abuse. Among other things, the center operates the website State Statutes (http://www.ndaa.org/ncpca_state_statutes.html), which lists state statutes that deal with criminal child abuse offenses.

Under state civil laws, child protective services agencies coordinate with juvenile courts (or dependency or family courts, as they are known) in cases in which the state believes that children should be removed from their home and placed in temporary foster care. In addition, the state can pursue legal action to terminate the parental or custody rights of child abusers. The Children's Bureau maintains the website State Statutes Search (https://www .childwelfare.gov/systemwide/laws_policies/state), which lists state civil statutes that deal with child abuse and neglect, child welfare, and adoption.

In *Definitions of Child Abuse and Neglect*, the Children's Bureau notes that state civil laws typically cover four types of child abuse:

- Physical abuse—this is commonly described in state statues as "any nonaccidental physical injury to the child" and includes behaviors such as striking, kicking,

FIGURE 1.2

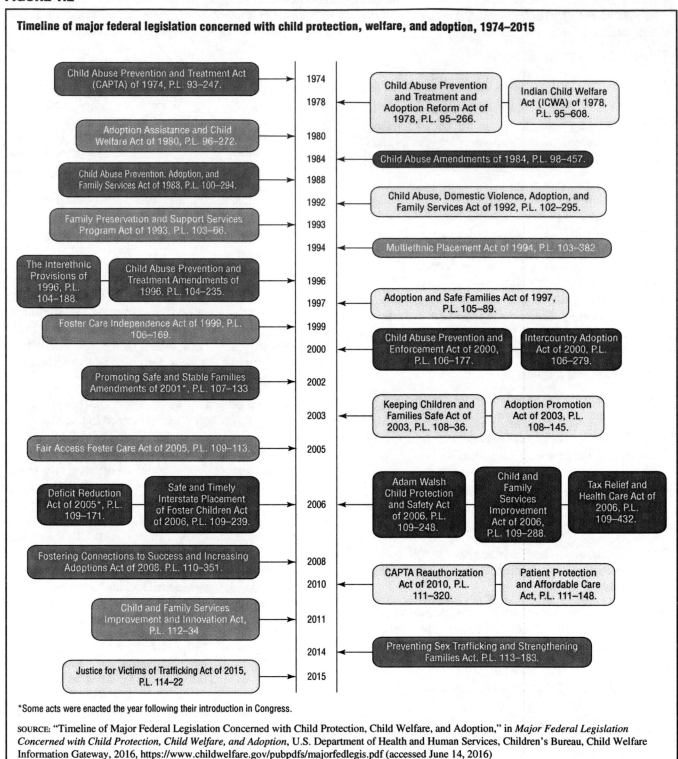

Timeline of major federal legislation concerned with child protection, welfare, and adoption, 1974–2015

	Year	
Child Abuse Prevention and Treatment Act (CAPTA) of 1974, P.L. 93–247.	1974	
	1978	Child Abuse Prevention and Treatment and Adoption Reform Act of 1978, P.L. 95–266. / Indian Child Welfare Act (ICWA) of 1978, P.L. 95–608.
Adoption Assistance and Child Welfare Act of 1980, P.L. 96–272.	1980	
	1984	Child Abuse Amendments of 1984, P.L. 98–457.
Child Abuse Prevention, Adoption, and Family Services Act of 1988, P.L. 100–294.	1988	
	1992	Child Abuse, Domestic Violence, Adoption, and Family Services Act of 1992, P.L. 102–295.
Family Preservation and Support Services Program Act of 1993, P.L. 103–66.	1993	
	1994	Multiethnic Placement Act of 1994, P.L. 103–382
The Interethnic Provisions of 1996, P.L. 104–188. / Child Abuse Prevention and Treatment Amendments of 1996, P.L. 104–235.	1996	
	1997	Adoption and Safe Families Act of 1997, P.L. 105–89.
Foster Care Independence Act of 1999, P.L. 106–169.	1999	
	2000	Child Abuse Prevention and Enforcement Act of 2000, P.L. 106–177. / Intercountry Adoption Act of 2000, P.L. 106–279.
Promoting Safe and Stable Families Amendments of 2001*, P.L. 107–133	2002	
	2003	Keeping Children and Families Safe Act of 2003, P.L. 108–36. / Adoption Promotion Act of 2003, P.L. 108–145.
Fair Access Foster Care Act of 2005, P.L. 109–113.	2005	
Deficit Reduction Act of 2005*, P.L. 109–171. / Safe and Timely Interstate Placement of Foster Children Act of 2006, P.L. 109–239.	2006	Adam Walsh Child Protection and Safety Act of 2006, P.L. 109–248. / Child and Family Services Improvement Act of 2006, P.L. 109–288. / Tax Relief and Health Care Act of 2006, P.L. 109–432.
Fostering Connections to Success and Increasing Adoptions Act of 2008, P.L. 110–351.	2008	
	2010	CAPTA Reauthorization Act of 2010, P.L. 111–320. / Patient Protection and Affordable Care Act, P.L. 111–148.
Child and Family Services Improvement and Innovation Act, P.L. 112–34	2011	
	2014	Preventing Sex Trafficking and Strengthening Families Act, P.L. 113–183.
Justice for Victims of Trafficking Act of 2015, P.L. 114–22	2015	

*Some acts were enacted the year following their introduction in Congress.

SOURCE: "Timeline of Major Federal Legislation Concerned with Child Protection, Child Welfare, and Adoption," in *Major Federal Legislation Concerned with Child Protection, Child Welfare, and Adoption*, U.S. Department of Health and Human Services, Children's Bureau, Child Welfare Information Gateway, 2016, https://www.childwelfare.gov/pubpdfs/majorfedlegis.pdf (accessed June 14, 2016)

burning, or biting the child or otherwise causing physical impairment. Many states also include "acts or circumstances that threaten the child with harm or create a substantial risk of harm to the child's health or welfare."

- Neglect—neglect is typically defined as "failure of a parent or other person with responsibility for the child to provide needed food, clothing, shelter, medical care,

or supervision to the degree that the child's health, safety, and well-being are threatened with harm." Some states also include education neglect (failing to educate a child as required by law) and medical neglect (failing to provide needed medical treatment).

- Sexual abuse/exploitation—sexual abuse involves physically sexual acts that are conducted with children. These acts may be defined by law in general or specific terms. In addition, sexual exploitation involves using a child for the purposes of sexual gratification, for example, through prostitution or pornography.

- Emotional abuse—emotional abuse is commonly defined as "injury to the psychological capacity or emotional stability of the child as evidenced by an observable or substantial change in behavior, emotional response, or cognition." Evidence of injury from emotional abuse typically includes "anxiety, depression, withdrawal, or aggressive behavior."

Besides the four major types of abuse, the Children's Bureau notes that some state civil laws pertaining to child abuse also cover parental substance abuse and abandonment of a child.

Domestic Violence Legislation

FEDERAL LEGISLATION. The Department of Health and Human Services indicates in "Information Memorandum" (March 28, 2011, http://www.acf.hhs.gov/sites/default/files/fysb/fvpsa_info_memo_2011_0.pdf) that via the Child Abuse Amendments of 1984 Congress enacted the Family Violence Prevention and Services Act (FVPSA), which provides federal funding to public and private entities that are devoted to domestic violence prevention and services. These entities include "States, Indian Tribes and Tribal organizations, local public agencies, nonprofit private organizations, and other persons seeking such assistance to implement programs to address the problem." The FVPSA has been amended and reauthorized over the years. As of September 2016, the most recent amendment occurred in December 2010 by way of passage of the CAPTA Reauthorization Act of 2010. The FVPSA (December 14, 2010, http://www.govtrack.us/congress/bills/111/s3817/text) provides funding for the following purposes:

- Assist States and Indian tribes in efforts to increase public awareness about, and primary and secondary prevention of, family violence, domestic violence, and dating violence

- Assist States and Indian tribes in efforts to provide immediate shelter and supportive services for victims of family violence, domestic violence, or dating violence, and their dependents

- Provide for a national domestic violence hotline

- Provide for technical assistance and training relating to family violence, domestic violence, and dating violence programs to States and Indian tribes, local public agencies (including law enforcement agencies, courts, and legal, social service, and health care professionals in public agencies), nonprofit private organizations (including faith-based and charitable organizations, community-based organizations, and

voluntary associations), tribal organizations, and other persons seeking such assistance and training

As with CAPTA, the FVPSA expired in September 2015 and had yet to be reauthorized as of September 2016.

In 1994 Congress passed the Violence against Women Act (VAWA) to enhance the investigation and prosecution of violent crimes against women, such as domestic violence, sexual assaults, and stalking. The following year the Office on Violence against Women (OVW) was created within the U.S. Department of Justice (DOJ). In "About the Office" (December 16, 2014, https://www.justice.gov/ovw/about-office), the OVW explains that the VAWA "emerged from the efforts of a broad, grassroots coalition of advocates and survivors who informed the work of Congress." The agency administers financial and technical assistance to state and local programs that are devoted to the prevention of domestic violence, dating violence, sexual assault, and stalking.

The VAWA has been controversial since its passage. The original law granted female victims of violence, including battered women, federal civil rights protection. The civil rights section of the act was tested in 1996, when Christy Brzonkala filed a civil suit after allegedly being raped by two football players from Virginia Polytechnic Institute. In *United States v. Morrison et al.* (529 U.S. 598 [2000]), the U.S. Supreme Court ruled that Congress could not enact "a federal civil remedy for the victims of gender-motivated violence." Individuals who committed crimes motivated by a gender bias, the court stated, could not be held accountable at the federal level.

In 2000 Congress passed the Victims of Trafficking and Violence Protection Act (a revised VAWA), which included the sections Strengthening Law Enforcement to Reduce Violence against Women, Strengthening Services to Victims of Violence, Limiting the Effects of Violence on Children, and Strengthening Education and Training to Combat Violence against Women. As a result of the Supreme Court ruling, the new legislation made no mention of women's civil rights. The VAWA was renewed in 2005. The law was reauthorized again in March 2013 and included several new provisions aimed at extending protection to specific groups. Julia Dahl reports in "President Obama Signs Violence against Women Act" (CBSNews.com, March 7, 2013) that the reauthorized version of the law guaranteed Native American victims of domestic violence the right to pursue legal recourse against nonnative assailants. At the same time, the reauthorization of the VAWA granted lesbian, gay, bisexual, and transgendered (LGBT) groups the right to apply for grants aimed at protecting LGBT individuals from acts of violence. The law also granted new protections to immigrant women, while providing housing assistance for women who no longer felt safe in their home. Even after the passage of the VAWA reauthorization, lawmakers continued to craft additional legislation that was designed to establish further protections for victims of domestic violence. One notable effort was the Protecting Domestic Violence and Stalking Victims Act (https://www.congress.gov/bill/114th-congress/house-bill/2216), which aimed to prevent perpetrators of domestic violence from acquiring firearms. As of September 2016, the proposed law was still in committee.

In "Grant Programs" (May 2, 2016, https://www.justice.gov/ovw/grant-programs), the OVW describes 24 grant programs that it operates. Some grants fund projects involving violence prevention and victim services provided in certain settings (e.g., college campuses) and for specific victim types (e.g., disabled women). In addition, grants provide funds to law enforcement agencies and courts to enhance their responses to domestic violence, dating violence, sexual assault, and stalking.

STATE LEGISLATION. State criminal laws specify the actions that are considered to be criminal offenses. All states further specify certain types of criminal offenses as domestic violence. For example, California's Domestic Violence Prevention Act is codified at Family Code Sections 6200 to 6219 (2016, http://www.leginfo.ca.gov/cgi-bin/displaycode?section=fam&group=06001-07000&file=6200-6219). It defines domestic abuse in terms of the offenses committed and the victim-offender relationship. The latter includes current and former spouses, cohabitants, people having "a dating or engagement relationship," and people who have had a child together. The law also includes certain children and any person "related by consanguinity or affinity within the second degree." *Consanguinity* and *affinity* are terms that often appear in legal definitions of domestic violence. Although they have specific meanings as set forth in state laws, in general *consanguinity* refers to biological relationships and *affinity* refers to relationships that are established through marriage. The degrees of consanguinity and affinity refer to the relative "closeness" of two parties. For example, a father and daughter have first-degree consanguinity, whereas a niece and uncle have second-degree consanguinity. Likewise, a husband and wife have first-degree affinity, whereas a woman and her husband's brother have second-degree affinity.

Domestic violence cases are also covered by civil laws, in that victims can sue their alleged attackers for monetary damages. Civil lawsuits can be brought even in cases in which criminal charges fail to achieve convictions. This gives victims another legal avenue against their abusers. In addition, victims can file civil lawsuits against third parties that are accused of helping in some way to facilitate domestic violence or for failing in

legally required circumstances to interact on the victim's behalf. Chapter 9 describes major third-party lawsuits involving domestic violence that have shaped the legal system's responses to the problem.

Family Violence Reporting Requirements

One of the challenges of bringing family violence into the realm of the legal system is the secrecy that often surrounds such cases. In the past, authorities only became aware of problems if family members or perhaps concerned relatives or friends chose to notify the police or other public officials. To overcome this veil of secrecy, laws have been passed that require certain parties, such as teachers and doctors, to report to authorities any suspected or known cases of abuse that come to their attention.

In 1961 the pediatric radiologist C. Henry Kempe (1922–1984) and his associates proposed the term *battered-child syndrome* at a symposium on the problem of child abuse held under the auspices of the American Academy of Pediatrics. The term refers to the collection of injuries that are sustained by a child as a result of repeated mistreatment or beatings. The following year Kempe et al. published the landmark article "The Battered-Child Syndrome" (*Journal of the American Medical Association*, vol. 181, no. 1, July 7, 1962). The term *battered-child syndrome* eventually evolved into the word *maltreatment*, which encompasses not only physical assault but also other forms of abuse, such as malnourishment, failure to thrive, medical neglect, and sexual and emotional abuse.

Kempe et al. proposed that physicians be required to report child abuse. According to the National Association of Counsel for Children, by 1967, after Kempe et al.'s findings had gained general acceptance among health and welfare workers and the public, 44 states had passed legislation that required the reporting of child abuse to official agencies, and the remaining six states had voluntary reporting laws. Initially, only doctors were required to report and then only in cases of "serious physical injury" or "nonaccidental injury." In the 21st century all 50 states and the District of Columbia have laws that require not only doctors but also most professionals who serve children to report all forms of suspected abuse and either require or permit any citizen to report child abuse.

One of the reasons for the lack of prosecution of early child abuse cases was the difficulty in determining whether a physical injury was due to a deliberate assault or an accident. In the latter part of the 20th century, however, doctors of pediatric radiology were able to determine the incidence of repeated child abuse through sophisticated developments in x-ray technology. These advances allowed radiologists to see more clearly things such as subdural hematomas (blood clots around the brain resulting from blows to the head) and abnormal fractures. As a result, these advances brought about more recognition in the medical community of the widespread incidence of child abuse, along with growing public condemnation of abuse.

Reporting requirement laws have made a significant impact to the child protection system. The Children's Bureau indicates in *Child Maltreatment 2014* (2016, https://www.acf.hhs.gov/sites/default/files/cb/cm2014.pdf) that professionals, such as educators and medical providers, were the sources for nearly 1.3 million reports of suspected child abuse in 2014. As of September 2016, the reporting requirements for child abuse were extensive and still growing. As is discussed further in Chapter 4, highly publicized cases of child abuse, particularly sexual abuse, during the early years of the 21st century have spurred legislators to expand the requirements to more professions and more settings.

SOCIAL AND PUBLIC HEALTH ISSUES

Society expects that biological ties or personal intimate relations between people will facilitate peaceful interactions (i.e., interactions that are characterized by an interest in and a desire to maintain the other person's well-being). In child abuse and domestic violence cases such expectations are horribly dashed. The perpetrators of these crimes break the social code of conduct in which civilized people believe that parents will nurture and not harm their children and that adults in intimate relationships will not commit violence against each other. Therefore, child abuse and domestic violence are not just legal matters, they violate the social order of society.

In addition, child abuse and domestic violence have public health ramifications. As is explained in subsequent chapters, victims of these traumatic events can suffer both short-term and long-term consequences to their physical and emotional well-being. In 2005 the U.S. surgeon general held a workshop on child abuse, "Making Prevention of Child Maltreatment a National Priority: Implementing Innovations of a Public Health Approach" (http://www.ncbi.nlm.nih.gov/books/NBK47486), at which Charles Wilson, the director of the San Diego Children's Hospital and Health Center, stated that child maltreatment was "a public health crisis, the full scale of which is masked by secrecy and denial." In 2010 the National Center for Injury Prevention and Control, a part of the Centers for Disease Control and Prevention, conducted the National Intimate Partner and Sexual Violence Survey, a comprehensive survey that collected information from adults about their experiences of sexual violence, stalking, and intimate partner violence. In

National Intimate Partner and Sexual Violence Survey: 2010 Summary Report (November 2011, http://www .cdc.gov/violenceprevention/pdf/nisvs_report2010-a.pdf), Michele C. Black et al. describe the numerous health consequences that victims suffer and note that "sexual violence, stalking, and intimate partner violence are major public health problems in the United States."

The Status of U.S. Children

The Federal Interagency Forum on Child and Family Statistics (known simply as the Forum) regularly collects information about the well-being of U.S. children. Since 1997 the agency has published reports presenting its findings. In *America's Children: Key National Indicators of Well-Being, 2015* (July 2015, http://www.childstats .gov/pdf/ac2015/ac_15.pdf), the Forum reports on the status of U.S. children based on data compiled between 2013 and 2014. Table 1.3 summarizes selected data indicators. The child population in 2014 was 73.6 million, meaning that children made up nearly a quarter (23.1%) of the total U.S. population. More than half (51.9%) of children in 2014 were non-Hispanic white. As shown in Figure 1.3, this percentage has been dropping for decades and is expected to continue to decline through 2050, when non-Hispanic white children are projected to make up around 40% of the child population. By contrast, the Hispanic child population has been growing dramatically, and its share is expected to increase to about 35% by 2050.

In 2014 nearly two-thirds (64%) of U.S. children aged 17 years and younger lived with two married parents. (See Table 1.3.) Roughly half (49%) of children aged zero to four years received their primary child care from a relative in 2011, the most recent data as of September 2016; among children aged three to six years, more than half (61%) were in center-based care arrangements in 2012. (Table 1.4 lists the various kinds of child care arrangements that are commonly used.) As shown in Table 1.3, in 2013 the birth rate among unmarried women aged 15 to 44 years was 44 births per 1,000 women; among females aged 15 to 17 years, the birth rate was 12 births per 1,000 women.

The socioeconomic status of children is of particular concern as a public health matter and has implications to child abuse prevalence rates. Chapter 3 examines the risk factors that are associated with child maltreatment and describes studies that find higher risks for children of lower socioeconomic status. As shown in Table 1.3, one-fifth (20%) of U.S. children were "in poverty" in 2013. Although there are differing federal definitions for poverty, the Forum based its data on poverty income thresholds, which are determined by the Census Bureau. The thresholds are minimum income levels for different family sizes and compositions. For example, the Forum

TABLE 1.3

National indicators of children's well-being, 2013 and 2014

	Previous value (year)	Most recent value (year)	Change between years
Demographic background			
Child population[a]			
Children ages 0–17 in the United States	73.6 million (2013)	73.6 million (2014)	NS
Children as a percentage of the population[a]			
Children ages 0–17 in the United States	23.3% (2013)	23.1% (2014)	↓
Racial and ethnic composition[a]			
Children ages 0–17 by race and Hispanic origin[b]			
White, non-Hispanic	52.3% (2013)	51.9% (2014)	↓
Black, non-Hispanic	13.8% (2013)	13.8% (2014)	NS
American Indian or Alaska Native, non-Hispanic	0.9% (2013)	0.9% (2014)	NS
Asian, non-Hispanic	4.7% (2013)	4.8% (2014)	↑
Native Hawaiian or other Pacific Islander, non-Hispanic	0.2% (2013)	0.2% (2014)	NS
Two or more races, non-Hispanic	4.0% (2013)	4.1% (2014)	↑
Hispanic	24.1% (2013)	24.4% (2014)	↑
Family and social environment			
Family structure and children's living arrangements			
Children ages 0–17 living with two married parents	64% (2013)	64% (2014)	NS
Births to unmarried women			
Births to unmarried women ages 15–44	45 per 1,000 (2012)	44 per 1,000 (2013)	↓
Births to unmarried women among all births	40.7% (2012)	40.6% (2013)	↓
Child care			
Children ages 0–4, with employed mothers, whose primary child care arrangement is with a relative	48% (2010)	49% (2011)	NS
Children ages 3–6, not yet in kindergarten, who were in center-based care arrangements	55% (2007)	61% (2012)	↑
Children of at least one foreign-born parent			
Children ages 0–17 living with at least one foreign-born parent	24% (2013)	24% (2014)	NS
Language spoken at home and difficulty speaking English			
Children ages 5–17 who speak a language other than English at home	22.3% (2012)	21.8% (2013)	↓
Children ages 5–17 who speak a language other than English at home and who have difficulty speaking English	5% (2012)	5% (2013)	NS
Adolescent births			
Births to females ages 15–17	14 per 1,000 (2012)	12 per 1,000 (2013)	↓
Child maltreatment[a]			
Substantiated reports of maltreatment of children ages 0–17	9.8 per 1,000 (2012)	9.8 per 1,000 (2013)	NS
Economic circumstances			
Child poverty and family income			
Children ages 0–17 in poverty	22% (2012)	20% (2013)	↓
Secure parental employment			
Children ages 0–17 living with at least one parent employed year round, full time	73% (2012)	74% (2013)	↑
Food insecurity			
Children ages 0–17 in households classified by USDA as "food insecure"	22% (2012)	21% (2013)	NS
Health care			
Health insurance coverage			
Children ages 0–17 who were uninsured at the time of interview	7% (2012)	7% (2013)	NS
Usual source of health care			
Children ages 0–17 with no usual source of health care	4% (2012)	4% (2013)	NS
Immunization			
Children ages 19–35 months with the 4:3:1:3*:3:1:4 combined series	68% (2012)	70% (2013)	NS
Oral health			
Children ages 5–17 with a dental visit in the past year	88% (2012)	88% (2013)	NS

notes that in 2013 the poverty threshold limit for a family of four including two adults and two children was $23,624 annually. Thus, any family matching that description and making an income of less than $23,624 annually was considered to be in poverty. The Forum indicates that the percentage of children in poverty was

	Previous value (year)	Most recent value (year)	Change between years
Physical environment and safety			
Outdoor air quality			
Children ages 0–17 living in counties with pollutant concentrations above the levels of the current air quality standards	68% (2012)	50% (2013)	↓
Secondhand smoke			
Children ages 4–11 with any detectable blood cotinine level, a measure for recent exposure to secondhand smoke	42% (2009–2010)	40% (2011–2012)	NS
Drinking water quality			
Children served by community water systems that did not meet all applicable health-based drinking water standards	8% (2012)	6% (2013)	NS
Lead in the blood of children			
Children ages 1–5 with blood lead greater than or equal to 5 µg/dL	4% (2003–2006)	2% (2009–2012)	↓
Housing problems			
Households with children ages 0–17 reporting shelter cost burden, crowding, and/or physically inadequate housing	46% (2011)	40% (2013)	↓
Youth victims of serious violent crimes			
Serious violent crime victimization of youth ages 12–17	6 per 1,000 (2012)	9 per 1,000 (2013)	NS
Child injury and mortality			
Injury deaths of children ages 1–4	11 per 100,000 (2012)	11 per 100,000 (2013)	NS
Injury deaths of children ages 5–14	5 per 100,000 (2012)	5 per 100,000 (2013)	NS
Adolescent injury and mortality			
Injury deaths of adolescents ages 15–19	35 per 100,000 (2012)	33 per 100,000 (2013)	↓
Behavior			
Regular cigarette smoking			
Students who reported smoking daily in the past 30 days			
8th grade	2% (2013)	1% (2014)	NS
10th grade	4% (2013)	3% (2014)	↓
12th grade	9% (2013)	7% (2014)	↓
Alcohol use			
Students who reported having 5 or more alcoholic beverages in a row in the past 2 weeks			
8th grade	5% (2013)	4% (2014)	↓
10th grade	14% (2013)	13% (2014)	NS
12th grade	22% (2013)	19% (2014)	↓
Illicit drug use			
Students who reported using illicit drugs in the past 30 days			
8th grade	9% (2013)	8% (2014)	NS
10th grade	19% (2013)	19% (2014)	NS
12th grade	25% (2013)	24% (2014)	NS
Sexual activity			
High school students who reported ever having had sexual intercourse	47% (2011)	47% (2013)	NS
Youth perpetrators of serious violent crimes			
Youth offenders ages 12–17 involved in serious violent crimes	9 per 1,000 (2012)	9 per 1,000 (2013)	NS
Education			
Family reading to young children			
Children ages 3–5 who were read to 3 or more times in the last week	83% (2007)	83% (2012)	NS
Mathematics and reading achievement			
Average mathematics scale score of			
4th-graders (0–500 scale)	241 (2011)	242 (2013)	↑
8th-graders (0–500 scale)	284 (2011)	285 (2013)	↑
12th-graders (0–300 scale)	153 (2009)	153 (2013)	NS
Average reading scale score of			
4th-graders (0–500 scale)	221 (2011)	222 (2013)	NS
8th-graders (0–500 scale)	265 (2011)	268 (2013)	↑
12th-graders (0–500 scale)	288 (2009)	288 (2013)	NS

16% in 2000 and crept up to 17% in 2006. The rate of child poverty then increased each year through 2012, when it hit 22%, before dropping to 20% in 2013. The rise in child poverty by this measure may be linked to the Great Recession, which lasted from late 2007 to mid-2009.

TABLE 1.3

	Previous value (year)	Most recent value (year)	Change between years
Education—cont.			
High school academic coursetaking			
High school graduates who completed selected mathematics and science courses			
Algebra II	70% (2005)	76% (2009)	↑
Analysis/precalculus	29% (2005)	35% (2009)	↑
Biology and chemistry	64% (2005)	68% (2009)	↑
Biology, chemistry, and physics	27% (2005)	30% (2009)	↑
High school completion			
Young adults ages 18–24 who have completed high school	91% (2012)	92% (2013)	NS
Youth neither enrolled in school[c] nor working			
Youth ages 16–19 who are neither enrolled in school nor working	9% (2013)	9% (2014)	NS
College enrollment			
Recent high school completers enrolled in college the October immediately after completing high school	66% (2012)	66% (2013)	NS
Health			
Preterm birth and low birthweight			
Infants less than 37 completed weeks of gestation at birth	11.5% (2012)	11.4% (2013)	↓
Infants weighing less than 5 lb. 8 oz. at birth	8% (2012)	8% (2013)	NS
Infant mortality			
Deaths before first birthday	6 per 1,000 (2011)	6 per 1,000 (2012)	NS
Emotional and behavioral difficulties			
Children ages 4–17 reported by a parent to have serious difficulties with emotions, concentration, behavior, or getting along with other people	5% (2012)	5% (2013)	NS
Adolescent depression			
Youth ages 12–17 with major depressive episode in the past year	9% (2012)	11% (2013)	↑
Activity limitation			
Children ages 5–17 with activity limitation resulting from one or more chronic health conditions	9% (2012)	9% (2013)	NS
Diet quality			
Average diet scores for children ages 2–17, expressed as a percentage of Federal diet quality standards	51% (2007–2008)	52% (2009–2010)	NS
Obesity			
Children ages 6–17 who are obese	18% (2009–2010)	19% (2011–2012)	NS
Asthma			
Children ages 0–17 who currently have asthma	9% (2012)	8% (2013)	↓

NS = No statistically significant change; USDA = United States Department of Agriculture.
↑ = Statistically significant increase.
↓ = Statistically significant decrease.
[a]Population estimates are not sample derived and thus not subject to statistical testing. Change between years identifies differences in the proportionate size of these estimates.
[b]Percentages may not sum to 100 due to rounding.
[c]School refers to high school and college.

SOURCE: "America's Children at a Glance," in *America's Children: Key National Indicators of Well-Being, 2015*, Federal Interagency Forum on Child and Family Statistics, July 2015, http://www.childstats.gov/pdf/ac2015/ac_15.pdf (accessed June 9, 2016)

Figure 1.4 provides an overall child poverty breakdown by race, Hispanic origin, and family type between 1980 and 2013. Children living with married couples had, by far, the lowest poverty levels. In 2013 about 10% of these children were in poverty. By contrast, about 47% of the children living with female householders were in poverty. There were also striking differences by race and ethnic origin. Children in households headed by African American and Hispanic females had higher rates of poverty than did children in households headed by white females. Children of low socioeconomic status

living with female householders face particular risks for family violence. One threat is the higher risk of child maltreatment due to low socioeconomic status. The Forum notes that the percentage of children living in families in severe poverty (below 50% of the poverty threshold for that family composition) was 9% in 2013.

Nearly three-quarters (74%) of U.S. children in 2013 lived with at least one parent who was employed full time year round. (See Table 1.3.) However, as the Forum reports in *America's Children*, there was a wide difference

FIGURE 1.3

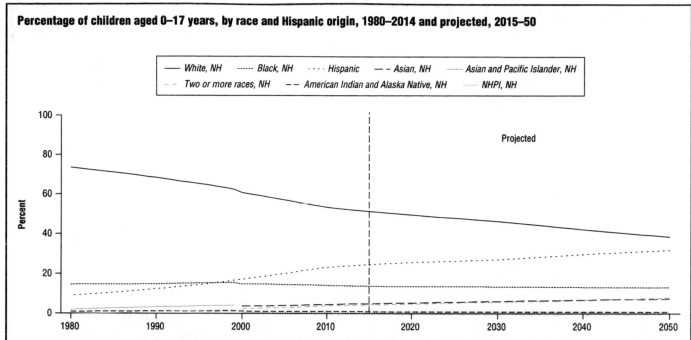

Percentage of children aged 0–17 years, by race and Hispanic origin, 1980–2014 and projected, 2015–50

Legend:
— White, NH ······ Black, NH ···· Hispanic — – Asian, NH ———— Asian and Pacific Islander, NH
– – Two or more races, NH — — American Indian and Alaska Native, NH ········ NHPI, NH

Projected

(y-axis: Percent, 0–100; x-axis: 1980, 1990, 2000, 2010, 2020, 2030, 2040, 2050)

Notes: The abbreviation NH refers to non-Hispanic origin. The abbreviation NHPI refers to the Native Hawaiian and Other Pacific Islander population. Each group represents the non-Hispanic population, with the exception of the Hispanic category itself. Race data from 2000 onward are not directly comparable with data from earlier years. Data on race and Hispanic origin are collected separately. Persons of Hispanic origin may be of any race.

SOURCE: "Indicator POP3. Percentage of Children Ages 0–17 in the United States by Race and Hispanic Origin, 1980–2014 and Projected 2015–2050," in *America's Children: Key National Indicators of Well-Being, 2015*, Federal Interagency Forum on Child and Family Statistics, July 2015, http://www.childstats.gov/pdf/ac2015/ac_15.pdf (accessed June 9, 2016)

TABLE 1.4

Types of child care

Type	Description
In-home care	Care provided in the child's home
Relative care	Care provided by someone related to the child other than the parents in any setting, typically in the child's or relative's home
Family child care	An individual provider who provides child care services as the sole caregiver in a private residence other than the child's home
Group home care	Two or more providers who provide child care services in a private residence other than the child's home (this does not include 24-hour residential facilities)
Child care centers	Nonresidential facilities that provide care for children and include full- and part-time group programs, such as nursery and preschool programs. Child care centers can be commercial, work-site based, school-based (preschool or after school), or a recreational program (such as camps or parks), and care can also be run by a religious organization or by federal, state, or local governments

SOURCE: "Table 1. Types of Child Care," in *Child Care: Overview of Relevant Employment Laws and Cases of Sex Offenders at Child Care Facilities*, U.S. Government Accountability Office, August 2011, http://www.gao.gov/assets/330/322722.pdf (accessed June 9, 2016)

in terms of full-time, year-round parental employment between those children who lived with two married parents (87%) and children living in families maintained by single mothers (42%).

In 2013 more than one-fifth (21%) of U.S. children lived in households that were classified by the U.S. Department of Agriculture (USDA) as "food insecure."

(See Table 1.3.) According to the Forum, food insecurity is assessed by the USDA through surveys that question parents and guardians about the adequacy of their household food supply. The Forum indicates that 1% of children lived in households that were deemed to have very low food security in 2013. This means that "at some time during the year one or more children were hungry, skipped a meal, or did not eat for a whole day because the household could not afford enough food."

The Forum notes that 93% of children had health insurance coverage at some point in 2013. This means that 7%, or roughly 5.2 million children, did not have health insurance coverage at any time in 2013. Chapter 2 describes the government programs that were in existence as of September 2016 to provide health insurance to low-income children. The Forum finds that 4% of children in 2013 had "no usual source of health care," meaning that they did not have "a particular person or place" to visit for preventive and sick care. The percentage of children falling into this category was higher for those who were uninsured (25%) than for those who had health insurance (2%).

According to the Forum, "inadequate, crowded, or too costly housing can pose serious problems to children's physical, psychological, and material well-being." Two-fifths (40%) of U.S. children in 2013 lived in households

FIGURE 1.4

Percentage of children aged 0–17 years living in poverty, by race, Hispanic origin, and family type, 1980–2013

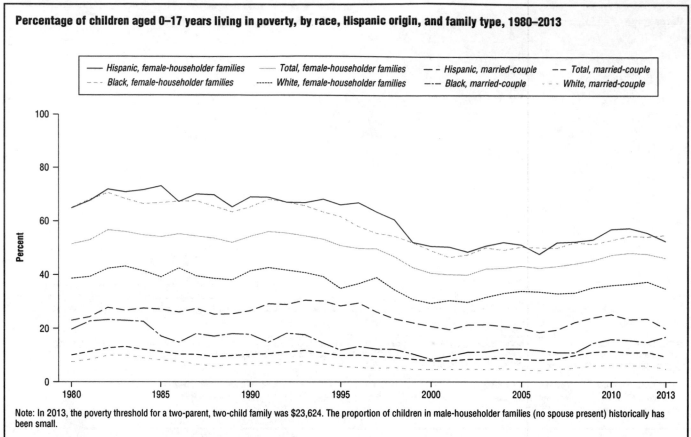

—— Hispanic, female-householder families	········ Total, female-householder families	— — Hispanic, married-couple	– – Total, married-couple
– – – Black, female-householder families	······ White, female-householder families	—·— Black, married-couple	··· — White, married-couple

Note: In 2013, the poverty threshold for a two-parent, two-child family was $23,624. The proportion of children in male-householder families (no spouse present) historically has been small.

SOURCE: "Indicator ECON1.A. Percentage of Children Ages 0–17 Living in Poverty by Race, Hispanic Origin, and Family Structure, 1980–2013," in *America's Children: Key National Indicators of Well-Being, 2015*, Federal Interagency Forum on Child and Family Statistics, July 2015, http://www .childstats.gov/pdf/ac2015/ac_15.pdf (accessed June 9, 2016)

that reported "shelter cost burden, crowding, and/or physically inadequate housing." The agency explains that a shelter cost burden indicates that a household was paying housing costs in excess of 30% of its income.

As shown in Table 1.3, 5% of U.S. children aged four to 17 years in 2013 were reported by a parent to have "serious difficulties with emotions, concentration, behavior, or getting along with other people." In addition, 9% of children aged five to 17 years had an "activity limitation resulting from one or more chronic health conditions." Studies described in Chapter 3 indicate that children with physical, emotional, and/or behavioral problems are at higher risk for maltreatment than other children.

VIOLENT ENVIRONMENTS

Researchers are increasingly focusing on the environments in which family violence occurs. What they are finding is that some children experience a shocking amount of violence in their home and neighborhood. In addition, violence follows some people from childhood through adulthood in that child victims of violence tend to continue to be victimized by violence as adults. For example, Black et al. note that "violence often begins at

an early age and commonly leads to negative health consequences across the lifespan."

The National Crime Victimization Survey

Since 1972 the Bureau of Justice Statistics (BJS), a part of the U.S. Department of Justice, has overseen an annual survey called the National Crime Victimization Survey (NCVS) in which the Census Bureau surveys a nationally representative sample of tens of thousands of households and asks people aged 12 years and older about their experiences of being victimized by certain crimes within the previous six months. The incidents include victimizations that were and were not reported to authorities. As is explained in Chapter 6, the NCVS is a major source of data regarding domestic violence in the United States. In addition, researchers use NCVS data to assess other areas of interest. For example, in *Nonfatal Domestic Violence, 2003–2012* (April 2014, http://www .bjs.gov/content/pub/pdf/ndv0312.pdf), the most recent source of domestic violence data as of September 2016, Jennifer L. Truman and Rachel E. Morgan of the BJS examine NCVS data between 2003 and 2012 to determine what percentage of violent victimizations were perpetrated by intimate partners, immediate family members or other relatives, or friends/acquaintances. According to Truman and Morgan, more than half (53.1%) of all violent victimizations reported between 2003 and 2012 occurred between individuals who knew each other, 38.5% of violent victimizations were perpetrated by strangers, and in 8.5% of cases the identity of the assailant was unknown. Assaults perpetrated by well-known or casual acquaintances accounted for 31.8% of all violent victimizations during this span, whereas 21.3% of incidents occurred between intimate partners or family members. Overall, the rate of violent victimizations that occurred between intimate partners fell dramatically between 1994 and 2012.

According to Truman and Morgan, between 2003 and 2012 there were 5.6 domestic violence victims per 1,000 people aged 12 years and older. During this period women (8.4 per 1,000 individuals) were three times more likely than men (2.8 per 1,000) to be victims of domestic violence; women (6.2 per 1,000) were also considerably more likely than men (1.4 per 1,000) to be victimized by an intimate partner. Individuals between the ages of 18 and 24 (11.6 per 1,000 people) were more likely to be victims of domestic violence than those of any other age group. Among various racial categories, individuals who identified as belonging to two or more races (22.5 per 1,000) were considerably more likely than non-Hispanic African Americans (6.7 per 1,000), non-Hispanic whites (5.7 per 1,000), Hispanics (4 per 1,000), or members of other races (3.7 per 1,000) to have been domestic violence victims between 2003 and 2012.

Truman and Morgan report that between 2003 and 2012 women were considerably more likely than men to be victims of domestic violence perpetrated by an intimate partner. Girlfriends who were victimized by their boyfriends accounted for 39% of all victimizations involving intimate partner violence during this span; female spouses accounted for one-quarter (25%) of all victimizations, and female ex-spouses accounted for 10% of victimizations. In domestic violence situations involving an immediate family member rather than an intimate partner, males were more likely to be victims of abuse. Male victims of parental abuse accounted for 10.2% of violent victimizations involving an immediate family member; this rate was more than double that of female victims of parental abuse, who accounted for 4.3% of violent victimizations involving immediate family members.

The National Survey of Children's Exposure to Violence

In 2008 the DOJ's Office of Juvenile Justice and Delinquency Prevention and the Centers for Disease Control and Prevention oversaw a survey to measure lifetime and past-year exposure to violence for children. The National Survey of Children's Exposure to Violence (NatSCEV) was designed and conducted by the Crimes against Children Research Center at the University of New Hampshire. The result of this landmark study,

Children's Exposure to Violence: A Comprehensive National Survey (October 2009, https://www.ncjrs.gov/pdffiles1/ojjdp/227744.pdf) by David Finkelhor et al., was released in October 2009.

Finkelhor et al. note that 10.2% of the children had been subjected to child maltreatment and that 9.8% had witnessed a family assault. Other types of violence exposure that children had experienced during the previous year were assault with no weapon or injury (36.7%), witnessing a community assault (19.2%), assault with a weapon and/or injury (14.9%), sexual victimization (6.1%), and dating violence (1.4%).

David Finkelhor, Heather Turner, and Sherry Hamby explain in "Questions and Answers about the National Survey of Children's Exposure to Violence" (October 2011, https://www.ncjrs.gov/pdffiles1/ojjdp/235163.pdf) that the survey included a nationally representative sample of more than 4,500 children aged 17 years and younger. Children aged 10 years and older were questioned directly; the parents or other caregivers of younger children were questioned in place of the younger children. The survey participants were asked about past-year and lifetime exposures to violence, including direct exposure (through personal victimization) and indirect exposure (witnessing violent acts against others). In addition, the participants were asked about psychological and emotional victimizations, such as bullying, neglect by a parent/caregiver, and Internet victimization.

Finkelhor, Turner, and Hamby find that 61% of the children had been exposed to violence, crime, or abuse during the previous year. According to the survey, physical assault (including by siblings and other children) was the most common type of victimization across almost all ages. It was slightly outranked among children aged 15 to 17 years by an experience of witnessing violence. The percentages of children experiencing past-year maltreatment and sexual victimizations were higher for older children than for younger children.

POLYVICTIMS. One of the significant findings from the NatSCEV data was that some children had been exposed to multiple types of violence, and these experiences had greatly stressed them. In *Polyvictimization: Children's Exposure to Multiple Types of Violence, Crime, and Abuse* (October 2011, https://www.ncjrs.gov/pdffiles1/ojjdp/235504.pdf), the most recent report on the subject as of September 2016, Finkelhor et al. note that 49% of the surveyed children reported two or more victimization types including direct and indirect victimizations during the previous year. The largest number of victimization types suffered was 18 victimizations. The researchers refer to the 8% of the children who had experienced seven or more victimizations during the previous year as "polyvictims" because these children showed significantly higher distress levels than did victims with less victimization types.

Finkelhor et al. assess distress levels among all the surveyed children using standardized trauma checklists. As expected, nonvictims had the lowest trauma symptom scores. Distress levels were higher for victims classified as low chronic victims (those exposed to less than the average frequency of only one type of victimization) and high chronic victims (those exposed to more than the average frequency of only one type of victimization). Trauma symptom scores were the highest for the polyvictims. Finkelhor et al. theorize that these children scored so high because "there are relatively few areas of safety for them."

Finkelhor et al. note that physical assault was the most common type of victimization, with nearly all (98%) the victims having experienced a physical assault during the previous year. Other victimization types that were experienced by at least three-fourths of the polyvictims included any property crime (88%) and any exposure to community violence (84%). The researchers find that polyvictims suffered more injuries than nonpolyvictims and experienced "a disproportionate share of the most serious kinds of victimizations." For example, more than half (55%) of the polyvictims suffered an injury, compared with 12% of nonpolyvictims. In addition, the polyvictims had greater rates than did nonpolyvictims for the most serious types of victimizations: caregiver perpetration (53% versus 14%), weapons victimizations (42% versus 6%), and sexual victimizations (36% versus 6%).

Finkelhor et al. also observe the demographic characteristics of polyvictims. Overall, males had a higher rate (8.4%) than did females (7.5%), and older children aged 14 to 17 years were more likely to be polyvictims than younger children. Children in the middle socioeconomic category (8.8%) had a higher polyvictimization rate than children in the low (7.3%) or high (4.7%) economic groups. Non-Hispanic African American children (12.8%) suffered the highest rate among the racial and ethnic groups. Family structure also played a role. Children in two-parent families had a significantly lower rate at 5.2% than did children in other family structures (12.4% to 13.9%). Lastly, children living in cities with a population of 300,000 or more had a slightly higher rate (8.3%) than children in cities or towns with lower populations (7.8%).

Finkelhor et al. indicate that there are four pathways that children become polyvictims: dangerous families (i.e., families that experience "considerable violence and conflict"), family disruption and adversity (e.g., families that are beset with financial problems or substance abuse), dangerous neighborhoods, and emotional problems (i.e., children whose preexisting emotional problems cause them to engage in risky behavior, antagonize others, or limit their abilities to defend themselves). (See Figure 1.5.) Child maltreatment, domestic violence, and sexual victimization are factors that contribute to polyvictimization.

FIGURE 1.5

Pathways by which children become polyvictims

SOURCE: David Finkelhor et al., "Figure 6. Conceptual Models of Pathways to Polyvictimization," in "Polyvictimization: Children's Exposure to Multiple Types of Violence, Crime, and Abuse," *Juvenile Justice Bulletin*, U.S. Department of Justice, Office of Justice Programs, Office of Juvenile Justice and Delinquency Prevention, October 2011, https://www.ncjrs.gov/pdffiles1/ojjdp/235504.pdf (accessed June 9, 2016)

CORPORAL PUNISHMENT: CHILD ABUSE OR NOT?

Corporal punishment is physical punishment intended to inflict pain on the person being punished. Although the term is a catch-all for various physical punishments, it is widely used to refer to spanking and other physical methods of discipline used against children. In the United States all 50 states allow parents to use corporal punishment for purposes of disciplining their children. As long as the children do not suffer injury, parents may use their hand or even an object such as a belt. When states passed child abuse laws during the 1960s, provisions allowing parents to use corporal punishment helped facilitate passage of the legislation. Despite its acceptance in the United States, corporal punishment against children is outlawed by some nations. The Global Initiative to End All Corporal Punishment of Children reports in "States Which Have Prohibited All Corporal Punishment" (http://www.endcorporalpunishment.org/progress/prohibiting-states/) that as of September 2016 corporal punishment by parents, caretakers, and teachers was completely banned in 49 countries.

Studies on the Effects of Corporal Punishment

In "Parents' Discipline of Young Children: Results from the National Survey of Early Childhood Health" (*Pediatrics*, vol. 113, no. 6, June 2004), Michael Regalado et al. report on the parental use of corporal punishment for discipline in regard to the health and development of children under three years of age. Six percent of parents surveyed indicated they had spanked their children when they were four to nine months old, 29% spanked their children when they were 10 to 18 months old, and 64% spanked their children when they were 19 to 35 months old. Frequent spankings were also administered by some parents of children 10 to 18 months old (11%) and 19 to 35 months old (26%).

Studies on the spanking of children have mostly used sample populations of children aged two years and older. In "Spanking in Early Childhood and Later Behavior Problems: A Prospective Study of Infants and Young Toddlers" (*Pediatrics*, vol. 113, no. 5, May 2004), Eric P. Slade and Lawrence S. Wissow of the Johns Hopkins Bloomberg School of Public Health conducted the first study of its kind in the United States by following a group of children younger than two years old to test "the hypothesis that spanking frequency before age 2 is positively associated with the probability of having significant behavior problems 4 years later."

Slade and Wissow collected data on 1,966 children and their mothers who participated in the National Longitudinal Survey of Mother-Child Sample, a large-scale national study of youth aged 14 to 21 years old. Some of these young people were mothers with children.

Data were collected on the mother-children groups when the children were under two years of age. Four years later, after the children had entered elementary school, Slade and Wissow interviewed the mothers to explore their hypothesis. Mothers were asked if they spanked their child the previous week and how frequently they spanked their children. They were also questioned about the child's temperament, mother-child interactions, and whether they had ever met with the child's teacher because of behavioral problems.

Slade and Wissow find that, when compared with children who were never spanked, non-Hispanic white children who were frequently spanked (five times per week) before age two were four times more likely to have behavioral problems by the time they started school. No connection was found between spanking and later behavioral problems among African American and Hispanic children. According to Slade and Wissow, the same results were found in studies involving children older than two years. The researchers surmise that the way non-Hispanic white families and other ethnic families view the spanking of children may influence the effects of spanking. For example, African American families typically do not consider spanking as "harsh or unfair."

Catherine A. Taylor et al. examine the relationship between the spanking of three-year-old children and later aggressive behavior in "Mothers' Spanking of 3-Year-Old Children and Subsequent Risk of Children's Aggressive Behavior" (*Pediatrics*, vol. 125, no. 5, May 2010). The researchers find that frequent use of corporal punishment on three-year-olds (spanking more than twice over the course of a month) was associated with increased aggressive behavior at five years of age. The increased risk held true even when the researchers controlled for the level of aggression at age three as well as for key demographic features. Taylor et al. conclude that even "minor" forms of corporal punishment, including spanking, increase children's risk of aggressive behavior.

Matthew K. Mulvaney and Carolyn J. Mebert of the University of New Hampshire report in "Stress Appraisal and Attitudes towards Corporal Punishment as Intervening Processes between Corporal Punishment and Subsequent Mental Health" (*Journal of Family Violence*, vol. 25, no. 4, May 2010) that negative attitudes about corporal punishment affect its degree of harm. The researchers report that children's evaluations of corporal punishment as threatening were more significantly associated with the adverse mental health effects than with the actual frequency of the punishment. Mulvaney and Mebert also find that the mother-child relationship was more impacted by corporal punishment than was the father-child relationship.

In "Corporal Punishment and Child Behavioural and Cognitive Outcomes through 5 Years of Age: Evidence from a Contemporary Urban Birth Cohort Study"

(*Infant and Child Development*, vol. 21, no. 1, January–February 2012), Michael J. McKenzie et al. report that corporal punishment can also exert a negative impact on a child's cognitive progress at a young age. The researchers find evidence that frequent spanking can inhibit the verbal development of children between the ages of three and five years. According to McKenzie et al., children who experienced a high level of corporal punishment at the age of three tended to test lower on the Peabody Picture Vocabulary Test, a standard that measures vocabulary, academic aptitude, and other indicators of verbal intelligence.

Sabrina Fréchette, Michael Zoratti, and Elisa Romano identify in "What Is the Link between Corporal Punishment and Child Physical Abuse?" (*Journal of Family Violence*, vol. 30, no. 2, February 2015) a strong link between spanking and physical child abuse. Although the frequency of corporal punishment is tied to increased rates of child abuse, the researchers note that any incidences of spanking can be indicators of potential physical abuse. Furthermore, Fréchette, Zoratti, and Romano observe that the presence of other violent or unstable behavior, such as intimate partner violence and "parental impulsiveness during disciplinary moments," put children at a higher risk of being physically abused.

In spite of studies demonstrating the negative impacts of corporal punishment on a child's well-being and development, spanking and other forms of physical discipline remain deeply ingrained within American culture. The notion that spanking or hitting is a traditional, and therefore normal, form of discipline is often used as a justification for corporal punishment. Indeed, as McKenzie et al.

note, adults who were spanked during their own childhoods are more likely to use corporal punishment to discipline their own children. At the same time, corporal punishment in the United States is not limited to family settings. Melinda D. Anderson reports in "Where Teachers Are Still Allowed to Spank Students" (Atlantic.com, December 15, 2015) that as of 2015, 19 states still allowed teachers to administer corporal punishment to their students in the classroom.

The question of corporal punishment became the subject of intense national debate in September 2014, when the Minnesota Vikings running back Adrian Peterson (1985–) was suspended by the National Football League after it was revealed that he had hit his four-year-old son with a switch. The incident had left the boy covered with cuts and bruises. Although Peterson subsequently expressed remorse for his actions on Twitter (September 15, 2014, https://twitter.com/AdrianPeterson/status/511586600346599424), he also attempted to justify his actions within the context of his own upbringing. "I have always believed that the way my parents disciplined me has a great deal to do with the success I have enjoyed as a man," Peterson stated. Despite facing felony charges of causing injury to a child, Peterson also insisted that he was "without a doubt, not a child abuser." Indeed, in 2014 a majority of Americans continued to believe that corporal punishment did not constitute actual abuse. As Tara Fowler writes in "Adrian Peterson Controversy: Is It OK to Spank Your Children?" (People.com, September 16, 2014), nearly three-quarters (74%) of mothers in the United States believed that spanking children between the ages of one and three was an acceptable form of discipline.

CHAPTER 2
DETECTING, MEASURING, AND PREVENTING CHILD ABUSE

CHILD ABUSE DATA SOURCES

Statistics on child abuse are difficult to interpret and compare because there is little consistency in how information is collected. The definitions of abuse vary from study to study, as do the methods of counting incidents of abuse. Some methods count only reported cases of abuse. Some statistics are based on estimates that are projected from a small study, whereas others are based on interviews.

As of September 2016, three federal government sources had published updated comprehensive data on child abuse:

- *Child Maltreatment*—an annual report published by the Children's Bureau, an agency within the U.S. Department of Health and Human Services (HHS).

- The National Survey of Child and Adolescent Well-Being (NSCAW)—a research project of the Office of Planning, Research, and Evaluation (OPRE) within the Administration for Children and Families. Numerous reports have been published by the OPRE and private researchers based on NSCAW data.

- National Incidence Study of Child Abuse and Neglect (NIS)—as of September 2016, four NIS studies had been conducted by the private research company Westat under contract to the OPRE.

CHILD MALTREATMENT

The Child Abuse Prevention, Adoption, and Family Services Act of 1988 mandated that the HHS establish a national data collection program on child maltreatment. In 1990 the National Child Abuse and Neglect Data System (NCANDS) began operating. The database includes child maltreatment data from child protective services (CPS) agencies in the 50 states and the District of Columbia. The Children's Bureau publishes summary NCANDS data on an annual basis. As of September 2016, the most recent publication was *Child Maltreatment 2014* (January 25, 2016, https://www.acf.hhs.gov/sites/default/files/cb/cm2014.pdf).

Referrals and Reports

Figure 2.1 indicates that in 2014 CPS agencies received an estimated 3.6 million referrals relating to 6.6 million children. Many referrals are made by phone, for example, to special hotlines that are maintained for the reporting of abuse allegations. The Children's Bureau notes that states differ in how they count the number of referrals they receive. For example, one state counted every call received via its hotline as a referral, even calls that were misdialed. About 2.2 million (61%) of the referrals received in 2014 were screened in, and approximately 1.4 million (39%) were screened out (not further acted on by CPS agencies). According to the Children's Bureau, screened-out referrals include calls that do not concern child abuse and neglect, calls that do not include enough information for the agency to act on, calls that are related to matters better handled by other agencies, and calls that concern children who are older than 18 years old.

Referrals that are screened in are called reports. As shown in Figure 2.1, nearly two-thirds (63%) of the 2014 reports originated from professional sources. Another 19% were from nonprofessional sources, and 19% were unclassified, meaning the professional status of the caller was unknown. Table 2.1 provides detailed information about report sources between 2010 and 2014. Overall, education and legal and law enforcement personnel accounted for more than one-third of all reports that were received in 2014. That year legal and law enforcement personnel (18.1%) accounted for most of the reports from professional sources, followed by education personnel (17.7%) and social services personnel (11%). Most reports from nonprofessional sources came from parents (6.8%) and other relatives (7%) of the children involved.

FIGURE 2.1

Child maltreatment referrals and dispositions, 2014

3.6 million[a] referrals alleging maltreatment to CPS involving 6.6 million children[a]

61% referrals screened in (become reports)

39% referrals screened out

2.2 million reports received a disposition[b]

Submitted by
• 63% professional
• 19% nonprofessional
• 19% unclassified
• Exceeds 100% due to rounding

3.2 million children[b] received either an investigation or alternative response

702,000 victims[a]
Includes 1,580 fatalities[a]

2,498,000 nonvictims[a,c]

410,448 victims received postresponse services

890,889 nonvictims received postresponse services

147,462 victims received foster care services

94,457 nonvictims received foster care services

[a]Indicates a nationally estimated number.
[b]Average 1.83 children per referral.
[c]The estimated number of unique nonvictims was calculated by subtracting the unique count of estimated victims from the unique count of estimated children.

SOURCE: "Exhibit S-1. Statistics at a Glance 2014," in *Child Maltreatment 2014*, U.S. Department of Health and Human Services, Administration for Children and Families, Administration on Children, Youth, and Families, Children's Bureau, January 25, 2016, https://www.acf.hhs.gov/sites/default/files/cb/cm2014.pdf (accessed June 9, 2016)

Child Victims

The 2014 reports concerned 3.2 million unique children. (See Figure 2.1.) Nearly 2.5 million of the uniquely counted children were determined to be nonvictims. The remaining 702,000 were determined to be child maltreatment victims; this number included 1,580 children who died from maltreatment. Many victims and nonvictims received in-home services and/or foster care services from CSA agencies in 2014.

Table 2.2 lists the child victimization rates for uniquely counted children between 2010 and 2014. These rates were calculated by dividing the estimated number of unique victims each year by the nation's child population for that year. A victimization rate of 9.4 victims per 1,000 children was reported in 2014. This value was up slightly from 9.1 victims per 1,000 children reported in 2012.

According to the Children's Bureau, in *Child Maltreatment 2014*, 50.7% of the child maltreatment victims in 2014 were girls and 48.9% were boys. The sex of the remaining 0.4% of victims was unknown. Table 2.3 shows a victim breakdown by race and ethnicity for

TABLE 2.1

Sources of reports for alleged child maltreatment, 2010–14

Report sources	Number					Percent				
	2010	2011	2012	2013	2014	2010	2011	2012	2013	2014
Professional										
Child daycare providers	14,189	14,494	14,545	13,863	13,974	0.8	0.7	0.7	0.7	0.7
Education personnel	313,763	326,072	347,840	346,930	364,782	16.9	16.7	17.3	17.5	17.7
Foster care providers	10,130	9,380	9,189	9,181	9,324	0.5	0.5	0.5	0.5	0.5
Legal and law enforcement personnel	318,347	339,428	349,168	347,892	372,750	17.1	17.4	17.4	17.6	18.1
Medical personnel	156,675	169,424	177,802	178,650	190,298	8.4	8.7	8.9	9.0	9.2
Mental health personnel	89,335	95,809	97,914	108,597	116,148	4.8	4.9	4.9	5.5	5.6
Social services personnel	219,634	214,867	230,713	218,135	226,083	11.8	11.0	11.5	11.0	11.0
Total professionals	**1,122,073**	**1,169,474**	**1,227,171**	**1,223,248**	**1,293,359**	**60.3**	**60.0**	**61.1**	**61.7**	**62.7**
Nonprofessional										
Alleged perpetrators	879	734	708	788	1,129	0.0	0.0	0.0	0.0	0.1
Alleged victims	8,047	7,847	7,643	6,477	6,432	0.4	0.4	0.4	0.3	0.3
Friends and neighbors	83,962	89,594	92,981	92,723	89,759	4.5	4.6	4.6	4.7	4.4
Other relatives	132,411	136,290	138,602	136,690	145,128	7.1	7.0	6.9	6.9	7.0
Parents	130,730	132,246	134,647	131,506	140,900	7.0	6.8	6.7	6.6	6.8
Total nonprofessionals	**356,029**	**366,711**	**374,581**	**368,184**	**383,348**	**19.1**	**18.8**	**18.6**	**18.6**	**18.6**
Unclassified										
Anonymous sources	171,179	177,386	179,094	177,152	167,406	9.2	9.1	8.9	8.9	8.1
Other	151,836	157,463	156,723	148,892	157,260	8.2	8.1	7.8	7.5	7.6
Unknown	59,974	79,120	71,340	64,270	59,934	3.2	4.1	3.6	3.2	2.9
Total unclassified	**382,989**	**413,969**	**407,157**	**390,314**	**384,600**	**20.6**	**21.2**	**20.3**	**19.7**	**18.7**
National	**1,861,091**	**1,950,154**	**2,008,909**	**1,981,746**	**2,061,307**	**100.0**	**100.0**	**100.0**	**100.0**	**100.0**
Reporting states	**50**	**50**	**50**	**49**	**50**					

SOURCE: "Table 2-2. Report Sources, 2010–2014," in *Child Maltreatment 2014*, U.S. Department of Health and Human Services, Administration for Children and Families, Administration on Children, Youth, and Families, Children's Bureau, January 25, 2016, https://www.acf.hhs.gov/sites/default/files/cb/cm2014.pdf (accessed June 9, 2016)

TABLE 2.2

Child maltreatment rates, 2010–14

Year	Reporting states	Child population of reporting states	Victims (unique count) from reporting states	National victimization rate per 1,000 children	Child population of all 52 states	National estimate of victims (unique count)
2010	51	74,154,952	688,099	9.3	75,020,077	698,000
2011	51	73,924,391	676,505	9.2	74,786,700	688,000
2012	52	74,549,295	680,198	9.1	74,549,295	680,000
2013	52	74,414,936	682,307	9.2	74,414,936	682,000
2014	52	74,356,370	702,208	9.4	74,356,370	702,000

Note: The national victimization rate was calculated by dividing the number of victims from reporting states by the child population of reporting states and multiplying by 1,000.
If fewer than 52 states reported data in a given year, the national estimate of victims was calculated by multiplying the national victimization rate by the child population of all 52 states and dividing by 1,000. The result was rounded to the nearest 1,000. If 52 states reported data in a given year, the number of estimated victims was calculated by taking the number of reported victims and rounding it to the nearest 1,000. Because of the rounding rule, the national estimate could have fewer victims than the actual reported number of victims.

SOURCE: "Exhibit 3-D. Child Victimization Rates, 2010–14," in *Child Maltreatment 2014*, U.S. Department of Health and Human Services, Administration for Children and Families, Administration on Children, Youth, and Families, Children's Bureau, January 25, 2016, https://www.acf.hhs.gov/sites/default/files/cb/cm2014.pdf (accessed June 9, 2016)

2014, by state. African American children suffered the highest rate of child maltreatment that year, with 15.3 victimizations per 1,000 children, followed by Native Americans and Alaskan Natives (13.4 per 1,000 children), children claiming multiple races (10.6 per 1,000 children), Hispanics (8.8 per 1,000 children), Pacific Islanders (8.6 per 1,000 children), and whites (8.4 per 1,000 children). By comparison to these groups, Asian Americans had a significantly lower rate of child maltreatment in 2014, with 1.7 victimizations per 1,000 children.

As shown in Figure 2.2, children younger than one year old accounted for the largest share of victims in 2014. Within this age group, there were 24.4 victims per 1,000 children, compared with a rate of 11.4 per 1,000 children between the ages of one and five. As Figure 2.3 reveals, boys aged five years and younger were more likely to be the victims of child maltreatment than girls in that age group, while girls between the ages of six and 17 years were more likely than boys in that age group to suffer abuse. Overall, girls (9.7 victims per 1,000 female children) were more likely than boys

TABLE 2.3

Child maltreatment victims, by race and ethnicity and state, 2014

State	African-American	American Indian or Alaska Native	Asian	Hispanic	Multiple race	Pacific Islander	White	Unknown	Total
Alabama	2,478	5	11	338		3	5,521	341	8,697
Alaska	40	1,315	11	71	189	23	472	363	2,484
Arizona	1,123	661	46	5,397	497	16	5,245	900	13,885
Arkansas	1,423	8	15	562	599	31	6,264	69	8,971
California	10,214	622	1,899	41,799	1,489	257	15,988	2,765	75,033
Colorado	861	83	48	3,796	394	14	4,510	273	9,979
Connecticut	1,556	13	45	2,417	383	8	2,925	304	7,651
Delaware	666		9	185	48		569	5	1,482
District of Columbia	977		3	176	16		13	343	1,528
Florida	14,379	53	159	8,379	2,011	8	19,518	1,231	45,738
Georgia	8,741	10	101	1,595	801	5	10,713	197	22,163
Hawaii	28	5	114	34	603	233	231	83	1,331
Idaho	15	80	2	236	19	1	1,194	48	1,595
Illinois	10,193	18	249	4,755		19	13,987	450	29,671
Indiana	4,333	10	60	2,037	1,621	12	15,259	27	23,359
Iowa	907	96	48	797	272	22	5,266	663	8,071
Kansas	174	13	8	268	106		1,420	9	1,998
Kentucky	2,257	11	27	822	877	9	15,234	1,596	20,833
Louisiana	5,331	42	22	298	256	4	5,756	348	12,057
Maine	63	29	10	168	118	5	2,288	1,142	3,823
Maryland	6,442	11	150	1,377	352	6	5,481	1,943	15,762
Massachusetts	4,232	54	392	8,338	1,267	11	12,241	5,328	31,863
Michigan	6,770	117	47	1,453	2,439	5	16,740	3,134	30,705
Minnesota	806	275	112	456	684	1	1,762	47	4,143
Mississippi	3,402	13	15	196	127		4,413	269	8,435
Missouri	881	4	16	217	83	7	3,936	178	5,322
Montana	22	225	5	71	78		778	12	1,191
Nebraska	591	208	24	673	223		2,021	200	3,940
Nevada	975	22	45	1,217	285	40	1,547	166	4,297
New Hampshire	14			41	14	1	538	38	646
New Jersey	3,639	6	138	2,759	229	12	3,732	1,327	11,842
New Mexico	195	636	8	4,556	165	8	1,792	246	7,606
New York	18,298	243	1,140	16,908	2,079	14	20,951	6,022	65,655
North Carolina	6,085	722	52	2,120	1,143	36	10,592	216	20,966
North Dakota	61	386	3	75	137	10	880	64	1,616
Ohio	6,117	8	60	1,271	1,772	9	15,262	432	24,931
Oklahoma	1,169	886	14	2,253	3,339	20	5,498	4	13,183
Oregon	445	236	85	1,348	397	44	6,047	1,486	10,088
Pennsylvania									
Puerto Rico									
Rhode Island	382	10	37	903	226		1,616	236	3,410
South Carolina	4,595	20	14	525	443	2	6,372	468	12,439
South Dakota	23	368	1	52	92	1	332	17	886
Tennessee									
Texas	11,024	80	253	28,909	2,293	58	21,437	1,280	65,334
Utah	235	163	53	2,034	180	143	6,987	81	9,876
Vermont	10		2	7			758	36	813
Virginia	1,697	1	42	698	368	28	3,404	226	6,464
Washington	529	417	111	1,114	713	95	3,906	456	7,341
West Virginia	115	2	5	55	272		4,281	232	4,962
Wisconsin	920	172	53	467	228	3	2,401	398	4,642
Wyoming	33	13	1	141	19		643	11	861
National	**145,466**	**8,372**	**5,765**	**154,364**	**29,946**	**1,224**	**298,721**	**35,710**	**679,568**

(9 victims per 1,000 male children) to suffer maltreatment in 2014.

FATALITIES. As noted earlier, an estimated 1,580 children died as a result of maltreatment in 2014. This equaled a national child fatality rate of 2.1 fatalities per 100,000 children. (See Table 2.4.) The fatality rate was down from that reported in 2012, but represented an increase over the rate reported in 2013. Table 2.5 provides a detailed age breakdown of the fatalities in 2014. Children under the age of one year had, by far, the highest fatality rate at nearly 18 fatalities per 100,000 population in that age group. Overall, fatality rates declined with increasing age, dropping to 6.5 fatalities per 100,000 population for children aged one year and 4.2 fatalities per 100,000 population for children aged two years. By comparison, the fatality rates for children aged 10 to 17 years ranged from 0.3 to 0.5 fatalities per 100,000 population in that age range.

The Children's Bureau notes in *Child Maltreatment 2014* that boys made up 58.3% of child fatalities due

TABLE 2.3

Child maltreatment victims, by race and ethnicity and state, 2014 [CONTINUED]

	Rate per 1,000 children						
State	African-American	American Indian or Alaska Native	Asian	Hispanic	Multiple race	Pacific Islander	White
Alabama	7.5	0.9	0.8	4.4		4.8	8.5
Alaska	6.4	39.6	1.1	4.2	8.3	7.3	5.0
Arizona	15.4	8.1	1.1	7.7	8.3	5.7	8.0
Arkansas	11.1	1.4	1.4	6.9	24.1	10.0	13.8
California	20.9	17.8	1.9	8.8	3.5	7.9	6.6
Colorado	16.4	11.1	1.3	9.8	7.6	7.8	6.4
Connecticut	17.8	6.7	1.2	14.0	13.5	22.3	6.5
Delaware	13.0		1.1	6.2	4.6		5.5
District of Columbia	14.7		1.1	10.4	3.6		0.5
Florida	17.4	5.5	1.5	7.0	14.3	2.8	11.0
Georgia	10.5	2.0	1.1	4.6	9.5	3.0	9.5
Hawaii	4.3	7.6	1.5	0.6	6.4	6.6	5.4
Idaho	3.9	16.1	0.4	3.1	1.4	1.3	3.7
Illinois	21.9	4.2	1.7	6.5		21.9	9.0
Indiana	24.8	3.2	1.9	12.3	26.9	20.7	13.3
Iowa	27.5	37.9	2.9	11.5	10.1	27.3	9.1
Kansas	3.8	2.3	0.4	2.1	2.9		2.9
Kentucky	24.1	7.0	1.8	14.5	22.5	11.8	18.9
Louisiana	12.9	5.6	1.2	4.5	8.1	8.9	10.0
Maine	9.2	14.4	2.6	24.2	13.3	50.0	9.9
Maryland	15.2	3.7	1.8	7.6	5.3	9.1	9.2
Massachusetts	37.2	20.8	4.4	35.6	24.5	18.1	13.6
Michigan	18.9	8.7	0.7	8.2	24.6	8.4	11.1
Minnesota	7.6	15.3	1.5	4.2	11.1	1.6	1.9
Mississippi	10.9	2.9	2.3	6.7	7.7		12.2
Missouri	4.7	0.7	0.6	2.5	1.4	3.1	3.8
Montana	13.4	10.5	3.0	5.5	7.7		4.4
Nebraska	21.9	40.2	2.4	8.7	12.5		6.1
Nevada	16.8	3.9	1.1	4.5	7.2	9.4	6.2
New Hampshire	3.0			2.8	1.6	12.3	2.3
New Jersey	13.1	1.8	0.7	5.5	3.8	17.4	3.8
New Mexico	23.2	12.4	1.4	15.3	13.0	24.6	14.2
New York	27.5	17.3	3.5	16.7	14.9	7.2	10.1
North Carolina	11.5	25.6	0.8	6.1	12.6	18.7	8.6
North Dakota	13.4	28.2	1.8	8.5	20.6	88.5	6.6
Ohio	15.8	1.9	1.1	8.5	15.1	7.9	7.9
Oklahoma	15.1	9.2	0.8	14.9	37.5	12.2	10.6
Oregon	24.4	22.7	2.5	7.2	7.9	10.8	10.9
Pennsylvania							
Puerto Rico							
Rhode Island	25.0	8.7	5.1	18.3	24.4		12.4
South Carolina	13.6	5.2	0.9	5.7	11.4	3.0	10.7
South Dakota	4.7	13.6	0.4	4.2	10.2	11.6	2.2
Tennessee							
Texas	13.2	4.3	0.9	8.3	13.5	10.0	9.2
Utah	22.1	19.1	3.4	13.2	6.0	15.2	10.3
Vermont	4.4		0.9	2.3			6.9
Virginia	4.5	0.2	0.4	3.0	3.7	20.7	3.3
Washington	8.0	17.7	1.0	3.4	5.8	7.3	4.2
West Virginia	8.0	3.4	1.8	6.6	19.3		12.6
Wisconsin	8.2	12.4	1.2	3.2	4.8	6.5	2.6
Wyoming	16.7	3.1	1.0	7.2	4.4		6.0
National	**15.3**	**13.4**	**1.7**	**8.8**	**10.6**	**8.6**	**8.4**

SOURCE: "Table 3-6. Victims by Race and Ethnicity, 2014," in *Child Maltreatment 2014*, U.S. Department of Health and Human Services, Administration for Children and Families, Administration on Children, Youth, and Families, Children's Bureau, January 25, 2016, https://www.acf.hhs.gov/sites/default/files/cb/cm2014.pdf (accessed June 9, 2016)

to maltreatment in 2014, whereas girls accounted for 40.9%. For 0.8% of the fatalities the sex of the children was unknown. White children (43%) made up the largest share of the fatalities, followed by African American children (30.3%) and Hispanic children (15.1%). Victimization rates were highest for African American children (4.4 fatalities per 100,000 children of that race), followed by white children (1.8 fatalities per 100,000), Hispanic children (1.5 per 100,000), and Native American or Alaskan Native children (1.5 per 100,000).

According to the Children's Bureau, the vast majority (72.3%) of child maltreatment fatalities in 2014 were due to neglect, either alone or combined with other maltreatment types. The second-largest cause was physical abuse (41.3%), again either alone or combined with other maltreatment types.

FIGURE 2.2

Child maltreatment victims, by age group, 2010–14

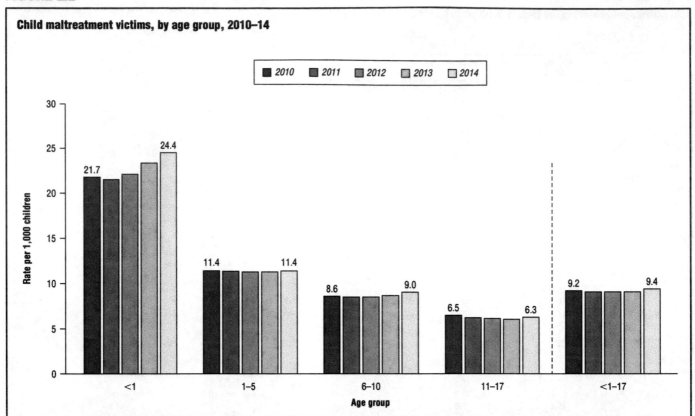

Notes: Based on data from 51 states for 2010–2011, and 52 states for 2012–2014. Data are from the Child File. This analysis does not include the categories of unborn, children ages 18–21, and children with unknown age.

SOURCE: "Exhibit 3-H. The victimization rate of children age <1 had the largest increase of all age groups for the past 5 years," in *Child Maltreatment 2014*, U.S. Department of Health and Human Services, Administration for Children and Families, Administration on Children, Youth, and Families, Children's Bureau, January 25, 2016, https://www.acf.hhs.gov/sites/default/files/cb/cm2014.pdf (accessed June 9, 2016)

Perpetrators

In *Child Maltreatment 2014*, the Children's Bureau reports that 91.6% of child abuse victims in 2014 were maltreated by a parent who either acted alone or with someone else. (See Table 2.6.) More than a two-fifths (40.7%) were maltreated by their mother acting alone. The second-largest category was the mother and father together (21.3%). Overall, 12.6% of child maltreatment cases were attributed to nonparents in 2014. Among specified nonparent perpetrators, male relatives (3%) and male partners (2.6%) made up the two largest groups of perpetrators.

Figure 2.4 provides a breakdown by age of child maltreatment perpetrators in 2014. Adults between the ages of 25 and 34 years had the highest rate of child maltreatment that year, with five perpetrators per 1,000 adults in that age group. The Children's Bureau notes that 54.1% of the perpetrators in 2014 were women, and 44.8% were men. The sex of the remaining 1.1% was unknown. Figure 2.5 shows perpetrator race and ethnicity for 2014. The largest percentage was white (48.8%), followed by African American (20%) and Hispanic (19.8%).

Categories of child neglect are shown in Table 2.7. As Figure 2.6 indicates, chronic neglect can stem from a range of factors and can arise from external social circumstances (such as poverty), personal issues that impact the ability of parents to raise their children effectively, or specific childhood trauma.

NATIONAL SURVEY OF CHILD AND ADOLESCENT WELL-BEING

In *NSCAW II Baseline Report: Introduction to NSCAW II* (August 1, 2011, http://www.acf.hhs.gov/sites/default/files/opre/nscaw2_intro.pdf), Melissa Dolan et al. explain that the NSCAW studies were authorized under the Personal Responsibility and Work Opportunity Reconciliation Act of 1996. The studies are longitudinal studies, meaning that they involve research that was conducted on the same test subjects over long periods, typically years. The first NSCAW study (now known as NSCAW I) tracked 5,501 children aged birth to 14 years between 1999 and 2007. The children were selected for the study because they were the subjects of maltreatment investigations by CPS agencies or because they were in foster care. NSCAW II began in 2008 and was ongoing as

FIGURE 2.3

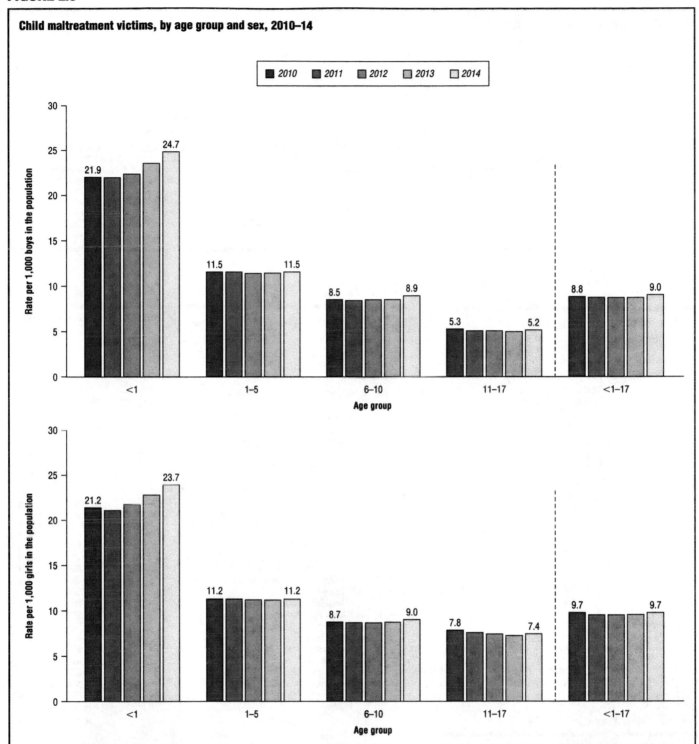

Child maltreatment victims, by age group and sex, 2010–14

Notes: Based on data from 51 states for 2010–2011, and 52 states for 2012–2014. Data are from the child file. This analysis does not include the categories of unborn, children ages 18–21, and children with unknown age.

SOURCE: "Exhibit 3-I. The victimization rates for younger boys are consistently higher than girls of the same age, while the victimization rates for older girls are consistently higher than boys of the same age," in *Child Maltreatment 2014*, U.S. Department of Health and Human Services, Administration for Children and Families, Administration on Children, Youth, and Families, Children's Bureau, January 25, 2016, https://www.acf.hhs.gov/sites/default/files/cb/cm2014.pdf (accessed June 9, 2016)

of September 2016. It was tracking 5,873 children for which maltreatment investigations were closed by CPS agencies between February 2008 and April 2009. The children were in the age range of birth to 17.5 years at that time. As of September 2016, two NSCAW II data collections (or waves) had taken place. Baseline data were collected about the children between March 2008 and September 2009 during Wave 1. Wave 2 data

TABLE 2.4

Child maltreatment fatality rates, 2010–14

Year	Reporting states	Child population of reporting states	Child fatalities from reporting states	National fatality rate per 100,000 children	Child population of all 52 states	National estimate of child fatalities
2010	52	75,020,077	1,563	2.08	75,020,077	1,560
2011	52	74,786,700	1,571	2.10	74,786,700	1,570
2012	51	74,284,172	1,622	2.18	74,549,295	1,630
2013	50	72,756,605	1,500	2.06	74,414,936	1,530
2014	50	72,706,925	1,546	2.13	74,356,370	1,580

Notes: Data are from the child file and agency file or the summary data component (SDC). National fatality rates per 100,000 children were calculated by dividing the number of child fatalities by the population of reporting states and multiplying by 100,000. If fewer than 52 states reported data, the national estimate of child fatalities was calculated by multiplying the national fatality rate by the child population of all 52 states and dividing by 100,000. The estimate was rounded to the nearest 10. If 52 states reported data, the national estimate of child fatalities was calculated by taking the number of reported child fatalities and rounding to the nearest 10. Because of the rounding rule, the national estimate could have fewer fatalities than the actual reported number of fatalities.

SOURCE: "Exhibit 4-A. Child Fatality Rates per 100,000 Children, 2010–2014," in *Child Maltreatment 2014*, U.S. Department of Health and Human Services, Administration for Children and Families, Administration on Children, Youth, and Families, Children's Bureau, January 25, 2016, https://www.acf.hhs.gov/sites/default/files/cb/cm2014.pdf (accessed June 9, 2016)

TABLE 2.5

Child maltreatment fatalities, by age, 2014

[Data based on 44 states]

		Child fatalities		
Age	Child population	Number	Percent	Rate per 100,000 children
<1	3,017,714	542	44.2	17.96
1	3,027,792	197	16.1	6.51
2	3,033,612	128	10.4	4.22
3	3,061,060	88	7.2	2.87
4	3,069,006	51	4.2	1.66
5	3,070,911	34	2.8	1.11
6	3,168,027	29	2.4	0.92
7	3,184,184	28	2.3	0.88
8	3,160,678	18	1.5	0.57
9	3,150,500	16	1.3	0.51
10	3,157,901	16	1.3	0.51
11	3,136,742	13	1.1	0.41
12	3,126,702	13	1.1	0.42
13	3,202,872	13	1.1	0.41
14	3,251,924	9	0.7	0.28
15	3,191,371	8	0.7	0.25
16	3,189,362	12	1.0	0.38
17	3,194,790	8	0.7	0.25
Unborn, unknown, and 18–21		3	0.2	
National	**56,395,148**	**1,226**	**100.0**	

SOURCE: "Table 4-3. Child Fatalities by Age, 2014," in *Child Maltreatment 2014*, U.S. Department of Health and Human Services, Administration for Children and Families, Administration on Children, Youth, and Families, Children's Bureau, January 25, 2016, https://www.acf.hhs.gov/sites/default/files/cb/cm2014.pdf (accessed June 9, 2016)

TABLE 2.6

Perpetrators of child maltreatment, by relationship to victim, 2014

[Data based on 47 states]

Perpetrator	Victims (unique count)	Reported relationships (duplicate count) Number	Reported relationships (duplicate count) Percent
Parent			
Father		124,870	20.5
Father and nonparent(s)		6,592	1.1
Mother		247,616	40.7
Mother and nonparent(s)		42,177	6.9
Mother and father		129,599	21.3
Mother, father, and nonparent		5,946	1.0
Total parents		**556,800**	**91.6**
Nonparent			
Child daycare provider		2,474	0.4
Foster parent (female relative)		280	0.0
Foster parent (male relative)		65	0.0
Foster parent (nonrelative)		856	0.1
Foster parent (unknown relationship)		155	0.0
Friend and neighbor		2,307	0.4
Group home and residential facility staff		508	0.1
Legal guardian (female)		858	0.1
Legal guardian (male)		236	0.0
More than one nonparental perpetrator		6,333	1.0
Other professional		1,035	0.2
Partner of parent (female)		1,816	0.3
Partner of parent (male)		15,669	2.6
Relative (female)		10,429	1.7
Relative (male)		18,375	3.0
Other		15,485	2.5
Total nonparents		**76,881**	**12.6**
Unknown			
Unknown only		21,481	3.5
Total unknown		**21,481**	**3.5**
National	607,851	655,162	107.8

SOURCE: "Table 3-10. Victims by Relationship to Their Perpetrators, 2014," in *Child Maltreatment 2014*, U.S. Department of Health and Human Services, Administration for Children and Families, Administration on Children, Youth, and Families, Children's Bureau, January 25, 2016, https://www.acf.hhs.gov/sites/default/files/cb/cm2014.pdf (accessed June 9, 2016)

collection for the same children occurred between October 2009 and January 2011, while Wave 3 data were compiled between June 2011 and December 2012.

The NSCAW studies are notable because they follow children as they progress through the child welfare system by monitoring their physical, mental, academic, health, social, and developmental well-being through interviews or assessments that are conducted with the children themselves, their parents, their caseworkers, and nonparent caregivers. Reports from caseworkers, teachers, and administrative records are also reviewed. The children's families and/or caregivers are assessed to

FIGURE 2.4

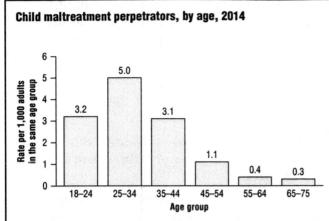

Child maltreatment perpetrators, by age, 2014

SOURCE: "Exhibit 5-C. Adults in the age group of 25–34 had the highest perpetrator rate," in *Child Maltreatment 2014*, U.S. Department of Health and Human Services, Administration for Children and Families, Administration on Children, Youth, and Families, Children's Bureau, January 25, 2016, https://www.acf.hhs.gov/sites/default/files/cb/cm2014.pdf (accessed June 9, 2016)

FIGURE 2.5

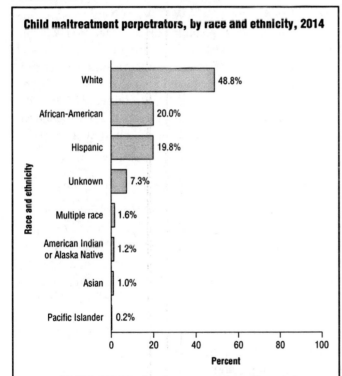

Child maltreatment perpetrators, by race and ethnicity, 2014

SOURCE: "Exhibit 5-D. The three largest percentages of perpetrators were of White, African-American, and Hispanic racial or ethnic descent," in *Child Maltreatment 2014*, U.S. Department of Health and Human Services, Administration for Children and Families, Administration on Children, Youth, and Families, Children's Bureau, January 25, 2016, https://www.acf.hhs.gov/sites/default/files/cb/cm2014.pdf (accessed June 9, 2016)

determine their status in terms of physical and mental health, substance use, domestic violence and other criminal acts, and services received from welfare agencies. In addition, NSCAW data include information about the

TABLE 2.7

Types and examples of child neglect

Types of neglect	Examples
Abandonment	Abandonment by parents/caregivers
Physical	• Inadequate nutrition • Inadequate or unsuitable seasonal clothing • Unreasonably unclean clothing • Inadequate hygiene • Exposure to chronically unhygienic, unsafe, chaotic or cluttered environment
Medical	• Delays in medical/health care • Parental/caregiver failure to seek health care • Parental/caregiver failure to seek therapy for developmental delay
Psychological/emotional	• Deprivation of emotional nurturance • Emotional absence of parent/caregiver
Developmental	• Parental/caregiver failure to recognize developmental capacities/limits • Parent/caregiver failure to address developmental needs • Parent/caregiver failure to foster ordinary developmental milestones
Supervisory	• Being left alone for extended or prolonged periods given the child's age and capacities • Being left in a locked, closed vehicle • Parental/caregiver incapacitation
Guidance	• Exposure to antisocial/criminal behaviors by parents/caregivers • Exposure to illicit drug use by parents/caregivers • Parental/caregiver failure to prevent/discourage risk taking or criminal behavior
Educational	• Parental/caregiver failure to ensure school enrollment or other necessary educational institutions • Parent/caregiver failure to discourage frequent absenteeism

SOURCE: "Types of Neglect," in *Chronic Child Neglect*, U.S. Department for Health and Human Services, Administration for Children and Families, Administration on Children, Youth, and Families, Children's Bureau, January 2013, https://www.childwelfare.gov/pubs/chronic_neglect.pdf (accessed June 9, 2016)

maltreatment investigations that were conducted and any interventions and services that resulted. Risk factors for maltreatment are also examined, as is explained in Chapter 3.

NSCAW II Data

In *NSCAW II Wave 2 Report: Child Safety* (August 2012, http://www.acf.hhs.gov/sites/default/files/opre/nscaw_child_safety.pdf), the most recent report of its kind as of September 2016, Cecilia Casanueva et al. provide characteristics about the 4,972 children who were evaluated in NSCAW II Wave 2. It should be noted that these data describe the children at the time the baseline data were collected, which was between October 2009 and January 2011. Casanueva et al. explain that the children were selected to be as nationally representative as possible of children who come into contact with the child welfare system. However, extra infants and children in out-of-home placement were added because the OPRE considers these to be "high-risk groups." In addition, the proportion of

FIGURE 2.6

Tiers of chronic child neglect

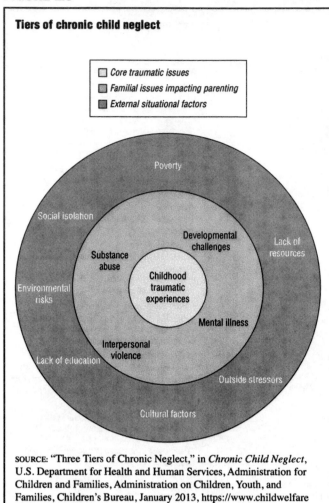

SOURCE: "Three Tiers of Chronic Neglect," in *Chronic Child Neglect*, U.S. Department for Health and Human Services, Administration for Children and Families, Administration on Children, Youth, and Families, Children's Bureau, January 2013, https://www.childwelfare .gov/pubs/chronic_neglect.pdf (accessed June 9, 2016)

children receiving services to those not receiving services was adjusted to include more children receiving services.

Investigatory

Casanueva et al. examine the types of maltreatment that the children were alleged to have received or the other reasons why the children were investigated by CPS agency caseworkers. It should be noted that children can fall under more than one category, for example, if they suffered from more than one type of maltreatment. Overall, neglect in the form of lack of supervision was the primary maltreatment type reported (980 incidences), followed by physical abuse (846 incidences) and failure to provide (446 incidences). Among problems other than maltreatment, a substance-abusing parent was by far the most common problem, with 605 incidences. Substance exposure (495 incidences) and domestic violence (466 incidences) were also notable factors.

Casanueva et al. report that, overall, when caseworkers were asked to name the "most serious" problem that spurred an investigation, the results were neglect in the form of lack of supervision (23.3%), physical abuse (21.9%), and substance-abusing parent (10.6%). Combined, these three problems accounted for more than half (55.8%) of the "most serious" problems cited.

CPS agency investigations of reports of child maltreatment result in a disposition, or finding, for each report. Although disposition terms differ from state to state, possible dispositions include:

- Substantiated or founded—sufficient evidence exists to support the allegation of maltreatment or risk of maltreatment

- Indicated or reason to suspect—the abuse and/or neglect cannot be confirmed, but there is reason to suspect that the child is maltreated or is at risk of maltreatment

- Unsubstantiated or unfounded—no maltreatment has occurred or sufficient evidence does not exist to conclude that the child is maltreated or is at risk of being maltreated

According to Casanueva et al., of 4,611 investigations analyzed in the NSCAW II Wave 2 report, less than one-quarter (22.1%) resulted in substantiated claims. Another 7.6% of investigations produced an indicated status, while 70.4% of investigations resulted in unsubstantiated claims. Children aged zero to two years had the highest percentage of substantiated claims (31.7%), followed by children aged 11 to 17 years (22.1%), children aged three to five years (21.3%), and children aged six to 10 years (15.6%).

Self-Reported Violence, Aggression, and Neglect

As noted earlier, the NSCAW studies include interviews with the children and their parents and/or caregivers. Among the data compiled by Casanueva et al. are child reports of violent acts that were committed by people who were living at home with the children. Only children aged eight to 17 years were questioned. Many of the children reported seeing acts that involved adults yelling and other children being spanked at home. Fewer percentages reported more serious acts, such as drug dealing, stabbings, and shootings. Overall, 11.1% of the children had seen a person arrested at their home, and 2.5% of the children had witnessed such an event within the previous month. When asked about violent acts that were committed against them personally by adults in the home, 42.3% said they had been yelled at and 24.6% said they had been spanked. Smaller percentages said they had experienced an adult throwing something at them or shoving or slapping them "really hard." For the most violent acts, 3.2% of the children said an adult in the home had beat them up, and 0.3% said they had a gun or knife pointed at them by an adult.

Casanueva et al. also examine acts of caregiver aggression reported by children to have occurred within the previous year. Only children aged 11 to 17 years were questioned. Overall, 83.9% of the children reported experiencing nonviolent discipline by their caregivers (e.g., being told that a behavior was wrong). More than half (53.4%) reported psychological aggression (e.g., yelling or shouting), and 31% reported "minor" physical assault or corporal punishment (e.g., spanking on the bottom or slapping a hand). Approximately one out of 10 (10.6%) of the children reported experiencing "severe physical assault" (e.g., hitting with a fist or knocking a child down), and 8.2% reported experiencing "very severe physical assault" (e.g., choking, burning, or threatening with a knife or gun) within the previous year from their caregivers.

Casanueva et al. also report on in-home parental aggression against the children within the previous year as self-reported by the parents. Overall, 96.7% of the parents reported using nonviolent discipline on the children. More than three-quarters (75.4%) reported using psychological aggression, and 47.9% reported conducting "minor" physical assault or corporal punishment. Only 3.3% of the parents reported inflicting "severe physical assault" and 0.9% reported inflicting "very severe physical assault" within the previous year on the children. In addition, 21.1% of the parents admitted to neglect, while 1.2% admitted to committing sexual abuse of the children.

NATIONAL INCIDENCE STUDY OF CHILD ABUSE AND NEGLECT

As part of the 1974 Child Abuse Prevention and Treatment Act (CAPTA), Congress mandated the HHS to conduct a periodic National Incidence Study of Child Abuse and Neglect (NIS). As of September 2016, four NIS studies had been conducted by the private research company Westat under contract to the OPRE. The most recent report was *Fourth National Incidence Study of Child Abuse and Neglect (NIS-4) Report to Congress* (January 2010, http://www.acf.hhs.gov/sites/default/files/opre/nis4_report_congress_full_pdf_jan2010.pdf), written by Andrea J. Sedlak et al. and published jointly by the OPRE and the Children's Bureau.

During the NIS studies, data on maltreated children were collected not only from CPS agencies but also from professionals in community agencies, such as law enforcement, public health, juvenile probation, mental health, and voluntary social services, as well as from hospitals, schools, and day care centers. As such, the NIS reports are considered to be comprehensive sources of information about the incidence of child maltreatment in the United States.

Conducted during two three-month periods in 2005 and 2006, the studies described by Sedlak et al. constitute the most extensive report on child maltreatment in the United States as of September 2016. These studies were based on a nationally representative sample of 10,791 professionals in 1,094 agencies serving 122 counties. The study group included not only child victims investigated by CPS agencies but also children seen by professionals in community institutions (such as day care centers, schools, homeless shelters, and hospitals) and in other investigating agencies (such as public health departments, police, and courts). In addition, victim counts were unduplicated, meaning that each child was counted only once.

Definition Standards

Sedlak et al. use two standardized definitions of abuse and neglect:

- Harm Standard—requires that an abusive act or incident of neglect result in demonstrable harm to be counted
- Endangerment Standard—allows children who had not yet demonstrated harm by maltreatment to be counted in the estimates of maltreated children if a non-CPS agency professional considered them to be at risk of harm or if their maltreatment was substantiated or indicated in a CPS agency investigation

Sedlak et al. report that over the course of their study 1.3 million children were victims of maltreatment under the Harm Standard. This was a 19.1% decrease from the Third National Incidence Study of Child Abuse and Neglect (NIS-3; 1996) estimate of 1.6 million children in 1993. The rate of maltreatment per 1,000 children under the age of 18 years was 17.1 in 2005–06, which was not significantly different from the rate of maltreatment in 1986. Declines in the rates of all forms of abuse were at least marginally statistically significant between 1993 and 2005–06, although declines in rates of neglect were not.

Under the Endangerment Standard more than 2.9 million children experienced some type of maltreatment in 2005–06. This estimate was not significantly different from the 1993 estimate, but it was double the 1986 estimate of 1.4 million children. The rates of abuse under the Endangerment Standard declined from 18.2 per 1,000 children in 1993 to 11.3 per 1,000 children in 2005–06, whereas the rates of all forms of neglect remained about the same. The exception was emotional neglect, which rose significantly between 1993 and 2005–06.

NIS-4 data provide detailed information about maltreatment by child demographics, such as gender, age, and race and ethnicity. In addition, the data are broken down by family characteristics, including socioeconomic status.

Gender of Victims

NIS data allow comparisons of types of maltreatment suffered by boys and girls. Under both the Harm and Endangerment Standards of NIS-4, more girls were subjected to maltreatment than were boys. About 8.5 girls per 1,000 children and 6.5 boys per 1,000 children experienced Harm Standard abuse in 2005–06. Under the Harm Standard girls (3 per 1,000 children) were sexually abused about five times more often than were boys (0.6 per 1,000 children). Between 1993 and 2005–06 the rates of serious harm declined 33% for boys and 11% for girls. Although boys were more likely to suffer serious harm than were girls in 1993, Sedlak et al. indicate that by 2005–06 boys' and girls' rates of experiencing serious harm were approximately the same.

The girls' rate of Endangerment Standard abuse (12 per 1,000 children) was slightly higher than the boys' rate (10 per 1,000 children) in 2005–06. Under the Endangerment Standard girls (3.8 per 1,000 children) suffered sexual abuse at 3.8 times the rate of boys (1 per 1,000 children).

Age of Victims

Sedlak et al. find a low incidence of maltreatment in younger children, particularly among those under the age of five years. This may be because, before reaching school age, children are less observable to community professionals, especially educators (the group most likely to report suspected maltreatment). The researchers explain that there was a disproportionate increase in the incidence of maltreatment among children as they reached ages six to 14. Sedlak et al. note that the incidence of maltreatment among children older than the age of 14 years decreased. Older children are more likely to escape if the abuse becomes more prevalent or severe. They are also more able to defend themselves and/or fight back.

Under the Harm Standard only 8.5 per 1,000 children in the zero-to-two age group experienced overall maltreatment. The numbers were significantly higher for children aged six to 17 years. Under the Endangerment Standard 33.4 per 1,000 children aged zero to two years were subjected to overall maltreatment. The oldest age group (15- to 17-year-olds) had a lower rate of maltreatment under the Endangerment Standard, at 29 per 1,000 children. As with the Harm Standard, children between the ages of six and 14 years had a higher incidence of maltreatment.

Race and Ethnicity of Victims

Sedlak et al. find that African American children had a Harm Standard maltreatment rate of 24 per 1,000 children in 2005–06, which was nearly twice the maltreatment rate among white children, at 12.5 per 1,000 children. The Harm Standard maltreatment rate among Hispanic children was 14.2 per 1,000 children. The most significant differences between white and African American children were found for physical abuse; differences between white and African American children for neglect and sexual abuse were marginal. Findings for Endangerment Standard maltreatment revealed similar differences. These findings were different from those of previous years. NIS-3 and the Second National Incidence Study of Child Abuse and Neglect (1991) did not find any disproportionate differences in race in relation to maltreatment incidence.

NIS-4 was the first national survey of child maltreatment to include data on children with disabilities. According to Sedlak et al., in 2005–06 children with disabilities (3.1 per 1,000 children) had a significantly lower rate of maltreatment under the Harm Standard than did children without disabilities (4.2 per 1,000 children). However, children with disabilities (4.7 per 1,000 children) were at a significantly higher risk of emotional neglect under the Harm Standard than were children without disabilities (2.3 per 1,000 children). Under the Endangerment Standard, however, children with disabilities were less likely than children without disabilities to suffer physical abuse, sexual abuse, physical neglect, and emotional neglect. Even so, children with disabilities (9.1 per 1,000 children) had a much higher rate of serious harm resulting from maltreatment under the Endangerment Standard than did children without disabilities (6 per 1,000 children).

Family Characteristics of Victims

Under the Harm Standard children living with a single parent and an unmarried partner were most at risk for child maltreatment (57.2 per 1,000 children) in 2005–06, which was more than eight times the rate of children living with married biological parents (6.8 per 1,000 children). Children living with neither parent also had a high rate of maltreatment (33.2 per 1,000 children), as did children living with a single parent with no partner (28.4 per 1,000 children). These relative risks by family composition were similar for all types of abuse and neglect. According to Sedlak et al., children living with a single parent and an unmarried partner also had a much greater risk of suffering serious injury (20.8 per 1,000 children) than did children living with married biological parents (2.6 per 1,000 children).

Under the Endangerment Standard an estimated 136.1 per 1,000 children living with a single parent and an unmarried partner suffered some type of maltreatment in 2005–06, compared with 15.8 per 1,000 children living with married biological parents. In other words, nearly one out of every eight children living in a household with a single parent and an unmarried partner were maltreated under the Endangerment Standard. Children living with unmarried parents (88.9 per 1,000 children), single parents with no partner (66.3 per 1,000 children), neither parent (66 per 1,000 children), and other married parents (51.5 per 1,000 children) also had substantially higher rates of maltreatment than did children living with married biological parents (15.8 per 1,000 children) under the Endangerment Standard.

SOCIOECONOMIC STATUS. Sedlak et al. report that socioeconomic status (SES) was significantly related to the incidence rates of child maltreatment. A family was considered to have low SES if the household income was below $15,000 per year, if the parents had less than a high school education, or any household member participated in a poverty-related social program. Under the Harm Standard children in families with low SES (22.5 per 1,000 children) had much higher rates of maltreatment than did children not in low SES families (4.4 per 1,000 children) in 2005–06. Under the Endangerment Standard children in low SES families (55.1 per 1,000 children) were nearly six times more likely to experience maltreatment than children not in low SES families (9.5 per 1,000 children). Children in low SES families (10.3 per 1,000 children) also had higher rates of serious harm than children not in low SES families (1.8 per 1,000 children).

Perpetrators of Child Maltreatment

Sedlak et al. indicate that in 2005–06, 81% of child victims were maltreated by their biological parents. Biological parents perpetrated 72% of physical abuse and 73% of emotional abuse. However, 40% of sexually abused children were violated by someone other than a biological or nonbiological parent. Nearly two out of five (37%) children were sexually abused by a biological parent, and almost a quarter (23%) were sexually abused by a nonbiological parent or parent substitute, such as a stepparent or a mother's boyfriend.

Overall, children were somewhat more likely to be maltreated by female perpetrators (68%) than by male perpetrators (48%) in 2005–06. Among children maltreated by their biological parents, 75% were maltreated by their mother and 43% were maltreated by their father (with some children being maltreated by both parents). Children who were maltreated by nonbiological parents or partners were more likely to be maltreated by male perpetrators (64%) than by female perpetrators (48%), as were children who were maltreated by other adults (75% were mistreated by male perpetrators and 20% by female perpetrators).

Neglected children differed from abused children with regard to the gender of the perpetrators in 2005–06. Because mothers or other females tended to be the primary caretakers, children were more likely to suffer all forms of neglect by female perpetrators (86%) than by

male perpetrators (38%). In contrast, children were more often abused by male perpetrators (62%) than by female perpetrators (41%).

REPORTING CHILD ABUSE
Mandatory Reporting

In 1974 Congress enacted the first CAPTA, which set guidelines for the reporting, investigation, and treatment of child maltreatment. States had to meet these requirements to receive federal funding to assist child victims of abuse and neglect. Among its many provisions, CAPTA required the states to enact mandatory reporting laws and procedures so that CPS agencies could take action to protect children from further abuse. Each state now designates mandatory reporters, which typically include health care workers, mental health professionals, social workers, school personnel, child care providers, and law enforcement officers. Some states require all people to report suspected abuse or neglect, not just designated professionals. Most states do not recognize the right for communications between certain professionals and their clients to remain confidential (called "privileged communications") in the case of suspected child abuse. In addition, all states offer immunity to individuals who report incidents of child maltreatment "in good faith" or with sincerity. Besides physical injury and neglect, most states include mental injury, sexual abuse, and the sexual exploitation of minors as cases to be reported. Many states impose penalties, either a fine and/or imprisonment, for failure to report child maltreatment. A mandated reporter, such as a physician, may also be sued for negligence for failing to protect a child from harm.

It should be noted that state statutes regarding mandatory reporting differ significantly and are constantly changing. In *Mandatory Reporters of Child Abuse and Neglect* (August 2015, https://www.childwelfare.gov/pubPDFs/manda.pdf), the Children's Bureau lists state statutes that deal with mandatory reporting. As of 2015, mandatory reporting bills existed in 48 states and the District of Columbia and included professionals such as teachers and school administrators, child care providers, social workers, doctors and other health care professionals, mental health professionals, medical examiners, and law enforcement officers.

CHILD ABUSE PREVENTION THROUGH INTERVENTION

One of the main functions of the nation's child welfare system is child abuse prevention. Most of the system's resources are geared toward intervention—that is, responding to reports of suspected child maltreatment and implementing measures to prevent these children (and any other children in the household) from suffering future maltreatment. Thus, the system is largely reactive in that it takes action after problems come to light.

Investigations and Assessments

As shown in Figure 2.7, screened-in maltreatment reports trigger CPS agency investigations or family assessments, depending on the perceived safety concerns to the child and the future risk of maltreatment. Family assessments, which are also known as "alternative responses," are typically conducted in cases with lower safety concerns and risks. As Figure 2.7 shows, family assessments can result in child welfare or community-based services being offered to the child's family or a referral to other sources for assistance.

According to the Children's Bureau, in *Child Maltreatment: 2014*, 69% of the 3.2 million cases in which child maltreatment referrals received an investigation of alternative response in 2014 were found to be unsubstantiated.

FIGURE 2.7

The child welfare system

SOURCE: "Appendix. The Child Welfare System," in *How the Child Welfare System Works*, U.S. Department of Health and Human Services, Administration for Children and Families, Administration on Children, Youth, and Families, Children's Bureau, February 2013, https://www.childwelfare.gov/pubs/factsheets/cpswork.pdf (accessed June 9, 2016)

Another 21.9% were substantiated and 1% were indicated. As shown in Figure 2.7, substantiated or founded cases are categorized by the level of harm to the child and the risk of future abuse. When a child is deemed to be at low or no risk, the case is typically closed, and the child's family may be referred for voluntary services. However, cases in which the child has been harmed and is at future risk of abuse or there are concerns about ongoing safety issues trigger more serious responses, including court action.

Judicial System Measures

State laws dictate the measures that authorities can take in dealing with children who are the subject of substantiated or founded maltreatment cases. These measures include two possible actions: protective custody and intervention by a state juvenile court.

PROTECTIVE CUSTODY. Protective custody is used when children are believed to be in such imminent danger that there is no time to obtain court approval before removing the children from their home. State laws prescribe who has the authority to place children in protective custody, notifications that must take place (e.g., to the children's parents, CPS agencies, and the court), how long a child can be held in protective custody, and the legal actions that are triggered. Protective custody is the means by which some children enter the child welfare system in the first place if, for example, they are found by police in a dangerous situation.

STATE JUVENILE COURT INTERVENTIONS. CPS agencies can petition state juvenile courts for intervention in child maltreatment cases. The juvenile court system handles legal matters that are related to minors (children under the age of 17 or 18 years, depending on state law). Offenses committed by minors are handled by the delinquency component of the court, while child maltreatment matters are handled by the dependency component of the court. In the fact sheet *How the Child Welfare System Works* (February 2013, https://www.childwelfare.gov/pubPDFs/cpswork.pdf), the Children's Bureau indicates that in substantiated or found cases in which families refuse voluntary in-home services offered by CPS agencies, the agencies can petition the juvenile dependency court for "a judicial determination that abuse or neglect occurred." If granted, the court can require the family to participate in in-home services.

In addition, CPS agencies file juvenile court petitions in maltreatment cases in which they believe a child has been seriously harmed and is at high risk for further harm or in danger due to other safety threats. If the court agrees, it can authorize the removal of the child from the home. Removed children are often called wards or dependents of the state or court.

The juvenile court (or family court, depending on the state) also has the authority to terminate parental rights

under certain circumstances. As with other child abuse laws, guidelines for terminating parental rights vary from state to state. The Children's Bureau provides an overview of state statutes in *Grounds for Involuntary Termination of Parental Rights* (January 2013, https://www.childwelfare.gov/pubPDFs/groundtermin.pdf). According to the Children's Bureau, the Adoption and Safe Families Act of 1997 requires all states to initiate petitions terminating parental rights in cases when:

- A child has been in foster care for 15 of the previous 22 months

- A court has determined a child to be an abandoned infant

- A court has found the parent to be guilty of felony murder or manslaughter charges involving another child of the parent; of conspiring in, aiding, or abetting such a murder or manslaughter; or to be guilty of felony assault causing significant physical harm to the child or another child of the parent

However, the Children's Bureau indicates that 32 states and the District of Columbia allow for some exceptions to these requirements. These include instances when a child has been placed in the care of another relative or when a state agency finds a "compelling reason to believe that terminating the parent's rights is not in the best interests of the child."

Foster Care

Children who are removed from their home under court order become part of the foster care system, which is administered at the state and local levels. As shown in Figure 2.7, foster children receive out-of-home care and services. Foster home choices include the homes of relatives, the homes of foster families, and group homes or institutions. Foster care is considered to be a temporary measure for child protection. In most cases, the ultimate goal is to reunite fostered children with their parents. In *How the Child Welfare System Works*, the Children's Bureau notes that administrators are supposed to develop a permanency plan for every child in foster care. These plans are typically based on input from the child's family. According to the Children's Bureau, federal law requires states to hold regular permanency hearings for every child who enters foster care. The first hearing must be held within 12 months from the time of entry into the system. Subsequent hearings must be held every 12 months thereafter. The agency explains that "reunification with parents, except in unusual and extreme circumstances, is the permanency plan for most children."

Table 2.8 shows national foster care statistics for fiscal years (FYs) 2010 to 2014. (The federal fiscal year extends from October 1 through September 30.) As of September 2014, there were 415,129 children in foster

TABLE 2.8

Foster care summary, fiscal years 2010–14

	2010	2011	2012	2013	2014
Number in foster care on September 30 of the fiscal year	404,878	398,057	397,153	400,989	415,129
Number entered foster care during the fiscal year	256,092	251,958	251,850	255,080	264,746
Number exited foster care during the fiscal year	257,806	247,607	240,987	240,392	238,230
Number waiting to be adopted on September 30 of the fiscal year	108,746	106,561	102,058	104,493	107,918
Number waiting to be adopted whose parental rights (for all living parents) were terminated during fiscal year	65,747	62,852	59,147	59,662	60,898
Number adopted with public child welfare agency involvement during fiscal year	53,547	50,901	52,046	50,841	50,644

SOURCE: "Numbers at a Glance," in *The AFCARS Report: Preliminary FY 2014 Estimates as of July 2015*, no. 22, U.S. Department of Health and Human Services, Administration for Children and Families, Administration on Children, Youth, and Families, Children's Bureau, July 2015, http://www.acf.hhs.gov/sites/default/files/cb/afcarsreport22.pdf (accessed June 9, 2016)

care throughout the country. Approximately a quarter (107,918) of them were waiting to be adopted. In FY 2014, 50,644 foster care children were adopted through the involvement of public child welfare agencies.

Table 2.9 provides detailed data about the children who were in foster care as of September 30, 2014. There was a slightly higher percentage of boys (52%) than girls (48%) in foster care at that time, and the mean (average) age was 8.7 years. Nearly half (49%) the children were aged seven years or younger. The largest single contingent was one-year-olds, which accounted for 8% of all children in foster care. There were also thousands of young adults aged 18 to 20 years in the system. Depending on state laws and policies, these are the ages at which children typically achieve emancipation (leave the foster care system) because they are legally considered to be adults.

In "The AFCARS Report: Preliminary FY 2014 Estimates as of July 2015" (July 2015, http://www.acf.hhs.gov/sites/default/files/cb/afcarsreport22.pdf), the Children's Bureau indicates that on a race and ethnicity basis, the largest shares of foster children were white (42%), African American (24%), and Hispanic (22%). (See Table 2.9.) As Table 2.10 shows, whites (45%) also represented the largest proportion of children who entered foster care in FY 2014.

The average time spent in foster care was 20.8 months. (See Table 2.9.) Overall, 48% of the children had been in foster care for less than a year, while 25% had spent at least a year, but less than two years, and 12% had spent at least two years, but less than three years. Another 9% of the children had been in foster care for three to four years and 7% for five years or more. (It should be noted that the individual percentages do not sum to 100% due to rounding.)

As of September 30, 2014, nearly half (46%) of the children were living in the homes of foster families to whom they were not related, and 29% were living with relatives designated as foster parents. (See Table 2.9.)

Smaller percentages were in institutions (8%) and group homes (6%). The permanency plan for just over half (55%) of all the children was to be reunited with their parent(s) or principal caretaker(s) at some point. Adoption was the goal for another 25% of the children.

More children entered the foster care system (264,746 entries) than exited it (238,230 exits) in FY 2014. (See Table 2.8.) Table 2.11 provides detailed information about the children who exited the system. The mean age was nine years. Approximately half (49%) of those exiting were aged seven years or younger. Whites (45%) made up the largest contingent of the children who exited, followed by African Americans (23%) and Hispanics (21%). On average, a child who exited the system in FY 2014 had spent 19.5 months in foster care. Nearly three-quarters (74%) of the children who left had been in foster care for less than two years. Another 13% had spent at least two years, but less than three years in care, while 8% had been in care for three to four years and 5% had spent five years or more in foster care. (It should be noted that the individual percentages do not sum to 100% due to rounding.) Just over half (51%) of the children who left the foster system were reunited with their parent(s) or principal caretaker(s), 21% were adopted, and 9% were emancipated.

The Debate about Family Preservation

The Adoption Assistance and Child Welfare Act of 1980 mandated: "In each case, reasonable efforts would be made (1) prior to the placement of a child in foster care, to prevent or eliminate the need for removal of the child from his home, and (2) to make it possible for the child to return to his home." However, because the law did not define the term *reasonable efforts*, states and courts interpreted the term in different ways. In many cases child welfare personnel took the "reasonable efforts" of providing family counseling, respite care, and substance abuse treatment, thus preventing the child from being removed from abusive parents.

TABLE 2.9

Children in foster care as of September 30, 2014

Age as of September 30th		Years
Mean		8.7
Median		8.0

Age as of September 30th	Percent	Number
Less than 1 year	7%	28,607
1 year	8%	33,264
2 years	7%	29,726
3 years	6%	26,512
4 years	6%	23,719
5 years	5%	22,714
6 years	5%	22,070
7 years	5%	20,456
8 years	5%	18,770
9 years	4%	17,216
10 years	4%	15,500
11 years	4%	14,974
12 years	4%	14,983
13 years	4%	16,651
14 years	5%	19,138
15 years	5%	22,622
16 years	6%	26,119
17 years	6%	26,476
18 years	2%	9,561
19 years	1%	3,245
20 years	1%	2,386
Race/ethnicity		
American Indian/Alaskan Native	2%	9,517
Asian	1%	2,107
Black or African American	24%	97,540
Native Hawaiian/other Pacific Islander	0%	693
Hispanic (of any race)	22%	90,299
White	42%	174,477
Unknown/unable to determine	3%	12,747
Two or more races	7%	27,179
Sex		
Male	52%	216,645
Female	48%	198,426
Most recent placement setting		
Pre-adoptive home	4%	15,554
Foster family home (relative)	29%	120,334
Foster family home (non-relative)	46%	190,454
Group home	6%	23,233
Institution	8%	32,955
Supervised independent living	1%	4,474
Runaway	1%	4,544
Trial home visit	5%	21,989
Case plan goal		
Reunify with parent(s) or principal caretaker(s)	55%	218,889
Live with other relative(s)	3%	12,351
Adoption	25%	99,521
Long term foster care	4%	15,008
Emancipation	5%	18,934
Guardianship	4%	14,739
Case plan goal not yet established	5%	18,408
Time in care		Months
Mean		20.8
Median		12.6
Time in care (months)		Number
Less than 1 month	5%	22,129
1–5 months	23%	94,358
6–11 months	20%	83,978
12–17 months	15%	62,447
18–23 months	10%	39,620
24–29 months	7%	29,401
30–35 months	5%	18,833
3–4 years	9%	36,292
5 years or more	7%	28,058

The law was a reaction to what was seen as over-zealousness during the 1960s and 1970s, when children,

TABLE 2.9

Children in foster care as of September 30, 2014 [CONTINUED]

Note: All races exclude children of Hispanic origin. Children of Hispanic ethnicity may be any race.

SOURCE: "Children in Foster Care on September 30, 2014," in *The AFCARS Report: Preliminary FY 2014 Estimates as of July 2015*, no. 22, U.S. Department of Health and Human Services, Administration for Children and Families, Administration on Children, Youth, and Families, Children's Bureau, July 2015, http://www.acf.hhs.gov/sites/default/files/cb/afcarsreport22.pdf (accessed June 9, 2016)

especially African American children, were taken from their homes because their parents were poor. In the 21st century, however, some believe that problems of drug or substance abuse can mean that returning the child to the home is likely a guarantee of further abuse. Others note that some situations exist where a parent's live-in partner, who sometimes has no emotional attachment to the child, may also present risks to the child.

Richard J. Gelles, a prominent family violence expert and once a vocal advocate of family preservation, had a change of heart after studying the case of 15-month-old David Edwards, who was suffocated by his mother after the child welfare system failed to come to his rescue. Although David's parents had lost custody of their first child because of abuse, and despite reports of David's abuse, the CPS agency made reasonable efforts to let the parents keep the child. In *The Book of David: How Preserving Families Can Cost Children's Lives* (1996), Gelles points out that CPS agencies need to abandon their blanket solution to child abuse in their attempt to use reasonable efforts to reunite the victims and their perpetrators. He contends that those parents who seriously abuse their children are incapable of changing their behavior.

By contrast, in "Foster Care vs. Family Preservation: The Track Record on Safety and Well-Being" (January 3, 2011, http://www.nccpr.org/reports/01SAFETY.pdf), the National Coalition for Child Protection Reform, a nonprofit organization of experts on child abuse and foster care who are committed to the reform of the child welfare system, contends that many allegedly maltreated children are unnecessarily removed from their home and that children are in more danger when placed in foster care than when given services to help preserve the family. The coalition recognizes that although there are cases in which the only way to save a child is to remove him or her from an abusive home, in many cases providing support services to the family in crisis, while letting the child remain at home, helps ensure child safety.

How Successful Is Intervention?

The nation's child welfare system has achieved many successes. Thousands of maltreated children have been

TABLE 2.10

Children entering foster care in fiscal year 2014

Age at entry		Years
Mean		7.4
Median		6.4

Age at entry	Percent	Number
Less than 1 year	17%	45,535
1 year	7%	19,442
2 years	6%	17,061
3 years	6%	15,461
4 years	5%	14,500
5 years	5%	14,092
6 years	5%	13,338
7 years	5%	12,355
8 years	4%	10,933
9 years	4%	9,925
10 years	3%	9,139
11 years	3%	8,863
12 years	3%	9,217
13 years	4%	10,904
14 years	5%	12,600
15 years	6%	14,672
16 years	6%	14,795
17 years	4%	10,403
18 years	0%	1,020
19 years	0%	345
20 years	0%	137

Race/ethnicity	Percent	Number
American Indian/Alaskan Native	2%	5,960
Asian	1%	1,635
Black or African American	22%	57,324
Native Hawaiian/other Pacific Islander	0%	559
Hispanic (of any race)	21%	56,207
White	45%	118,168
Unknown/unable to determine	3%	7,928
Two or more races	6%	16,338

Note: All races exclude children of Hispanic origin. Children of Hispanic ethnicity may be any race.

SOURCE: "Children Entering Foster Care during FY 2014," in *The AFCARS Report: Preliminary FY 2014 Estimates as of July 2015*, no. 22, U.S. Department of Health and Human Services, Administration for Children and Families, Administration on Children, Youth, and Families, Children's Bureau, July 2015, http://www.acf.hhs.gov/sites/default/files/cb/afcarsreport22.pdf (accessed June 9, 2016)

TABLE 2.11

Children exiting foster care in fiscal year 2014

Age at exit		Years
Mean		9.0
Median		8.0

Age at exit	Percent	Number
Less than 1 year	4%	10,636
1 year	8%	18,768
2 years	8%	18,551
3 years	7%	16,348
4 years	6%	14,916
5 years	6%	14,007
6 years	5%	12,983
7 years	5%	11,874
8 years	4%	10,424
9 years	4%	9,446
10 years	4%	8,665
11 years	3%	7,980
12 years	3%	7,477
13 years	3%	7,691
14 years	4%	8,643
15 years	4%	10,026
16 years	5%	11,711
17 years	5%	12,051
18 years	8%	18,320
19 years	2%	5,114
20 years	0%	923

Time in care		Months
Mean		19.5
Median		13.3

Time in care	Percent	Number
Less than 1 month	11%	26,316
1–5 months	15%	36,532
6–11 months	20%	46,920
12–17 months	16%	37,860
18–23 months	12%	27,568
24–29 months	8%	19,041
30–35 months	5%	12,162
3–4 years	8%	20,091
5 years or more	5%	11,534

Race/ethnicity	Percent	Number
American Indian/Alaskan Native	2%	4,786
Asian	1%	1,518
Black or African American	23%	53,969
Native Hawaiian/other Pacific Islander	0%	525
Hispanic (of any race)	21%	50,613
White	45%	106,000
Unknown/unable to determine	2%	5,485
Two or more races	6%	15,026

Reasons for discharge	Percent	Number
Reunification with parent(s) or primary caretaker(s)	51%	121,241
Living with other relative(s)	7%	15,774
Adoption	21%	49,693
Emancipation	9%	22,392
Guardianship	9%	21,055
Transfer to another agency	2%	4,173
Runaway	0%	1,138
Death of child	0%	326

Note: All races exclude children of Hispanic origin. Children of Hispanic ethnicity may be any race.

SOURCE: "Children Exiting Foster Care during FY 2014," in *The AFCARS Report: Preliminary FY 2014 Estimates as of July 2015*, no. 22, U.S. Department of Health and Human Services, Administration for Children and Families, Administration on Children, Youth, and Families, Children's Bureau, July 2015, http://www.acf.hhs.gov/sites/default/files/cb/afcarsreport22.pdf (accessed June 9, 2016)

identified, many lives have been saved, and many more have been taken out of dangerous environments. It is impossible to tally the number of child abuse cases that might have ended in death; these children have been saved by changes in the laws, by awareness and reporting, and by the efforts of the professionals who intervened on their behalf. Mandatory reporting laws have brought many maltreated children into the system who might have gone unnoticed otherwise.

Although many CPS agencies are conscientiously and effectively doing their job, they sometimes commit mistakes that result in great harm and even death to the children under their care. During the first decade of the 21st century there were several high-profile cases in which CPS agencies appear to have utterly failed the children they were supposed to be protecting.

For example, the Florida Department of Children and Families could not account for the disappearance of a five-year-old foster child, Rilya Wilson, who had been missing for more than a year before the agency noticed her absence in April 2002. At that time the agency had reportedly lost track of more than 530 children. Rilya's disappearance was discovered only after her caseworker was fired, and the new caseworker could not locate the child. The former caseworker had reported that Rilya was fine, although that caseworker had not visited the child at her foster home for months. The article "Trial in Rilya Wilson Case Continues" (FLCourier.com, December 20, 2012) notes that in 2005 Geralyn Graham, the live-in lover of Pamela Graham, who was Rilya's foster mother, was indicted for murdering the girl. During Geralyn's December 2012 trial, Pamela testified that Geralyn abused the girl by keeping her in a small room, tying her to her bed, and dipping her into "extremely hot bathtub water." Pamela claimed that her own fears of Geralyn and of being blamed by authorities prompted her to cover up Rilya's disappearance. She reportedly pleaded guilty to reduced charges in exchange for her testimony against Geralyn and was not expected to face jail time. Geralyn was facing a term of life in prison if convicted of murdering Rilya. In February 2013 Geralyn was convicted on charges of kidnapping and child abuse and sentenced to 55 years in prison. Rilya's body was never found.

More generally, overcrowding and lack of effective oversight continue to plague the nation's foster care system. The problem is particularly acute among private foster care providers. Evey Rosenbloom reports in "Where Do the Children Go When They Are Taken Away?" (HuffingtonPost.com, December 7, 2015) that high demand for foster care within the California child welfare system has forced the state to allow private agencies to waive certain basic qualifications among foster care parents. As of December 2015, private agencies had granted more than 5,000 waivers, accepting applications from registered sex offenders and individuals with criminal records. Rosenbloom also notes that the state government's dependence on private agencies has limited its ability to monitor the performance and safety of foster homes, leading to widespread abuses within the system. According to Rosenbloom, children living in private foster care arrangements in California are 33% more likely to suffer neglect or abuse than in state-managed homes.

In *Child Maltreatment 2014*, the Children's Bureau provides limited data about children in the child welfare system who died due to maltreatment in 2014. The agency notes that 29 states specified how many of their total fatalities were of children whose families had received preservation services in the previous five years. Overall, 93 (12.2%) of the 764 fatalities fell into this category. It should be noted, however, that the 29 reporting states did not include some of the states with the largest numbers of maltreatment fatalities, specifically California and New York. According to the Children's

Bureau, 38 states with a total of 1,053 maltreatment fatalities in 2014 reported that 19 of those fatalities were of children who had been reunited with their family within the previous five years. California was not among the reporting states.

The Children's Bureau also provides data on the number of children under CPS agency protection who are found to have been maltreated by foster parents and other sanctioned caregivers. In 2014 there were 1,356 duplicate victims (a duplicate count tallies a child for each reported incidence of abuse, so a victim may be counted more than once) involving maltreatment by foster parents (both relatives and nonrelatives) and 508 involving maltreatment by group home and residential facility staff. These cases are particularly troubling because the victims were most likely in foster care after having already been maltreated by their parents or other caregivers. In addition, these cases raise questions about the CPS agencies' thoroughness in screening potential foster parents and the personnel who are employed to work at group homes and residential facilities.

Another area of interest regarding CPS agency performance is the appropriate response in cases where child maltreatment claims are not substantiated. As noted earlier, 702,000 of the 3.2 million unique children maltreatment claims investigated in 2014 were found to be substantiated or indicated, while nearly 2.5 million were determined to be unsubstantiated. (See Figure 2.1.) As part of the NSCAW II longitudinal study, researchers are following the well-being of children with substantiated and unsubstantiated cases of maltreatment.

Child Welfare Workforce

Child welfare caseworkers perform multiple tasks in the course of their jobs. Among other things, they investigate reports of child maltreatment, coordinate various services (mental health, substance abuse, and so on) to help keep families together, find foster care placements for children if needed, make regular visits to children and families, arrange placement of children in permanent homes when they cannot be safely returned to their parents or caretakers, and document all details pertaining to their cases. Caseworker supervisors monitor and support their caseworkers, sometimes taking on some of the cases when there is a staff shortage or heavy caseload. Child welfare caseworkers must typically earn at least a four-year bachelor's degree in social work to become a licensed baccalaureate social worker. This degree path typically includes several hours of fieldwork as a prerequisite for graduating.

Workers in the child welfare system face particular emotional stresses in their job that can lead to burnout. The Children's Bureau notes in "Burnout/Secondary Trauma" (2016, https://www.childwelfare.gov/topics/

management/workforce/retention/workforce-retention/turn over/burnout/) that workers can develop what is called vicarious trauma or secondary trauma from dealing with traumatized children and their families. As a result, workforce retention is a significant challenge for CPS agencies. According to the Children's Bureau, in "Worker Turnover" (2016, https://www.childwelfare.gov/topics/manage ment/workforce/retention/workforce-retention/turnover/), in some jurisdictions worker turnover is as high as 90% per year.

MEASURING STATE PERFORMANCE. The Adoption and Safe Families Act of 1997 requires the HHS to submit an annual report to Congress regarding state performance in operating CPS and other child welfare programs. In *Child Welfare Outcomes 2010–2013 Report to Congress* (January 2016, http://www.acf.hhs.gov/sites/ default/files/cb/cwo10_13.pdf), the Children's Bureau notes that the first report to Congress included child welfare data from 1998 and addressed seven national goals or desired outcomes:

- Outcome 1: Reduce recurrence of child abuse and/or neglect

- Outcome 2: Reduce the incidence of child abuse and/ or neglect in foster care

- Outcome 3: Increase permanency for children in foster care

- Outcome 4: Reduce time in foster care to reunification without increasing reentry

- Outcome 5: Reduce time in foster care to adoption

- Outcome 6: Increase placement stability

- Outcome 7: Reduce placements of young children in group homes or institutions

Twelve measures, called the original outcome measures, were developed and are used to assess state performance in meeting these desired outcomes. The Children's Bureau notes that it includes 52 "states" in its assessment because it includes the District of Columbia and Puerto Rico.

Table 2.12 shows the original outcome measure performance between 2010 and 2013. It should be noted that the desirable trend over time for Measures 1.1, 2.1, 3.4, and 7.1 is for values to decrease, whereas the desirable trend for all other measures is for values to increase. In general, states improved their performance between 2010 and 2013 in seven of the measures, and performed worse in five measures. The measure showing the greatest improvement, Measure 6.1b, assessed the states in terms of the percentage of children in foster care for a period of between 12 and 24 months who experienced no more than two placement settings during that span. Overall, this percentage increased from 61.4% to 64.8%. Another

TABLE 2.12

State performance on original outcome measures of child welfare, 2010–13

Outcome measures[a]	Median performance by year			
	2010	2011	2012	2013
[b]Measure 1.1: Of all children who were victims of substantiated or indicated child abuse and/or neglect during the first six months of the year, what percentage had another substantiated or indicated report within a six-month period?	5.0%	5.2%	5.1%	5.4%
[b]Measure 2.1: Of all children who were in foster care during the year, what percentage were the subject of substantiated or indicated maltreatment by a foster parent or facility sta member?	0.33%	0.29%	0.28%	0.34%
Measure 3.1: Of all children who exited foster care during the year, what percentage left to either reunification, adoption, or legal guardianship (i.e., were discharged to a permanent home)?	86.3%	87.2%	87.4%	89.1%
Measure 3.2: Of all children who exited foster care during the year and were identified as having a diagnosed disability, what percentage left to either reunification, adoption, or legal guardianship (i.e., were discharged to a permanent home)?	76.0%	76.8%	77.8%	78.7%
Measure 3.3: Of all children who exited foster care during the year and were older than age 12 at the time of their most recent entry into care, what percentage left either to reunification, adoption, or legal guardianship (i.e., were discharged to a permanent home)?	65.2%	65.1%	64.8%	65.8%
[b]Measure 3.4: Of all children exiting foster care in the year to emancipation, what percentage were age 12 or younger at the time of entry into care?	24.5%	25.4%	23.5%	22.6%
Measure 4.1: Of all children reunified with their parents or caretakers at the time of discharge from foster care during the year, what percentage were reunified in less than 12 months from the time of entry into foster care?	69.1%	68.3%	65.5%	65.8%
Measure 5.1a: Of all children discharged from care during the year to a finalized adoption, what percentage were discharged in less than 12 months from the date of the latest removal from home?	4.0%	3.7%	4.4%	3.2%
Measure 6.1a: Of all children served in foster care during the year who were in care for less than 12 months, what percentage had no more than two placement settings?	85.2%	85.7%	85.1%	85.1%
Measure 6.1b: Of all children served in foster care during the year who were in foster care for at least 12 months but less than 24 months, what percentage had no more than two placement settings?	61.4%	62.9%	64.2%	64.8%
Measure 6.1c: Of all children served in foster care during the year who were in foster care for at least 24 months, what percentage had no more than two placement settings?	32.0%	32.8%	34.2%	34.7%
[b]Measure 7.1: Of all children who entered foster care during the year and were age 12 or younger at the time of their most recent placement, what percentage were placed in a group home or institution?	4.5%	4.4%	4.5%	4.0%

[a]Data for this table include all states for which adequate data are available.
[b]For these measures, a lower number indicates better performance.

SOURCE: "Table 1. Median State Performance, 2010–2013: Original Outcome Measures," in *Child Welfare Outcomes 2010–2013 Report to Congress*, U.S. Department of Health and Human Services, Administration for Children and Families, Administration on Children, Youth, and Families, Children's Bureau, February 1, 2016, http://www.acf.hhs.gov/sites/default/files/cb/cwo10_13.pdf (accessed June 9, 2016) area that showed strong improvement between 2010 and 2013 was Measure 3.1, which assessed states in terms of the percentage of children who achieved reunification (i.e., were reunited with parents, caretakers, or other relatives), left foster care to live with a legal guardian in a permanent residence, or were adopted. This percentage rose steadily over this span, from 86.3% in 2010 to 89.1% in 2013.

In 2005 the Children's Bureau developed an additional set of 12 outcome measures that it calls the composite measures. The agency indicates that the composite measures also address the seven national goals listed earlier, but provide more detailed information than do the original outcome measures. Table 2.13 shows the national results for the composite measures between 2010 and 2013. The desirable trend over time for Measures C1.2, C1.4, C2.2, and C3.3 is downward, whereas the desirable trend for all other measures is upward. Overall, there was improvement in 10 of 12 composite measures between 2010 and 2013. The largest improvement was for Measure C3.3, which measures the percentage of children who were in foster care for three or more years before either being emancipated or reaching their 18th birthday. In 2010, 44.1% of foster children lived in foster care for three or more years before either becoming emancipated or turning 18; by 2013, this percentage fell to 38.7%.

It should be noted that not all 52 "states" (including the District of Columbia and Puerto Rico) reported data

TABLE 2.13

State performance on composite outcome measures of child welfare, 2010–13

Composite measures	Median performance by year			
	2010	2011	2012	2013
Measure C1.1: Of all children discharged from foster care to reunification during the year who had been in care for eight days or longer, what percentage were reunified in less than 12 months from the date of the latest removal from home? (Includes trial home visit adjustment)	67.9%	70.6%	68.7%	69.8%
*Measure C1.2: Of all children discharged from foster care to reunification during the year who had been in care for eight days or longer, what was the median length of stay (in months) from the date of the latest removal from home until the date of discharge to reunification? (Includes trial home visit adjustment)	7.5 months	7.5 months	8.0 months	7.9 months
Measure C1.3: Of all children who entered foster care for the first time in the six-month period just prior to the year shown, and who remained in care for eight days or longer, what percentage were discharged from foster care to reunification in less than 12 months from the date of the latest removal from home? (Includes trial home visit adjustment)	42.1%	41.2%	38.6%	37.2%
*Measure C1.4: Of all children discharged from foster care to reunification in the 12-month period prior to the year shown, what percentage reentered care in less than 12 months from the date of discharge?	12.6%	11.8%	11.8%	11.8%
Measure C2.1: Of all children discharged from foster care to a finalized adoption during the year, what percentage were discharged in less than 24 months from the date of the latest removal from home?[b]	32.6%	33.0%	32.6%	34.8%
*Measure C2.2: Of all children discharged from foster care to a finalized adoption during the year, what was the median length of stay in care (in months) from the date of latest removal from home to the date of discharge to adoption?	29.6 months	29.4 months	29.0 months	28.3 months
Measure C2.3: Of all children in foster care on the first day of the year who were in care for 17 continuous months or longer, what percentage was discharged from foster care to a finalized adoption by the last day of the year?[c]	24.9%	25.4%	29.0%	27.9%
Measure C2.4: Of all children in foster care on the first day of the year who were in foster care for 17 continuous months or longer, and who were not legally free for adoption prior to that day, what percentage became legally free for adoption during the first six months of the year? (N = 47 states)[d]	11.8%	13.3%	13.6%	14.3%
Measure C2.5: Of all children who became legally free for adoption in the 12-month period prior to the year shown, what percentage were discharged from foster care to a finalized adoption in less than 12 months from the date of becoming legally free?	58.4%	59.8%	63.0%	62.9%
Measure C3.1: Of all children in foster care for 24 months or longer on the first day of the year, what percentage were discharged to a permanent home prior to their 18th birthday and by the end of the year?	29.8%	32.0%	33.1%	32.8%
Measure C3.2: Of all children who were discharged from foster care during the year, and who were legally free for adoption at the time of discharge, what percentage were discharged to a permanent home prior to their 18th birthday?[e]	94.9%	94.3%	95.7%	96.0%
*Measure C3.3: Of all children who, during the year shown, either (1) were discharged from foster care prior to age 18 with a discharge reason of emancipation, or (2) reached their 18th birthday while in foster care, what percentage were in foster care for three years or longer?	44.1%	43.4%	41.9%	38.7%

*For these measures, a lower number indicates better performance.
Notes: Data for this table include all states for which adequate data are available. Individual measures developed for Composite 4: Placement stability are not shown in this table because the measures are nearly identical to the original measures of placement stability incorporated into measure 6.1.
Although measure C2.1 is calculated exactly the same way as original measure 5.1b, the results can vary slightly because the source files are different for the composite measures. In the source les for measure C2.1, all children are excluded who were not age 17 for at least 1 day. No such exclusion exists for measure 5.1b. In addition, composites are calculated at the county level and then are aggregated to the state level, which also could influence slightly performance on C2.1 compared to 5.1b.
The denominator for this measure excludes children who, by the last day of the year, were discharged from foster care with a discharge reason of reunification with parents or primary caretakers, living with relatives, or guardianship.
A child is considered to be "legally free" for adoption if there is a date for parental rights termination reported to AFCARS for both mother and father. Also, the denominator for this measure excludes children who, during the first 6 months of the year, were discharged from foster care with a discharge reason of reunification with parents or primary caretakers, living with other relatives, or guardianship.
A child is considered to be "legally free" for adoption if there is a date for the parental rights termination reported to AFCARS for both mother and father.

SOURCE: "Table 2. Median State Performance, 2010–2013: Composite Measures," in *Child Welfare Outcomes 2010–2013 Report to Congress*, U.S. Department of Health and Human Services, Administration for Children and Families, Administration on Children, Youth, and Families, Children's Bureau, February 1, 2016, http://www.acf.hhs.gov/sites/default/files/cb/cwo10_13.pdf (accessed June 9, 2016) for every outcome measure. In addition, the Children's Bureau indicates that results differed significantly between states for some outcome measures. Thus, readers are advised to refer to *Child Welfare Outcomes 2010– 2013 Report to Congress* for a state-by-state breakdown of the performance data.

Funding the Child Welfare System

The nation's child welfare system is funded through federal, state, and local government budgets. Thus, determining total national spending is difficult. However, some private organizations publish spending estimates based on their own data collection efforts. Child Trends is a nonprofit research organization located in Washington, D.C. In *Federal, State, and Local Spending to Address Child Abuse and Neglect in SFY 2012* (September 2014, http:// www.childtrends.org/wp-content/uploads/2014/09/2014-61 ChildWelfareSpending-2012-2nd-revision-march.pdf), Kerry DeVooght, Megan Fletcher, and Hope Cooper of Child Trends present child welfare spending data for the 50 states, the District of Columbia, and Puerto Rico. As noted earlier, the federal government operates on a fiscal year that runs from October 1 to September 30. State fiscal years (SFYs) may or may not coincide with the federal fiscal year. According to DeVooght, Fletcher, and Cooper, national government spending for child welfare purposes was $28.2 billion in SFY 2012, broken down as follows:

- Federal government funds—$12.7 billion (or 45% of the total)

- State government funds—$10.9 billion (or 39% of the total)

- Local government funds—$4.6 billion (or 16% of the total)

Overall, total child welfare spending fell from $30.6 billion in 2010 to $28.2 billion in 2012, a decrease of 8%. According to DeVooght, Fletcher, and Cooper, this decrease represented the first two-year decline since the survey was first conducted in 1996.

PROACTIVE CHILD ABUSE PREVENTION

Besides the interventional measures described earlier, the government also operates programs that function to proactively prevent child maltreatment from occurring in the first place. One component of this approach is public awareness. The HHS notes on the National Child Abuse Prevention Month website (2016, https://www.childwelfare .gov/preventing/preventionmonth/about) that in April 1983 the federal government held the first National Child Abuse Prevention Month. Since then the event has been held annually in April and has featured public awareness activities, proclamations from federal and state leaders, and conferences devoted to child well-being.

As is explained in Chapter 3, poverty is one of the primary risk factors associated with child maltreatment. Major government programs that assist families and children in need include:

- The U.S. Department of Agriculture's (USDA) Women, Infants, and Children program (http:// www.fns.usda.gov/wic/women-infants-and-children-wic) provides federal grants to states so that they can offer food assistance, nutrition education, and health care referrals to low-income pregnant women and women with infants and children up to age five who are at risk of poor nutrition.

- The USDA's Supplemental Nutrition Assistance Program (http://www.fns.usda.gov/snap/supplemental-nutrition-assistance-program-snap) is a federally administered program through which states provide financial assistance so that needy people can purchase food.

- The USDA's Child and Adult Care Food Program (http://www.fns.usda.gov/cacfp/child-and-adult-care-food-program) is a federally funded program through which states provide meals to low-income children and elderly adults. Children's programs include free and reduced-price breakfasts and lunches that are served at schools and day care facilities.

- The Office of Head Start (http://eclkc.ohs.acf.hhs .gov/hslc/hs) within the HHS's Administration for Children and Families provides federal grants to public and private agencies that operate programs for low-income preschoolers that enhance the children's school readiness and their cognitive, social, and emotional development.

- Medicaid (https://www.medicaid.gov/) is a federal-state program that provides health coverage to individuals, including low-income children, who meet certain eligibility requirements.

- The Children's Health Insurance Program (https://www .medicaid.gov/chip/chip-program-information.html) is a federal-state program that provides free or low-cost health insurance to low-income children whose family income is too high to qualify for Medicaid.

- The Office of Family Assistance within the HHS operates Temporary Assistance for Needy Families (http://www.acf.hhs.gov/programs/ofa/programs/tanf), a federal grant program that provides funds to states to operate welfare programs for needy families.

- The Federal Home Visiting Program (http://mchb .hrsa.gov/programs/homevisiting) is a federal grant program created by the Patient Protection and Affordable Care Act of 2010. Overseen by the HHS's Health Resources and Services Administration, the program facilitates home visits by experienced counselors to priority populations in local communities.

CHAPTER 3
CAUSES AND EFFECTS OF CHILD ABUSE

CAUSES OF CHILD ABUSE

Investigations into the possible causes of child abuse typically focus on examining the factors that characterize children who have been maltreated in the past. This includes data about the children themselves and their living circumstances, parents and other caregivers, families, and communities. Shared characteristics are seen as risk factors that indicate a higher likelihood that other children with the same characteristics may be subjected to maltreatment. The effects of child abuse can be devastating for many maltreated children. Emerging research is showing that the psychological consequences of maltreatment are particularly debilitating and long-lasting. As a result, child protective service (CPS) agencies are beginning to focus more resources on the emotional, social, and behavioral needs of children who come into contact with the child welfare system.

RISK FACTORS IDENTIFIED IN MAJOR MALTREATMENT STUDIES
National Incidence Studies

As is explained in Chapter 2, the 1974 Child Abuse Prevention and Treatment Act mandated that the U.S. Department of Health and Human Services (HHS) conduct a periodic National Incidence Study of Child Abuse and Neglect (NIS). The findings from the first NIS study (NIS-1) were published in 1981 by the Children's Bureau (which is operated by the HHS) and included information that was gathered from CPS agencies between 1979 and 1980. Although the researchers' primary focus was determining the prevalence of child maltreatment, they correlated data on a handful of demographic characteristics between alleged maltreatment victims and children in the U.S. population as a whole. In *Study Findings: National Study of the Incidence and Severity of Child Abuse and Neglect* (September 1981), the Children's Bureau noted significantly higher representation of young children (aged five years and younger) and children in families

with low annual incomes (less than $15,000) among alleged maltreatment victims when compared with the total U.S. child population. No significant differences were found based on race.

NIS-2 studies were conducted during the 1980s; the original findings report was published in 1988, but technical errors prompted the Children's Bureau to publish a revised edition in 1991. In *National Incidence and Prevalence of Child Abuse and Neglect 1988, Revised Report* (September 1991), Andrea J. Sedlak began using the term *risk factors* to refer to shared characteristics of maltreated children and their families. Overall, Sedlak determined that low income was a "highly significant risk factor for child maltreatment." The significance of other characteristics, including child age, sex, and race/ethnicity; family size; and county type (e.g., metropolitan or rural) was less definitive. The NIS-2 data did indicate that incidences of abuse increased with child age, but that younger children were most at risk for serious injury and death. Sedlak noted, "Overall, it appeared that, while the youngest children were not as frequently maltreated as older ones, when they did experience maltreatment it tended to be more injurious, perhaps due to their greater physical frailty in comparison to older children." In addition, Sedlak reported that children living in families with four or more children had higher rates of maltreatment than did children living in smaller families.

Another report based on NIS-2 data was published in 1993 and specifically looked at risk factors that were associated with child maltreatment. The HHS's National Center on Child Abuse and Neglect examined in *A Report to Congress: The National Center on Child Abuse and Neglect Study of High Risk Child Abuse and Neglect Groups, Appendix B: NIS-2 Reanalysis Report* (1993) seven key factors (family income, child's age, family structure, child's race/ethnicity, county metropolitan status, family size, and child's sex) and rated their strengths as predictors of risk for maltreatment. Overall, the center found family income to be the "most important predictor of risk for all maltreatment types" and indicated that children in low-income families were at "much higher risk in all categories of abuse and neglect." In addition, maltreatment risk "generally increased" with the child's age and was higher for females, only children, and children living in urban counties. The predictive nature of family structure as a risk factor varied across maltreatment types, and no single racial/ethnic group was found to be "consistently at higher risk."

NIS-3 studies were conducted throughout the early 1990s. The overall findings were reported by Andrea J. Sedlak and Diane D. Broadhurst in *Third National Incidence Study of Child Abuse and Neglect: Final Report* (September 1996). In regards to risk factors, Sedlak and Broadhurst reached the following conclusions:

- Girls were sexually abused three times more often than boys, but boys had a greater risk than girls of being subjected to emotional neglect and to physical abuse resulting in serious injury.

- There were no significant differences in maltreatment incidence by race.

- Compared with children living with both parents, children living with a single parent had a 77% greater risk of being harmed by physical abuse, an 80% greater risk of suffering serious injury or harm from abuse or neglect, and an 87% greater risk of being harmed by physical neglect.

- Compared with children in families with higher annual incomes, children in the lower income brackets were 22 times more likely to experience maltreatment fitting the Harm Standard and 25 times more likely to experience maltreatment fitting the Endangerment Standard. (See Chapter 2 for complete definitions of these standards; in brief, the Harm Standard requires that demonstrable harm to a child be present, whereas the Endangerment Standard requires only that a professional consider a child to be at risk of harm.) In addition, low-income children were 18 times more likely than higher-income children to be sexually abused and 56 times more likely to be educationally neglected.

As is noted in Chapter 2, another round of NIS studies was conducted between 2005 and 2006, and the results were reported in *Fourth National Incidence Study of Child Abuse and Neglect (NIS-4) Report to Congress* (January 2010, http://www.acf.hhs.gov/sites/default/files/opre/nis4_report_congress_full_pdf_jan2010.pdf), which was authored by Andrea J. Sedlak et al. and published jointly by the HHS's Office of Planning, Research, and Evaluation (OPRE) and the Children's Bureau. Sedlak et al. assess various child, family, and community characteristics in terms of maltreatment incidence rates (the number of children maltreated per 1,000 children). The rates are calculated under both the Harm Standard and the Endangerment Standard and for different maltreatment types, depending on data availability. Sedlak et al. find that family structure, number of children in household, parental employment, and socioeconomic status are relevant factors to child abuse and neglect. In addition, the researchers provide data on the perceived role of perpetrator alcohol abuse, drug abuse, and mental illness in maltreatment cases.

As of September 2016, a release date for a fifth NIS study had not yet been announced.

Some Findings from NIS-4

FAMILY STRUCTURE. Single-parent families in which an unmarried partner was living in the household had the greatest risk of child maltreatment, whereas families headed by married biological parents had the lowest risk. In NIS-4 Sedlak et al. report the following incidence rates (number of children per 1,000 children) under the Harm Standard for maltreatment by family structure:

- All maltreatment—57.2 per 1,000 children for single parent with a cohabiting partner, compared with a range of 6.8 for married biological parents to 33.2 for neither parent living in household

- All abuse types—33.6 per 1,000 children for single parent with a cohabiting partner, compared with a range of 2.9 for married biological parents to 17.4 for other married parents living in household

- All neglect types—27 per 1,000 children for single parent with a cohabiting partner, compared with a range of 4.2 for married biological parents to 20.4 for neither parent living in household

NUMBER OF CHILDREN IN HOUSEHOLD. Sedlak et al. note that the number of children in a household is a risk factor in maltreatment rates. Under the Harm Standard for all maltreatment types the incidence rates by number of children in the household were 21.2 per 1,000 children (four or more children), 17.9 (one child), 15.7 (three children), and 11.9 (two children). Likewise, under the Endangerment Standard the rates were 62.9 per 1,000 children (four or more children), 38.2 (three children), 36.6 (one child), and 27.2 (two children). Under both standards, the presence of four or more children in the household was a significant risk factor for maltreatment.

PARENTAL EMPLOYMENT. According to Sedlak et al. in NIS-4, the incidence rates for all maltreatment types under the Harm Standard were 22.6 per 1,000 children for parent(s) not in the labor force, 15.9 for unemployed parent(s), and 7.6 for employed parent(s). Under the Endangerment Standard the rates were 57.7 per 1,000 children for parent(s) not in the labor force, 39.9 for unemployed parent(s), and 17.1 for employed parent(s). Thus, parental employment substantially lowered the risk for child maltreatment.

SOCIOECONOMIC STATUS. In their NIS-4 report, Sedlak et al. assess maltreatment incidence rates using a composite measure of socioeconomic status that incorporates household income, parental education level, and household member participation in a poverty-related program. The researchers designated children as having "low socioeconomic status" if their household income was less than $15,000 annually, their parents' highest education level was less than high school, or any household member participated in a poverty-related program. The incidence rate for all maltreatment types under the Harm Standard was 22.5 per 1,000 children for children of low socioeconomic status, compared with 4.4 for other children. Likewise, the incidence rate for all maltreatment types under the Endangerment Standard was 55.1 per 1,000 children for children of low socioeconomic status, compared with 9.5 for other children. Overall, children of low socioeconomic status were at "significantly" greater risk of maltreatment than other children.

PERPETRATOR PROBLEMS. As part of the NIS-4 data collection effort, researchers asked their sources (typically CPS agencies) if they believed that perpetrator alcohol use, drug use, and/or mental illness were factors in the specific child maltreatment cases they had investigated. Sedlak et al. note that under the Harm Standard for all maltreatment types, the sources indicated they believed that 11.4% of the children they investigated had been maltreated by a perpetrator with an alcohol abuse problem. The percentages for drug abuse and mental illness were 10.8% and 7.2%, respectively.

National Survey of Child and Adolescent Well-Being

As is explained in Chapter 2, the Personal Responsibility and Work Opportunity Reconciliation Act of 1996 authorized the performance of the National Survey of Child and Adolescent Well-Being (NSCAW) studies by the OPRE. The longitudinal studies (studies of the same group of people over time) began in 1997 with NSCAW I, which tracked 5,501 children aged birth to 14 years who had been the subjects of maltreatment investigations by CPS agencies or were in foster care. NSCAW I ran through 2007. NSCAW II began in 2008 and was ongoing as of September 2016. It was tracking 5,873 children aged birth to 17.5 years for which maltreatment investigations were closed by CPS agencies between February 2008 and April 2009. As of September 2016, three NSCAW II waves had taken place: Wave 1 (March 2008 to September 2009) featured baseline data collection, Wave 2 (October 2009 to January 2011) featured follow-up data collection on the same children, and Wave

3 (June 2011 to December 2012) included further follow-up data relating to the children and their families.

From a risk factor standpoint, the NSCAW studies are informative because they include detailed characteristics about the children, their families, and/or their caregivers. NSCAW I data, in particular, provide insight into maltreatment risk factors that had not previously been comprehensively studied. These include child health problems, domestic violence in the household, and the parents' mental health status, substance abuse status, and own history of being abused. For example, the OPRE notes in "National Survey of Child and Adolescent Well-Being, Research Brief No. 7: Special Health Care Needs among Children in Child Welfare" (June 2007, http://www.acf.hhs.gov/sites/default/files/opre/special_health.pdf) that NSCAW I data indicate that 35% of the children who were the subjects of maltreatment investigations by CPS agencies had a chronic health problem or special need, such as emotional disturbance, speech impairment, and/or developmental delay, at the time of their baseline assessment (two to six months following the close of the maltreatment investigation).

In NSCAW II Wave 3 Report: Wave 3 Tables (June 2014, http://www.acf.hhs.gov/sites/default/files/opre/nscaw_wave_3_tables_june_2014_clean.pdf), Cecilia Casanueva et al. assess some of the lingering effects of maltreatment on NSCAW participants. As presented in Table 3.1, 37.4% of maltreated children between the ages of two and five showed signs of developmental difficulties at the time the Wave 3 data were compiled. In this age range, boys (42.3%) were considerably more likely than girls (30.8%) to show signs of developmental problems during the Wave 3 study. Among racial and ethnic groups, Hispanic children (40.9%) between the ages of two and five were the most likely to suffer from developmental issues, followed by whites (38.9%) and African Americans (32.8%).

Risks of behavioral, emotional, and other issues were also prevalent among NSCAW participants between the ages of 11 and 20. As Table 3.2 shows, more than one-third (37.6%) of participants in this age group demonstrated a risk of developing either behavioral or emotional problems, or a problem with substance abuse, at the time the Wave 3 data were compiled. This issue was most prevalent among children between the ages of 15 and 17, with nearly half (47.1%) of participants in this age group demonstrating a risk for behavioral, emotional, or substance abuse problems. When accounting for living arrangements, participants who lived in group homes or other residential programs demonstrated the highest level of risk, with more than three-quarters (77.2%) of individuals in this category in danger of developing behavioral, emotional, or substance abuse issues. At the same time, individuals in this category were also the most likely to

TABLE 3.1

Children with developmental problems reported in the National Survey of Child and Adolescent Well-Being II, Wave 3, by sex, age, race and ethnicity, home setting, and insurance status, 2011–12

	Developmental problems[a]
	%
Total	37.4
Gender	
Male	42.3
Female	30.8
Age (years)	
2	26.3
3–5	37.4
Race/ethnicity	
Black	32.8
White	38.9
Hispanic	40.9
Other	33.4
Setting	
In-home	38.7
Formal kin care	50.3
Informal kin care	19.5
Foster care	58.2
Insurance status	
Private	30.1
Public[b]	38.6
Other	21.0
Uninsured	42.5

[a]Developmental problem was defined based on young children having a diagnosed mental or medical condition that has a high probability of resulting in developmental delay (e.g., Down syndrome). Areas included cognitive development based on the Battelle Developmental Inventory (BDI) or Kaufman Brief Intelligence Test (K-BIT), communication development based on the Preschool Language Scale-3 (PLS-3), and adaptive development based on the Vineland Daily Living Skills.
[b]"Public" includes children who did not have private coverage at the time of interview, but who had Medicaid and/or a State Children's Health Insurace Program (SCHIP).
Note: All analyses were on weighted National Survey of Child and Adolescent Well-Being II, Wave 3 data.

SOURCE: Adapted from Cecelia Casanueva et al., "Exhibit 7. Developmental Problems among Children 2 to 5 Years Old at Wave 3," in *NSCAW II Wave 3 Report: Wave 3 Tables*, U.S. Department of Health and Human Services, Administration for Children and Families, Office of Planning, Research, and Evaluation, June 5, 2014, http://www.acf.hhs.gov/sites/default/files/opre/nscaw_wave_3_tables_june_2014_clean.pdf (accessed June 16, 2016)

have been arrested or picked up by the police. As Table 3.3 shows, 4.1% of participants between the ages of 11 and 20 who were living in group homes or residential programs at the time of the Wave 3 report had been arrested within the previous six months. By comparison, 2.6% of participants who were living at home had been arrested or picked up by police.

Casanueva et al. find that NSCAW participants also demonstrated a range of basic health needs at the time of the Wave 3 study. For example, about three-fifths (60.2%) of all participants needed a routine medical checkup or immunizations at the time the Wave 3 information was collected, while more than half (56.2%) needed basic dental care. (See Table 3.4.) As Table 3.4 shows, a high proportion of participants needing specific health services eventually received some form of care.

For example, 97.6% of children referred by caseworkers for medical checkups or immunizations went on to receive care, and 96.6% of children referred for dental care later visited a dentist.

A history of maltreatment can also impact future sexual behavior, particularly among girls. Table 3.5 offers an overview of sexual activities among female NSCAW participants between the ages of 11 and 20. Nearly half (46.1%) of all participants had had sex by the time of the Wave 3 report; 41.2% had had sex in the previous year. In addition, one out of five (20.5%) female NSCAW participants had experienced a pregnancy at some point during their life. Casanueva et al. report in *Child Well-Being Spotlight: Teenage Girls in the Child Welfare System Report High Rates of Risky Sexual Activity and Pregnancy* (June 12, 2014, http://www.acf.hhs.gov/sites/default/files/opre/sexual_outcomes_spotlight_13.pdf) that female victims of maltreatment also experienced high incidences of forced sexual intercourse. Among female maltreatment victims between the ages of 14 and 17, 14.4% had been forced to have sex at some point during their life; this figure more than doubled for female maltreatment victims between the ages of 18 and 20, with nearly one-third (29.1%) of young women in that age group having experienced forced sexual intercourse. (See Figure 3.1.)

According to the Casanueva et al., achieving stability can prove to be a significant challenge for child victims of maltreatment. Table 3.6 examines the living arrangements of NSCAW participants at the time of the Wave 3 report. The HHS explains on its Child Welfare Information website (2016, https://www.childwelfare.gov/permanency/overview) that maltreated children achieve permanency when they have left foster care for a permanent legal living situation, whether they have reunited with their parents, gone to live with other relatives, or been adopted. As Table 3.6 shows, about half (49.9%) of NSCAW participants had achieved permanency by 2012. Of these, nearly three-quarters (73.3%) were reunited with their parents, 24.4% were adopted, and 2.3% went to live with relatives. Even still, permanency did not necessarily indicate an improvement in the quality of care received by participants. Among children who had achieved permanency at the time of the Wave 3 report, a majority reported living with a primary caretaker who suffered from serious mental health issues (56.4%), who actively abused substances (53.2%), or who exhibited poor parenting skills (52.6%). (See Table 3.6.)

Of the caregivers represented in the Wave 3 report, nearly half (47.3%) lived in poverty, while a comparable proportion (48.2%) either did not work or were currently unemployed and looking for work. (See Table 3.7.) Table 3.7 also shows that female caregivers (88.8%) outnumbered male caregivers (11.2%) by a considerable

TABLE 3.2

Children at risk of emotional/behavioral or substance abuse problems reported in the National Survey of Child and Adolescent Well-Being II, Wave 3, by sex, age, race and ethnicity, home setting, and insurance status, 2011–12

	Risk of a behavioral/ emotional problem[a]	Risk of a substance abuse problem[b]	Risk of a behavioral/ emotional or substance abuse problem
	%	%	%
Total	32.9	14.4	37.6
Gender			
Male	31.9	15.4	38.6
Female	33.7	13.6	36.8
Age (years)			
11–12	28.6	0.1	28.7
13–14	34.0	4.6	35.6
15–17	41.5	17.0	47.1
18–20	26.6	30.4	37.0
Race/ethnicity			
Black	33.0	7.3	36.0
White	33.1	15.6	38.7
Hispanic	29.5	13.2	33.3
Other	43.3	28.6	50.8
Setting			
In-home	33.6	8.2	36.3
Formal kin care	52.5	2.0	53.1
Informal kin care	35.3	6.4	37.2
Foster care	58.6	8.2	63.6
Group home or residential program	72.7	13.2	77.2
Insurance status			
Private	21.9	16.4	29.6
Public[c]	37.5	12.2	41.3
Other	31.0	12.4	36.3
Uninsured	26.2	21.9	31.4

[a]Risk of a behavioral/emotional problem was defined as scores in the clinical range on any of the following standardized measures among children 1.5 to 17 years old: Internalizing, Externalizing or Total Problems scales of the Child Behavior Checklist (CBCL: administered for children 1.5 to 18 years old), Youth Self Report (YSR; administered to children 11 years old and older), or the Teacher Report From (TRF; administered for children 6 to 18 years old); the Child Depression Inventory (CDI; administered to children 7 years old and older); or the PTSD section Intrusive Experiences and Dissociation subscales of the Trauma Symptoms Checklist (administered to children 8 years old and older). For young adults 18 to 20 years old, risk of a behavioral/emotional problem was defined as scores in the clinical range on the Internalizing, Externalizing or Total Problems scales of the Adult Self Report (ASF), the Composite International Diagnostic Interview Form, Short-Form Depression section (CIDI-SF), and the PTSD section of the Trauma Symptom Checklist for Adults (TSCA).
[b]Risk of a substance abuse problem was defined by a Total score of 2 or more on the CRAFFT (Car, Relax, Alone, Forget, Friends, Trouble) substance abuse screening test (CRAFFT). A CRAFFT total score of 2 or more is higahly correlated with having a substance-related diagnosis and the need for substance abuse treatment.
[c]"Public" includes children who did not have private coverage at the time of interview, but who had Medicaid and/or a State Children's Health Insurance Plan (SCHIP).
Note: All analyses were on weighted National Survey of Child and Adolescent Well-Being II Wave 3 data.

SOURCE: Adapted from Cecelia Casanueva et al., "Exhibit 14. Risk of a Behavioral/Emotional Problem or Substance Abuse Problem among Children 11 to 20 Years Old at Wave 3," in *NSCAW II Wave 3 Report: Wave 3 Tables*, U.S. Department of Health and Human Services, Administration for Children and Families, Office of Planning, Research, and Evaluation, June 5, 2014, http://www.acf.hhs.gov/sites/default/files/opre/nscaw_wave_3_tables_june_2014_clean .pdf (accessed June 16, 2016)

margin. Despite this wide discrepancy, male caregivers showed considerably greater likelihood of exhibiting behavioral problems or other issues that might negatively impact their ability to provide adequate care. For example, at the time of the Wave 3 report, fathers (30%) were considerably more likely than mothers (19.7%) to demonstrate a need for alcohol or substance abuse treatment. (See Table 3.8.) Conversely, mothers (23.1%) were significantly more likely than fathers (13.6%) to take prescription drugs for mental health issues at the time the Wave 3 data were compiled. (See Table 3.9.)

According to Casanueva et al., problems of maltreatment persisted well after the initial NSCAW baseline report was completed. At the time the Wave 3 information was collected in 2011 and 2012, nearly one-quarter (24.3%) of NSCAW participants were involved in a

re-report of maltreatment; of these, nearly one-third (29.7%) were substantiated by a caseworker. (See Table 3.10.) Among maltreatment victims between the ages of 11 and 17, roughly half (49.9%) reported experiencing an incidence of psychological aggression (e.g., yelling or shouting) in the 12 months prior to the Wave 3 study, more than one-quarter (28.8%) reported experiencing corporal punishment (e.g., being spanked on the bottom or slapped on the hand), while one out of 10 (9.8%) were victims of serious physical assault (e.g., being punched with a fist or being knocked down). (See Table 3.11.)

Exposure to domestic violence is another serious issue confronting maltreatment victims. In "Child Well-Being Spotlight: Parents Reported for Maltreatment Experience High Rates of Domestic Violence" (February 13, 2013, http://www.acf.hhs.gov/sites/default/files/opre/

TABLE 3.3

Arrests in prior six months among adolescents reported in the National Survey of Child and Adolescent Well-Being II, Wave 3, by gender, age, race and ethnicity, and home setting, 2011–12

	Arrested or picked up by police in past 6 months
	%
Total	3.4
Gender	
Male	2.8
Female	3.8
Age (years)	
11–12	0.3
13–14	4.9
15–17	2.2
18–20	5.9
Race/ethnicity	
Black	3.9
White	1.8
Hispanic	4.1
Other	7.5
Setting	
In-home	2.6
Formal kin care	0.8
Informal kin care	1.2
Foster care	1.4
Group home or residential program	4.1

Note: All analyses were on weighted National Survey of Child and Adolescent Well-Being II Wave 3 data.

SOURCE: Adapted from Cecelia Casanueva et al., "Exhibit 16. Arrest in Past 6 Months of Adolescents 11 to 20 Years Old by Adolescent and Young Adult Report at Wave 3," in *NSCAW II Wave 3 Report: Wave 3 Tables*, U.S. Department of Health and Human Services, Administration for Children and Families, Office of Planning, Research, and Evaluation, June 5, 2014, http://www.acf.hhs.gov/sites/default/files/opre/nscaw_wave_3_tables_june_2014_clean.pdf (accessed June 16, 2016)

TABLE 3.4

Child service needs reported in the National Survey of Child and Adolescent Well-Being II, Wave 3, by referral status, 2011–12

Number of weeks	Needed service %	Referred to service %	Received service* %
Routine check-up/immunizations	60.2	62.1	97.6
Dental	56.2	48.7	96.6
Independent living training	32.9	28.2	75.6
Screening for learning or developmental disability	24.9	17.9	84.0
Emotional/behavioral/attention problem	45.0	34.8	94.3
Vision	22.5	12.1	98.7
Hearing	11.9	7.5	97.5
Health problem	13.4	9.0	98.1
Special education	23.1	9.7	96.9
Substance use	3.5	2.7	81.7
Delinquency	6.3	4.1	94.3

*Caseworkers are asked about service receipt only when a service referral is reported. The "Received" category represents the subset of children who were referred to a service and who received that service.
Note: All analyses were on weighted National Survey of Child and Adolescent Well-Being II, Wave 3 data.

SOURCE: Adapted from Cecelia Casanueva et al., "Exhibit 18. Child Service Need, Referral, and Receipt by Caseworker Report at Wave 3," in *NSCAW II Wave 3 Report: Wave 3 Tables*, U.S. Department of Health and Human Services, Administration for Children and Families, Office of Planning, Research, and Evaluation, June 5, 2014, http://www.acf.hhs.gov/sites/default/files/opre/nscaw_wave_3_tables_june_2014_clean.pdf (accessed June 16, 2016)

parentsinhome_v2.pdf), Casanueva et al. report that about one-quarter (24.7%) of parents involved in the NSCAW study reported being involved in a domestic violence incident within the previous year. Furthermore, Carlos A. Cuevas et al. indicate in *Children's Exposure to Violence and the Intersection between Delinquency and Victimization* (October 2013, http://www.ojjdp.gov/pubs/240555.pdf) that exposure to violence at home can lead to future incidences of delinquency among children. Specifically, more than one out of five (20.8%) boys between the ages of 10 and 17 who had been exposed to violent behavior later engaged in some form of juvenile delinquency, another 17.9% reported being victims of delinquency, and 18.1% reported being both victims and perpetrators. By contrast, only 13% of girls in this age group who had encountered violent behavior later engaged in juvenile delinquency. For boys, delinquency rates were highest among 16-year-olds, with one-third (33.6%) of boys in that age group engaging in some form of delinquent behavior. Delinquency among adolescent girls also peaked at the age of 16, with 18.2% of girls in that age group engaging in delinquent behavior.

Child Maltreatment 2014

As is noted in Chapter 2, the Children's Bureau publishes an annual summary report about maltreatment claims reported to CPS agencies in the 50 states, the District of Columbia, and Puerto Rico. As of September 2016, the most recent report was *Child Maltreatment 2014* (January 25, 2016, https://www.acf.hhs.gov/sites/default/files/cb/cm2014.pdf). In 2014 CPS agencies handled maltreatment reports concerning 3.2 million unique children. Nearly 2.5 million of the uniquely counted children were found to be nonvictims of child maltreatment. This group includes children whose cases were investigated but not substantiated and those who received a response other than a formal CPS investigation, such as a caseworker working with a family to identify appropriate services. (Note that a child determined to be a nonvictim of maltreatment may still need and receive follow-up services.) The remaining 702,000 were determined to be victims; this number included 1,580 children who died from maltreatment.

Table 3.12 shows the numbers and percentages of unique victims by state whose caregivers had an alcohol abuse risk factor. For the 30 states that reported data for unique victims, 9.2% of the children had the risk factor. This risk was considerably higher than for children who were determined to be nonvictims of abuse. Twenty-one states reported data for unique nonvictims. Overall, 3.8%

TABLE 3.5

Rates of sexual experience and pregnancy among females aged 11 to 20 reported in the National Survey of Child and Adolescent Well-Being II, Wave 3, by age, race and ethnicity, home setting, type of sexual experience, and pregnancy status, 2011–12

	Ever had sex	Had sex in past 12 months	Ever had forced sex	Ever been pregnant
	%	%	%	%
Total	**46.1**	**41.2**	**14.7**	**20.5**
Age (years)				
11–12	1.5	0.1	0.5	0.0
13–14	11.9	10.9	2.9	0.8
15–17	51.3	45.9	16.7	21.2
18–20	92.5	83.4	29.1	45.1
Race/ethnicity				
Black	45.9	40.9	13.7	24.2
White	46.4	40.3	13.1	19.0
Hispanic	39.3	35.6	10.4	19.5
Other	61.3	58.7	32.6	21.9
Setting				
In-home	24.7	22.0	8.5	8.8
Formal kin care	35.2	29.1	5.4	14.4
Informal kin care	34.0	32.3	6.5	14.4
Foster care	21.8	17.5	2.8	3.5
Group home or residential program	27.4	11.0	17.9	3.4

Note: All analyses were on weighted National Survey of Child and Adolescent Well-Being II Wave 3 data. "Sex" was defined as vaginal sex.

SOURCE: Adapted from Cecelia Casanueva et al., "Exhibit 15. Sexual Experience and Pregnancy by Female 11 to 20 Years Old by Adolescent and Young Adult Report at Wave 3," in *NSCAW II Wave 3 Report: Wave 3 Tables*, U.S. Department of Health and Human Services, Administration for Children and Families, Office of Planning, Research, and Evaluation, June 5, 2014, http://www.acf.hhs.gov/sites/default/files/opre/nscaw_wave_3_tables_june_2014_clean.pdf (accessed June 16, 2016)

FIGURE 3.1

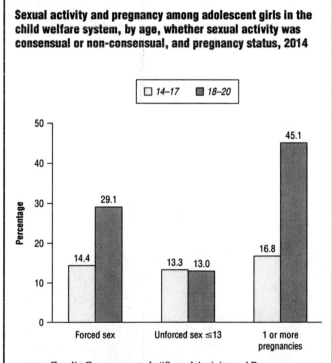

Sexual activity and pregnancy among adolescent girls in the child welfare system, by age, whether sexual activity was consensual or non-consensual, and pregnancy status, 2014

SOURCE: Cecelia Casanueva et al., "Sexual Activity and Pregnancy among Teenage Girls," in *Child Well-Being Spotlight: Teenage Girls in the Child Welfare System Report High Rates of Risky Sexual Activity and Pregnancy*, U.S. Department of Health and Human Services, Administration for Children and Families, Office of Planning, Research and Evaluation, June 12, 2014, http://www.acf.hhs.gov/sites/default/files/opre/sexual_outcomes_spotlight_13.pdf (accessed June 10, 2016)

of these children had the alcohol abuse caregiver risk factor. A similar summary is presented in Table 3.13 for the drug abuse caregiver risk factor. The risk factor was present for 26% of the unique victims (with 33 states reporting data) and for 8.2% of the unique nonvictims (with 25 states reporting data). The Children's Bureau indicates that some states do not differentiate between alcohol abuse and drug abuse and report both risk factors for a child whose caregiver has any substance abuse problem.

According to the Children's Bureau, in *Child Abuse and Neglect Fatalities 2013: Statistics and Interventions* (April 2015, https://www.childwelfare.gov/pubPDFs/fatality.pdf), 1,520 children died from maltreatment in 2013. Of these, nearly half (46.5%) were under the age of one year old. (See Figure 3.2.) Of all child fatalities that year, 71.4% were caused by neglect and 46.8% were caused by physical abuse. (See Figure 3.3.) As shown in Table 3.14, the Children's Bureau assesses three specific caregiver risk factors for child maltreatment fatalities. However, data on caregiver risk factors were not available for all of these children because not all states reported the data. For the 26 to 29 states reporting caregiver risk factors, the data indicate that 6.9% of the child maltreatment fatalities were associated with a caregiver with alcohol abuse problems, while 17.9% were associated with a caregiver with drug abuse problems.

TABLE 3.6

Risks in children's homes at time of maltreatment investigation as reported in the National Survey of Child and Adolescent Well-Being II, Wave 3, 2011–12

| | Total achieving permanency | | Type of permanency | | | | Discharged to relatives |
| | | | Adoption | | Reunification | | |
	Population	%	Population	%	%		%
Total	3,066	49.9	1,799	24.4	73.3		2.3
Gender							
Male	1,597	50.8	948	23.7	73.2		3.0
Female	1,469	48.9	851	25.2	73.3		1.4
Age (years) at baseline							
0–2	1,897	59.9	1,213	21.9	75.1		3
3–5	372	49.9	210	20.1	76.4		3.5
6–10	467	45.4	237	38.1	60.5		1.4
11–12	134	33.7	58	14.0	85.8		0.2
13–17	196	47.0	81	18.1	81.3		0.6
Race/ethnicity							
Black	1,057	41.2	515	29.4	69.6		0.9
White	946	52.3	580	25.1	71.9		3.1
Hispanic	845	51.9	569	21.8	75.5		2.7
Other	203	57.8	127	17.1	82.8		0.1
Setting at baseline							
In-home	969	57.5	630	18.4	79.2		2.4
Formal kin care	480	37.7	233	38.1	61.4		0.5
Informal kin care	506	29.2	255	20.4	75.8		3.7
Foster care	1,043	58.7	651	51.3	46.6		2.1
Group home or residential program	44	23.4	17	10.9	89.1		0
Developmental need at baseline (birth to 5 years old)*							
Yes	558	45.3	338	31.4	67.9		0.7
No	1,711	59.8	1,085	17.8	78.2		4.1
Risk of any behavioral/emotional or cognitive problems at baseline (children 6 to 17 years old)							
Yes	488	46.5	233	28.5	71.0		0.5
No	249	38.4	114	32.1	65.8		2.1
Caseworker risk assessment at baseline							
Active drug abuse by primary caregiver							
Yes	1,057	53.2	700	27.5	64.4		8
No	2,009	49.1	1,099	23.6	75.6		0.8
Primary caregiver had serious mental health problem							
Yes	965	56.4	610	25.0	73.9		1.1
No	2,101	48.0	1,189	24.2	73.1		2.7
Primary caregiver had poor parenting skills							
Yes	1,353	52.6	824	23.8	74.7		1.5
No	1,713	48.7	975	24.7	72.6		2.7
History of domestic violence against caregiver							
Yes	976	54.7	623	15.8	80.9		3.3
No	2,090	48.1	1,176	28.1	70.1		1.9
History of abuse or neglect of primary caregiver							
Yes	919	53.4	594	25.1	71.4		3.5
No	2,147	48.9	1,205	24.2	73.9		1.9
High stress on the family (e.g., unemployment, drug use, poverty, or neighborhood violence)							
Yes	1,840	54.8	1,124	19.8	78.1		2.1
No	1,226	44.3	675	30.8	66.6		2.6
Low social support							
Yes	1,120	54.9	701	26.3	70.2		3.5
No	1,946	48.0	1,098	23.6	74.6		1.8
Family have trouble paying basic necessities							
Yes	1,053	48.0	674	25.7	71.0		3.2
No	2,013	50.6	1,125	24.0	74.1		2.0

THE SOCIOECONOMIC EFFECT

As noted earlier, low socioeconomic status has long been considered to be a major risk factor for child maltreatment. The NIS studies, in particular, found a strong correlation between low family income and child maltreatment incidence rates. For example, using NIS-4

TABLE 3.6

Risks in children's homes at time of maltreatment investigation as reported in the National Survey of Child and Adolescent Well-Being II, Wave 3, 2011–12 [CONTINUED]

*Developmental need was defined based on young children having a diagnosed mental or medical condition that has a high probability of resulting in developmental delay (e.g., Down syndrome).

Areas included cognitive development based on the Battelle Developmental Inventory (BDI) or Kaufman Brief Intelligence Test (K-BIT), communication development based on the Preschool Language Scale-3 (PLS-3), and adaptive development based on the Vineland Daily Living Skills.

Note: Caseworkers were asked about reunification plans if the child was in out of home care at the time of the interview. Estimates of reunification may represent an underestimate of reunification attempts, as situations where the child was placed out of home and then reunified between interview waves would not be captured. All analyses were on weighted National Survey of Child and Adolescent Well-Being baseline, Adoption and Foster Care Analysis and Reporting System (AFCARS), Wave 2 and Wave 3 data; populations are unweighted and, therefore, direct percentages cannot be calculated by hand. Reported populations vary slightly across analyses because of missing data in some variable categories.

SOURCE: Cecelia Casanueva et al., "Exhibit 31. Permanency of Children Placed in Out-of-Home Care by Caseworker Report through Wave 3 and Adoption and Foster Care Analysis and Reporting System (AFCARS) Data," in *NSCAW II Wave 3 Report: Wave 3 Tables*, U.S. Department of Health and Human Services, Administration for Children and Families, Office of Planning, Research, and Evaluation, June 5, 2014, http://www.acf.hhs.gov/sites/default/files/opre/nscaw_wave_3_tables_june_2014_clean.pdf (accessed June 16, 2016)

data from 2005–06, Sedlak et al. estimate that incidence rates for all maltreatment types were five to six times higher for children of low socioeconomic status than for other children. The researchers used household income data, parental education level, and household participation in poverty-related programs to assign families to socioeconomic brackets. As shown in Table 3.7 and described earlier, data collected for the NSCAW II Wave 3 assessment indicate that 52.7% of the families who came to the attention of CPS agencies in 2011–12 lived below the federal poverty level (16.8% of these families had incomes below 50% of the federal poverty level and 35.9% had incomes in the range of 50% to 99% of the federal poverty level).

Because of the evidential link between low socioeconomic status and child maltreatment rates, it would be expected that child maltreatment rates would increase during times of national economic downturns. From late 2007 to mid-2009 the United States experienced an economic downturn of such historic proportions that it has been dubbed the Great Recession. Unemployment rates rose dramatically during this period, as did the number of homeowners who lost their homes because they could not afford to pay their mortgages. The latter phenomenon actually began several years earlier as the United States suffered from a housing industry slowdown and banking industry crisis that pushed many homeowners into financial difficulties. Rates increased dramatically for mortgage delinquencies (late mortgage payments) and foreclosures (seizures by banks and other mortgage holders of the homes of people who stop making mortgage payments). Although the national economy began to improve by mid-2009, the recovery was slow and halting. As a result, the negative effects of the Great Recession lingered into 2014.

Table 2.2 in Chapter 2 lists child maltreatment victimization rates between 2010 and 2014 as estimated by the Children's Bureau based on data reported by CPS agencies. The rates fell from 9.3 victims per 1,000 children in 2010 to 9.1 victims per 1,000 children in 2012, before rising to 9.4 victims per 1,000 children in 2014. Despite this slight rise, on the whole child maltreatment victimization rates have declined since the first decade of the 21st century. The Children's Bureau indicates in *Child Maltreatment 2005* (March 2007, http://archive.acf.hhs.gov/programs/cb/pubs/cm05/cm05.pdf) that the child maltreatment victimization rate was 12.1 victims per 1,000 children in 2005. Some analysts believe the decreasing child maltreatment rates reflect the broader trend of less violence in American society. Others claim that tightened state budgets during and immediately after the Great Recession forced CPS agencies to reduce the number of cases they could investigate, which artificially lowered the child maltreatment victimization rates. This assertion is particularly controversial and is difficult to support evidentially given that the rates were already falling before the Great Recession began.

CONSEQUENCES OF CHILDHOOD MALTREATMENT

The consequences of childhood maltreatment can be severe and long lasting. The immediate and most obvious consequences are from maltreatment incidents that cause physical harm, such as injuries and even deaths. Neglect does not necessarily leave obvious physical marks like abuse does, and it often involves infants and young children who lack the language skills to describe their abuse. However, children subjected to neglect may show obvious signs of malnourishment or lack of proper medical care. Likewise, victims of sexual abuse may have telltale injuries or sexually transmitted diseases. These problems are readily evident and relatively easy to treat. More insidious and difficult to diagnose and treat are the long-term biological and psychological consequences of maltreatment. Exposure to severe and/or chronic trauma during childhood is blamed for what researchers call sequelae (diseases or disorders that emerge later in life,

TABLE 3.7

Caregivers represented in the National Survey of Child and Adolescent Well-Being II, Wave 3, 2011–12

Caregiver characteristics	Population	Total sample size = 3,893 %	In-home parents sample size = 3,145 %	Informal kin caregivers sample size = 342 %	Formal kin caregivers sample size = 193 %	Foster caregivers sample size = 213 %
Total	3,893	100	86.6	8.8	2.0	2.6
Gender						
Male	422	11.2	10.5	15.2	17.1	18.5
Female	3,471	88.8	89.6	84.8	83.0	81.5
Age (years)						
19 and under	24	0.2	0.2	0.0	3.0	0.0
20–29	1,043	24.2	27.4	4.5	3.1	0.7
30–49	2,138	61.9	66.8	30.2	18.9	38.1
50–59	479	10.3	4.9	47.5	41.1	40.4
60 and older	209	3.4	0.7	17.9	34.0	20.8
Race/ethnicity						
Black	1,037	22.2	21.6	20.9	36.2	37.3
White	1,670	48.1	47.8	54.8	45.2	36.8
Hispanic	950	24.9	25.7	18.1	17.1	24.9
Other	221	4.9	4.9	6.2	1.5	1.1
Education						
Less than high school	843	21.7	22.3	19.6	20.3	8.0
High school	1,648	43.2	43.9	38.5	51.0	31.6
More than high school	1,395	35.1	33.8	41.9	28.7	60.5
Percentage of federal poverty level						
<50	665	16.8	17.1	19.4	5.1	6.4
50–99	1,147	35.9	37.8	26.2	34.8	2.5
100–200	1,082	28.8	28.8	24.0	34.8	42.4
>200	811	18.5	16.3	30.4	25.3	48.8
Employment status						
Work, full time	1,225	34.0	33.5	37.5	33.8	37.6
Work, part time	592	15.6	16.4	10.1	8.7	13.7
Unemployed, looking for work	620	15.6	17.3	4.6	7.3	3.0
Does not work	1,367	32.6	30.7	46.4	49.9	34.5
Other	90	2.3	2.1	1.5	0.2	11.2
Marital status						
Married	1,332	34.8	33.8	34.4	43.1	65.2
Separated	375	10.1	10.2	13.2	6.3	1.9
Divorced	688	21.1	20.5	28.3	19.7	14.9
Widowed	121	3.0	1.5	11.9	15.7	12.3
Never married	1,377	31.0	34.0	12.2	15.3	5.6
Number of children in home						
1	970	22.5	20.5	42.9	27.2	17.7
2	1,016	26.6	27.3	18.6	23.8	36.1
3	841	24.6	24.4	29.6	19.2	17.3
4	539	14.6	15.8	1.5	18.1	15.9
5 or more	528	11.7	12.1	7.4	11.7	13.1
Number of adults in home						
1	1,205	31.0	31.4	27.9	28.6	28.9
2	1,875	47.8	48.0	45.5	54.8	43.8
3	540	14.9	14.3	19.1	13.5	23.0
4 or more	274	6.3	6.3	7.5	3.2	4.4

Note: All analyses were on weighted National Survey of Child and Adolescent Well-Being II, Wave 3 data; populations are unweighted and, therefore, direct percentages cannot be calculated by hand. Reported populations vary slightly across analyses because of missing data in some variable categories.

SOURCE: Cecelia Casanueva et al., "Exhibit 19. Caregiver and Household Characteristics at Wave 3," in *NSCAW II Wave 3 Report: Wave 3 Tables*, U.S. Department of Health and Human Services, Administration for Children and Families, Office of Planning, Research, and Evaluation, June 5, 2014, http://www.acf.hhs.gov/sites/default/files/opre/nscaw_wave_3_tables_june_2014_clean.pdf (accessed June 16, 2016)

but are linked to previous experiences of disease, injury, or other trauma). Casanueva et al. list in *National Survey of Child and Adolescent Well-Being, Research Brief No. 18: Instability and Early Life Changes among Children in the Child Welfare System* (September 2012, http://www.acf.hhs.gov/sites/default/files/opre/early_life.pdf) the following psychological sequelae that are associated with childhood traumas, such as maltreatment:

- Alcohol and drug abuse and dependence
- Depression
- Anxiety

TABLE 3.8

Need for alcohol and substance abuse treatment among parents reported in the National Survey of Child and Adolescent Well-Being II, Wave 3, by type of service, 2011–12

	Need for substance abuse services[a]	Received inpatient alcohol or substance abuse service[b]	Received outpatient alcohol or substance abuse service[c]
	%	%	%
Total	20.8	0.3	0.9
Parent gender			
Male	30.0	0.0	0.5
Female	19.7	0.3	0.9
Parent age (years)			
Under 20	1.0	0.0	0.0
20–29	21.0	0.7	1.2
30–49	20.3	0.1	0.8
50–59	25.9	0.4	0.5
60 and older	25.4	0.0	0.0
Parent race/ethnicity			
Black	19.9	0.0	0.0
White	18.2	0.5	1.5
Hispanic	26.2	0.0	0.6
Other	20.9	0.0	0.3
Parent insurance status			
Public	23.0	0.3	1.2
Private	14.0	0.0	0.0
Uninsured	22.2	0.5	1.0

[a]Parents were determined to have a need for substance abuse services if they met any one of four criteria: (1) caseworker report of parent's need for services for a drug or alcohol problem at Wave 3, (2) AUDIT Total score ≥5, (3) DAST-20 Total score 2–4 or 5 or higher, or (4) the parent's self-reported need ("a lot" or "somewhat") for alcohol or substance abuse services in the past year, if she or he had not received a substance abuse service.

[b]Inpatient alcohol or substance abuse services include having been admitted overnight to hospital or medical facility for alcohol/drug problem in the last 12 months, having stayed overnight in a facility that provides alcohol or drug treatment in the last 12 months, or having used an emergency room for alcohol/drug abuse in past 12 months.

[c]Outpatient alcohol or substance abuse services include having been to a clinic or doctor regarding an alcohol or drug problem in the past 12 months.

Note: The term "in-home parents" refers to the parents of children living at home at Wave 3. Only permanent caregivers were asked about substance abuse service receipt; responses here reflect only those of in-home parents. Parents who indicated that they had not ever received substance abuse services were included as not having received these services in the past 12 months. All analyses were on weighted National Survey of Child and Adolescent Well-Being II Wave 3 data.

SOURCE: Adapted from Cecelia Casanueva et al., "Exhibit 23. In-Home Parents' Need for and Receipt of Alcohol or Substance Abuse Services in Past 12 Months (Wave 3)," in *NSCAW II Wave 3 Report: Wave 3 Tables*, U.S. Department of Health and Human Services, Administration for Children and Families, Office of Planning, Research, and Evaluation, June 5, 2014, http://www.acf.hhs.gov/sites/default/files/opre/nscaw_wave_3_tables_june_2014_clean.pdf (accessed June 16, 2016)

- Conduct problems

- Schizophrenia

- Personality disorders

- Post-traumatic stress disorder

- Acute stress disorder

- Suicide

- Unfavorable psychological adjustment to subsequent traumatic events

- Difficulties with emotion regulation

- Greater vulnerability to developing traumatic symptoms when exposed to new traumatic events

It is important to note that the actions taken by CPS agencies after a maltreatment incident occurs, for example, removing a child from the home and putting him or her into the foster care system, are also traumatic events. Casanueva et al. indicate that the Child and Family Services Improvement and Innovation Act of 2011 includes "new language" that requires the states to develop plans to "monitor and treat emotional trauma associated with a child's maltreatment and removal."

In the information memorandum "Promoting Social and Emotional Well-Being for Children and Youth Receiving Child Welfare Services" (April 17, 2012, http://www.acf.hhs.gov/sites/default/files/cb/im1204.pdf), the Administration on Children, Youth, and Families (ACYF) examines six domains that are associated with childhood maltreatment: neurobiology, traumatic traits, behavioral problems, relational competence, mental health, and use of psychotropic medications. The domains are not stand-alone, but can have significant overlap. In other words, maltreated children can experience multiple problems across the domains. It is also important to understand that most problems are assessed in maltreated children months or even years after the maltreatment occurred. Thus, it is not entirely clear whether the problems existed beforehand or developed as a result of the maltreatment and/or subsequent interventions, such as removal from the home. In addition, there are few longitudinal studies that follow maltreated

TABLE 3.9

Need for mental health services among parents reported in the National Survey of Child and Adolescent Well-Being II, Wave 3, by type of service, 2011–12

	Need for mental health services[a]	Received inpatient mental health service[b]	Received outpatient mental health service[c]	Used prescription medication for mental health problem[d]
	%	%	%	%
Total	26.5	1.2	11.9	22.1
Parent gender				
Male	12.5	0.2	4.7	13.6
Female	28.2	1.3	12.7	23.1
Parent age (years)				
Under 20	29.6	0.0	17.4	16.2
20–29	23.5	1.0	11.2	16.2
30–49	28.0	1.2	12.0	24.2
50–59	26.2	1.1	14.7	27.0
60 and older	11.9	0.0	3.4	4.7
Parent race/ethnicity				
Black	26.3	1.4	5.3	10.4
White	27.4	1.4	17.2	30.3
Hispanic	25.8	0.3	8.1	16.8
Other	26.9	2.0	10.7	25.2
Parent insurance status				
Public	33.6	1.6	15.7	29.3
Private	20.7	0.1	9.6	20.1
Uninsured	20.0	1.2	7.7	12.5

[a]Parents were determined to have a need for mental health services if they met any one of four criteria: (1) caseworker report of a parent's need for services for an emotional, psychological, or other mental health problem at Wave 3, (2) self-reported scores were within the clinical range on the major depression scale of the CIDI-SF, (3) a score exceeded 1.5 standard deviations below the norm (i.e., a score ≤35) on the Mental Health Component of the SF-12, or (4) the parent's self-reported need ("a lot" or "somewhat") for mental health services in the past year, if she or he had not received a mental health service.
[b]Inpatient mental health services include having been admitted overnight to hospital or medical facility for a mental health problem in the last 12 months or having used the emergency room for a mental health problem in past 12 months.
[c]Outpatient mental health services include having had one or more sessions of psychological counseling for emotional problems with any type of professional in the past 12 months or day treatment or partial hospitalization for mental health problem in past 12 months.
[d]This category includes the use of prescription medication for one's emotions, nerves, or mental health from any type of professional in past 12 months.
Note: The term "in-home parents" refers to the parents of children living at home at Wave 3. Only permanent caregivers were asked about mental health service receipt; responses here reflect only those of in-home parents. Parents who indicated that they had not ever received mental health services were included as not having received these services in the past 12 months. All analyses were on weighted National Survey of Child and Adolescent Well-Being II Wave 3 data.

SOURCE: Adapted from Cecelia Casanueva et al., "Exhibit 24. In-Home Parents' Need for and Receipt of Mental Health Services in Past 12 Months (Wave 3)," in *NSCAW II Wave 3 Report: Wave 3 Tables*, U.S. Department of Health and Human Services, Administration for Children and Families, Office of Planning, Research, and Evaluation, June 5, 2014, http://www.acf.hhs.gov/sites/default/files/opre/nscaw_wave_3_tables_june_2014_clean.pdf (accessed June 16, 2016)

children into adulthood. Most studies that examine adults rely on self-reports from the test subjects regarding their childhood experiences. This introduces a certain element of uncertainty to the adverse impact data that are reported by adults.

The following sections summarize the ACYF findings on domain effects and support them with separate, but relevant, published scientific studies.

Neurobiology

As the ACYF points out, early childhood is a key time for development of the neurological system, including the brain. Brain development, or learning, is the process of creating connections between neurons in the brain, called synapses. Neurons, or nerve cells, send signals to one another through synapses, which in turn form the neuronal pathways that enable the brain to respond to specific environments. An infant is born with very few formed synapses; however, sufficient numbers

are present to accommodate breathing, eating, and sleeping. During the early years of life the brain develops synapses at a fast rate. Scientists find that repeated experiences strengthen the neuronal pathways, making them sensitive to similar experiences that may occur later on in life. If these early life experiences are of a negative nature, the development of the brain may be impaired. For example, if an infant who cries for attention constantly gets ignored, his or her brain creates the neuronal pathways that enable him or her to cope with being ignored. If the infant continually fails to get the attention he or she craves, the brain strengthens those same neuronal pathways.

NSCAW II DATA. In *NSCAW II Baseline Report: Child Well-Being* (August 1, 2011, http://www.acf.hhs.gov/sites/default/files/opre/nscaw2_child.pdf), Casanueva et al. report scores on a neurodevelopment test for thousands of children who were assessed during the baseline assessment of the NSCAW II studies. As described

TABLE 3.10

Re-reports of maltreatment among children reported in the National Survey of Child and Adolescent Well-Being II, Wave 3, by select characteristics and report status, 2011–12

	Re-reports sample size = 1,376	Substantiated sample size = 412	Indicated sample size = 75	Unsubstantiated sample size = 759
	%	%	%	%
Total	**24.3**	**29.7**	**1.8**	**68.5**
Gender				
Male	27.4	26.9	1.2	72.0
Female	21.1	33.7	2.5	63.8
Age (years) at baseline				
0–2	24.1	37.1	2.6	60.2
3–5	22.3	18.2	1.8	80.0
6–10	28.6	23.8	1.0	75.2
11–17	21.9	39.8	1.9	58.3
Race/ethnicity				
Black	21.7	28.8	1.4	69.8
White	27.5	29.6	1.9	68.5
Hispanic	22.9	29.2	1.6	69.2
Other	19.6	33.3	2.3	64.5
Setting at baseline*				
In-home bio and adoptive	24.0	29.7	1.6	68.7
Formal kin care	14.2	29.1	6.6	64.3
Informal kin care	28.5	23.6	1.2	75.3
Foster care	28.3	45.8	3.9	50.3
Group home or residential program	51.1	21.9	0.7	77.3

*During a period of reunification, children could have been reported again for maltreatment, and that could have prompted a return to an out-of-home placement. Thus, even if a child was at a foster care placement at the baseline and 18-month or 36-month follow-up, the re-report could have happened during a period of no foster home placement. Of the children who were at any point placed out of home, 54.4% were in-home with biological parents at baseline. Of those, 49.3% were reunified or had at least one reunification attempt across time. Of the children who were in out-of-home placement at baseline, at least one reunification attempt was made for 35.0% of those in formal kin care, 21.4% of those in informal kin care, 29.3% of those in foster care, and 35.8% of those in group home/residential treatment. Caseworkers were asked about reunification plans if the child was in out of home care at the time of the interview. Estimates may represent an underestimate of reunification attempts, as situations where the child was placed out of home and then reunified between interview waves would not be captured. Of those placed out of home at the time of interview, 39.2% had at least one attempt of reunification.

Note: All analyses were on weighted National Survey of Child and Adolescent Well-Being II baseline, National Child Abuse and Neglect System, Wave 2, and Wave 3 data.

SOURCE: Adapted from Cecelia Casanueva et al., "Exhibit 25. Re-reports of Maltreatment and Substantiation Status by Caseworker Report through Wave 3 and NCANDS," in *NSCAW II Wave 3 Report: Wave 3 Tables*, U.S. Department of Health and Human Services, Administration for Children and Families, Office of Planning, Research, and Evaluation, June 5, 2014, http://www.acf.hhs.gov/sites/default/files/opre/nscaw_wave_3_tables_june_2014_clean.pdf (accessed June 16, 2016)

earlier, NSCAW II baseline data collection was conducted between March 2008 and April 2009 on children for which maltreatment investigations were closed by CPS agencies between February 2008 and April 2009. According to Casanueva et al., 2,177 infants aged three months to 24 months were administered the Bayley Infant Neurodevelopmental Screener (BINS), a test that was developed by Glen Aylward, a professor of pediatrics and psychiatry. The BINS test identifies infants with developmental delays and/or neurological impairments that need further diagnostic testing. The test assesses functions of the central nervous system, sensation and perception, motor skills, and cognitive processes, such as memory, learning, thinking, and reasoning. Overall, approximately half (50.8%) of the NSCAW II infants had scores indicating "high risk" for developmental delay or neurological impairment. This compares with 9% to 16% of the children in the general population with scores in this range. The latter cohort (group) does not include children with clinically diagnosed risk factors such as premature births, low birth weights, and respiratory distress syndrome. Overall, more than five times as many NSCAW II infants as infants in the general population (without clinically diagnosed risk factors) had "high risk" BINS scores.

Casanueva et al. provide the results of five other tests of cognitive development and abilities in thousands of NSCAW II children and compare the scores with those of children in the general population or a comparable norm. In all cases five to eight times more of the NSCAW II children than general population or comparable norm children showed poor testing results.

A RETROSPECTIVE STUDY. Scientists find that childhood maltreatment has distinct negative effects on the biological development of the brain. For example, in "Childhood Maltreatment Is Associated with Reduced Volume in the Hippocampal Subfields CA3, Dentate Gyrus, and Subiculum" (*Proceedings of the National Academy of Sciences*, vol. 109, no. 9, February 28, 2012), a study that focuses on the hippocampus (a portion of the brain that plays a major role in memory and learning processes), Martin H. Teicher, Carl M. Anderson, and Ann

TABLE 3.11

Incidences of caretaker aggression and neglect experienced by children reported in the National Survey of Child and Adolescent Well-Being II, Wave 3, by select characteristics and type of maltreatment, 2011–12

	CTS-PC Nonviolent discipline	CTS-PC Psychological aggression	CTS-PC Minor physical assault (corporal punishment)	CTS-PC Severe physical assault	CTS-PC Very severe physical assault
	%	%	%	%	%
Total	80.0	49.9	28.8	9.8	3.0
Gender					
Male	76.5	41.2	26.9	7.0	3.2
Female	82.8	56.6	30.3	12.0	2.9
Age (years)					
11–12	71.1	43.9	32.5	10.1	3.3
13–14	86.1	55.2	37.8	12.0	3.3
15–17	81.7	49.6	19.8	8.0	2.6
Race/ethnicity					
Black	77.0	51.6	34.1	15.1	6.0
White	78.1	42.9	27.0	6.8	0.9
Hispanic	83.6	58.6	26.0	10.0	3.5
Other	85.1	46.3	36.6	10.0	5.2

Notes: CTS-PC = Conflict Tactics Scale Parent-Child. All analyses were on weighted National Survey of Child and Adolescent Well-Being II Wave 3 data.

SOURCE: Adapted from Cecelia Casanueva et al., "Exhibit 26. Caregiver Aggression and Neglect of Children 11 to 17 Years Old from a Caregiver in the Past Year by Child Report at Wave 3," in *NSCAW II Wave 3 Report: Wave 3 Tables*, U.S. Department of Health and Human Services, Administration for Children and Families, Office of Planning, Research, and Evaluation, June 5, 2014, http://www.acf.hhs.gov/sites/default/files/opre/nscaw_wave_3_tables_june_2014_clean.pdf (accessed July 21, 2014)

Polcari of McLean Hospital in Belmont, Massachusetts, examine the brain scans of 193 young adults aged 18 to 25 years, who are described as "ethnically diverse" and "predominantly middle-class and well-educated." The childhood history of the subjects was determined using two surveys: the Adverse Childhood Experience Questionnaire and the Childhood Trauma Questionnaire. These are screening tools that are widely used by researchers to ascertain whether or not adults experienced traumatic events during childhood. As such, the surveys are known as retrospective (looking back) tests. Overall, 46% of the test group had no self-reported childhood exposure to maltreatment, while 16% reported exposure to three or more types of maltreatment, mainly physical abuse and parental verbal abuse. Medicated subjects and subjects who had experienced nonmaltreatment-related childhood traumas (e.g., car wrecks) were not included in the study.

According to Teicher, Anderson, and Polcari, test subjects with high childhood maltreatment scores showed lower hippocampus volumes than did test subjects with low scores. Reduced hippocampal volume is associated with psychiatric disorders, such as depression, posttraumatic stress disorder, borderline personality disorder, and schizophrenia. The researchers note that their findings support other studies showing that early exposure to stress, particularly maltreatment between the ages of three and five years, negatively affects hippocampal development. These effects are not obvious until several years later. The researchers acknowledge that their test group of well-educated mostly middle-class adults is not representative of the overall maltreated population, which tends to be less educated and less privileged. However, Teicher, Anderson, and Polcari suspect that the latter population would show hippocampal reductions "to at least the same degree."

Indeed, other studies have seemed to corroborate Teicher, Anderson, and Polcari's findings. For example, in "Childhood Maltreatment and Psychopathology Affect Brain Development during Adolescence" (*Journal of the American Academy of Child and Adolescent Psychiatry*, vol. 52, no. 9, September 2013), Sarah Whittle et al. conclude that experiences of childhood maltreatment can have a negative impact on brain development during early adolescence. As part of their study, Whittle et al. conducted magnetic resonance imaging (MRI) exams on adolescent boys aged 12 and 13 years with follow-up testing at a later date. The results of the tests reveal diminished development in the left hippocampus of childhood trauma victims. At the same time, the MRIs revealed that victims of childhood trauma experienced increased growth of the left amygdala, the portion of the brain responsible for moderating emotions. Christopher Bergland reports in "The Size and Connectivity of the Amygdala Predicts Anxiety" (PsychologyToday.com, November 20, 2013) that an enlarged amygdala has been linked to higher incidences of chronic anxiety in children.

STRESS IMPAIRMENTS. Another neurobiological impact of childhood maltreatment is the occurrence of abnormally high levels of cortisol, a hormone that is

TABLE 3.12

Child maltreatment victims and nonvictims with alcohol abuse caregiver risk factors, by state, 2014

State	Victims (unique count)	Victims (unique count) with an alcohol abuse caregiver risk factor		Nonvictims (unique count)	Nonvictims (unique count) with an alcohol abuse caregiver risk factor	
		Number	Percent		Number	Percent
Alabama						
Alaska	2,484	427	17.2	7,631	415	5.4
Arizona	13,885	2,147	15.5	59,256	1,913	3.2
Arkansas						
California						
Colorado						
Connecticut						
Delaware	1,482	536	36.2	11,780	234	2.0
District of Columbia						
Florida						
Georgia	22,163	1,732	7.8	115,059	1,314	1.1
Hawaii	1,331	156	11.7	1,974	233	11.8
Idaho						
Illinois						
Indiana	23,359	1,042	4.5			
Iowa						
Kansas						
Kentucky	20,833	2,521	12.1	50,841	1,730	3.4
Louisiana						
Maine	3,823	731	19.1	9,463	522	5.5
Maryland	15,762	185	1.2			
Massachusetts						
Michigan	30,705	719	2.3			
Minnesota	4,143	677	16.3	22,252	1,712	7.7
Mississippi	8,435	235	2.8			
Missouri	5,322	553	10.4	69,980	1,611	2.3
Montana	1,191	63	5.3	8,989	98	1.1
Nebraska	3,940	45	1.1			
Nevada						
New Hampshire	646	73	11.3	10,990	358	3.3
New Jersey	11,842	1,783	15.1	63,849	2,570	4.0
New Mexico	7,606	2,843	37.4	19,199	3,545	18.5
New York						
North Carolina						
North Dakota	1,616	499	30.9	4,781	788	16.5
Ohio	24,931	423	1.7	77,581	922	1.2
Oklahoma	13,183	2,233	16.9	42,901	1,305	3.0
Oregon						
Pennsylvania						
Puerto Rico	7,683	661	8.6			
Rhode Island	3,410	145	4.3	5,964	75	1.3
South Carolina						
South Dakota	886	313	35.3	3,517	477	13.6
Tennessee						
Texas	65,334	5,591	8.6	187,439	7,351	3.9
Utah	9,876	544	5.5			
Vermont						
Virginia						
Washington	7,341	2,275	31.0	35,231	4,265	12.1
West Virginia	4,962	63	1.3			
Wisconsin	4,642	209	4.5	28,109	541	1.9
Wyoming	861	217	25.2			
National	**323,677**	**29,641**	**9.2**	**836,786**	**31,979**	**3.8**

SOURCE: "Table 3-8. Children with Alcohol Abuse Caregiver Risk Factor, 2014," in *Child Maltreatment 2014*, U.S. Department of Health and Human Services, Administration for Children and Families, Administration on Children, Youth, and Families, Children's Bureau, January 25, 2016, https://www.acf.hhs.gov/sites/default/files/cb/cm2014.pdf (accessed June 10, 2016)

released by the body during times of stress. The ACYF notes that scientific studies show that heightened stress impairs development of the prefrontal cortex, an area of the brain that engages in planning, decision making, focusing, and self-regulation.

The National Scientific Council on the Developing Child is a project of the Center on the Developing Child at Harvard University. As of September 2016, the council had published a series of 12 working papers (http://developingchild.harvard.edu/resources/reports_and_working_papers/working_papers) that summarize research on brain and neurological system development and the adverse effects of childhood traumas, such as abuse and neglect. In *Building the Brain's "Air Traffic Control" System: How Early Experiences Shape the Development*

TABLE 3.13

Child maltreatment victims and nonvictims with drug abuse caregiver risk factors, by state, 2014

State	Victims (unique count)	Victims (unique count) with a drug abuse caregiver risk factor		Nonvictims (unique count)	Nonvictims (unique count) with a drug abuse caregiver risk factor	
		Number	Percent		Number	Percent
Alabama	8,697	478	5.5			
Alaska	2,484	212	8.5	7,631	249	3.3
Arizona	13,885	7,366	53.1	59,256	6,079	10.3
Arkansas	8,971	278	3.1			
California						
Colorado						
Connecticut						
Delaware	1,482	489	33.0	11,780	235	2.0
District of Columbia						
Florida						
Georgia	22,163	5,870	26.5	115,059	5,467	4.8
Hawaii	1,331	543	40.8	1,974	598	30.3
Idaho						
Illinois						
Indiana	23,359	4,365	18.7	103,978	3,307	3.2
Iowa						
Kansas						
Kentucky	20,833	6,815	32.7	50,841	3,561	7.0
Louisiana						
Maine	3,823	1,276	33.4	9,463	1,123	11.9
Maryland	15,762	566	3.6			
Massachusetts						
Michigan	30,705	8,499	27.7	121,706	7,727	6.3
Minnesota	4,143	964	23.3	22,252	1,784	8.0
Mississippi	8,435	689	8.2			
Missouri	5,322	990	18.6	69,980	2,754	3.9
Montana	1,191	258	21.7	8,989	195	2.2
Nebraska	3,940	249	6.3	18,499	644	3.5
Nevada						
New Hampshire	646	152	23.5	10,990	889	8.1
New Jersey	11,842	3,732	31.5	63,849	6,678	10.5
New Mexico	7,606	5,002	65.8	19,199	5,767	30.0
New York						
North Carolina						
North Dakota	1,616	794	49.1	4,781	803	16.8
Ohio	24,931	9,576	38.4	77,581	9,647	12.4
Oklahoma	13,183	6,015	45.6	42,901	3,911	9.1
Oregon						
Pennsylvania						
Puerto Rico	7,683	565	7.4			
Rhode Island	3,410	323	9.5	5,964	193	3.2
South Carolina						
South Dakota	886	324	36.6	3,517	376	10.7
Tennessee	11,695	1,229	10.5	82,962	1,527	1.8
Texas	65,334	18,884	28.9	187,439	23,486	12.5
Utah	9,876	926	9.4			
Vermont						
Virginia						
Washington	7,341	3,420	46.6	35,231	7,734	22.0
West Virginia	4,962	357	7.2			
Wisconsin	4,642	330	7.1	28,109	709	2.5
Wyoming	861	367	42.6			
National	**353,040**	**91,903**	**26.0**	**1,163,931**	**95,443**	**8.2**

SOURCE: "Table 3-9. Children with Drug Abuse Caregiver Risk Factor, 2014," in *Child Maltreatment 2014*, U.S. Department of Health and Human Services, Administration for Children and Families, Administration on Children, Youth, and Families, Children's Bureau, January 25, 2016, https://www.acf.hhs.gov/sites/default/files/cb/cm2014.pdf (accessed June 10, 2016)

of Executive Function: Working Paper No. 11 (2011, http://developingchild.harvard.edu/), the council concludes that "adverse environments resulting from neglect, abuse, and/or exposure to violence can impair the development of executive function skills as a result of the disruptive effects of toxic stress on the developing architecture of the brain." Likewise, in *The Science of*

Neglect: The Persistent Absence of Responsive Care Disrupts the Developing Brain: Working Paper No. 12 (2012, http://developingchild.harvard.edu/), the council notes that "children who have experienced severe neglect are more likely to have cognitive problems, academic delays, deficits in executive function skills, and difficulties with attention regulation."

FIGURE 3.2

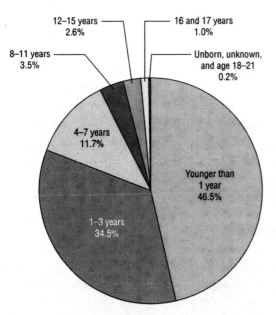

Child abuse and neglect fatalities, by age of victim, 2013

- 12–15 years 2.6%
- 16 and 17 years 1.0%
- 8–11 years 3.5%
- Unborn, unknown, and age 18–21 0.2%
- 4–7 years 11.7%
- Younger than 1 year 46.5%
- 1–3 years 34.5%

SOURCE: "Child Abuse and Neglect Fatality Victims by Age, 2013," in *Child Abuse and Neglect Fatalities 2013: Statistics and Interventions*, U.S. Department of Health and Human Services, Children's Bureau, April 2015, https://www.childwelfare.gov/pubPDFs/fatality.pdf (accessed June 10, 2016))

FIGURE 3.3

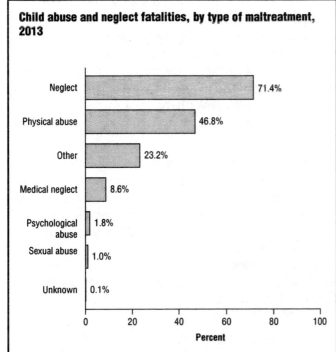

Child abuse and neglect fatalities, by type of maltreatment, 2013

- Neglect 71.4%
- Physical abuse 46.8%
- Other 23.2%
- Medical neglect 8.6%
- Psychological abuse 1.8%
- Sexual abuse 1.0%
- Unknown 0.1%

Percent (0, 20, 40, 60, 80, 100)

SOURCE: "Child Abuse and Neglect Fatalities by Reported Maltreatment Type, 2013," in *Child Abuse and Neglect Fatalities 2013: Statistics and Interventions*, U.S. Department of Health and Human Services, Children's Bureau, April 2015, https://www.childwelfare.gov/pubPDFs/fatality.pdf (accessed June 10, 2016)

TABLE 3.14

Child fatalities due to mistreatment, by selected caregiver risk factors, 2014

Caregiver risk factor	Reporting states	Child fatalities from reporting states	Child fatalities with a caregiver risk factor	
			Number	Percent
Alcohol abuse	26	620	43	6.9
Drug abuse	29	686	123	17.9

Notes: For each caregiver risk factor, the analysis includes only those states that reported at least 1 percent of child victims' caregiver with the risk factor. States were excluded from this analyses if they were not able to differentiate between alcohol abuse and drug abuse caregiver risk factors and reported both risk factors for the same children in both caregiver risk factor categories.

SOURCE: "Exhibit 4-G. Child Fatalities with Selected Caregiver Risk Factors, 2014," in *Child Maltreatment 2014*, U.S. Department of Health and Human Services, Administration for Children and Families, Administration on Children, Youth, and Families, Children's Bureau, January 25, 2016, https://www.acf.hhs.gov/sites/default/files/cb/cm2014.pdf (accessed June 10, 2016)

Traumatic Traits

The ACYF notes that traumatic events in childhood can cause children to develop chronic response tactics called hyperarousal and dissociation. During the state of hyperarousal, the brain is always attuned to what it perceives as a threatening situation. The brain has "learned" that the world is a dangerous place and that it has to be constantly on the alert. The victim experiences extreme anxiety toward any perceived threat, or he or she may use aggression to control the situation. For example, children who have been physically abused may start a fight just so they can control the conflict and be able to choose their adversary. Males and older children are more likely to exhibit hyperarousal, whereas females and younger children are more likely to show dissociation. In the dissociative state, victims disconnect themselves from the negative experience. By "pretending" not to be there, their body and mind do not react to the abusive experience.

According to the ACYF, if maltreated children do not receive treatment to overcome these learned traits, the traits can become their standard responses to everyday experiences that are not threatening. As a result, the children have trouble forming interpersonal relationships and experience other difficulties, including managing intense emotions, such as anger and anxiety. In addition, they are prone to forming incorrect perceptions of themselves and others and interpreting communications from others inaccurately.

Behavioral Problems

The ACYF indicates that the prevalence of behavioral problems is high among maltreated children. Researchers commonly assess behavioral problems using standardized surveys for which behaviors are reported by the children themselves or by parents, caregivers, or schoolteachers. One example is the Child Behavior

Checklist, which was developed by Thomas Achenbach of the University of Vermont. The Child Behavior Checklist assesses internalizing behaviors (e.g., withdrawal and anxiety) and externalizing behaviors (e.g., acting up and aggression) based on parent and caregiver information.

In *NSCAW II Baseline Report: Child Well-Being*, Casanueva et al. report scores on behavioral tests for thousands of children who were assessed during the NSCAW II baseline assessment studies, which were conducted between March 2008 and April 2009. According to Casanueva et al., 3,417 children aged 1.5 to 17 years were administered the Child Behavior Checklist. The results show that 22.9% of them had a standardized score of 64 or more, indicating "clinical range" behavioral problems. For comparison, Casanueva et al. note that 8% of children in the general population or a comparable norm would be expected to have a Child Behavior Checklist score in the clinical range. Thus, the percentage of children with clinical-level behavioral problems was nearly three times higher among the NSCAW II children than among children in the general population or a comparable norm.

The percentage of NSCAW II children with scores in the clinical range was slightly higher for boys (24.5%) than for girls (21.2%). The percentages by child age were: aged 11 to 17 years (30.4%), aged six to 10 years (25.8%), aged three to five years (15.7%), and aged 1.5 to two years (9.7%). There were small to negligible differences in the percentages based on race and ethnicity. However, children in different settings showed decidedly different scores. Children who stayed in their home or lived with relatives had the lowest percentage (22.4%) of clinical range scores, compared with children in foster care (32.2%) and children in group homes or other residential programs (47.3%).

Overall, the NSCAW II data indicate that 57.6% of the children aged 11 to 14 years and 56.9% of the children aged 15 to 17 years had emotional and/or behavioral problems. More than a quarter of the children aged 11 to 14 years old had poor social skills (28.2%) or had ever repeated a grade (25.5%). Smaller percentages had run away during the previous six months (12.6%), had a substance use disorder (12.3%), had made a court appearance during the previous year (8.2%), or had ever been pregnant (1.9% of girls).

Although the percentage of older youths exhibiting poor social skills (27.2%) was similar to that seen in younger youths (28.2%), on all other well-being indicators higher percentages of older youths than younger youths showed problem behaviors. Among youths aged 15 to 17 years, the percentages experiencing problems were 42.5% for repeating a grade, 33.2% for a substance use disorder, 20.7% for having made a court appearance

during the previous year, and 18.4% for running away during the previous six months. In addition, 10.5% of the girls in this age group had ever been pregnant. Furthermore, Casaneuva et al. note in *Child Well-Being Spotlight: Teenage Girls in the Child Welfare System Report High Rates of Risky Sexual Activity and Pregnancy* that, three years after the baseline report of maltreatment, 16.8% of NSCAW participants between the ages of 14 and 17, and 45.1% of participants between the ages of 18 and 20, had experienced at least one pregnancy.

A DECADES-LONG STUDY. During the 1980s Cathy S. Widom of the State University of New York, Albany, led a study in which researchers tracked down and interviewed hundreds of young adults who were known through court records to have been maltreated as children. Widom is widely known for her work on the cycle of violence theory. This theory suggests that childhood physical abuse increases the likelihood that the child victim will later be arrested or commit a violent crime as a teen or adult. Widom's study is considered to be one of the most detailed longitudinal studies of the consequences of childhood maltreatment.

Widom explains in "Childhood Victimization: Early Adversity, Later Psychopathology" (*National Institute of Justice Journal*, January 2000) that she began the study in 1986 by tracking down 908 children in a midwestern metropolitan region who were six to 11 years old when they were maltreated (between 1967 and 1971). A control group of 667 children with no history of childhood maltreatment was used for comparison. Each group contained about two-thirds whites and one-third African Americans and about an equal number of males and females. Widom examined the long-term consequences of childhood maltreatment on the subjects' intellectual, behavioral, social, and psychological development. When the two groups were first interviewed for the study, they had a median age (half were older, half were younger) of about 29 years.

Widom finds that although a large proportion of maltreated children did not become juvenile delinquents or criminals, those who suffered childhood abuse or neglect were more likely than those with no reported maltreatment to be arrested as juveniles (31.2% versus 19%) and as adults (48.4% versus 36.2%) when surveyed in 1986. The maltreated victims (21%) were also more likely than those with no reported childhood maltreatment history (15.6%) to be arrested for a violent crime during their teen years or adulthood.

Widom notes that the victims' later psychopathology (psychological disorders that result from maltreatment during childhood) manifested itself in suicide attempts, antisocial personality, and alcohol abuse and/or dependence. When surveyed in 1989, victims of maltreatment were more likely than individuals in the control group to report having attempted suicide (18.8% versus 7.7%) and having manifested antisocial personality disorder (18.4% versus 11.2%). Both groups, however, did not differ much in the rates of alcohol abuse and/or dependence.

Widom finds that gender plays a role in the development of psychological disorders in adolescence and adulthood. In 1989 females (24.3%) with a history of childhood maltreatment reported being more likely to attempt suicide, compared with their male counterparts (13.4%). In contrast, a significantly larger percentage of male victims (27%) than female victims (9.8%) developed an antisocial personality disorder. Although mistreated males (64.4%) and control subjects (67%) had similar proportions of alcohol abuse or dependence, females who experienced abuse or neglect were more likely than the control group to have alcohol problems (43.8% versus 32.8%).

Another phase of Widom's cycle of violence research was conducted when the maltreated and control groups had a median age of 32.5 years. Aside from collecting arrest records from federal, state, and local law enforcement agencies, Widom and Michael G. Maxfield also conducted interviews in 1994 with the subjects and reported their findings in *An Update on the "Cycle of Violence"* (February 2001, http://www.ncjrs.gov/pdffiles1/nij/184894.pdf). Overall, Widom and Maxfield find that childhood abuse or neglect increased the likelihood of arrest in adolescence by 59% and in adulthood by 28%. Childhood maltreatment also increased the likelihood of committing a violent crime by 30%.

Although earlier analysis of the maltreated group found that most of the victims did not become offenders, Widom and Maxfield's study shows that nearly half (49%) of the victims had experienced a nontraffic offense as teenagers or adults. Comparison by race shows that although both white and African American maltreated children had more arrests than the control group, there was no significant difference among whites in the maltreated and control groups. Among African American children, however, the maltreated group had higher rates of arrests. Maltreated African Americans were nearly twice as likely as their counterparts in the control group to be arrested as juveniles (40.6% versus 20.9%).

Widom and Maxfield also examined the type of childhood maltreatment that might lead to violence later in life. They find that physically abused children (21.1%) were the most likely to commit a violent crime in their teen or adult years and were closely followed by those who experienced neglect (20.2%). Although their study shows that just 8.8% of children who had been sexually abused were arrested for violence, Widom and Maxfield note that the victims were mostly females and that "females less often had a record of violent offenses."

In 2008 Widom reported on yet another phase of her longitudinal study. In "Childhood Victimization and Lifetime Revictimization" (*Child Abuse and Neglect*, vol. 32, no. 8, August 2008), Widom, Sally J. Czaja, and Mary Ann Dutton describe the results of interviews that were conducted between 2000 and 2002 with members of the two original cohorts. At the time of the interviews the average age of the participants was 39.5 years. The researchers note that 896 of the original participants were interviewed again for the study. Some of the original participants could not be located, had died, were incapacitated, or refused to participate. However, the subjects interviewed between 2000 and 2002 were similar in demographics and maltreatment history to the original participants. Widom, Czaja, and Dutton find that higher percentages of the abused/neglected group had suffered violent victimizations than did the control group. For example, 54% of the abused/neglected group reported having been threatened with a weapon, compared with 45% of the control group. Other significant differences were seen when the participants reported having been physically harmed (76% of abused/neglected group, compared with 60% of control group), been coerced into unwanted sex (36% of abused/neglected group, compared with 18% of control group), and been the victim of a mugging (16% of abused/neglected group, compared with 11% of control group). The researchers conclude that the childhood victims of maltreatment, regardless of the type of maltreatment, had a greater risk than did the control group members of lifetime revictimization.

Helen W. Wilson and Cathy S. Widom report in "Pathways from Childhood Abuse and Neglect to HIV-Risk Sexual Behavior in Middle Adulthood" (*Journal of Consulting and Clinical Psychology*, vol. 79, no. 2, April 2011) on interviews that were conducted between 2003 and 2004 with 800 of the original survey participants. At that time the average age of the participants was 41 years. The researchers find that the subjects who were abused/neglected as children self-reported riskier sexual behavior than did members of the control group. In particular, the abused/neglected individuals reported sexual behavior that was more likely to expose them to the human immunodeficiency virus, a virus that causes the acquired immunodeficiency syndrome.

A number of scholars have also identified a link between childhood abuse or neglect and intimate partner violence during adulthood. For example, in "Exposure to Family Violence and Attachment Styles as Predictors of Dating Violence Perpetration among Men and Women: A Mediational Model" (*Journal of Interpersonal Violence*, vol. 29, no. 1, January 2014), Mary Lee, Marla Reese-Weber, and Jeffrey H. Kahn find that individuals who were abused as children have a higher likelihood of perpetrating acts of violence against their partners while dating as adults. According to the researchers, this higher tendency toward dating violence was prevalent in both male and female victims of child abuse and neglect. Furthermore, intimate partner violence, particularly when it occurs during adolescence, can lead to a range of health and behavioral issues in adulthood. Deinera Exner-Cortens, John Eckenrode, and Emily Rothman note in "Longitudinal Associations between Teen Dating Violence Victimization and Adverse Health Outcomes" (*Pediatrics*, vol. 131, no. 1, January 2013) that teenage victims of dating violence, whether physical or psychological, demonstrate a higher tendency to struggle with substance abuse problems, antisocial attitudes, and intimate partner violence as adults.

Relational Competence

Relational competence is the competence with which people enter into relationships and socially interact with each other. These interactions begin at birth and are particularly important for infants, who must form strong bonds with their caregivers to thrive. Such relationships form the basis for future emotional connections. Childhood maltreatment and subsequent interventions by the child welfare system can disrupt the attachment process, resulting in severe consequences for the child's healthy emotional development.

In *NSCAW II Wave 3 Report: Wave 3 Tables*, Casanueva et al. report on the prevalence of placement instability (changes in caregiver and household) among NSCAW participants. As Casanueva et al. note, among children who were under the age of two at the time of the NSCAW baseline report, nearly one-third (30.4%) had experienced two placements at the time Wave 3 data were compiled; another 5.2% had experienced three placements during this period, and 3% had experienced four or more placements.

Placement instability is a serious problem for very young children. As Casanueva et al. note in *National Survey of Child and Adolescent Well-Being, Research Brief No. 18: Instability and Early Life Changes among Children in the Child Welfare System*, infants are "hardwired" to form emotional attachments to their primary caregivers. Scientists find that attachment disruptions can cause children to suffer emotional problems, internalized and externalized behavior problems, and subsequent psychopathology. Infants who are removed from their home and placed into foster care are at substantial risk for these poor outcomes because they face significant challenges in forming healthy attachments to new caregivers. This is particularly true if the infants "experienced difficult and harsh rearing conditions" before they left their home. Casanueva et al. indicate that maltreated infants who enter foster care "exhibit behaviors like avoidance, rejection, and opposition to care by new caregivers, pushing away foster parents even when they are distressed."

Foster parents who are unable to overcome these difficulties are likely to return the children to the child welfare system, thus increasing the placement instability in the children's lives. According to Casanueva et al., young children who have been adopted after multiple foster home placements exhibit more emotional and behavioral problems than do children who had never been placed in foster care or children who had only one "stable" placement following removal from their original home.

In *NSCAW II Baseline Report: Child Well-Being*, Casanueva et al. report scores on social skills tests for thousands of children who were part of the studies. According to Casanueva et al., 618 children aged 12 months to 18 months were assessed using the Brief Infant Toddler Social and Emotional Assessment (BITSEA), a test that was developed by the psychologists Margaret Briggs-Gowan and Alice Carter. The test has two subscales that score children on social-emotional problems and social-emotional competence. Casanueva et al. indicate that 34.6% of the NSCAW II infants who were administered the BITSEA problem test had scores in the "possible problem" range. For comparison, 25% of the infants in the general population or a comparable norm would be expected to have a score in this range. On the BITSEA competence subscale, 21.2% of the NSCAW II infants had scores in the "possible deficit/delay" range, indicating that they may not have acquired the social and emotional skills that are expected for children of their age and sex. This percentage was higher than the 15% of the infants in the general population or a comparable norm that would be expected to score in this range. Overall, NSCAW II infants living in their own home with their parents had higher scores on the BITSEA competence subscale than did NSCAW II infants living in foster care.

NSCAW II children aged three to 17 years were assessed using the Social Skills Rating System (SSRS), which was developed by the psychologists Frank Gresham and Stephen Elliott. SSRS results were based on caregiver reports and divided the children into three broad groups: fewer skills, average skills, and more skills. Overall, 34.3% of the NSCAW II children were rated as having fewer skills. This compares with 15% of the children in the general population or a comparable norm who would be expected to fall into this category. The percentages of NSCAW II children rated as having fewer skills by placement setting were: kin care (32.5%), in-home (34.1%), foster care (43.3%), and group home or residential program (43.8%). Thus, children in group homes or residential programs were more likely than children in other settings to rate poorly in social skills.

Mental Health

The ACYF notes that scientific studies show high rates of mental illness among older children in foster care. In the United States mental illnesses are typically classified in accordance with the definitions and criteria outlined in the *Diagnostic and Statistical Manual of Mental Disorders* (*DSM*), which is published by the American Psychiatric Association (APA). Other less stringent screening tools are also used by researchers, particularly to assess children.

NSCAW II DATA. In *NSCAW II Baseline Report: Child Well-Being*, Casanueva et al. report the results obtained during the NSCAW II baseline assessment studies, which were conducted between March 2008 and April 2009. Researchers assessed depression symptoms in 1,720 children aged seven to 17 years using the Children's Depression Inventory, a screening tool that was developed by the psychologist Maria Kovacs. The results show that 11.4% of the children had a score within the clinical range for depression based on self-reported results for the previous two weeks. The percentages within the clinical range varied strongly by placement setting: kin care (8.5%), in-home care (11.6%), foster care (13.2%), and group home or residential program (20.1%). For comparison, Casanueva et al. note that an estimated 6.7% of children aged seven to 17 years in the general population or a comparable norm would be expected to have a score within the clinical range for depression.

OLDER YOUTHS IN FOSTER CARE. J. Curtis McMillen et al. report in "Prevalence of Psychiatric Disorders among Older Youths in the Foster Care System" (*Journal of the American Academy of Child and Adolescent Psychology*, vol. 44, no. 1, January 2005) their findings from interviews that were conducted between December 2001 and June 2003 with 373 youths aged 17 years old in the foster care system of eight Missouri counties. The researchers used the diagnostic interview procedures from the fourth edition of the *DSM* to estimate the previous-year and lifetime prevalence of psychiatric disorders in the youths. Overall, 62% of the youths were assessed as having had at least one psychiatric disorder during their lifetime. More than one-third (37%) of the youths met the criteria for having had a psychiatric disorder in the previous year.

McMillen et al. indicate that nearly half (47%) of the youths met the lifetime prevalence criteria for conduct disorder. In the fifth edition of the *DSM* (2013, http://dsm.psychiatryonline.org/doi/book/10.1176/appi.books.9780890425596), the APA describes "Disruptive, Impulse-Control, and Conduct Disorders" as "conditions involving problems in the self-control of emotions and behaviors." More specifically, the APA explains that these particular disorders are generally "manifested in behaviors that violate the rights of others (e.g., aggression, destruction of property) and/or that bring the individual into significant conflict with societal norms or authority figures." According to McMillen et al., the

percentages of youths who met the lifetime prevalence criteria for other psychiatric disorders were: major depression (27%), attention deficit/hyperactivity disorder (ADHD; 20%), and post-traumatic stress disorder (PTSD; 14%). In "Parent Training for Attention Deficit Hyperactivity Disorder (ADHD) in Children Aged 5 to 18 Years" (2012, http://www.ncbi.nlm.nih.gov/pubmedhealth/PMH0032947), the Cochrane Database of Systematic Reviews defines ADHD as "a neurodevelopmental disorder characterised by high levels of inattention, hyperactivity and impulsivity that are present before the age of seven years, seen in a range of situations, inconsistent with the child's developmental level and causing social or academic impairment." PTSD is an anxiety disorder that can develop in people who experience or witness a traumatic event involving actual or threatened injury or death. People with PTSD may experience flashbacks (reexperience the trauma), sleep disturbances, emotional numbness, depression, rage, memory loss, concentration problems, anxiety, and physical symptoms.

Use of Psychotropic Medications

Psychotropic medications are drugs that affect psychological functions, such as moods and emotions. In "Promoting Social and Emotional Well-Being for Children and Youth Receiving Child Welfare Services," the ACYF indicates that a study published in 2010 by Rutgers University found that among children covered by Medicare (a federal health insurance program for people aged 65 years and older and people with disabilities), children in foster care were prescribed psychotropic medications at a much higher rate than were children not in foster care. The ACYF admits that "numerous studies" show that psychotropic medication rates are "comparatively high" for foster children; however, the agency notes that this discrepancy is due in part to the high rates of emotional and behavioral disorders among foster care children.

Leyla F. Stambaugh et al. examine in *National Survey of Child and Adolescent Well-Being, Child Well-Being Spotlight: Children in Out-of-Home Placements Receive More Psychotropic Medications and Other Mental Health Services Than Children Who Remain In-Home Following a Maltreatment Investigation* (August 15, 2012, http://www.acf.hhs.gov/sites/default/files/opre/nscaw2_child_out.pdf) NSCAW II Wave 2 data that were collected between 2008 and 2010 for 1,371 children aged 16 months to 19 years. The vast majority (1,057) of the children were living in-home, while 314 were living out of the home. More than half (58.2%) of the in-home children were receiving no mental health services or psychotropic medications. The remainder of the in-home children were receiving specialty mental health services and medications (21.5%), specialty mental health services only (18.5%), or medications only (1.8%). Only 30%

of the out-of-home children were receiving no services. Of the remainder, about one-third (33.1%) were receiving specialty mental health services and medications, 27.5% were receiving specialty mental health services only, and 9.4% were receiving medications only. Overall, the percentages of children receiving psychotropic medications and/or specialty mental health services were higher among the out-of-home children than among the in-home children.

Developing New Strategies

Although the ACYF has identified clear domains that are associated with child maltreatment, the agency continues to seek new ways to address these issues effectively. In "Promoting Social and Emotional Well-Being for Children and Youth Receiving Child Welfare Services," the ACYF acknowledges that emerging scientific evidence shows that its historical child welfare priorities of "ensuring safety and achieving permanency" are no longer sufficient. The agency notes that it intends to place much greater focus on the behavioral, social, and emotional domains, because recent research shows that most adverse effects of maltreatment are concentrated in these areas and cause problems "that ripple across the lifespan." The ACYF states, "These effects can keep children from developing the skills and capacities they need to be successful in the classroom, in the workplace, in their communities, and in interpersonal relationships."

The ACYF examines new strategies to addressing the problem of child maltreatment in *2015–2016 Strategic Plan* (March 2015, https://www.acf.hhs.gov/sites/default/files/assets/acf_2015_2016_strategic_plan.pdf). It describes a need for a "two-generational, whole family" approach to improving child welfare. The agency notes that "it is fundamental that to get better outcomes for children, we need to also work with their parents, and that any strategy for effectively working with adults must recognize their needs and responsibilities as parents." As part of this strategy, the ACYF outlines five core objectives:

- Promote economic, health, and social well-being for individuals, families, and communities

- Promote healthy development and school readiness for children, especially those in low-income families

- Promote safety and well-being of children, youth, and families

- Support underserved and underrepresented populations

- Upgrade the capacity of the Administration for Children and Families to make a difference for families and communities

In outlining these goals, the ACYF cites several congressional acts as having the potential to strengthen its efforts to develop and implement a comprehensive plan to tackle childhood maltreatment. Notable legislation passed in 2014 included the Workforce Innovation and Opportunity Act and the Preventing Sex Trafficking and Strengthening Families Act. According to the ACYF, "These new laws create important new opportunities to address health, safety and quality in child care; broaden the responsibilities of child welfare agencies in addressing sex trafficking and promoting better outcomes for young people in foster care; and build linkages between human services and workforce agencies in a stronger workforce system."

CHAPTER 4
CHILD SEXUAL ABUSE

Child sexual abuse is a horrendous misuse of an adult's trust and power over a child. When the abuser is particularly close to the victim, the child feels betrayed and trapped in a situation in which an adult who claims to care for the child is assaulting him or her. Many experts believe sexual abuse is the most underreported type of child maltreatment. A victim, especially a young child, may not know what he or she is experiencing. In many cases, the child is threatened to keep the abuse secret or feels embarrassed or guilty about it. Adults who may be aware of the abuse sometimes get involved in a conspiracy of silence. The effects of childhood sexual abuse can be severe and long-lasting by contributing to behavioral, mental, and physical problems years after the abuse occurs.

WHAT IS CHILD SEXUAL ABUSE?

It is important to understand that there are two types of laws in the United States that deal with the sexual abuse of children. Criminal laws define the types of sexual conduct for which offenders can be prosecuted in criminal court. Sexual acts committed against children by family members (interfamilial sexual abuse) and by nonfamily members may rise to the legal definition of criminal behavior. Because children (up to a certain age) are deemed incapable of voluntarily consenting to sexual activity, all sexual acts perpetrated on children are considered to be coercive. This distinction protects children, particularly older children, against claims from adult perpetrators that the sexual activity was voluntary on the part of the child. In addition, criminal laws generally forbid certain types of sexual conduct no matter the age of those involved. One example is incest, which is sexual activity between closely related family members.

Civil laws typically focus on interfamilial child sexual abuse. Under civil law, the parents (and other caretakers with custody rights) of children who are sexually abused can be investigated by child protective services (CPS) agencies and have their parental or custody rights terminated if they played a role in the abuse. In addition, civil laws include reporting requirements, as is described in Chapter 2, that require certain professionals (such as educators) to report all forms of suspected child abuse to authorities.

Civil law definitions of child sexual abuse differ by jurisdiction. At the federal level, the Child Abuse Prevention and Treatment Act of 2010 defines sexual abuse at 42 USC Section 5106g (2016, http://www.law.cornell.edu/uscode/text/42/5106g) as follows:

The term "sexual abuse" includes—

(A) the employment, use, persuasion, inducement, enticement, or coercion of any child to engage in, or assist any other person to engage in, any sexually explicit conduct or simulation of such conduct for the purpose of producing a visual depiction of such conduct; or

(B) the rape, and in cases of caretaker or inter-familial relationships, statutory rape, molestation, prostitution, or other form of sexual exploitation of children, or incest with children.

In *Definitions of Child Abuse and Neglect* (June 2014, https://www.childwelfare.gov/pubPDFs/define.pdf), the Children's Bureau within the U.S. Department of Health and Human Services (HHS) indicates that nearly all 50 U.S. states, the District of Columbia, Puerto Rico, and U.S. territories include civil definitions of child sexual abuse in their laws; however, these definitions vary. The agency provides a summary of the laws by jurisdiction. For example, Texas defines child sexual abuse as including the following acts:

- Sexual conduct harmful to a child's mental, emotional, or physical welfare, including conduct that constitutes the offense of continuous sexual abuse of a young child, indecency with a child, sexual assault, or aggravated sexual assault

- Failure to make a reasonable effort to prevent sexual conduct harmful to a child

- Compelling or encouraging a child to engage in sexual conduct, including conduct that constitutes an offense of trafficking of persons, prostitution, or compelling prostitution

- Causing, permitting, encouraging, engaging in, or allowing the photographing, filming, or depicting of a child if the person knew or should have known that the resulting photograph, film, or depiction of the child is obscene or pornographic

- Causing, permitting, encouraging, engaging in, or allowing a sexual performance by a child

Under both criminal and civil laws child sexual abuse encompasses activities that fall into two broad categories. Physical contact acts involve intercourse or other penetrating and invasive sexual actions. Fondling and other inappropriate touching also fall into this category. Nonphysical contact acts include exposure (i.e., indecently exposing oneself to a child), voyeurism (spying on or secretly videotaping a child for the purposes of sexual gratification), allowing a child to be sexually abused by someone else (e.g., through prostitution), and using a child for pornographic purposes (e.g., in the production of sexually explicit photographs or videos).

CHILD SEXUAL ABUSE DATA

Data about child sexual abuse are available from two primary types of sources. First are CPS agencies and other social service agencies or institutions that compile data about child abuse cases as they are reported and investigated. Second are surveys or interviews in which adults or children (typically youths) are asked about childhood sexual abuse. Survey-based studies are known as retrospective studies because they rely on subjects "looking back" at past events. Each type of data source has its drawbacks and limitations. For example, CPS agencies may only be aware of a fraction of the child sexual abuse cases occurring in their communities because it is likely that not all cases are reported to the authorities. Surveys and other retrospective studies depend on the accurate memories of the subjects who are questioned. In addition, these studies typically feature small and geographically limited populations. Nevertheless, both types of sources provide clues about the prevalence of child sexual abuse and the victims, perpetrators, and risk factors that are involved.

NATIONAL INCIDENCE STUDIES

As is explained in Chapter 2, there have been four comprehensive studies conducted as part of the National Incidence Study of Child Abuse and Neglect (NIS):

- NIS-1—data collection between 1979 and 1980
- NIS-2—data collection in 1986
- NIS-3—data collection in 1993
- NIS-4—data collection between 2005 and 2006

Child Sex Abuse Prevalence

The Children's Bureau notes in *Study Findings: National Study of the Incidence and Severity of Child Abuse and Neglect* (September 1981) that in regards to sexual abuse, NIS-1 researchers only counted cases in which an in-home parent or other adult caretaker was implicated. The Children's Bureau provides an estimated incidence rate for sexual exploitation (i.e., child sexual abuse) of 0.7 per 1,000 children in the U.S. population in 1979–80.

For the NIS-2, NIS-3, and NIS-4 studies researchers used two standards to assess abuse and neglect: the Harm Standard and the Endangerment Standard. (See Chapter 2 for complete definitions of these standards; in brief, the Harm Standard requires that demonstrable harm to a child be present, whereas the Endangerment Standard requires only that a professional consider a child to be at risk of harm.) In addition, the criteria for child sexual abuse cases were expanded to include more types of perpetrators. In *National Incidence and Prevalence of Child Abuse and Neglect 1988, Revised Report* (September 1991), Andrea J. Sedlak notes that during NIS-2 researchers began including cases in which adult caretakers other than parents or parent substitutes (e.g., foster parents and stepparents) "permitted" sexual abuse to happen. The researchers also counted cases in which "nonparental teenage caretakers had perpetrated or permitted the abuse." The NIS-1 through NIS-3 studies generally divided child sexual abuse acts into broad categories based on whether or not penetration or genital contact occurred. For example, in *Third National Incidence Study of Child Abuse and Neglect: Final Report* (September 1996), Andrea J. Sedlak and Diane D. Broadhurst divide sexual actions against children into three categories:

- Intrusion—oral, anal, or genital penile penetration or anal or genital digital or other penetration

- Molestation with genital contact—acts in which some form of actual genital contact occurred, but intrusion did not occur

- Other or unknown sexual abuse—unspecified acts not known to have involved intrusion or actual genital contact

By the time the NIS-4 studies were conducted in 2005–06, a more refined list had been developed for classifying various types of child sexual abuse. Andrea J. Sedlak et al. provide in *Fourth National Incidence*

Study of Child Abuse and Neglect (NIS-4) Report to Congress (January 2010, http://www.acf.hhs.gov/sites/default/files/opre/nis4_report_congress_full_pdf_jan2010.pdf) a list of the types of sexual abuse that were cataloged by NIS-4 researchers:

- Intrusion sex without force
- Intrusion sex involving use of force
- Child's prostitution or involvement in pornography with intrusion
- Molestation with genital contact
- Providing sexually explicit materials
- Child's involvement in pornography without intrusion
- Failure to supervise child's voluntary sexual activity
- Attempted/threatened sexual abuse with physical contact
- Other/unknown sexual abuse

Because of the criteria and standard differences between NIS-1 and the succeeding NIS studies, the prevalence rates from NIS-2, NIS-3, and NIS-4 are not directly comparable to the rate of 0.7 per 1,000 children in population that was calculated in NIS-1. Sedlak et al. report the following incidence rates for child sexual abuse based on NIS-4 data:

Under the Harm Standard:

- NIS-2 (1986)—1.9 per 1,000 child population
- NIS-3 (1993)—3.2 per 1,000 child population
- NIS-4 (2005–06)—1.8 per 1,000 child population

Under the Endangerment Standard:

- NIS-2 (1986)—2.1 per 1,000 child population
- NIS-3 (1993)—4.5 per 1,000 child population
- NIS-4 (2005–06)—2.4 per 1,000 child population

Child Sex Abuse Victims, Perpetrators, and Risk Factors

According to the Children's Bureau, the NIS-1 data indicate that girls made up 83% of the victims, whereas boys accounted for 17% of the victims. The vast majority (88%) of the victims were white. Older children accounted for more than half of the victims, with the largest percentages for children aged 15 to 17 years (32%), 12 to 14 years (28%), and nine to 11 years (21%). Fathers and father substitutes acting alone accounted for 36% of the perpetrators, followed by both mothers/substitutes and fathers/substitutes at 21%. In regards to household characteristics, the Children's Bureau reports that nearly half (46%) of the households involved in child sexual abuse cases were in rural counties. Most (80%) of the households were in the two lowest annual family income brackets, which included incomes up to $15,000 per year.

Sedlak et al. note that the NIS-2 data indicated a higher prevalence rate for child sexual abuse among females (3.3 per 1,000 child population) than among males (1 per 1,000 child population). In addition, the abuse was six times more frequent among children in low-income families than among children in high-income families. In *A Report to Congress: The National Center on Child Abuse and Neglect, Study of High Risk Child Abuse and Neglect Groups, Appendix B: NIS-2 Reanalysis Report* (1993), the HHS's National Center on Child Abuse and Neglect examines risk factors for the occurrence of various types of child maltreatment, including sexual abuse. According to the center, in addition to females and children in lower income families, the children at the greatest risk include older children in white, African American, and Hispanic families and older children in father-only households. No relationship was found between risk and county metropolitan status or between risk and number of children in the household.

Sedlak and Broadhurst note the following findings regarding child sexual abuse:

- Girls were sexually abused about three times more often than boys under both the Harm Standard and the Endangerment Standard.
- Children were "consistently vulnerable" to sexual abuse from the age of three years upward.
- Low-income children were 18 times more likely than high-income children to be sexually abused under both the Harm Standard and the Endangerment Standard.

For nearly half (46%) of the sexually abused children, the perpetrators were people other than a parent or parent figure. Another 29% of the victims were sexually abused by a birth parent and 25% by other parent or parent-substitute (e.g., stepparent or father's girlfriend). The incidence rates under the Harm Standard for children living with both parents or a single parent of either sex were 2.5 to 2.6 per 1,000 child population. The comparable rate for children living with neither parent was much higher, at 6.3 per 1,000 child population.

The NIS-4 studies were conducted between 2005 and 2006. As is described in Chapter 3, Sedlak et al. assess various child and household characteristics in terms of incidence rates for maltreatment overall and for specific types of maltreatment. The rates for sexually abused children were calculated for many, but not all, of the characteristics based on data availability. According to Sedlak et al.:

- The incidence rates for sexual abuse under the Harm Standard were 3 per 1,000 child population for girls and 0.6 per 1,000 child population for boys. Under the

Endangerment Standard the rates were 3.8 per 1,000 child population for girls and 1 per 1,000 child population for boys.

- Most (87%) of the sexually abused children were abused by a male, compared with only 11% who were abused by a female.

- The perpetrators in child sexual abuse cases were much more likely to be male when they were the child's nonbiological parent. However, children who were sexually abused by their biological parents had the highest percentage of female perpetrators (22% versus 6% or less in other relationship categories).

- The incidence rates under the Harm Standard by race/ethnicity were: African American (2.6 per 1,000 African American child population), Hispanic (1.8 per 1,000 Hispanic child population), and white (1.4 per 1,000 white child population).

- For 42% of the sexually abused children, the perpetrators were people other than a parent (whether biological or nonbiological) or a parent's partner; 36% of the victims were sexually abused by a biological parent.

- The incidence rates under the Harm Standard by parental employment status were: parents not in the labor force (3.7 per 1,000 child population), parents steadily employed (1.1 per 1,000 child population), and parents unemployed (0.9 per 1,000 child population).

- The incidence rates under the Harm Standard by socioeconomic status were: families with low socioeconomic status (1.7 per 1,000 child population) and families without low socioeconomic status (0.6 per 1,000 child population). Under the Endangerment Standard the rates were: families with low socioeconomic status (2.4 per 1,000 child population) and families without low socioeconomic status (0.7 per 1,000 child population). (For a description of how Sedlak et al. categorize families via socioeconomic status, see Chapter 3.)

Unlike in previous NIS studies, NIS-4 researchers compiled detailed information about the family structures and living arrangements of the children. Sedlak et al. report the following incidence rates in descending order for child sexual abuse.

Under the Harm Standard:

- Single parent with partner (9.9 per 1,000 child population)

- Neither parent (5.3 per 1,000 child population)

- Other married parents (4.3 per 1,000 child population)

- Single parent with no partner (2.4 per 1,000 child population)

- Unmarried parents (2.4 per 1,000 child population)

- Married biological parents (0.5 per 1,000 child population)

Under the Endangerment Standard:

- Single parent with partner (12.1 per 1,000 child population)

- Neither parent (6.3 per 1,000 child population)

- Other married parents (5.5 per 1,000 child population)

- Single parent with no partner (3.4 per 1,000 child population)

- Unmarried parents (3.2 per 1,000 child population)

- Married biological parents (0.7 per 1,000 child population)

As is noted in Chapter 3, the NIS-4 study was the most recent report of its kind as of September 2016.

NATIONAL SURVEY OF CHILD AND ADOLESCENT WELL-BEING

Chapter 2 describes the National Survey of Child and Adolescent Well-Being (NSCAW) studies, which are longitudinal studies (studies of the same groups of people over time) that cover thousands of children. NSCAW I ran from 1997 to 2007; and NSCAW II began in 2008 and was ongoing as of September 2016. NSCAW II has included three data collections or waves: Wave 1 (March 2008 to September 2009) featured baseline data collection, while Wave 2 (October 2009 to January 2011) and Wave 3 (June 2011 to December 2012) featured follow-up data collection on the same children. Although NSCAW researchers did not specifically focus on sexual abuse, they did collect some data regarding this maltreatment type.

The NSCAW studies include interviews by researchers with the children and their parents and/or caregivers. In *NSCAW II Baseline Report: Maltreatment* (August 1, 2011, http://www.acf.hhs.gov/sites/default/files/opre/nscaw2_mal treatment.pdf), Cecilia Casanueva et al. indicate that 4.2% of the in-home parents/caregivers reported that their child "was touched in a sexual way or was forced to have sex by an adult or older child, including a member of the family or anyone outside the family." Casaneuva et al. note in *NSCAW II Wave 2 Report: Child Safety* (August 2012, http://www.acf.hhs.gov/sites/default/files/opre/nscaw_child_safety.pdf) that in-home parents and caregivers of children aged 11 to 17 years (2.2%) were more likely to report sexual abuse than those of children aged three to five years (0.8%).

CHILD MALTREATMENT

Each year the HHS's National Child Abuse and Neglect Data System collects child maltreatment data from CPS agencies in the 50 states and the District of

Columbia and Puerto Rico (which are collectively known as the 52 states). Summaries of the compiled information are published annually by the Children's Bureau in the report *Child Maltreatment*. As of September 2016, the most recent report was *Child Maltreatment 2014* (January 25, 2016, https://www.acf.hhs.gov/sites/default/files/cb/cm2014.pdf).

According to the Children's Bureau, the maltreatment types by uniquely counted victims were neglect (75%), physical abuse (17%), and sexual abuse (8.3%); other categories of maltreatment include psychological abuse (6%), medical neglect (2.2%), and other forms of neglect or abuse (6.8%). (See Table 4.1.) It should be noted that these percentages add up to more than 100% because some victims experienced more than one type of maltreatment. Table 4.1 provides a state-by-state break-down for childhood sexual abuse victims in 2014 based on reporting data from the 50 states, the District of Columbia, and Puerto Rico. The proportion of sexual abuse victims as a percentage of all maltreatment victims was highest in Pennsylvania (61.7%) and Vermont

TABLE 4.1

Abused children, by type of maltreatment and state, 2014

State	Victims (unique count)	Medical neglect	Neglect	Other	Physical abuse	Psychological maltreatment	Sexual abuse	Unknown	Total maltreatment types
Alabama	8,697	59	3,491		4,114	22	1,763		9,449
Alaska	2,484	74	2,006		340	546	137		3,103
Arizona	13,885		13,048		1,250	22	413		14,733
Arkansas	8,971	1,065	4,902	5	1,929	113	1,962		9,976
California	75,033		64,029	99	6,840	9,940	3,652		84,560
Colorado	9,979	142	7,949		1,166	288	984	44	10,573
Connecticut	7,651	302	6,297		470	2,504	408		9,981
Delaware	1,482	16	488	146	282	515	158		1,605
District of Columbia	1,528	39	1,213	6	300	115	75		1,748
Florida	45,738	1,023	23,973	21,582	4,596	786	2,498		54,458
Georgia	22,163	950	15,585		2,232	5,738	663		25,168
Hawaii	1,331	25	211	1,080	142	11	66		1,535
Idaho	1,595	14	1,205	16	369		78		1,682
Illinois	29,671	626	20,572		6,579	33	4,502		32,312
Indiana	23,359	425	19,618		2,187	73	2,658		24,961
Iowa	8,071	86	6,086	851	1,218	40	564		8,845
Kansas	1,998	53	419	516	424	262	575		2,249
Kentucky	20,833	295	19,020		1,998	81	875		22,269
Louisiana	12,057		10,300		2,011	60	605	31	13,007
Maine	3,823		2,560		935	1,354	278		5,127
Maryland	15,762		10,608		4,304	21	1,597		16,530
Massachusetts	31,863		29,888	19	3,451	36	841		34,235
Michigan	30,705	698	25,430	13	7,560	158	982		34,841
Minnesota	4,143	40	2,879		760	29	853		4,561
Mississippi	8,435	359	6,026	26	1,478	1,308	994		10,191
Missouri	5,322	213	3,296	1	1,685	477	1,368		7,040
Montana	1,191	12	1,097		109	48	66		1,332
Nebraska	3,940	3	3,318		499	38	302		4,160
Nevada	4,297	89	3,164		1,493	35	204		4,985
New Hampshire	646	22	511		56	6	100		695
New Jersey	11,842	237	9,402		1,747	55	1,111		12,552
New Mexico	7,606	248	6,265		1,021	1,661	250		9,445
New York	65,655	3,867	62,616	17,311	6,369	469	2,067		92,699
North Carolina	20,966	497	16,586	115	2,214	97	1,654	159	21,322
North Dakota	1,616	45	1,138		170	609	69		2,031
Ohio	24,931	465	10,838		10,838	1,097	4,610		27,848
Oklahoma	13,183	212	9,291		2,919	3,425	695		16,542
Oregon	10,088	142	5,371	4,767	928	200	816		12,224
Pennsylvania	3,262	128	110		1,063	28	2,014		3,343
Puerto Rico	7,683	619	4,736	79	2,080	3,886	201		11,601
Rhode Island	3,410	60	2,496		433	667	135		3,791
South Carolina	12,439	387	7,952	178	5,364	107	767		14,755
South Dakota	886		759		109	6	53		927
Tennessee	11,695	177	8,080		1,353	310	2,714		12,634
Texas	65,334	1,690	53,045		11,746	429	5,581	6	72,497
Utah	9,876	29	2,508	584	4,078	2,875	1,982		12,056
Vermont	813	21	14		374	1	442		852
Virginia	6,464	146	4,178	4	1,934	109	804		7,175
Washington	7,341		5,996		1,388		454		7,838
West Virginia	4,962	38	2,663	615	1,720	1,384	237		6,657
Wisconsin	4,642		2,881		869	33	1,127		4,910
Wyoming	861	7	630	3	23	183	101		947
National	**702,208**	**15,645**	**526,744**	**48,016**	**119,517**	**42,290**	**58,105**	**240**	**810,557**

TABLE 4.1

Abused children, by type of maltreatment and state, 2014 [CONTINUED]

State	Medical neglect	Neglect	Other	Physical abuse	Psychological maltreatment	Sexual abuse	Unknown	Total maltreatment types
							Percent	
Alabama	0.7	40.1		47.3	0.3	20.3		108.6
Alaska	3.0	80.8		13.7	22.0	5.5		124.9
Arizona		94.0		9.0	0.2	3.0		106.1
Arkansas	11.9	54.6	0.1	21.5	1.3	21.9		111.2
California		85.3	0.1	9.1	13.2	4.9		112.7
Colorado	1.4	79.7		11.7	2.9	9.9	0.4	106.0
Connecticut	3.9	82.3		6.1	32.7	5.3		130.5
Delaware	1.1	32.9	9.9	19.0	34.8	10.7		108.3
District of Columbia	2.6	79.4	0.4	19.6	7.5	4.9		114.4
Florida	2.2	52.4	47.2	10.0	1.7	5.5		119.1
Georgia	4.3	70.3		10.1	25.9	3.0		113.6
Hawaii	1.9	15.9	81.1	10.7	0.8	5.0		115.3
Idaho	0.9	75.5	1.0	23.1		4.9		105.5
Illinois	2.1	69.3		22.2	0.1	15.2		108.9
Indiana	1.8	84.0		9.4	0.3	11.4		106.9
Iowa	1.1	75.4	10.5	15.1	0.5	7.0		109.6
Kansas	2.7	21.0	25.8	21.2	13.1	28.8		112.6
Kentucky	1.4	91.3		9.6	0.4	4.2		106.9
Louisiana		85.4		16.7	0.5	5.0	0.3	107.9
Maine		67.0		24.5	35.4	7.3		134.1
Maryland		67.3		27.3	0.1	10.1		104.9
Massachusetts		93.8	0.1	10.8	0.1	2.6		107.4
Michigan	2.3	82.8	0.0	24.6	0.5	3.2		113.5
Minnesota	1.0	69.5		18.3	0.7	20.6		110.1
Mississippi	4.3	71.4	0.3	17.5	15.5	11.8		120.8
Missouri	4.0	61.9	0.0	31.7	9.0	25.7		132.3
Montana	1.0	92.1		9.2	4.0	5.5		111.8
Nebraska	0.1	84.2		12.7	1.0	7.7		105.6
Nevada	2.1	73.6		34.7	0.8	4.7		116.0
New Hampshire	3.4	79.1		8.7	0.9	15.5		107.6
New Jersey	2.0	79.4		14.8	0.5	9.4		106.0
New Mexico	3.3	82.4		13.4	21.8	3.3		124.2
New York	5.9	95.4	26.4	9.7	0.7	3.1		141.2
North Carolina	2.4	79.1	0.5	10.6	0.5	7.9	0.8	101.7
North Dakota	2.8	70.4		10.5	37.7	4.3		125.7
Ohio	1.9	43.5		43.5	4.4	18.5		111.7
Oklahoma	1.6	70.5		22.1	26.0	5.3		125.5
Oregon	1.4	53.2	47.3	9.2	2.0	8.1		121.2
Pennsylvania	3.9	3.4		32.6	0.9	61.7		102.5
Puerto Rico	8.1	61.6	1.0	27.1	50.6	2.6		151.0
Rhode Island	1.8	73.2		12.7	19.6	4.0		111.2
South Carolina	3.1	63.9	1.4	43.1	0.9	6.2		118.6
South Dakota		85.7		12.3	0.7	6.0		104.6
Tennessee	1.5	69.1		11.6	2.7	23.2		108.0
Texas	2.6	81.2		18.0	0.7	8.5	0.0	111.0
Utah	0.3	25.4	5.9	41.3	29.1	20.1		122.1
Vermont	2.6	1.7		46.0	0.1	54.4		104.8
Virginia	2.3	64.6	0.1	29.9	1.7	12.4		111.0
Washington		81.7		18.9		6.2		106.8
West Virginia	0.8	53.7	12.4	34.7	27.9	4.8		134.2
Wisconsin		62.1		18.7	0.7	24.3		105.8
Wyoming	0.8	73.2	0.3	2.7	21.3	11.7		110.0
National	**2.2**	**75.0**	**6.8**	**17.0**	**6.0**	**8.3**	**0.0**	**115.4**

SOURCE: "Table 3-7. Maltreatment Types of Victims, 2014," in *Child Maltreatment 2014*, U.S. Department of Health and Human Services, Administration for Children and Families, Administration on Children, Youth, and Families, Children's Bureau, January 25, 2016, https://www.acf.hhs.gov/sites/default/files/cb/cm2014.pdf (accessed June 10, 2016)

(54.4%) in 2014, whereas Puerto Rico (2.6%) and Massachusetts (2.6%) reported the lowest proportion of sexual abuse victims.

RETROSPECTIVE SURVEYS ABOUT CHILD SEXUAL ABUSE

As noted earlier, retrospective surveys are another major source of data on child sexual abuse prevalence. Survey-based studies rely on the truthfulness and accurate recollections of the test subjects. In rare cases, the researchers may have access to external evidence, such as childhood medical reports, that can lend credence to claims from adults that they suffered sexual abuse as children. However, most surveys depend solely on memories, as no collaborating evidence is available. As a result, survey methodologies are very important.

Considerations include the number and types of questions that are asked, how they are asked, and by whom. The population size and demographics of the survey subjects are also key variables that affect results. Subject age is particularly relevant because older memories may be less reliable than those formed more recently. As noted earlier, there is no single legal definition of what constitutes sexual abuse. Thus, researchers conducting retrospective surveys about childhood sexual abuse may question subjects about certain sexual activities and not others. In addition, some subjects may not consider sexual events to rise to the level of "abuse"; thus the choice of terminology can influence survey results.

Another confounding factor is the stigma that is associated with certain sexual activities. As such, survey participants may be reluctant to admit to events about which they feel embarrassed or ashamed. Furthermore, the subjects may not remember childhood sexual abuse. Some researchers believe that memory repression (repression by the mind of painful or unpleasant memories) causes some people to be unable to remember childhood traumas. Overall, there are numerous factors that affect the reliability of retrospective survey data and the relevance of the data to the population at large.

Adult Surveys Reveal High Prevalence Rates

Numerous retrospective surveys related to childhood sexual abuse have been conducted since the 1970s, and they consistently show much higher rates of child sexual abuse than the rates indicated by agency reports, such as *Child Maltreatment*. This discrepancy underlies the oft-stated claim that child sexual abuse cases are vastly underreported to authorities.

One of the early landmark retrospective studies of child sexual abuse was conducted in 1978 by the sociologist Diana E. H. Russell of Mills College. Russell surveyed 930 adult women in San Francisco, California, about their early sexual experiences and reported her findings in *The Secret Trauma: Incest in the Lives of Girls and Women* (1986). Russell noted that 38% of the women had suffered sexual abuse before their 18th birthday. About 16% had been abused by a family member. Russell's study is one of many cited by people who believe that much more child sexual abuse occurs than is officially reported by government studies. They suggest the high results recorded in her study reflect the thoroughness of her preparation and the fact that she asked the participants 14 different questions, any one of which might have triggered a memory of sexual abuse.

In *The Epidemic of Rape and Child Sexual Abuse in the United States* (2000), Russell and Rebecca M. Bolen revisit the prevalence rates reported in Russell's 1978 survey. They believe those rates are underestimated.

The 1978 survey subjects did not include two groups that are regarded to be highly probable victims of child sexual abuse: females in institutions and those not living at home. Russell and Bolen also find that some women were reluctant to reveal experiences of abuse to survey interviewers, whereas others did not recall these experiences.

David Finkelhor is a national authority on child sexual abuse and is the director of the Crimes against Children Research Center at the University of New Hampshire. In "Current Information on the Scope and Nature of Child Sexual Abuse" (*Future of Children: Sexual Abuse of Children*, vol. 4, no. 2, Summer–Fall 1994), Finkelhor states his opinion that surveys of adults regarding their childhood experiences probably give the most complete estimates of the actual extent of child sexual abuse. He reviews 19 adult retrospective surveys and finds that the proportion of adults who indicated sexual abuse during childhood ranged widely, from 2% to 62% for females and from 3% to 16% for males. Finkelhor observes that the surveys that reported higher levels of abuse were those that asked multiple questions about the possibility of abuse. Multiple questions are more effective because they provide respondents various cues about the different kinds of experiences the researchers are asking about in their surveys. Multiple questions also give the respondents ample time to overcome their embarrassment. In his 2009 study "The Prevention of Childhood Sexual Abuse" (*Future of Children*, vol. 19, no. 2, Fall 2009), Finkelhor offers different estimates concerning percentages of adult victims of childhood sexual abuse, with the proportion of female victims falling somewhere between 25% and 40%, and male victims between 8% and 13%. Finkelhor et al. find in "Child Maltreatment Rates Assessed in a National Household Survey of Caregivers and Youth" (*Child Abuse and Neglect*, vol. 39, no. 9, September 2014), a 2011 survey based on interviews with caregivers of children under the age of nine, as well as with children between the ages of 10 and 17, that 2.2% of children had suffered sexual abuse within the past year.

Between 1995 and 1997 the Centers for Disease Control and Prevention (CDC) collaborated with the insurance company Kaiser Permanente to survey more than 17,000 adults regarding their childhood experiences. The CDC explains in "About the CDC-Kaiser ACE Study" (June 14, 2016, http://www.cdc.gov/violencepre vention/acestudy/about.html) that the Adverse Childhood Experiences (ACEs) Study "is one of the largest investigations of childhood abuse and neglect and later-life health and well-being." The survey subjects were all members of a Kaiser Permanente health maintenance organization and were questioned during their physical examinations at a clinic in San Diego, California. The CDC indicates in *Adverse Childhood Experiences (ACE):*

What Happens Early Can Change Lives (November 2014, http://www.cdc.gov/violenceprevention/acestudy/prevalence.html) that 20.7% of the 17,337 subjects said they had experienced sexual abuse in childhood. The rates by sex were 24.7% for women and 16% for men. The agency (June 14, 2016, http://www.cdc.gov/violenceprevention/acestudy/about.html) explains that childhood sexual abuse was defined as: "An adult, relative, family friend, or stranger who was at least 5 years older than you ever touched or fondled your body in a sexual way, made you touch his/her body in a sexual way, attempted to have any type of sexual intercourse with you." As of September 2016, researchers continued to track the medical status of the survey subjects.

As retrospective studies of childhood sexual abuse gain in popularity, some standardized surveying tools are being developed. For example, David DiLillo et al. compare in "Retrospective Assessment of Childhood Sexual and Physical Abuse: A Comparison of Scaled and Behaviorally Specific Approaches" (*Assessment*, vol. 13, no. 3, September 2006) two of the most common screening tools: the Childhood Trauma Questionnaire (CTQ) and the Computer Assisted Maltreatment Inventory (CAMI). The researchers used both scales to assess 1,195 undergraduate students at the University of Nebraska, Lincoln; Miami University; and the University of Southern California. The sample population included 863 women and 332 men, and the average age was 20.3 years. Overall, the CTQ and the CAMI provided consistent agreement in that 92% of the subjects were classified equivalently by both tools in terms of sexual abuse victimization. The results indicate that 7% of the subjects were deemed by both tools to be childhood victims of sexual abuse.

The willingness to disclose a history of sexual abuse is crucial to treating psychological problems suffered by adult victims of child sexual abuse. Over the years, psychologists and other counseling professionals have developed a range of methods aimed at combating the lingering negative effects of sexual abuse in adult patients. Michael D. Earley et al. report in "Mindfulness Intervention for Child Abuse Survivors: A 2.5-Year Follow-Up" (*Journal of Clinical Psychology*, vol. 70, no. 10, October 2014) that one approach that has shown positive results is mindfulness-based treatment. Mindfulness is a form of cognitive therapy that helps patients attain emotional awareness through education, meditation, and other methods. According to Earley et al., mindfulness has been shown to be effective in treating disorders caused by sexual abuse, including anxiety, depression, and post-traumatic stress disorder (PTSD).

Experiences of childhood sexual abuse can also be indicators of future criminal behavior among victims. In "Child Maltreatment Victimization by Type in Relation to Criminal Recidivism in Juvenile Offenders" (*BMC*

TABLE 4.2

Prevalence of child maltreatment among juvenile offenders, by type of maltreatment and sex, 2014

	Male juvenile offenders	Female juvenile offenders
Victim of sexual abuse	8.0%	33.2%
Victim of physical abuse	23.6%	36.0%
Victim of neglect	20.8%	29.4%
General criminal recidivism	46.6%	34.0%
Violent felony recidivism	8.5%	3.2%

SOURCE: Adapted from Claudia E. van der Put and Corine de Ruiter, "Table 1. Prevalence of Child Maltreatment and Criminal Recidivism Rates Separately for Male and Female Juvenile Offenders," in "Child Maltreatment Victimization by Type in Relation to Criminal Recidivism in Juvenile Offenders," *BMC Psychiatry*, vol. 16, February 2016, https://bmcpsychiatry.biomedcentral.com/track/pdf/10.1186/s12888-016-0731-y?site=bmcpsychiatry.biomedcentral.com (accessed June 16, 2016)

Psychiatry, vol. 16, February 2016), Claudia E. van der Put and Corine de Ruiter report that 33.2% of female juvenile offenders and 8% of male juvenile offenders surveyed had suffered some form of sexual abuse during childhood. (See Table 4.2.)

Youth and Children Surveys

Some retrospective studies target youths and children for their recollections of previous sexual abuse. The surveys may focus on the lifetime prevalence of such victimizations or the incidences during a particular period, typically the previous year.

NATIONAL SURVEY OF ADOLESCENTS (1995). Rochelle F. Hanson et al. report in "Correlates of Adolescent Reports of Sexual Assault: Findings from the National Survey of Adolescents" (*Child Maltreatment*, vol. 8, no. 4, November 2003) the results from the National Survey of Adolescents, which was conducted in 1995. A random sample of 4,023 U.S. adolescents aged 12 to 17 years included 51.3% males and 48.7% females. A majority (70.2%) were non-Hispanic whites. The children were grouped into several age cohorts (groups). Interviews were conducted by telephone, with the consent of the parent or guardian.

A total of 326 (8.1%) adolescents indicated that they had experienced child sexual abuse. Approximately four out of five (78.1%) of those reporting child sexual abuse were female, and one out of five (21.9%) were male. Most (58.2%) were white, 23.6% were African American, and 9.4% were Hispanic. Other ethnic groups made up the remaining 8.8% of child sexual abuse victims.

Of the 326 victims, 30.7% had been raped, 26.8% reported fearing for their life during the assault, and 10% had suffered physical injuries. Alcohol or drugs were involved in 6.7% of the incidents. Single incidents were reported by about two-thirds (64.1%) of the victims. Three-quarters (76.4%) knew the perpetrator. Specifically, 4.3% identified their father or stepfather as the abuser, 17.5% named another relative, 52.8% reported an unrelated acquaintance, and 1.8% knew the perpetrator but did not identify the person. Nearly a quarter (23%) said the perpetrator was a stranger, and two victims did not identify the perpetrator.

DEVELOPMENTAL VICTIMIZATION SURVEY (2002–03). In "The Victimization of Children and Youth: A Comprehensive, National Survey" (*Child Maltreatment*, vol. 10, no. 1, February 2005), Finkelhor et al. describe the Developmental Victimization Survey, which was conducted in 2002–03 using a nationally representative sample of 2,030 children and youth aged two to 17 years. The purpose of the study was to ascertain any violent victimizations of the children during the previous year. Researchers directly interviewed older children (those aged 10 years and older) and interviewed the caretakers of younger children.

Finkelhor et al. find that more than half of the children had been victimized during the previous year by a physical assault, a property offense, a form of child maltreatment, a form of sexual victimization, or a form of indirect victimization, such as witnessing an act of violence. One youth out of 12 had been sexually victimized during the study year. This provided an incidence rate of 82 sexual victimizations per 1,000 child population. The rate for girls was 96 per 1,000 girls, and the rate for boys was 67 per 1,000 boys. The incidence rates by victim age were: youths aged 13 to 17 years (168 per 1,000 child population), children aged six to 12 years (53 per 1,000 child population), and children aged two to five years (15 per 1,000 child population). The vast majority (86%) of the sexual perpetrators were juveniles. In addition, 91% of the perpetrators were acquaintances of the victims, 7% were strangers, and 2% were family members.

The overall rates for particular types of sexual victimization were sexual assault (32 per 1,000 child population), completed rape (4 per 1,000 child population), and flashing or sexual exposure by an adult perpetrator (4 per 1,000 child population). For sexual assaults, the breakdown by perpetrator type was 21 per 1,000 child population for a peer (i.e., another youth), 6 per 1,000 child population for a known adult, and 4 per 1,000 child population for an adult stranger.

NATIONAL SURVEY OF CHILDREN'S EXPOSURE TO VIOLENCE. The National Survey of Children's Exposure to Violence (NatSCEV; http://www.unh.edu/ccrc/projects/natscev.html) is a project of the University of New Hampshire's Crimes against Children Research Center, conducted with funding from the U.S. Department of Justice's Office of Juvenile Justice and Delinquency Prevention (OJJDP) and the CDC. The first survey, NatSCEV I, was conducted in 2008 using a nationally representative sample of 4,549 children aged zero to 17 years who were assessed for their one-year and lifetime experiences of violence.

In "Violence, Abuse, and Crime Exposure in a National Sample of Children and Youth" (*Pediatrics*, vol. 124, no. 5, November 2009), Finkelhor et al. report on the results of the first NatSCEV study, a survey that repeated many of the elements that were used in the Developmental Victimization Survey in 2002–03. According to the researchers, NatSCEV data indicate an overall previous year sexual victimization rate of 6.1% (7.4% among females and 4.8% among males). The highest percentages were for youths aged 14 to 17 years (16.3%) and those aged 10 to 13 years (7.7%). In regards to lifetime victimization, the overall prevalence rate was 9.8% (12.2% among females and 7.5% among males). Again, the highest percentages were for youths aged 14 to 17 years (27.8%) and those aged 10 to 13 years (9.4%).

The NatSCEV results for particular types of sexual victimization were sexual assault (1.8% previous year and 3.9% lifetime), completed rape (0.2% previous year and 0.7% lifetime), and flashing or sexual exposure by an adult perpetrator (0.4% previous year and 0.6% lifetime). For sexual assaults, the breakdown by perpetrator type for previous year victimizations was 1.3% for a peer (i.e., another youth), 0.3% for a known adult, and 0.3% for an adult stranger. The percentages for lifetime sexual assaults by perpetrator type were 2.7% for a peer, 1.2% for a known adult, and 0.5% for an adult stranger.

Since 2009, the OJJDP has published the *Juvenile Justice Bulletin: National Survey of Children's Exposure to Violence* (2016, http://www.ojjdp.gov/publications/pubresults.asp?sei=94#2009), a periodic report covering various issues relating to child victimization. The OJJDP had published six bulletins as of September 2016. In *Children's Exposure to Violence and the Intersection between Delinquency and Victimization* (October 2013, http://www.ojjdp.gov/pubs/240555.pdf), Carlos A. Cuevas et al. examine rates of sexual victimization among both perpetrators and victims of juvenile delinquency between the ages of 10 and 17. The researchers note that children who have been both perpetrators and victims of delinquent acts are considerably more likely to report being sexually victimized than children who have solely been victims of juvenile delinquency. For example, two out of five (40%) boys who were both perpetrators and victims of juvenile delinquency experienced some form of sexual victimization, compared with 13% of boys who were only victims of juvenile delinquency. These rates are even higher among female perpetrators and victims. According to Cuevas et al., 58% girls who were both perpetrators and victims of delinquency reported experiencing sexual victimization; by comparison, 27% of girls who were only victims reported being sexually victimized.

Meanwhile, a final report on NatSCEV I, *National Survey of Children's Exposure to Violence (NATSCEV I), Final Report* (https://www.ncjrs.gov/pdffiles1/ojjdp/grants/248444.pdf), was released in October 2014. In addition, Finkelhor has spearheaded two subsequent NatSCEV projects: NatSCEV II, which was conducted in 2011 using a representative sample of 4,503 children aged zero to 17 years, and NatSCEV 2014, which was conducted between August 2013 and April 2014 using a representative sample of 4,000 children aged zero to 17 years.

Findings from NatSCEV II appeared in *Children's Exposure to Violence, Crime, and Abuse: An Update* (September 2015, http://www.ojjdp.gov/pubs/248547.pdf), a report in the *Juvenile Justice Bulletin: National Survey of Children's Exposure to Violence* series. Finkelhor et al. reveal that nearly one out of 10 (9.5%) of all children surveyed in the NatSCEV II study had experienced some form of sexual victimization during their lifetime. This figure was considerably higher among teenagers. The researchers note that more than a quarter (27.4%) of all teens aged 14 to 17 years claimed to have been a victim of sexual abuse at some point during their lifetime. In addition, 16.4% of 14- to 17-year-olds had experienced sexual abuse during the past year. According to Finkelhor et al., girls were considerably more likely than boys to be victims of some form of sexual abuse. As findings from the NatSCEV II study show, more than one out of 10 (11.4%) of all girls aged zero to 17 years experienced some form of sexual victimization during their lifetime, compared with 7.8% of all boys in that age range.

Finkelhor et al. also published results from the NatSCEV 2014 study in "Prevalence of Childhood Exposure to Violence, Crime, and Abuse: Results from the National Survey of Children's Exposure to Violence" (*JAMA Pediatrics*, vol. 169, no. 8, August 2015). The researchers reveal that 14.3% of girls aged 14 to 17 years had been sexually assaulted during their lifetime, compared with 6% of boys in that age group. Girls were also considerably more likely than boys to have experienced some form of sexual harassment during their lifetime. According to Finkelhor et al., more than one out of five (20.5%) girls aged 14 to 17 years had been the victim of sexual harassment during their lifetime, compared with only 3.4% of boys in that age group.

NATIONAL CRIME VICTIMIZATION SURVEYS (1994– 2010). Since 1972 the Bureau of Justice Statistics (BJS), an agency within the U.S. Department of Justice, has conducted an annual survey called the National Crime Victimization Survey (NCVS). The BJS surveys tens of thousands of households and compiles data from subjects aged 12 years and older regarding crime victimizations, both reported and not reported to authorities. Only certain crimes, including rape and sexual assault, are included in the survey questions.

As of September 2016, the most recent NCVS report to address the subject of child sexual abuse was *Violent Crime against Youth, 1994–2010* (December 2012, http://www.bjs.gov/content/pub/pdf/vcay9410.pdf). In the report, Nicole White and Janet L. Lauritsen of the University of Missouri, St. Louis, describe trends in violent crimes that were committed against youths between 1994 and 2010 based on NCVS data. Approximately 41,000 households and 73,300 individual subjects were interviewed as part of the 2010 NCVS. According to White and Lauritsen, the rate of rape and sexual assault against youths aged 12 to 17 years declined from 7 victimizations per 1,000 youths in 1994 to 2.2 victimizations per 1,000 youths in 2010, a decrease of 68%.

What Makes Victims Disclose?

Hanson et al. report on the factors that contribute to the likelihood that an adolescent will disclose sexual abuse. The researchers also examine whether, among the different ethnic and racial groups, adolescents differ in the rates of disclosure and in the factors contributing to that disclosure. About two-thirds (68.1%) of the victims told interviewers they disclosed their sexual abuse to someone. Just 4.5% of those who disclosed first told a police officer or social worker. One-third (34.3%) told their mother or stepmother and nearly four out of 10 (39.3%) told a close friend. The other victims told another relative (6.1%), a teacher (1.8%), a father or stepfather (1.7%), or a doctor or other health professional (1.3%). About 3.4% indicated they disclosed the abuse to someone but did not say who it was. Another 3.9% would not say whom they told of the abuse or could not remember whom they first told. Overall, just 33.6% indicated they ever reported the abuse to police or other authorities.

According to Hanson et al., more females (74%) than males (46.5%) disclosed to someone that they had been sexually abused. White victims (75.1%) were more likely than Hispanics (67.7%) and African Americans (55.8%) to tell someone of their abuse. Those who feared for their life during the assault (80.7%) were especially likely to disclose the abuse. Other factors that were related to high levels of disclosure were having experienced a penetration assault (72%), having suffered physical injury (70.6%), having used substances (68.2%), or having been assaulted once (67.9%). The likelihood of telling someone of the abuse was also influenced by the relationship between the victim and the perpetrator. Hanson et al. grouped perpetrators into four categories: father/stepfather, another relative (e.g., uncle or grandparent), unrelated acquaintance, and stranger. Those who were abused by a relative other than a father/stepfather (87.7%) and those who were abused by a stranger (70.7%) were more likely to report the abuse than those who were sexually abused by an unrelated acquaintance (62.2%) or by a father/stepfather (57.1%).

In "Children's Disclosures of Sexual Abuse: Learning from Direct Inquiry" (*Child Abuse and Neglect*, vol. 35, no. 5, May 2011), Paula Schaeffer, John M. Leventhal, and Andrea Gottsegen Asnes report on the results of 191 interviews of child sexual abuse victims aged three to 18 years. The researchers note three primary reasons that children disclosed the abuse: internal incentives (e.g., nightmares), external prompts (e.g., someone questioned the child about whether abuse occurred), and direct evidence (e.g., someone witnessed the abuse). In addition, Schaeffer, Leventhal, and Asnes find five major factors that influenced children to delay disclosure: perpetrator threats (e.g., that the child would get into trouble for disclosing), internal fears (e.g., that disclosure would have bad consequences), lack of opportunity to disclose the abuse, lack of understanding that the abuse constituted unacceptable behavior, and relationship factors (e.g., the victim considered the perpetrator to be a friend). Rosaleen McElvaney, Sheila Greene, and Diane Hogan identify in "To Tell or Not to Tell? Factors Influencing Young People's Informal Disclosures of Child Sexual Abuse" (*Journal of Interpersonal Violence*, vol. 29, no. 5, March 2014) other psychological factors that influence a child's decision to disclose incidents of sexual abuse. These factors include shame, apprehension about being believed, concern about the consequences of disclosure, and peer pressure. According to McElvaney, Greene, and Hogan, engaging children directly about their emotional well-being remains vital to helping urge them to disclose incidences of sexual victimization.

NONFAMILY PERPETRATORS IN POSITIONS OF TRUST

As described earlier, agency reports and retrospective studies dealing with child sexual abuse tend to categorize perpetrators into broad groups, such as parents, other relatives, acquaintances, peers, and strangers. Sexual attacks on children by strangers, although much less common than other types of attacks, capture national attention and tend to dominate media reports on the subject. Another category of perpetrators that attracts intense public scrutiny consists of nonfamily members who hold positions of trust in the community and interact with children regularly. Examples include teachers, coaches, religious leaders, pediatricians, and employees and volunteers who are affiliated with child organizations and clubs. Child sex scandals involving perpetrators in these positions make headlines and cause widespread outrage. These cases are particularly upsetting because the perpetrators are considered by other community members to be respectable, trustworthy, and commendable for their work with children.

Depending on the circumstances, the sexual misdeeds may be viewed by the public as individual failings or as institutional failings. For example, a case in which a perpetrator worked for an organization that took swift action to notify authorities once allegations came to light is likely to be seen as an instance of deviant behavior by the individual. However, if there is any evidence that others in an organization suspected or knew of the abuse and failed to take appropriate action, the case is seen as proof of gross institutional misconduct by the organization involved. In 2012 media reports surfaced that the Boy Scouts of America (BSA) kept secret for decades allegations of sexual abuse by troop leaders. The article "Report Dredges up Boy Scouts Sex Abuse Scandal" (Associated Press, September 16, 2012) notes that the *Los Angeles Times* gained access to some of the BSA's "perversion" files dating from 1970 to 1991. In hundreds of cases the files reveal that leaders within the organization did not report sexual abuse allegations to authorities. However, the article indicates that a BSA spokesperson released a statement ensuring the public that this practice no longer occurs in the organization and that all abuse suspicions are reported to local authorities.

Educators

Child sexual abuse by educators began attracting widespread public attention during the 1990s. At that time it was common for teachers accused of sexual misconduct with students to be allowed by school administrators to quietly resign. Because of lax screening procedures, these teachers could then move to another school district or state and obtain a new teaching position. In "Dirty Secrets: Why Sexually Abusive Teachers Aren't Stopped" (Post-Gazette.com, October 31, 1999), Jane Elizabeth Zemel and Steve Twedt summarize more than a dozen cases of teachers who were accused, and sometimes convicted, of sexually abusing students. Many of the teachers were so-called mobile molesters because they were able to move from school to school after being quietly fired or allowed to resign after allegations surfaced about their misconduct. Besides describing these egregious examples, the reports note that they uncovered 727 cases between 1994 and 1999 across the United States in which educators lost their teaching licenses for "sex offenses." Zemel and Twedt complain that some of the offending teachers were caught "only after they had been molesting students for many years."

Since the late 1990s, greater public awareness, tighter screening, and stricter laws have helped alleviate some of the worst problems described by Zemel and Twedt. Nevertheless, child sexual abuse cases involving teachers continue to occur. Because there is no central clearinghouse that tracks and reports the cases, it is difficult to know the prevalence of sexual misconduct by teachers with children. Charol Shakeshaft of Hofstra University notes in *Educator Sexual Misconduct: A Synthesis of Existing Literature* (June 2004, http://www2.ed.gov/rschstat/research/pubs/misconductreview/report.pdf), a study commissioned by the U.S. Department of Education, that her literature review revealed few empirical studies (studies based on observational data and statistical analyses) related to educator sexual misconduct. As a result, she relied on two Hostile Hallways surveys that she had overseen for the American Association of University Women. The surveys were conducted in 1993 and 2001 and involved 3,695 public school students in grades eight to 11. Shakeshaft projects the numbers in her surveys to the whole public school system. She estimates that 9.6% of public school children (or around 4.5 million students at that time) had experienced sexual misconduct by educators ranging from being told sexual jokes, to being shown pictures of a sexual nature, to sexual intercourse. Educators included teachers and other school officials, such as principals, coaches, counselors, substitute teachers, teacher's aides, security guards, bus drivers, custodians, and other employees.

In the early 21st century, revelations of pervasive childhood sexual abuse at some of the nation's most prestigious private schools have also emerged. In "Private Schools, Painful Secrets" (BostonGlobe.com, May 7, 2016), Jenn Abelson et al. reveal that between 1991 and 2016 faculty members and staff at 67 New England preparatory schools were confronted with charges of sexual abuse. According to the reports, some of the incidents under investigation occurred as far back as the 1950s. During the first half of 2016 alone, at least eight preparatory schools from the region, including Phillips Exeter Academy in New Hampshire and St. George's School in Rhode Island, were in the midst of investigating cases of sexual misconduct. Overall, at least 200 students had come forward with claims of sexual misconduct as of May 2016. However, Abelson et al. suggest that these figures likely fall far short of the actual number of sexual misconduct cases that occurred during this span, primarily because of the confidentiality policies at many of the schools, as well as a reluctance on the part of many victims to make their experiences of abuse public.

Priests

Public concern about sexual abuse by priests skyrocketed during the first decade of the 21st century as a result of a scandal surrounding abuse and cover-ups within the Catholic Church. Thomas F. Reilly (1942–), the former attorney general of Massachusetts, explains in *The Sexual Abuse of Children in the Roman Catholic Archdiocese of Boston* (July 23, 2003, http://www.bishop-accountability.org/resources/resource-files/reports/ReillyReport.pdf) the culture of secrecy involving the sexual abuse of an estimated 1,000 minors in the archdiocese of Boston since 1940. Reilly's 18-month-long investigation finds that "there is overwhelming evidence that for many years Cardinal [Bernard] Law and his senior managers had direct, actual knowledge that substantial numbers of children in the Archdiocese had been sexually abused by substantial numbers of its priests."

Reilly started the investigation in March 2002, shortly after John J. Geoghan (1935–2003), a former priest in the archdiocese of Boston, was sentenced to nine to 10 years in prison for sexually abusing a 10-year-old boy. Reilly's investigators found that starting in 1979 the archdiocese had received complaints of child sexual abuse against Geoghan. Church documents, which had previously been sealed, revealed that the church had not only moved Geoghan from parish to parish but had also paid settlements amounting to $15 million to the victims' families. Reilly notes that the archdiocese's own files showed that 789 people had brought sexual complaints against the Boston clergy. However, Reilly believes the actual number of victims is higher. There were 237 priests and 13 church workers who had been accused of rape and sexual assault.

EXTENT OF CHILD SEXUAL ABUSE BY PRIESTS. Responding to emerging allegations of sexual abuse by priests, the U.S. Conference of Catholic Bishops commissioned in June 2002 a study of the nature and scope of the problem of child sexual abuse in the Catholic Church in the United States. The John Jay College of Criminal Justice of the City University of New York conducted the study based on information provided by 195 dioceses, which represented 98% of all diocesan priests in the United States. The researchers also collected data from 140 religious communities, which accounted for approximately 60% of religious communities and 80% of all priests in the religious communities.

The Nature and Scope of the Problem of Sexual Abuse of Minors by Catholic Priests and Deacons in the United States 1950–2002 (February 2004, http://www.usccb.org/issues-and-action/child-and-youth-protection/upload/The-Nature-and-Scope-of-Sexual-Abuse-of-Minors-by-Catholic-Priests-and-Deacons-in-the-United-States-1950-2002.pdf) indicates that of the 109,694 priests and deacons (collectively referred to as priests) who served between 1950 and 2002, 4,392 (4%) allegedly abused children under the age of 18 years. Most (55.7%) of these priests had a single allegation of abuse. Another 26.9% had two to three allegations, 13.9% had four to nine allegations, and 3.5% had 10 or more allegations.

The report shows that 10,667 individuals made allegations of child sexual abuse by priests between 1950 and 2002. About 81% of the victims were male and 19% were female. Approximately half (50.7%) were between the ages of 11 and 14. More than a quarter (26.7%) were aged 15 to 17 years, 16.5% were aged eight to 10 years, and 6.1% were aged seven years or younger. The number of allegations rose steadily between 1950 and 1980 before dropping off sharply.

At the time of the allegations, most of the priests were serving in the capacity of associate pastor (42.3%) or pastor (25.1%). One out of 10 (10.4%) were serving as resident priests. Most of the abuse occurred in the priest's home or parish residence (40.9%), in church (16.3%), and in the victim's home (12.4%). Nearly half (49.6%) of the priests socialized with the alleged victim's family, mostly (79.6%) in the family's home.

In "Child Sexual Abuse in the Catholic Church: How Situational Crime Prevention Strategies Can Help Create Safe Environments" (*Criminal Justice and Behavior*, vol. 35, no. 5, May 2008), a follow-up study, Karen J. Terry and Alissa Ackerman find that many victims of abuse by priests were groomed for the abuse: 7.8% of children were given gifts and 17% were given other enticements, such as alcohol, drugs, money, or trips. Only 7.8% of victims were threatened, usually psychologically rather than physically.

In 2010 allegations surfaced that Pope Benedict XVI (1927–) had acted to shield the Catholic Church from scandal rather than protect hundreds of children from the priests who abused them when he served as an archbishop in Germany and as the Vatican's chief doctrinal enforcer. Laurie Goodstein reports in "Vatican Declined to Defrock U.S. Priest Who Abused Boys" (NYTimes .com, March 24, 2010) that "top Vatican officials— including the future Pope Benedict XVI—did not defrock a priest who molested as many as 200 deaf boys" between 1950 and 1974. According to Goodstein, this case was only one of thousands that were forwarded to the Congregation for the Doctrine of the Faith, the Vatican office that decides whether accused priests should be brought to trial. The Vatican, she reports, continues to fight to keep the documents secret, noting that "the Vatican has tended to view the matter in terms of sin and repentance more than crime and punishment." Richard Owen notes in "Sins in the Church to Blame for Child Abuse Scandal, Admits Pope" (SundayTimes .co.uk, May 12, 2010) that Pope Benedict issued a statement in May 2010 indicating that the Catholic Church took responsibility for the child abuse that occurred within the church.

In 2013 Pope Benedict was succeeded by Pope Francis I (1936–). Pope Francis took an active stance in contending with the issue of child sexual abuse in the Catholic Church. Catherine Hornby indicates in "Pope Francis Targets Child Abuse, Leaks in Vatican Legal Reform" (Reuters.com, July 11, 2013) that in July 2013 he revised a law prohibiting crimes against children in Vatican City to cite a range of sex-related crimes, including sexual abuse, child prostitution, and child pornography. In March 2014 Pope Francis established the Pontifical Commission for the Protection of Minors, which is dedicated to developing and promoting initiatives aimed at ensuring the safety of young people in churches worldwide. However, despite the ambitious scope of the commission, as of 2016 efforts to protect minors from sexual misconduct had proven largely ineffective. For example, in "Catholic Bishops Not Obliged to Report Clerical Child Abuse, Vatican Says" (Guardian.com, February 10, 2016), Stephanie Kirchgaessner reveals that the commission's guidelines did not require bishops to report incidences of childhood sexual misconduct to the police, leaving it to the victims to initiate legal action in cases of abuse.

Notorious Predators in Positions of Trust

Two other cases involving child sexual predators in positions of trust are noteworthy because of the circumstances involved.

In 2010 Earl B. Bradley (1953–), a pediatrician in Delaware, was indicted on hundreds of counts of sexually abusing child patients. In "Delaware Crime: Dr. Earl Bradley Sex Case Ignites Outrage" (DelawareOnline .com, February 24, 2010), Cris Barrish reports that Bradley was accused of raping or sexually assaulting more than 100 children. Much of the evidence against Bradley was obtained from videos that he made of the attacks, which date back to 1998. According to Barrish, all but one of the victims were girls. In August 2011 Bradley was found guilty of 24 counts and sentenced to 14 life terms plus 164 years in prison with no possibility of parole.

Another case of note is that of Jerry Sandusky (1944–), a former assistant football coach at Pennsylvania State University (Penn State). In "Timeline of Jerry Sandusky Sex Abuse Case; State Files Suit over Related NCAA Sanctions" (PennLive.com, January 2, 2013), Penn Live indicates that in 1977 Sandusky founded a charity called the Second Mile that was "dedicated to helping children with absent or dysfunctional families." In this capacity Sandusky interacted with boys who were typically aged seven to 13 years and sexually victimized at least eight of them. Some of the incidents took place in the locker and shower rooms that were used by the football team on the Penn State campus. In addition, he took some of the victims on trips to bowl games in which the Penn State football team competed. On two occasions fellow employees at the university reportedly witnessed Sandusky having sexual relations with boys in the shower room. The first witness told coworkers, but failed to notify authorities. The second witness notified Joe Paterno (1926–2012), the head coach of the Penn State football team, the day after he witnessed the sex act. Although Paterno alerted university officials to the allegations, neither the campus police nor the city police were notified. In 2011 Sandusky was arrested after one of his victims told authorities about being sexually abused. The resulting scandal and apparent cover-up by Penn State officials cost Paterno and other top university officials—including the university president Graham Spanier (1948–), the athletic director Tim Curley (1954–), and the university administrator Gary Schultz—their jobs. In addition, Spanier, Curley, and Schultz faced multiple charges for their role in the cover-up. In June 2012 Sandusky was found guilty of 45 abuse counts; months later he was sentenced to 30 to 60 years in prison. Although Spanier, Curley, and Schultz were eventually cleared of a number of allegations, including perjury and obstruction of justice, they still faced indictments on child endangerment and related conspiracy charges. Debra Erdley reports in "Kane Preps for Trial of 3 Former Penn State Officials" (TribLive.com, April 29, 2016) that in April 2016 Kathleen Kane (1966–), the attorney general of Pennsylvania, announced her intention to pursue the criminal case against the three former Penn State officials. As of September 2016, a trial date had not yet been set.

The Bradley and Sandusky cases both triggered the passage of new legislation designed to prevent such events from happening again. In the press release "Nine Bills Stemming from Earl Bradley Case Become Law" (June 30, 2010, http://governor.delaware.gov/news/2010/1006 june/20100630-legislation.shtml), the state of Delaware indicates that its legislature passed nine bills in June 2010 that, among other things, strengthened the state's mandatory reporting system, provided new measures for screening doctors, and required another adult to be present when doctors examine children aged 15 years or younger who are undressed or undergoing specific physical examinations. According to the article "Jerry Sandusky Sex Abuse Case Has States Re-examining Mandatory Reporter Laws" (Associated Press, June 9, 2012), by June 2012 six states had expanded their mandatory reporting requirements and/or developed new policies and reporting procedures in response to the Sandusky case. Florida passed a particularly strict law that makes it a felony for mandated reporters to fail to report suspected child abuse. In addition, Florida institutions, such as universities, can face hefty fines and be denied state funding for failing to comply with the new law. The Sandusky case also prompted some lawmakers to seek tougher mandatory reporting laws at the national level. Beth Brelje notes in "Sandusky Case Leads to Tougher Stand on Reporting Child Abuse" (PoconoRecord.com, May 17, 2014) that in May 2014 Senator Robert P. Casey Jr. (1960–; D-PA) proposed a new federal statute that would legally require members of certain professions, including doctors, school employees, and camp counselors, among others, to report any incidences of child abuse to law enforcement.

SEXUAL PREDATORS ON THE INTERNET

The Internet presents an attractive venue to child predators because they can act anonymously. Internet chat rooms, social networking sites, e-mail, and other computer-mediated communication methods provide adults with opportunities to form online relationships with children, engage in sexual banter with them, solicit or provide sexually explicit photographs or videos, and even arrange for personal meetings. Older children, particularly preteens and teenagers, tend to be highly active on the Internet. Adults who are sexually interested in youths can pose online as youths themselves in an effort to appear less threatening to children who might spurn sexually charged conversations with adults.

In 2000, 2005, and 2010 Finkelhor and his colleagues at the University of New Hampshire's Crimes against Children Research Center spearheaded national telephone surveys of thousands of youths across the country to determine to what extent the children had experienced unwanted online sexual communications. Lisa M. Jones, Kimberly J. Mitchell, and David Finkelhor discuss in "Trends in Youth Internet Victimization: Findings from Three Youth Internet Safety Surveys 2000–2010" (*Journal of Adolescent Health*, vol. 50, no. 2, February 2012) the results from the three surveys. Each survey included approximately 1,500 children aged 10 to 17 years who were Internet users. The youths were asked if they had ever experienced any of three types of online communications: unwanted sexual solicitations, harassment, or exposure to pornography. Overall, 9% of the youths who participated in the 2010 survey reported experiencing unwanted sexual solicitations, down from 13% in the 2005 survey and 19% in the 2000 survey. According to Kimberly J. Mitchell et al., in "Understanding the Decline in Unwanted Online Sexual Solicitations for U.S. Youth 2000–2010: Findings from Three Youth Internet Safety Surveys" (*Child Abuse and Neglect*, vol. 37, no. 12, December 2013), the decline in online sexual solicitations between 2000 and 2010 was primarily among preteens between the ages of 10 and 12. Finkelhor et al. reveal in "Prevalence of Childhood Exposure to Violence, Crime, and Abuse: Results from the National Survey of Children's Exposure to Violence" that online sexual misconduct involving minors remained a serious issue in 2014, particularly among teens aged 14 to 17 years. According to the researchers, 13.9% of all girls and 5.6% of all boys between the ages of 14 and 17 had been victimized by online sex talk during their lifetime.

In "The Internet and Family and Acquaintance Sexual Abuse" (*Child Maltreatment*, vol. 10, no. 1, February 2005), Kimberly J. Mitchell, David Finkelhor, and Janis Wolak find that although the percentage of youth who used the Internet rose between 2000 and 2005, the percentage of youth who communicated with people they knew only online dropped from 40% to 34%. This decline might be due to a heightened awareness of pedophiles (adults who have a sexual interest in prepubescent children) on the Internet. In fact, the researchers note that when youth were sexually solicited online, most were able to deal with the problem by blocking solicitors or leaving sites. Most did not report feeling distressed by the experience, but about 4% of youth did report feeling upset or distressed as a result of the online solicitation. Other studies have attempted to identify the personality traits of adolescents who develop online friendships. Wendy A. Walsh, Wolak, and Mitchell report in "Close Relationships with People Met Online in a National U.S. Sample of Adolescents" (*Cyberpsychology*, vol. 7, no. 3, 2013) that in 2013 one out of 10 teenage Internet users reported having formed a close relationship with someone they met over the Internet. According to the researchers, adolescents who were frequent Internet users, who suffered from depression, who engaged in delinquent activities, who searched for online pornography, and/or who had experienced harassment or sexual solicitations over the Internet were twice as likely as teens who did not belong in any of these categories to form close online relationships.

EFFECTS OF CHILD SEXUAL ABUSE

As is described in Chapter 2, all types of child abuse have negative consequences over the short term and long term to the mental and physical health of the victims. Table 4.3 is a list compiled by the Children's Bureau of typical symptoms seen in the victims of childhood sexual abuse. In *Trauma-Focused Cognitive Behavioral Therapy for Children Affected by Sexual Abuse or Trauma* (August 2012, https://www.childwelfare.gov/pubPDFs/trauma.pdf), the agency notes that the symptoms shown in Table 4.3 "can impact the child's daily life and affect

TABLE 4.3

Negative effects often seen in victims of child sexual abuse

- Maladaptive or unhelpful beliefs and attributions related to the abusive events, including:
  - A sense of guilt for their role in the abuse
  - Anger at parents for not knowing about the abuse
  - Feelings of powerlessness
  - A sense that they are in some way "damaged goods"
  - A fear that people will treat them differently because of the abuse
- Acting out behaviors, such as engaging in age-inappropriate sexual behaviors
- Mental health disorders, including major depression
- Posttraumatic stress disorder (PTSD) symptoms, which are characterized by:
- Intrusive and reoccurring thoughts of the traumatic experience
  - Avoidance of reminders of the trauma (often places, people, sounds, smells, and other sensory triggers)
  - Emotional numbing
  - Irritability
  - Trouble sleeping or concentrating
  - Physical and emotional hyperarousal (often characterized by emotional swings or rapidly accelerating anger or crying that is out of proportion to the apparent stimulus)

SOURCE: Adapted from "TF-CBT Addresses the Effects of Sexual Abuse and Trauma," in *Trauma-Focused Cognitive Behavioral Therapy for Children Affected by Sexual Abuse or Trauma*, U.S. Department of Health and Human Services, Administration for Children and Families, Administration on Children, Youth and Families, Children's Bureau, August 2012, https://www.childwelfare.gov/pubPDFs/trauma.pdf (accessed June 10, 2016)

behavior, school performance, attention, self-perception, and emotional regulation." A type of therapy called trauma-focused cognitive behavioral therapy (TF-CBT) has been clinically proven to help children, adolescents, and their parents and caregivers in dealing with the trauma inflicted by childhood sexual victimization. The Children's Bureau explains that TF-CBT combines elements of cognitive therapy, behavioral therapy, and family therapy to "reduce negative emotional and behavioral responses following child sexual abuse."

High-Risk Behaviors in Female Child Sexual Abuse Victims

In "Sexual At-Risk Behaviors of Sexually Abused Adolescent Girls" (*Journal of Child Sexual Abuse*, vol. 12, no. 2, 2003), a study of sexual at-risk behaviors of 125 female adolescents aged 12 to 17 years who had experienced sexual abuse, Caroline Cinq-Mars et al. administered a self-report questionnaire that asked about the subjects' sexual activities, not including sexual abuse experiences. Afterward, the subjects were interviewed regarding their sexual abuse experiences, including information about the perpetrator (both family and nonfamily members), the frequency and duration of the abuse, the severity of the abuse, and whether or not they told someone about the abuse.

Among offending family members, fathers were the perpetrators in 30.4% of incidents. Stepfathers and extended family members each were responsible for 28.8% of the sexual abuse, and brothers accounted for another 9.6% of abuse. The victims experienced more than one incident of sexual abuse, with the mean (average) number of incidents per victim being 1.8. The mean age for the start of abuse was 9.3 years. More than one-third (36.8%) of the victims experienced sexual abuse before the age of 11 years.

More than half (55.3%) of the subjects reported being sexually active, and 54.5% had their first consensual intercourse before the age of 15 years. The rate of pregnancy was 15%. Cinq-Mars et al. find three sexual abuse characteristics that were associated with the adolescents' sexual at-risk behavior. Adolescents who experienced abuse involving penetration were 13 times as likely to have been pregnant and twice as likely to have more than one consensual partner in the 12 months preceding the study. Having been abused by more than one perpetrator (in one or more incidents) was also closely associated with at-risk behaviors: pregnancy (eight times as likely), having more than one consensual sexual partner (four times as likely), and irregular condom use (three times as likely). Finally, physical coercion during abuse increased the odds of pregnancy (four times as likely), having more than one consensual sexual partner (five times as likely), and irregular condom use (three times as likely).

Brigitte Leeners et al. indicate in "Risk Factors for Unfavorable Pregnancy Outcome in Women with Adverse Childhood Experiences" (*Journal of Perinatal Medicine*, vol. 42, no. 2, March 2014) that female victims of sexual abuse are also more likely than nonvictims to engage in risky behavior during pregnancy. The researchers report that roughly one-third (31.7%) of child sexual abuse victims later smoked during pregnancy, a rate more than three times higher than that of pregnant women who were not victims of childhood sexual abuse (9.4%). At the same time, victims of childhood sexual abuse experienced high likelihoods of experiencing emotional abuse (44.7%), physical abuse (16.5%), and sexual abuse (12.9%) while they were pregnant.

In addition, Leeners et al. find that victims of child sexual abuse are susceptible to certain "triggers" that make them recall memories of their abuse during pregnancy. Nearly one out of five (19.2%) pregnant women in the study reported that the experience of having a vaginal examination triggered memories of the sexual abuse they endured as a child.

Substance Abuse

A number of studies, such as Christiane Brems et al.'s "Childhood Abuse History and Substance Use among Men and Women Receiving Detoxification Services" (*American Journal of Drug and Alcohol Abuse*, vol. 30, no. 4, November 2004), Patricia B. Moran, Sam Vuchinich, and Nancy K. Hall's "Associations between Types of Maltreatment and Substance Use during Adolescence" (*Child Abuse and Neglect: The International Journal*, vol. 28, no. 5, May 2004), and Cathy S. Widom et al.'s "Long-Term Effects of Child Abuse and Neglect on Alcohol Use and Excessive Drinking in Middle Adulthood" (*Journal of Studies on Alcohol and Drugs*, vol. 68, no. 3, May 2007), show that child sexual abuse increases the risk for substance abuse later in life. In "Abnormal T2 Relaxation Time in the Cerebellar Vermis of Adults Sexually Abused in Childhood: Potential Role of the Vermis in Stress-Enhanced Risk for Drug Abuse" (*Psychoneuroendocrinology*, vol. 27, nos. 1–2, January–February 2002), Carl M. Anderson et al. of Harvard Medical School uncover how this occurs. They find that the vermis, the region that is flanked by the cerebellar hemispheres of the brain, may play a key role in the risk for substance abuse among adults who have experienced child abuse. The vermis develops gradually and continues to produce neurons, or nerve cells, after birth. It is known to be sensitive to stress; as a result, stress can influence its development.

Anderson et al. compared young adults aged 18 to 22 years, including eight with a history of repeated sexual abuse in childhood and 16 others as the control group. Using functional magnetic resonance imaging technology,

the researchers measured the resting blood flow in the vermis. They find that the subjects who had been victims of sexual abuse had diminished blood flow. Anderson et al. suggest the stress experienced with repeated sexual abuse may have caused damage to the vermis, which in turn could not perform its job of controlling irritability in the limbic system (a collection of connected clusters of nerve cells). Located in the center of the brain, the limbic system is responsible for, among other things, regulating emotions and memory. Therefore, the damaged vermis induces a person to use drugs or alcohol to suppress the irritability.

Sunny Hyucksun Shin, Hyokyoung Grace Hong, and Andrea L. Hazen analyze in "Childhood Sexual Abuse and Adolescent Substance Use: A Latent Class Analysis" (*Drug and Alcohol Dependence*, vol. 109, nos. 1–3, June 1, 2010) data on 1,019 adolescents followed in the Patterns of Youth Mental Health Care Public Service Systems Study. The researchers find that not only is child sexual abuse associated with drug and alcohol use during adolescence but also that sexual abuse shapes the patterns of substance use of teen girls. Female adolescent victims of child sexual abuse were five times more likely than nonvictims to heavily use multiple kinds of drugs. These findings held true even when Shin, Hong, and Hazen controlled for peer substance use, family influences, mental disorders, and other types of child maltreatment. The researchers also note that male sexual abuse survivors were not more likely to use drugs and alcohol during adolescence than were nonvictims.

In "Contributions of Child Sexual Abuse, Self-Blame, Posttraumatic Stress Symptoms, and Alcohol Use to Women's Risk for Forcible and Substance-Facilitated Sexual Assault" (*Journal of Child Sexual Abuse*, vol. 25, no. 4, May–June 2016), Taylor R. Mokma, Lee R. Eshelman, and Terri L. Messman-Moore examine the link between childhood sexual abuse and incidents of rape and sexual assault among female adults. They find that female survivors of child sexual abuse demonstrate a greater likelihood of becoming victims of both forcible sexual assault and alcohol-facilitated sexual assault in adulthood. The researchers also observe that indications of self-blame and PTSD among female survivors of childhood sexual abuse are the strongest predictors of later adult sexual victimization.

Sexual Revictimization and Self-Harming Behaviors

Jennie G. Noll et al. report in "Revictimization and Self-Harm in Females Who Experienced Childhood Sexual Abuse: Results from a Prospective Study" (*Journal of Interpersonal Violence*, vol. 18, no. 12, December 2003) on a longitudinal study that examined the effects of child sexual abuse on female development. This was the first prospective study that followed children from the time sexual abuse was reported through adolescence and into early adulthood. Referred by CPS agencies, the participants had experienced sexual abuse by a family member before the age of 14 years. The median age (half were younger and half were older) at the start of sexual abuse was seven to eight years, and the median duration of abuse was two years. The study consisted of 84 abused children and a comparison group of 82 nonabused children. Two yearly interviews followed the first assessment of the group and two more interviews were conducted within five years of the sexual abuse report.

Noll et al. note that this study was the first to provide information about the revictimization of child sexual abuse survivors not long after their abuse (seven years after the abuse, when the participants were in their adolescence and early adulthood). The researchers find that participants who had been sexually abused during childhood were twice as likely as the comparison group to have experienced sexual revictimization, such as rape and sexual assault, and almost four times as likely to harm themselves through suicide attempts or self-mutilation. They also suffered 1.6 times more physical victimization, such as domestic violence. Compared with the nonabused group, the abused group reported 20% more significant lifetime traumas subsequent to being sexually abused. Significant lifetime traumas reported by the participants included separation and losses (e.g., having family or friends move away or die), emotional abuse and/or rejection by family, natural disasters, and witnessing violence.

In "Substance Use and PTSD Symptoms Impact the Likelihood of Rape and Revictimization in College Women" (*Journal of Interpersonal Violence*, vol. 24, no. 3, March 2009), Terri L. Messman-Moore, Rose Marie Ward, and Amy L. Brown find that substance use and PTSD increase the likelihood that college women will be raped or otherwise revictimized. They argue that PTSD sufferers use drugs and alcohol or maladaptive sexual behavior to cope with PTSD symptoms and that these coping behaviors increase their risk of further victimization.

Noll et al. observe that child sexual abuse is the "strongest predictor of self-harm," even when other types of abuse are present. They surmise that the victims may have negative feelings toward their own body and want to hurt it. Noll et al. indicate that some researchers believe victims may want to reveal internal pains through the outward manifestation of self-harm. Others wish to re-experience feelings of shame in an attempt to resolve it.

However, Jennifer J. Muehlenkamp et al. find a stronger correlation between physical abuse and self-injury than between sexual abuse and self-injury. In "Abuse Subtypes and Nonsuicidal Self-Injury: Preliminary Evidence of Complex Emotion Regulation Patterns" (*Journal of Nervous and Mental Disease*, vol. 198, no. 4,

April 2010), the researchers report that a relatively weak association exists between child sexual abuse and later nonsuicidal self-injury. They theorize that people with a history of sexual abuse may be more likely to engage in other self-destructive behaviors such as eating disorders and substance abuse than in externalizing self-injury. Muehlenkamp et al. suggest that more research is needed into the emotional difficulties that are experienced by child sexual abuse survivors and their association with self-harming behavior.

A Longitudinal Study of the Effects of Child Sexual Abuse

Ron Roberts et al. seek in "The Effects of Child Sexual Abuse in Later Family Life: Mental Health, Parenting, and Adjustment of Offspring" (*Child Abuse and Neglect: The International Journal*, vol. 28, no. 5, May 2004) to determine the effects of child sexual abuse on adult mental health, parenting relationships, and the adjustment of the children of mothers who had been victims of child sexual abuse. The researchers investigated 8,292 families, a subsample of the Avon Longitudinal Study of Parents and Children (2016, http://www.bristol.ac.uk/alspac/participants/coco90s/), which is a continuing study of women and their families in Avon, England. The participating women had self-reported experiences of sexual assault before adolescence. Four family groups were included:

- Single-mother families (9% of the study sample)—consist of a nonmarried woman with no partner and her children

- Biological families (79.5%)—consist of two parents and their biological children with no other children from previous relationships

- Stepmother/complex stepfamilies (4.6%)—consist of a father with at least one biological child (living in the household or visiting regularly) who is not the biological offspring of the mother

- Stepfather families (6.9%)—consist of a mother and at least one biological child (living in the household or visiting regularly) who is not the biological offspring of the father

The researchers report that 26% of survivors of child sexual abuse had teen pregnancies. These women were disproportionately likely to be currently living in a non-traditional family—single-mother families (3%) and stepfather families (2.9%)—than in a biological family (1.3%). Roberts et al. did not have a similar finding when it came to stepmother/complex stepfamilies. In this group just 0.8% reported child sexual abuse. The researchers surmise that a woman who has experienced child sexual abuse tends to choose a partner without children because she might feel inadequate to take care of more children.

Child sexual abuse also has consequences on the adult survivors' mental health. Mothers who reported child sexual abuse were likely to report more depression and anxiety and lower self-esteem. These mental problems in turn affect the mothers' relationships with their children and the children's adjustment. Mothers with a history of child sexual abuse reported less self-confidence and less positive relationships with their children. The children were hyperactive and had emotional, peer, and conduct problems. Debra R. Wilson et al. report in "Overcoming Sequelae of Childhood Sexual Abuse with Stress Management" (*Journal of Psychiatric and Mental Health Nursing*, vol. 19, no. 7, September 2012) that emotional issues stemming from childhood sexual abuse can lead victims to adopt poor coping skills when confronting stressful situations as adults, which can result in a range of both psychological and physiological health issues.

CHAPTER 5
CHILD ABUSE AND THE LAW

As is explained in earlier chapters, child abuse cases can fall under the jurisdiction of civil or criminal courts, depending on the circumstances. Chapter 2 describes the civil court proceedings that child protective services (CPS) agencies undertake in cases in which they remove a child from the home, provide in-home protective services, or require the abuser to get treatment. These cases are handled in juvenile or family courts and are broadly known as child abuse, child protection, dependency, or child welfare cases. Civil laws also allow adults who suffered abuse as children to file lawsuits seeking monetary damages from their alleged abusers and/or from third parties that played a role in the abuse. Criminal proceedings are initiated by a government prosecutor if an alleged abuser is charged with a crime, such as sexual abuse. These cases are handled in criminal courts.

CHILDREN'S LEGAL RIGHTS IN CHILD PROTECTION CASES

Historically, children who appeared in dependency court were not subject to constitutional due process rights or legal representation. This changed in 1972, when the U.S. Supreme Court ruled in *In re Gault* (387 U.S. 1) that children, whether they have committed a crime or are the victims of a crime, are entitled to due process and legal representation. The original case involved delinquency (a criminal offense committed by juveniles). However, the protections afforded by the Supreme Court's decision were soon applied to the civil court proceedings used in dependency cases.

In "Session 3: Children's Rights in the Context of Welfare, Dependency, and the Juvenile Court" (*Journal of Juvenile Law and Policy*, vol. 8, no. 2, 2004), John E. B. Myers of the University of the Pacific notes, "Prior to *Gault*, lawyers were uncommon in abuse and neglect cases. The child protection agency was represented by a social worker, who presented the agency's position to the judge. Parents, most of whom were poor, seldom had legal representation. Rules of evidence and procedure were downplayed or ignored, and informality was the order of the day." Ever since the *Gault* ruling, attorneys have played a much larger role in dependency court hearings. Judges in these hearings can appoint temporary guardians called guardians ad litem (guardians at law) to represent the children's interests during dependency hearings. The guardians may be attorneys working pro bono (without compensation) or specially trained volunteers. For example, the Florida Guardian ad Litem Program notes in "Volunteer FAQ" (2016, http://www.guardianadl item.org/vol_faq.asp) that "anyone with common sense, compassion and dedication to children can be a Guardian ad Litem."

Another program devoted to advocating for children involved in dependency hearings is the court-appointed special advocate (CASA) program. The National CASA Association indicates in *Annual Report 2014* (2016, http://nc.casaforchildren.org/apps/annualreport2014/index .html) that in 2014 more than 76,300 CASA and guardian ad litem volunteers helped more than 251,000 abused and neglected children.

Guardians ad litem and CASA volunteers try to ensure that the legal system serves the best interests of the child. A volunteer reviews all records pertaining to the maltreated child, including CPS reports and medical and school records. The volunteer also meets with the child, parents and family members, social workers, health care providers, school officials, and other people who may know of the child's history. The research compiled by the volunteer helps the child's lawyer (if one is involved) and the court in deciding what is best for the child.

Table 5.1 shows a state-by-state count of the number of duplicate victims and the number who experienced

TABLE 5.1

Child maltreatment victims with court action, 2014

State	Victims (duplicate count)	Victims (duplicate count) with court action	
		Number	Percent
Alabama	8,895	603	6.8
Alaska	2,922	816	27.9
Arizona	14,743	8,047	54.6
Arkansas	9,517	2,400	25.2
California	80,644	29,105	36.1
Colorado	10,498	2,020	19.2
Connecticut	8,221	2,131	25.9
Delaware	1,523	212	13.9
District of Columbia	1,615	273	16.9
Florida	48,343	14,294	29.6
Georgia	23,387	4,928	21.1
Hawaii	1,373	820	59.7
Idaho	1,652	952	57.6
Illinois			
Indiana	25,448	15,709	61.7
Iowa	9,076	3,274	36.1
Kansas	2,090	929	44.4
Kentucky	23,026	5,652	24.5
Louisiana	12,742	3,306	25.9
Maine	4,070	119	2.9
Maryland	16,824	1,557	9.3
Massachusetts	36,114	7,361	20.4
Michigan			
Minnesota	4,294	1,575	36.7
Mississippi	9,044	238	2.6
Missouri	5,546	1,858	33.5
Montana	1,224	791	64.6
Nebraska	4,196	1,719	41.0
Nevada	4,532	2,414	53.3
New Hampshire	652	341	52.3
New Jersey	12,682	2,473	19.5
New Mexico	8,801	1,539	17.5
New York			
North Carolina			
North Dakota	1,668	264	15.8
Ohio	27,006	5,860	21.7
Oklahoma	14,131	1,985	14.0
Oregon	10,661	2,845	26.7
Pennsylvania			
Puerto Rico	8,093	188	2.3
Rhode Island	3,702	1,222	33.0
South Carolina	12,821	2,814	21.9
South Dakota			
Tennessee	12,142	1,068	8.8
Texas	67,525	11,334	16.8
Utah	10,579	2,032	19.2
Vermont	932	211	22.6
Virginia	6,624	1,214	18.3
Washington	8,286	2,959	35.7
West Virginia	5,056	1,023	20.2
Wisconsin	4,915	567	11.5
Wyoming	893	241	27.0
National	**588,728**	**153,283**	**26.0**

SOURCE: "Table 6-5. Victims with Court Action, 2014," in *Child Maltreatment 2014*, U.S. Department of Health and Human Services, Administration for Children and Families, Administration on Children, Youth, and Families, Children's Bureau, January 25, 2016, https://www.acf.hhs.gov/sites/default/files/cb/cm2014.pdf (accessed June 10, 2016)

TABLE 5.2

Child maltreatment victims with court-appointed representatives, 2014

State	Victims (duplicate count)	Victims (duplicate count) with court-appointed representatives	
		Number	Percent
Alabama	8,895	698	7.8
Alaska	2,922	799	27.3
Arizona	14,743	9,847	66.8
Arkansas			
California	80,644	34,309	42.5
Colorado			
Connecticut			
Delaware	1,523	212	13.9
District of Columbia	1,615	59	3.7
Florida			
Georgia	23,387	4,711	20.1
Hawaii	1,373	768	55.9
Idaho			
Illinois			
Indiana	25,448	4,792	18.8
Iowa	9,076	1,737	19.1
Kansas			
Kentucky			
Louisiana			
Maine	4,070	990	24.3
Maryland			
Massachusetts	36,114	6,779	18.8
Michigan	33,016	1,631	4.9
Minnesota	4,294	1,441	33.6
Mississippi	9,044	2,922	32.3
Missouri			
Montana	1,224	336	27.5
Nebraska	4,196	1,767	42.1
Nevada	4,532	597	13.2
New Hampshire	652	341	52.3
New Jersey	12,682	268	2.1
New Mexico	8,801	1,539	17.5
New York			
North Carolina			
North Dakota	1,668	194	11.6
Ohio	27,006	3,168	11.7
Oklahoma	14,131	1,985	14.0
Oregon			
Pennsylvania			
Puerto Rico			
Rhode Island	3,702	1,136	30.7
South Carolina	12,821	135	1.1
South Dakota			
Tennessee			
Texas			
Utah	10,579	2,032	19.2
Vermont	932	211	22.6
Virginia			
Washington			
West Virginia	5,056	65	1.3
Wisconsin			
Wyoming	893	30	3.4
National	**365,039**	**85,499**	**23.4**

SOURCE: "Table 6-6. Victims with Court-Appointed Representatives, 2014," in *Child Maltreatment 2014*, U.S. Department of Health and Human Services, Administration for Children and Families, Administration on Children, Youth, and Families, Children's Bureau, January 25, 2016, https://www.acf.hhs.gov/sites/default/files/cb/cm2014.pdf (accessed June 10, 2016)

court actions in 2014. (A duplicate count tallies a child for each reported incidence of abuse, so a victim may be counted more than once.) It should be noted that data were not available from six states: Illinois, Michigan, New York, North Carolina, Pennsylvania, and South Dakota. Of the 588,728 duplicate victims reported, 153,283 (26%) had court actions in 2014. Table 5.2

shows the number of duplicate victims who had court-appointed representatives in 2014. Data from 29 states and the District of Columbia are presented. Of the 365,039 duplicate victims reported, 85,499 (23.4%) victims had court-appointed representatives.

DIFFICULTIES IN PROSECUTING CHILD ABUSERS

Abusive acts that are defined as criminal offenses are prosecuted in criminal court. In many cases the victim, a child, may be the key witness. This can present challenges for prosecutors, particularly when the victim is a young child (e.g., age six or younger) because the question of competency arises. Several studies have examined children's reliability in recalling and retelling past events. Researchers find that different settings and interview techniques may result in children remembering different details at different times.

Prosecutors also worry about the possible harm the child may suffer in having to relive the abuse and in being interrogated by adversarial defense attorneys. For instance, if the child is an adolescent making accusations of sexual abuse, the defendant's attorney may accuse the teenage victim of seducing the defendant or having willingly taken part in the acts. Other factors that prosecutors must consider include the slowness of the court process and the possibility that the case may be delayed, not just once, but several times. This is hard enough for adults to tolerate, but it is particularly difficult for children because the delay prolongs their pain. Children may become more reluctant to testify or may no longer be able to retell their stories accurately. There is a far greater difference between an 11-year-old retelling an event that happened at six years of age than a 31-year-old testifying about something that happened when he or she was 26 years old.

CONSIDERATIONS IN CHILD SEXUAL ABUSE PROSECUTIONS

In "Child Maltreatment and the Justice System: Predictors of Court Involvement" (*Research on Social Work Practice*, vol. 15, no. 5, September 2005), Andrea J. Sedlak et al. note that child sexual abuse cases have the highest likelihood among maltreatment cases of being tried in criminal court. William G. Jones explains in *Working with the Courts in Child Protection* (2010) that the types of maltreatment cases that are typically prosecuted are those that include sex offenses and those that cause serious injury or death.

Still, a number of obstacles confront the prosecution of child sexual assault cases. Indeed, a high percentage of rape and sexual assault cases ultimately go unreported to the authorities. Table 5.3 provides a breakdown of rape and sexual assault cases of minors aged 12 to 17 years between 2010 and 2014. Of the 9,114 rape and sexual assault cases involving children between the ages of 15 and 17 that were documented in 2014, roughly half (4,531, or 49.7%) were reported to the police. As Table 5.4 shows, all 4,531 cases of rape and sexual assault involving children aged 15 to 17 years that were reported to the police in 2014 also involved some form of injury to the victim.

Dena Nazer and Vincent J. Palusci of the Children's Hospital of Michigan in Detroit, Michigan, note in "Child Sexual Abuse: Can Anatomy Explain the Presentation?" (*Clinical Pediatrics*, vol. 47, no. 1, January 2008) that prosecuting a child sexual abuse case is particularly challenging. A child who is physically abused will often display unmistakable signs of the abuse, such as bruises and broken bones. Sexual abuse does not necessarily leave such visible marks. Therefore, the abuse is less likely to be noticed by others and is more difficult to verify once an accusation is made.

In "How Long to Prosecute Child Sexual Abuse for a Community Using a Children's Advocacy Center and Two Comparison Communities?" (*Child Maltreatment*, vol. 13, no. 1, February 2008), Wendy A. Walsh et al. examine the effect of the particular difficulties encountered in child sexual abuse cases on the length of time it took to resolve them. The researchers find that less than

TABLE 5.3

Victims of child sexual assault, by age and reporting to police, 2010–14

Crime type	2010	2011	2012	2013	2014
Rape/sexual assault					
12 to 14	32,781!	3,961!	26,606!	8,103!	6,180!
Yes, reported to the police	14,618!	—	13,528!	4,463!	—
No, did not report to the police	18,163!	3,961!	10,924!	3,640!	6,180!
Do not know	—	—	2,154!	—	—
15 to 17	20,531!	20,995!	12,060!	18,266!	9,114!
Yes, reported to the police	14,344!	7,202!	4,904!	15,230!	4,531!
No, did not report to the police	6,187!	13,792!	7,156!	3,036!	4,584!

—Estimate is equal to 0 sample cases.
!Interpret data with caution, based on 10 or fewer sample cases or the coefficient of variation is greater than 50%.
Notes: Special tabulations from the National Crime Victimization Survey (NCVS) Victimization Analysis Tool (NVAT). No unique link for individual data sets. Detail may not sum to total due to rounding and/or missing data.

SOURCE: Adapted from "Number of Rape/Sexual Assaults by Age and Reporting to the Police, 2010–2014," in *NCVS Victimization Analysis Tool (NVAT)*, U.S. Department of Justice, Office of Justice Programs, Bureau of Justice Statistics, June 10, 2016, http://www.bjs.gov/index.cfm?ty=nvat (accessed June 10, 2016)

TABLE 5.4

Victims of child sexual assault, by age and injury status, 2010–14

Crime type	2010	2011	2012	2013	2014
Rape/sexual assault					
12 to 14	32,781!	3,961!	26,606!	8,103!	6,180!
Not injured	23,687!	3,961!	20,365!	3,640!	6,180!
Injured	9,095!	—	6,241!	4,463!	—
15 to 17	20,531!	20,995!	12,060!	18,266!	9,114!
Not injured	16,689!	4,032!	8,404!	2,421!	4,584!
Injured	3,843!	16,963!	3,656!	15,845!	4,531!

—Estimate is equal to 0 sample cases.
!Interpret data with caution, based on 10 or fewer sample cases or the coefficient of variation is greater than 50%.
Notes: Special tabulations from the National Crime Victimization Survey (NCVS) Victimization Analysis Tool (NVAT). No unique link for individual data sets. Detail may not sum to total due to rounding and/or missing data.

SOURCE: Adapted from "Number of Rape/Sexual Assaults by Age and Injury, 2010–2014," in *NCVS Victimization Analysis Tool (NVAT)*, U.S. Department of Justice, Office of Justice Programs, Bureau of Justice Statistics, June 10, 2016, http://www.bjs.gov/index.cfm?ty=nvat (accessed June 10, 2016)

half (44%) of child sexual abuse cases in the legal system were resolved within one year, and nearly one-third (30%) remained unresolved at the two-year mark. Only one out of five was resolved within six months, which is the American Bar Association standard for felony cases.

According to Walsh et al., in "Prosecuting Child Sexual Abuse: The Importance of Evidence Type" (*Crime and Delinquency*, vol. 56, no. 3, July 2010), the sexual abuse cases that were the most likely to have charges filed had at least some of these types of evidence: a child disclosure, a corroborating witness, an offender confession, or an additional report against the alleged perpetrator. Cases lacking physical evidence were twice as likely to be filed if there was a corroborating witness. Regardless of whether or not a child disclosed the abuse, a case was much more likely to be filed if there were at least two types of evidence present.

Tisha R. Wiley of the Juvenile Protective Association finds in "Legal and Social Service Responses to Child Sexual Abuse: A Primer and Discussion of Relevant Research" (*Journal of Child Sexual Abuse*, vol. 18, no. 3, May–June 2009) that only a small proportion of child sexual abuse cases are ever prosecuted. Cases involving female victims and older victims are more likely to be prosecuted than those involving male victims or younger victims. The more severe the abuse, the more likely it will be prosecuted. If a child is inconsistent in his or her story or if the child's family is against the prosecution, the case is unlikely to be brought to court. Children must also be willing and able to testify in court.

The Question of Competency

Traditionally, judges protected juries from incompetent witnesses, which during the early years of the United States were considered to include women, slaves, and children. Children in particular were believed to live in a fantasy world, and their inability to understand terms such as *oath*, *testify*, and *solemnly swear* denied them the right to appear in court. In 1895 the U.S. Supreme Court established in *Wheeler v. United States* (159 U.S. 523) the status of child witnesses. The court explained:

> There is no precise age which determines the question of competency. This depends on the capacity and intelligence of the child, his appreciation of the difference between truth and falsehood, as well as of his duty to tell the former. The decision of this question rests primarily with the trial judge, who sees the proposed witness, notices his manner, his apparent possession or lack of intelligence, and may resort to any examination which will tend to disclose his capacity and intelligence, as well as his understanding of the obligations of an oath.... To exclude [a child] from the witness stand ... would sometimes result in staying the hand of justice.

As a result of this ruling, the courts formalized the *Wheeler* decision by requiring judges to interview all children to determine their competency. The Federal Rules of Evidence (http://www.law.cornell.edu/rules/fre) are rules that have been codified into law by Congress and dictate certain evidentiary practices and procedures that most federal courts have to follow. In general, the state courts also abide by the Federal Rules of Evidence, which were codified in 1975. Rule 601, Competency to Testify in General, states: "Every person is competent to be a witness unless these rules provide otherwise." Under U.S. Code (USC) Section 3509, Child Victims' and Child Witnesses' Rights (http://www.gpo.gov/fdsys/pkg/USCODE-2011-title18/pdf/USCODE-2011-title18-partII-chap223-sec 3509.pdf), a child is presumed to be competent, and a competency examination is only required upon written motion and an "offer of proof of incompetency."

Is a Child's Account Reliable?

Some experts believe children do not lie about sexual abuse. They point out that children cannot describe events unfamiliar to them. For example, the average six-year-old has no concept of how forced penetration feels or what semen tastes like. Experts also note that children lie to get themselves out of trouble, not into trouble, and reporting sexual abuse is definitely trouble. Children sometimes recant or deny that any abuse has happened, after they disclosed it. Perhaps the reaction to the disclosure is unfavorable, or the pain of talking about the experience is too great. The child's recanting under interrogation in a court of law may prove damaging to the case and may encourage claims that the child has made false accusations.

Kenneth V. Lanning surmises in "Criminal Investigation of Sexual Victimization of Children" (John E. B. Myers et al., eds., *The APSAC Handbook on Child Maltreatment*, 2002) that children rarely lie about sexual abuse. Some children, however, may recount what they believe in their mind to be the truth, although their account may turn out to be inaccurate. Lanning gives the following explanations for these inaccuracies:

- The child may be experiencing distorted memory because of trauma

- The child's story might be a reflection of normal childhood fears and fantasy

- The child may have been confused by the abuser's use of trickery or drugs

- The child's testimony may be influenced by the suggestive questions of investigators

- The child's account might reflect urban legends and cultural mythology

Nazer and Palusci point out that children's accounts of sexual abuse sometimes do contain bizarre or impossible events. This does not mean that the child was not sexually abused; instead, understanding sexual abuse may be beyond a child's ability at his or her developmental stage. For example, if a child is penetrated in the course of sexual abuse, the child may perceive the painful object to be a knife. In addition, when faced with sexual abuse and the emotional pain that surrounds the trauma of the abuse, children may have distorted memories of exactly what occurred.

CHILDREN CAN BE UNRELIABLE WITNESSES IF SUBJECTED TO SUGGESTED EVENTS. In "Children's Eyewitness Reports after Exposure to Misinformation from Parents" (*Journal of Experimental Psychology: Applied*, vol. 7, no. 1, March 2001), Debra Ann Poole and D. Stephen Lindsay examined children's eyewitness reports after the children were given misinformation by their parents and showed that children may not be able to distinguish fact from fiction when subjected to suggested events before formal interviews.

A total of 114 children aged three to eight years participated (on a one-to-one basis) in four science activities with a man called "Mr. Science." Three interviews

were conducted afterward. The first interview occurred right after the science activities in which an interviewer asked each child nonsuggestive questions about the activities. About three and a half months later the children's parents read them a story about their science experience. The story included two science activities they had experienced and two others that they had not experienced. The story also included an event in which the child experienced unpleasant touching by Mr. Science. In reality this event did not happen. The children were then interviewed. The final step in the interview consisted of a source-monitoring procedure, in which the children were reminded of their actual experiences, as well as the story, to help them distinguish fact from fiction. A final interview was conducted one month later. This time the children were not given any misinformation.

The interview conducted right after the science activities showed that the children recalled their experiences, with the amount of events reported increasing with the age of the child. When prompted for more information, the amount of new information reported also increased with age. The reports resulting from the promptings remained accurate. In the interview that occurred soon after the children were read the story with misleading suggestions, 35% (40) of the children reported 58 suggested events in free recall (without prompting from the interviewer), including 17 events about unpleasant touching by Mr. Science. In the last interview, with no additional misinformation given the children, 21% (24) of the children reported 27 suggested events, including nine suggested events that involved unpleasant touching by Mr. Science. Even when the children were prompted to provide more information about their experiences, they continued to report false events. Poole and Lindsay concluded that because children's credibility as eyewitnesses depends on their ability to distinguish their memories from other sources, interviewers will have to develop better procedures to help them do so.

Since the publication of Poole and Lindsay's study, other scholars have attempted to identify ways that children struggle to differentiate between fact and fiction under certain circumstances. For example, Lucy Akehurst, Natalie Burden, and Jane Buckle examine in "Effect of Socially Encountered Misinformation and Delay on Children's Eyewitness Testimony" (*Psychiatry, Psychology and Law*, vol. 16, suppl. 1, March 2009) the effects of misinformation and suggestibility on the ability of children aged nine to 11 years to recount events. The researchers report that children in that age group proved far more susceptible to suggestibility when misinformation was shared in a social situation by a fellow witness, than when the same misinformation was presented in a written narrative. Furthermore, Akehurst, Burden, and Buckle reveal that children who have been influenced by misinformation tend to exhibit fewer signs of suggestibility after the passage of several months. Scholars have also demonstrated that children are not merely susceptible to misinformation that is shared verbally or in writing. In "Handmade Memories: The Robustness of the Gestural Misinformation Effect in Children's Eyewitness Interviews" (*Journal of Nonverbal Behavior*, vol. 39, no. 3, September 2015), Elizabeth Kirk et al. observe that an interviewer's use of suggestive gestures during questioning can play a significant role in leading children into recapitulating misinformation, even immediately after an event has occurred.

Research also shows that susceptibility to suggestion can be conditioned by a child's sense of social identity. According to Kyla P. McDonald and Lili Ma, in "Preschoolers' Credulity toward Misinformation from Ingroup versus Outgroup Speakers" (*Journal of Experimental Child Psychology*, vol. 148, August 2016), four-year-olds are far more likely to believe misinformation when it is provided by someone with whom they share both common racial traits and a common speaking accent, than when it is provided by a representative of a different race who speaks in an unfamiliar accent. When the interviewer demonstrates either common racial traits or a common accent, but not both at the same time, four-year-olds show no particular likelihood of either credulity or skepticism when presented with misinformation. McDonald and Ma note that three-year-olds subjected to the same experiment show equal susceptibility to suggestion when presented with misinformation from both categories of the interviewer.

BEST INTERVIEWING TECHNIQUES. In "Toward a Better Way to Interview Child Victims of Sexual Abuse" (*NIJ Journal*, no. 267, Winter 2010), Sara Harris of Palladian Partners, Inc., notes that "in many child sexual abuse cases, there is no witness other than the child and no corroborating evidence—the entire case can hang on a child's recollection of the alleged abuse." The importance of obtaining reliable information from sexually abused children has prompted the development and testing of various interview protocols. Harris describes a protocol that was developed during the 1990s by the Eunice Kennedy Shriver National Institute of Child Health and Human Development (NICHD). This protocol organizes the interview process into several distinct phases, beginning with a rapport-building exercise before eventually moving toward the questioning phase. Generally speaking, the questioning is divided into a free-recall phase, during which the interviewer invites the child to recount a particular event from memory, and a direct-question phase, when the interviewer begins to solicit specific details about that event. Evidence shows that when compared with other protocols, the NICHD protocol elicits more information and information of greater

detail and accuracy. The U.S. Department of Justice's National Institute of Justice funded a study to assess the protocol's usefulness in a real-life situation. Researchers examined 1,280 child sexual abuse cases that were handled by the Salt Lake County, Utah, sheriff's office between 1994 and 2000. According to Harris, 551 of the interviews were conducted before the detectives were trained in the NICHD protocol, and 729 interviews were conducted using the protocol. The results indicate that more cases were accepted for prosecution after the protocol was implemented. In addition, prosecutors obtained a higher percentage of guilty verdicts in cases in which the protocol was used.

Wiley reviews the "best practices" for interviewing child victims of sexual abuse. According to Wiley, a single interview, rather than multiple interviews, is considered best for the child. Research also suggests that open-ended questions should be used as much as possible, to be followed up with specific questions when needed. Leading questions, complex questions, and intimidating techniques should be avoided. In contrast, other studies have concluded that multiple conversations with child sexual abuse victims can be more effective in helping interviewers create a more accurate and complete report. Carmit Katz and Irit Hershkowitz note in "Repeated Interviews with Children Who Are the Alleged Victims of Sexual Abuse" (*Research on Social Work Practice*, vol. 23, no. 2, March 2013) that research shows that repeated, open-ended questioning can provide investigators with evidence that would otherwise be unattainable in a single interview.

THE CONFRONTATION CLAUSE AND HEARSAY

The Sixth Amendment to the U.S. Constitution lays out the rights of people who are accused of crimes: "In all criminal prosecutions, the accused shall enjoy the right to a speedy and public trial, by an impartial jury of the state and district wherein the crime shall have been committed, which district shall have been previously ascertained by law, and to be informed of the nature and cause of the accusation; to be confronted with the witnesses against him; to have compulsory process for obtaining witnesses in his favor, and to have the assistance of counsel for his defense."

The so-called confrontation clause ("to be confronted with the witnesses against him") is a key consideration in the criminal prosecution of child abuse cases. It is particularly difficult for children to deal with the fear and intimidation of testifying in open court with their alleged abuser sitting in the room with them. In the past, live testimony of children in the courtroom was the only choice. However, video technologies developed during the 20th century have introduced new testimony options.

They have also raised issues of constitutionality that have been debated by the highest courts in the country.

Testimony by Closed-Circuit Television

Closed-circuit television (CCTV) is a system in which video is transmitted only to specific television monitors. Hence, the system is "closed" or limited to only certain participants. During trials, the use of CCTV allows witnesses to testify live from locations other than the courtroom. One-way CCTV systems only include television monitors in the courtroom, whereas two-way systems also include a television monitor at the witness's location. In other words, in a two-way CCTV setup the witness can see live what is happening in the courtroom.

In 1990 the U.S. Supreme Court upheld in *Maryland v. Craig* (497 U.S. 836) the use of one-way CCTV in a case where a six-year-old child had to testify against her prekindergarten teacher, Sandra Craig, who had been charged with sexual assault and battery. Justice Sandra Day O'Connor (1930–) noted in the majority opinion that the Sixth Amendment confrontation clause does not guarantee an "absolute" right to a face-to-face meeting with the witness. A CCTV system does permit cross-examination and observation of the witness's demeanor by those in the courtroom, including the defendant. Justice O'Connor declared, "We are therefore confident that use of the one-way closed-circuit television procedure, where necessary to further an important state interest, does not impinge upon the truth-seeking or symbolic purposes of the Confrontation Clause."

The National Center for Prosecution of Child Abuse (NCPCA) is a project of the National District Attorneys Association. District attorneys (or prosecutors as they are commonly called) prosecute cases on behalf of the government against defendants who are accused of criminal offenses. The NCPCA summarizes in *Closed-Circuit Televisions Statutes* (August 2012, http://www.ndaa.org/pdf/CCTV%20(2012).pdf) state statutes that deal with the use of CCTV testimony instead of in-court testimony for children. The conditions under which children testify and the age under which they are allowed vary considerably. In some states the jury stays in the courtroom while the child, the judge, the prosecutor, the defendant, and the defense attorney are in a different room, whereas in other states the child is alone in a room separate from the jury and other participants. Some states only allow the youngest children to testify via CCTV.

Hearsay

Another component of the confrontation clause is the issue of hearsay. In legal terminology, hearsay evidence is evidence other than the live testimony in the courtroom of a witness who is swearing to the truth of what he or she saw, heard, or otherwise experienced. As noted earlier, CCTV testimony is not considered hearsay evidence because of the U.S. Supreme Court's decision in *Maryland v. Craig*. However, there are many other kinds of evidence that may be considered hearsay. For example, a statement that a victim made to police, doctors, or other people after being victimized could be considered hearsay evidence if the original recipient of that statement cannot testify in court. Issues related to the admissibility of hearsay evidence are very controversial and have been the subject of many court cases.

Article VIII, Hearsay, of the Federal Rules of Evidence (2016, http://www.law.cornell.edu/rules/fre/rule_802) defines what constitutes hearsay evidence and includes the rule against hearsay (i.e., the hearsay rule), which simply states: "Hearsay is not admissible unless any of the following provides otherwise: a federal statute; these rules; or other rules prescribed by the Supreme Court." Hearsay law is constantly evolving and has elicited some confusing opinions from the courts, including the U.S. Supreme Court.

The hearsay rule is intended to prevent the conviction of defendants by reports of evidence offered by someone other than a witness. With a few exceptions, hearsay is inadmissible as testimony because the actual witness cannot be cross-examined and his or her demeanor cannot be assessed for credibility of testimony. Some courts consider spontaneous declarations or excited utterances made by a person right after a stressful experience as reliable hearsay. Courts also typically allow statements that individuals have made to physicians and other medical personnel for purposes of medical treatment or diagnosis. In this case it is generally assumed that people who consult with a physician are seeking treatment and, therefore, tell the physician the truth about their illness.

Hearsay Issues in Child Sexual Abuse Cases

Hearsay evidence is especially important in cases of child sexual abuse because these cases may rely on evidence such as videotaped out-of-court testimony and statements by child victims to physicians, parents, counselors, and other adults in the aftermath of an assault. In addition, cases can take years to come to trial, by which time a child may have forgotten the details of the abuse.

Videotaping children's statements is widely practiced in child abuse cases for several reasons. It limits the number of interviews the child must undergo. This is important because recounting abusive events can be highly traumatic. Also, a videotaped statement can be a powerful tool to deal with the problem of a child who recants his or her testimony when put on the witness stand. The case can still be prosecuted, with the jury witnessing the child's opposing statements. Some experts believe that a videotaped statement containing sufficient details from the child and elicited through nonleading questions makes for compelling evidence.

Whether to accept the hearsay evidence from a child's reports of abuse to a parent or other person has been frequently debated, as has the constitutionality of videotaped statements by children alleging abuse.

OHIO V. ROBERTS. In *Ohio v. Roberts* (448 U.S. 56 [1980]), a case that was not about child abuse, the U.S. Supreme Court established the basis for permitting hearsay evidence: the actual witness has to be unavailable and his or her statement has to be reliable enough to permit another person to repeat it to the jury. Many judges have chosen to interpret unavailability on physical standards rather than on the emotional unavailability that children who are afraid to testify may exhibit. Furthermore, legal experts insist that the reliability of a statement does not refer to whether the statement appears to be truthful, but only that it has sufficient reliability for the jury to decide whether it is true.

After *Ohio v. Roberts*, many courts decided that spontaneous statements by child abuse victims, especially victims of sexual assault, fulfilled the hearsay requirements. In *White v. Illinois* (502 U.S. 346 [1992]), the Supreme Court found that a four-year-old girl's statements to her babysitter, her mother, a police officer, an emergency department nurse, and a doctor fulfilled the hearsay requirements because they were all either spontaneous declarations or made for medical treatment. In *Bugh v. Mitchell* (329 F.3d 496 [2003]), the U.S. Court of Appeals for the Sixth Circuit ruled that a child's statements to her mother, a counselor, a county social services supervisor, and a doctor about sexual abuse by her father were admissible as hearsay evidence because a three-year-old would have limited ability to lie about the circumstances of an attack. However, in *Carpenter v. State* (786 N.E.2d 696 [2003]) the Indiana Supreme Court decided that out-of-court statements made by a three-year-old who had been sexually assaulted by her father to her mother and grandfather were inadmissible because the state could not establish the precise time of alleged molestation or whether the child's statements occurred immediately after the alleged molestation.

CRAWFORD V. WASHINGTON OVERRULES OHIO V. ROBERTS. In *Crawford v. Washington* (541 U.S. 36 [2004]), the U.S. Supreme Court overturned its ruling in *Ohio v. Roberts*. *Crawford v. Washington* concerned an out-of-court tape-recorded statement that a woman had made to police that seemed to implicate her husband in an assault of another man. Prosecutors could not force the woman to testify in court about the statement because most state laws prohibit one spouse from testifying against the other without the other's consent. The trial court found the wife's statement to be reliable and trustworthy and accepted it as evidence. Her husband was subsequently convicted of the crime. During the appeals process the U.S. Supreme Court agreed to hear the case to determine whether the state's use of the wife's statement violated the confrontation clause of the Sixth Amendment.

The U.S. Supreme Court held that when a hearsay statement is "testimonial," the confrontation clause bars the state from using that statement against a criminal defendant unless the person who made the statement is available to testify at trial or the defendant had a previous opportunity to cross-examine that person. The court did not, however, define what it meant by a "testimonial" statement, which precipitated more legal wrangling. In addition, some convictions that had been obtained based on hearsay evidence were overturned, including several child sexual abuse cases. According to Erin Thompson, in "Child Sex Abuse Victims: How Will Their Stories Be Heard after *Crawford v. Washington?*" (*Campbell Law Review*, vol. 27, no. 2, Spring 2005), convictions in *People v. Espinoza* (No. H026266, 204 WL 1560376, at 1 [Cal. App. 6 July 13, 2004]), *People v. Vigil* (104 P.3d 258, 261 [Colo. Ct. App. 2004]), *In the Interest of R.A.S.* (No. 03CA12092004 WL 1351383, at 1 [Colo. App. June 17, 2004]), and *Snowden v. State* (156 Md. App. 139; 846 A.2d 36, 42 [Md. Ct. App. 2004]) were all overturned because the perpetrators had been convicted based on videotaped testimony, with no opportunity for cross-examination of the child witnesses.

In 2006 the U.S. Supreme Court provided some guidance on what does and does not constitute "testimonial" evidence in its decisions in two cases: *Davis v. Washington* (547 U.S. 813) and *Hammon v. Indiana* (No. 05-5705). The court refused to provide an exhaustive list of testimonial and nontestimonial statements, but it did note in *Davis v. Washington* that "statements are nontestimonial when made in the course of police interrogation under circumstances objectively indicating that the primary purpose of interrogation is to enable police assistance to meet an ongoing emergency. They are testimonial when the circumstances objectively indicate that there is no such ongoing emergency, and that the primary purpose of the interrogation is to establish or prove past events potentially relevant to later criminal prosecution."

With this guidance, prosecutors have been left with the challenge of trying to ensure that any videotaped victim or witness statements introduced in child sexual abuse trials are either nontestimonial in nature or otherwise exempt from the hearsay rule.

STATUTE OF LIMITATIONS AND RECOVERED MEMORY

A statute of limitations is a law that sets the time within which criminal charges or civil claims can be filed and after which a victim loses the right to do so. State laws differ dramatically in their time limits regarding child sexual abuse claims and differentiate between criminal and civil claims. Most states allow delayed commencement dates for the time window during which cases of child sexual abuse can be prosecuted. In these cases, the clock for the statute of limitations does not begin ticking until the child reaches a prescribed age, such as 18 years. This distinction is important because it allows adults who were abused as children to bring cases against their alleged abusers years later.

In *Statutes of Limitation for Prosecution of Offenses against Children* (August 2012, http://www.ndaa.org/pdf/ Statute%20of%20Limitations%20for%20Prosecution%20of %20Offenses%20Against%20Children%202012.pdf), the NCPCA summarizes state criminal statutes that deal with statutes of limitation in crimes involving child victims. The provisions can be quite complex and depend on various factors, including the severity of the crime. For example, Maryland has no statute of limitations for felonies, a category into which most sexual offenses would fall. Thus, sexual abuse cases alleged to have occurred many decades ago can still be prosecuted in criminal court.

The National Center for Victims of Crime provides in *Statutes of Limitation for Sexual Assault* (August 21, 2013, https://victimsofcrime.org/docs/DNA%20Resource %20Center/sol-for-sexual-assault-check-chart---final--- copy.pdf?sfvrsn=2) a state-by-state listing of civil statutes of limitations that are relevant to child sexual abuse.

Repressed Memory Controversy

States delay the start of their statute of limitations window for cases involving child abuse because the thinking is that adults may have lacked the will to act when they were minors, perhaps out of fear of their abusers or because they did not understand the seriousness and criminal nature of what was being done to them. Increasingly, the courts are being asked to grant exceptions to statute of limitations time ranges by people who claim they were abused as children and then repressed the memories for many years before recovering them. This contention is extremely controversial both within the field of psychology and in the courts.

RESEARCHERS DISAGREE. During the late 1800s the Austrian psychoanalyst Sigmund Freud (1856–1939) first proposed the theory of repression, which hypothesizes that the mind can reject unpleasant ideas, desires, and memories by banishing them into the unconscious. Some clinicians believe that dissociative amnesia, as it is called, can occur through memory repression, thus allowing a victim of a traumatic experience, such as childhood sexual abuse, to forget the horrible incident. Some also believe that forgotten traumatic experiences can be eventually recovered.

Other memory researchers do not agree, explaining that children who have suffered serious psychological trauma do not repress the memory; rather, they can never forget it. They cite examples of survivors of World War II (1939–1945) concentration camps or children who have witnessed the murder of a parent who never forget. Their explanation for recovered memories is that the memories are inaccurate. These researchers point to studies that demonstrate that memory is unreliable and that it can be manipulated to "remember" events that never happened.

In the middle of this controversy are clinicians and memory researchers who believe that the workings of the mind have yet to be fully understood. They agree that, while it is possible for a trauma victim to forget and then remember a horrible experience, it is also possible for a person to have false memories.

COURT FINDINGS. From a legal standpoint, the scientific validity of repressed memory is important because recovered memories may serve as the impetus for an alleged victim's pursuit of criminal and/or civil charges against an accused abuser.

According to Anita Lipton, in "Recovered Memories in the Courts" (Sheila Taub, ed., *Recovered Memories of Child Sexual Abuse: Psychological, Social, and Legal Perspectives on a Contemporary Mental Health Controversy*, 1999), between 1983 and 1998 many individuals who had recovered memories of childhood sexual abuse sued their alleged abusers. During those years a total of 589 lawsuits based on repressed memory were filed, of which 506 were civil and 83 were criminal.

In 1991 Paula Hearndon sued her stepfather, Kenneth Graham, for sexually abusing her from 1968 to 1975 (when she was between the ages of eight and 15). According to Hearndon, the "traumatic amnesia" she experienced because of the abuse lasted until 1988. Because of Florida's four-year statute of limitations on felonies, the lawsuit did not proceed. However, in *Hearndon v. Graham* (767 So. 2d 1179, 1184 [2000]), the Florida Supreme Court ruled 5–2 that memory loss resulting from the trauma of childhood sexual abuse should be considered an exception to the statute of limitations. While observing that disagreements about recovered memory exist, the court stated, "It is widely recognized that the shock and confusion resultant from childhood molestation, often coupled with authoritative adult demands and threats for secrecy, may lead a child to deny or suppress such abuse from his or her consciousness."

The admissibility of child sexual abuse claims based on recovered memories varies by state. For example, the NCPCA cites in *Statutes of Limitation for Prosecution of Offenses against Children* the following statement from the Delaware criminal code: "No prosecution under this subsection shall be based upon the memory of the victim that has been recovered through psychotherapy unless there is some evidence of the corpus delicti [essence of the crime] independent of such repressed memory." By contrast, the NCPCA notes that Kansas law allows extension of its statute of limitations in cases of repressed memory, but only under certain conditions and when "there is substantially competent expert testimony indicating the victim psychologically repressed such witness' memory of the fact of the crime, and in the expert's professional opinion the recall of such memory is accurate and free of undue manipulation, and substantial corroborating evidence can be produced in support of the allegations contained in the complaint or information."

In "Repressed Memories in a Controversial Conviction" (*Journal of the American Academy of Psychiatry and the Law*, vol. 38, no. 4, December 2010), Anthony J. Wolf and Melvin J. Guyer relate a case brought to trial in 2005 in Massachusetts that centered around the recovered memories of a young adult, who testified that he was sexually abused as a boy during the late 1980s by a priest at his church school. The victim said he recovered memories of the abuse after learning that the priest had been accused of sexually abusing children. The victim was part of a successful civil lawsuit against the archdiocese of Boston over the alleged abuse and obtained $500,000 in the settlement. He then pursued criminal charges against the priest, who was convicted in 2005 of two counts of sexual abuse of a child. The defense appealed the case to the Massachusetts Supreme Court, which upheld the conviction in 2010 in *Commonwealth v. Shanley* (455 Mass. 752).

In 2012 the Minnesota Supreme Court sided with a lower court in ruling that a man who claimed to have recovered memories of being abused as a child could not get an extension of the state's statute of limitations. The article "Minnesota Supreme Court Rejects Church Abuse Case Based on Repressed Memories" (Associated Press, July 26, 2012) indicates the plaintiff filed his original claim in 2006, but it was rejected because it was "well outside the state's six-year statute of limitations." According to the article, the higher court agreed with the lower court's finding that "studies claiming to have proven the existence of repressed memory 'lacked foundational reliability.'"

LEGAL PROTECTIONS FOR CHILDREN
Child Pornography

Although the First Amendment protects pornography as an expression of free speech, it does not protect child pornography. Child pornography has been banned since 1982, when the U.S. Supreme Court ruled in *New York v. Ferber* (458 U.S. 747) that pornography depicting children engaged in sexually explicit acts can be banned, whether or not it is obscene, because of the state's interest in protecting children from sexual exploitation. In other words, such images are not protected by the First Amendment.

Since the Supreme Court's decision, federal and state legislators have strived to pass child pornography laws that can withstand constitutional challenges. As of September 2016, several federal laws applied, including 18 USC Chapter 110, Sexual Exploitation and Other Abuse of Children (http://www.law.cornell.edu/uscode/text/18/part-I/chapter-110) and 18 USC Chapter 71, Obscenity, particularly Section 1466A, Obscene Visual Representations of the Sexual Abuse of Children (http://www.law.cornell.edu/uscode/text/18/1466A). Child pornography laws specifically targeting online activities include 47 USC Section 231, Restriction of Access by Minors to Materials Commercially Distributed by Means of World Wide Web That Are Harmful to Minors (http://www.law.cornell.edu/uscode/text/47/231) and 47 USC Section 254, Universal Service (http://www.law.cornell.edu/uscode/text/47/254).

Federal agencies regularly conduct widespread sting operations in which dozens of people are arrested for child pornography offenses. In late 2012 U.S. Immigration and Customs Enforcement led Operation Sunflower, which netted more than 240 alleged perpetrators. Carol Cratty reports in "245 Arrested in U.S.-Led Child Sex Abuse Operation" (CNN.com, January 4, 2013) that authorities identified 123 victims and removed 44 children who were living with accused abusers. Most of the victims (110) lived in the United States, and the vast majority (222) of the people arrested were apprehended in the United States. Another major child pornography ring was uncovered in April 2016, when the U.S. Department of Homeland Security collaborated with Canadian law enforcement to arrest 80 perpetrators in Ontario, Canada. In "80 Arrested, 274 Charges Laid in Massive Ontario-wide Child Porn Bust" (GlobalNews.ca, April 28, 2016), David Shum notes that one of the individuals charged in the case, Steven Campbell, worked as a teacher at a day care center at the time of his arrest. According to Shum, 80% of the pornographic images discovered in the investigation involved children under the age of 12.

Ending the "Incest Exception"

As is described in Chapter 4, incest is a crime involving sexual activities between close relatives. Critics claim that in some states people who sexually abuse children receive penalties that are too light because they are prosecuted under incest laws rather than under child sexual abuse laws. Andrew Vachss is an advisory board member of the National Association to Protect Children, a nonprofit organization devoted to child protection issues. In the editorial "The Incest Loophole" (NYTimes.com,

November 20, 2005), Vachss notes that incest laws were "founded on biblical prohibitions and intended to prevent the conception of genetically impaired children." In other words, the laws were intended to keep adult close relatives (such as first cousins) from procreating.

Many of these laws have been on the books for more than a century and feature relatively lenient penalties for violations. A problem arises when people accused of sexually abusing biological relatives (such as their own children) are prosecuted under incest laws rather than under much tougher sexual abuse laws. According to the National Association to Protect Children, in "PROTECT Legislative Victories" (2016, http://www.protect.org/articles/our-victories), the organization has helped eliminate or reform the incest loophole in Arkansas, California, Illinois, and North Carolina. Under Arkansas's old incest laws, an adult who raped a child in his or her own family was considered guilty of incest and was either fined or given probation. In 2006 California repealed its incest exception law of 1981, which had allowed judges to grant a sentence of probation to men and women convicted of sexually abusing family members. In Illinois the laws had been deliberately revised in 1981 with a view to keeping families together by imposing a punishment of probation or two years of counseling rather than jail time for incestuous offenders. North Carolina's incest law had been on the books since 1879. Under the law, a father who raped his child was found guilty of a minor felony, which was punishable by probation, and an uncle who raped his niece was required to perform 45 days of community service for the misdemeanor offense of incest.

Prenatal Drug Exposure

In 1997 the South Carolina Supreme Court held in *Whitner v. South Carolina* (328 S.C. 1, 492 S.E.2d 777) that pregnant women who use drugs can be criminally prosecuted for child maltreatment. The court found that a viable fetus (potentially capable of surviving outside the womb) is a person covered by the state's child abuse and neglect laws. Cornelia Whitner's newborn tested positive for cocaine. She was prosecuted, pled guilty to child neglect, and was sentenced to eight years in prison in 1992. Whitner appealed the ruling to the South Carolina Supreme Court. The supreme court upheld the conviction, which was the first time the highest court of any state upheld the criminal conviction of a woman charged with such an offense.

Whitner's lawyer had argued that if a woman could be prosecuted for child abuse for having used drugs while pregnant, what was to keep the law from prosecuting her for smoking or drinking alcohol or even for failing to obtain prenatal care? Other critics of the law argued that women who are substance abusers and who fear prosecution might not seek prenatal care and counseling for their drug problems, which would further endanger the child.

In another South Carolina case Regina McKnight, a crack cocaine addict, was arrested in 1999 after giving birth to a stillborn infant (dead at birth). In 2001 she was convicted of homicide by child abuse and was sentenced to 12 years in prison. The jury found her guilty of killing a viable fetus, which is considered to be a child under South Carolina law. In January 2003 the South Carolina Supreme Court ruled in *State v. McKnight* (No. 25585) against McKnight. The court pointed out that the state legislature amended the homicide by child abuse statute in 2000, about three years after the court held in *Whitner v. South Carolina* that the term *child* includes a viable fetus. The court added, "The fact that the legislature was well aware of this Court's opinion in *Whitner*, yet failed to omit 'viable fetus' from the statute's applicability, is persuasive evidence that the legislature did not intend to exempt fetuses from the statute's operation." In October 2003 the U.S. Supreme Court refused to hear McKnight's case.

According to the Children's Bureau, in *Parental Drug Use as Child Abuse* (April 2015, https://www.childwelfare.gov/systemwide/laws_policies/statutes/drugexposed.pdf), the Child Abuse Prevention and Treatment Act of 2010 requires that all states have policies and procedures that ensure that CPS agencies are notified of substance-exposed newborns. In addition, the law requires that all states establish "a plan of safe care" for substance-exposed newborns. The Children's Bureau notes that as of April 2015 at least 19 states and the District of Columbia had substance-exposed-newborns reporting procedures in place. Furthermore, 14 states and the District of Columbia included prenatal substance exposure in their definitions of child abuse and neglect.

Critics complain that subjecting the mothers of newborns to civil and criminal penalties discourages them from seeking treatment for drug and alcohol problems during pregnancy. Jeanne Flavin and Lynn M. Paltrow highlight in "Punishing Pregnant Drug-Using Women: Defying Law, Medicine, and Common Sense" (*Journal of Addictive Diseases*, vol. 29, no. 2, April 2010) the "inherent unfairness of a system that expects low-income and drug-dependent pregnant women to provide their fetuses with the health care and safety that these women themselves are not provided and have not been guaranteed." The researchers surmise that "the arrests, detentions, prosecutions, and other legal actions taken against drug-dependent pregnant women distract attention from significant social problems, such as our lack of universal health care, the dearth of policies to support pregnant and parenting women, the absence of social supports for children, and the overall failure of the drug war."

CHAPTER 6

THE PREVALENCE OF DOMESTIC VIOLENCE

As is described in Chapter 1, there is no single legal definition of domestic violence. One factor is the scope of victim-offender relationships that are included in varying definitions. Some analysts count only cases that involve current and former intimate partners (i.e., spouses, girlfriends, and boyfriends), whereas other analysts also include cases that involve violence between relatives (other than spouses) and cases between nonintimate and nonfamily household cohabitants (e.g., roommates). This makes it difficult to compare domestic violence prevalence data that are collected from different studies. Another complication is the definition of violence itself. Some analysts consider only physical acts, such as assaults, as domestic violence incidents, whereas others also count threats. Thus, readers of publications that present domestic violence prevalence data should take note of the definitions and terms that are used by the authors.

Because many domestic violence cases may go unreported, it is impossible to be certain exactly how many cases occur each year. Variations in definitions, the types of questions posed by researchers, and the context in which they are asked compound the difficulty. For example, when victims are questioned in the presence of their abuser or other family members, they may be more reluctant to report instances of violence. Thus, studies on the prevalence of domestic violence can present statistics that differ widely. Many researchers fear that available data represent only a fraction of a problem of much larger proportions.

NATIONAL CRIME VICTIMIZATION SURVEY

The Bureau of Justice Statistics (BJS) is an agency within the U.S. Department of Justice. Since 1972 the BJS has overseen an annual survey called the National Crime Victimization Survey (NCVS), in which the U.S. Census Bureau surveys a nationally representative sample of tens of thousands of households and asks people aged 12 years and older about their experiences within the previous six months of being victimized by certain crimes. The participants are asked both about victimizations they reported and those they did not report to authorities. Only incidents that occurred within the United States are counted. The sample values are used to calculate national victimization estimates using U.S. population data. The survey participants are asked to provide demographic information about themselves, such as their age, sex, race and ethnicity, education level, marital status, and income. The participants reporting victimization incidents are asked for certain details about the events, including information about the offenders.

Each year the BJS publishes the report *Criminal Victimization*, which summarizes the collected data. Other summary reports are occasionally released that examine victimization trends over time for specific types of crimes. In addition, the agency maintains a searchable database of historical NCVS results that can be accessed online using the NCVS Victimization Analysis Tool (http://www.bjs.gov/index.cfm?ty=nvat).

Terms and Definitions

Because the NCVS only covers victimizations in which the victims can be interviewed, murders are not included in the data set. In "NCVS Victimization Analysis Tool (NVAT): Definitions" (2016, http://www.bjs.gov/index.cfm?ty=nvat), the BJS notes that violent victimizations include rapes, sexual assaults, personal robberies, and assaults. Specific crimes in these categories are defined by the agency as follows:

- Aggravated assault—an attack or attempted attack with a weapon, regardless of whether the victim is injured, or an attack without a weapon when serious injury results.

- Rape—unlawful penetration of a person against the will of the victim, with use or threatened use of force, or attempting such an act. Includes psychological coercion and physical force. Forced sexual intercourse means vaginal, anal, or oral penetration by the offender. Also includes incidents where penetration is from a foreign object, such as a bottle. Includes male and female victims, and both heterosexual and homosexual rape. Attempted rape includes verbal threats of rape.

- Robbery—the unlawful taking or attempted taking of property that is in the immediate possession of another, by force or threat of force, with or without a weapon, and with or without injury.

- Sexual assault—a wide range of victimizations, separate from rape or attempted rape. These crimes include attacks or attempted attacks generally involving unwanted sexual contact between victim and offender. Sexual assaults may or may not involve force and include grabbing or fondling. Sexual assault also includes verbal threats.

- Simple assault—an attack or attempted attack without a weapon that results in either no injury, minor injury (e.g., bruises, black eyes, cuts, scratches, or swelling), or an undetermined injury requiring less than two days of hospitalization.

According to the BJS, neither interviewers nor victims classify victimizations as specific crimes during the interviews. However, the interviewers do ask detailed questions about the nature of each event. A computer program uses the victims' answers to classify the victimizations as particular crimes. For incidents that include more than one crime (e.g., robbery and rape), only the most serious crime is counted using the following hierarchy: rape, sexual assault, robbery, and assault.

The BJS considers domestic violence as violence involving intimate partners or family members. Concerning victim-offender relationships, the following specific terms are used:

- Intimate partners—spouses or ex-spouses, boyfriends or girlfriends, and ex-boyfriends or ex-girlfriends

- Other relatives—parents or stepparents, children or stepchildren, brothers or sisters, and other relatives

Violent Victimizations

Jennifer L. Truman and Lynn Langton of the BJS summarize in *Criminal Victimization, 2014* (August 2015, http://www.bjs.gov/content/pub/pdf/cv14.pdf) NCVS data for 2014. They note that approximately 158,090 people aged 12 years and older from 90,380 households across the country were interviewed during the survey.

Table 6.1 shows the number of total violent victimizations calculated for 2005, 2013, and 2014 based on separate surveys that were conducted in those years. Overall, Truman and Langton estimate that 5.4 million total violent victimizations occurred in 2014. Of these, 1.1 million (20.7%) were considered to be domestic violence. Violent intimate partner victimizations numbered

TABLE 6.1

Violent victimizations, by crime type, 2005, 2013, and 2014

Type of violent crime	Number			Rate per 1,000 persons age 12 or older		
	2005	2013	2014[a]	2005	2013	2014[a]
Violent crime[b]	**6,947,800**	**6,126,420**	**5,359,570**	**28.4**	**23.2**	**20.1**
Rape/sexual assault	207,760	300,170	284,350	0.8	1.1	1.1
Robbery	769,150	645,650	664,210	3.1	2.4	2.5
Assault	5,970,890	5,180,610	4,411,010	24.4	19.6	16.5
Aggravated assault	1,281,490	994,220	1,092,090	5.2	3.8	4.1
Simple assault	4,689,400	4,186,390	3,318,920	19.2	15.8	12.4
Domestic violence[c]	1,242,290	1,116,090	1,109,880	5.1	4.2	4.2
Intimate partner violence[d]	816,010	748,800	634,610	3.3	2.8	2.4
Stranger violence	2,829,600	2,098,170	2,166,130	11.6	7.9	8.1
Violent crime involving injury	1,759,210	1,603,960	1,375,950	7.2	6.1	5.2
Serious violent crime[e]	**2,258,400**	**1,940,030**	**2,040,650**	**9.2**	**7.3**	**7.7**
Serious domestic violence[c]	425,270	464,730	400,030	1.7	1.8	1.5
Serious intimate partner violence[d]	311,480	360,820	265,890	1.3	1.4	1.0
Serious stranger violence	1,096,480	737,940	930,690	4.5	2.8	3.5
Serious violent crime involving weapons	1,659,030	1,174,370	1,306,900	6.8	4.4	4.9
Serious violent crime involving injury	824,800	739,210	692,470	3.4	2.8	2.6

[a]Comparison year.
[b]Excludes homicide because the National Crime Victimization Survey (NCVS) is based on interviews with victims and therefore cannot measure murder.
[c]Includes victimization committed by intimate partners and family members.
[d]Includes victimization committed by current or former spouses, boyfriends, or girlfriends.
[e]In the NCVS, serious violent crime includes rape or sexual assault, robbery, and aggravated assault.
Note: Detail may not sum to total due to rounding. Total population age 12 or older was 244,505,300 in 2005; 264,411,700 in 2013; and 266,665,160 in 2014.

SOURCE: Jennifer L. Truman and Lynn Langton, "Table 1. Violent Victimization, by Type of Violent Crime, 2005, 2013, and 2014," in *Criminal Victimization, 2014*, U.S. Department of Justice, Office of Justice Programs, Bureau of Justice Statistics, August 2015, http://www.bjs.gov/content/pub/pdf/cv14.pdf (accessed June 10, 2016)

TABLE 6.2

Violent victimizations, by victim-offender relationship, 2010–14

Crime type	2010	2011	2012	2013	2014
Violent victimization	4,935,983	5,812,523	6,842,593	6,126,423	5,359,570
Intimates	773,434	850,772	810,794	748,795	634,610
Other relatives	356,129	504,135	448,598	367,291	475,265
Well-known/casual acquaintances	1,573,294	1,779,618	2,263,252	2,445,099	1,709,366
Stranger	1,812,303	2,146,307	2,710,114	2,098,170	2,166,129
Do not know relationship	288,667	240,956	371,910	288,795	223,847
Do not know number of offenders	132,156	290,736	228,660	178,273	150,351

Notes: Special tabulations from the NCVS Victimization Analysis Tool (NVAT). (NCVS is National Crime Victimization Survey.) Detail may not sum to total due to rounding and/or missing data.

SOURCE: "Number of Violent Victimizations by Victim-Offender Relationship, 2010–2014," in *NCVS Victimization Analysis Tool (NVAT)*, U.S. Department of Justice, Office of Justice Programs, Bureau of Justice Statistics, June 10, 2016, http://www.bjs.gov/index.cfm?ty=nvat (accessed June 10, 2016)

634,610 and accounted for 57.2% of the domestic violence victimizations and 11.8% of the total violent victimizations.

The BJS considers rape, sexual assault, robbery, and aggravated assault to be serious violent crimes. In 2013 there were more than 1.9 million total victimizations involving serious violent crimes; in 2014 the number of victimizations involving serious violent crimes rose to more than 2 million. (See Table 6.1.) However, among serious violent crimes, the number of those victimized by serious domestic violence decreased from 464,730 in 2013 to 400,030 in 2014, and serious intimate partner violence victimizations dropped from 360,820 in 2013 to 265,890 in 2014. In 2014 approximately two-thirds (66.4%) of the serious domestic violence victimizations were between intimate partners.

Table 6.2 provides a breakdown of victim-offender relationships for NCVS data between 2010 and 2014. Strangers committed the largest number (2.2 million) of violent victimizations in 2014 and made up more than 40% of the total. Well-known and casual acquaintances followed, with 1.7 million victimizations, or 31.8% of the total.

Jennifer L. Truman and Rachel E. Morgan of the BJS examine domestic violence trends in *Nonfatal Domestic Violence, 2003–2012* (April 2014, http://www.bjs.gov/content/pub/pdf/ndv0312.pdf), the most recent report on this topic as of September 2016. Table 6.3 shows domestic violence rates between 2003 and 2012. During this span, 5.6 out of 1,000 male and female individuals aged 12 years and older were victims of some form of domestic violence. Of these, 3.9 out of 1,000 individuals were involved in a domestic violence incident with an intimate partner, 1.1 out of 1,000 involved an immediate family member, and 0.6 out of 1,000 involved another relative. Among victims of intimate partner violence, 2.1 out of 1,000 individuals were victimized by a boyfriend or girlfriend, 1.3 out of 1,000 were victimized by a spouse, and 0.5 out of 1,000 were victimized by an ex-spouse.

TABLE 6.3

Rates of violent victimization, by degree of violence and victim-offender relationship, 2003–12

Victim-offender relationship	Total violent crime	Serious violent crime[a]	Simple assault
Domestic	5.6	2.0	3.6
Intimate partner[b]	3.9	1.4	2.5
Spouse	1.3	0.5	0.8
Ex-spouse	0.5	0.1	0.4
Boy/girlfriend	2.1	0.8	1.3
Immediate family	1.1	0.4	0.7
Parent	0.3	0.1	0.2
Child	0.4	0.1	0.3
Sibling	0.4	0.1	0.3
Other relative	0.6	0.2	0.4
Well-known/casual acquaintance	8.4	2.3	6.1
Stranger	10.2	3.7	6.5

[a]Includes rape or sexual assault, robbery, and aggravated assault.
[b]Includes current or former spouses, boyfriends, and girlfriends.
Note: Victimization rates are per 1,000 persons age 12 or older. In a small percentage of victimizations, the victim-offender relationship was unknown or the number of offenders was unknown. These estimates are not shown.

SOURCE: Jennifer L. Truman and Rachel E. Morgan, "Table 2. Rate of Violent Victimization, by Victim–Offender Relationship, 2003–2012," in *Nonfatal Domestic Violence, 2003–2012*, U.S. Department of Justice, Office of Justice Programs, Bureau of Justice Statistics, April 2014, http://www.bjs.gov/content/pub/pdf/ndv0312.pdf (accessed June 17, 2016)

Overall, rates of intimate partner violence dropped dramatically between 2003 and 2012, while rates of domestic violence perpetrated by immediate family members or by other relatives experienced much smaller declines during that span. (See Figure 6.1.) As Figure 6.2 shows, female victims were far more likely than male victims to suffer abuse by an intimate partner between 2003 and 2012.

As shown in Table 6.4, female victims of serious violence are far more likely to be victimized by people they know than by strangers. Between 2003 and 2012 more than one-third (37%) of serious violent crimes involving female victims were domestic violence incidents; more than a quarter (26.6%) involved an intimate partner. Overall, nearly two-thirds (65%) of female victims of serious violent crimes knew their assailants. By

FIGURE 6.1

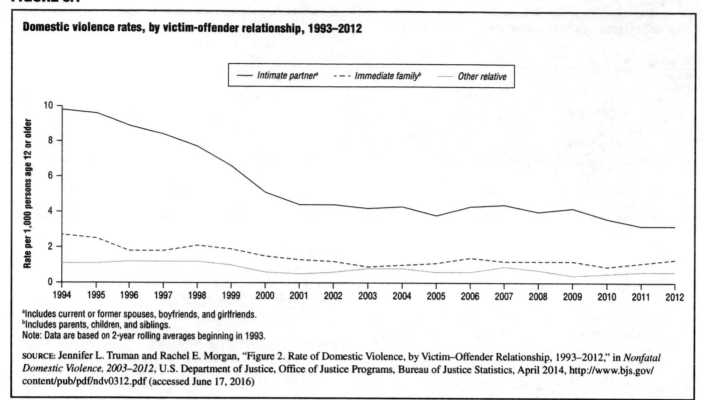

Domestic violence rates, by victim-offender relationship, 1993–2012

—— Intimate partner[a]   - - - Immediate family[b]   ······ Other relative

[a]Includes current or former spouses, boyfriends, and girlfriends.
[b]Includes parents, children, and siblings.
Note: Data are based on 2-year rolling averages beginning in 1993.

SOURCE: Jennifer L. Truman and Rachel E. Morgan, "Figure 2. Rate of Domestic Violence, by Victim–Offender Relationship, 1993–2012," in *Nonfatal Domestic Violence, 2003–2012*, U.S. Department of Justice, Office of Justice Programs, Bureau of Justice Statistics, April 2014, http://www.bjs.gov/content/pub/pdf/ndv0312.pdf (accessed June 17, 2016)

FIGURE 6.2

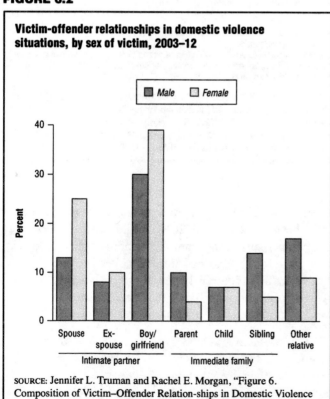

Victim-offender relationships in domestic violence situations, by sex of victim, 2003–12

■ Male   □ Female

SOURCE: Jennifer L. Truman and Rachel E. Morgan, "Figure 6. Composition of Victim–Offender Relation-ships in Domestic Violence Victimizations, by Victim's Sex, 2003–2012," in *Nonfatal Domestic Violence, 2003–2012*, U.S. Department of Justice, Office of Justice Programs, Bureau of Justice Statistics, April 2014, http://www.bjs.gov/content/pub/pdf/ndv0312.pdf (accessed June 17, 2016)

contrast, just over one-third (34.3%) of male victims were attacked by someone they knew.

Between 2003 and 2012 fewer than half (44.6%) of domestic violence victims were injured during a domestic dispute. (See Table 6.5.) This rate was slightly higher among victims of intimate partner violence. As Table 6.5 shows, 48.1% of intimate partner violence victims during this period sustained injuries. Of all domestic violence victims who suffered injuries between 2003 and 2012, more than one-third (36.6%) received medical treatment.

Of domestic violence incidents that occurred between 2003 and 2012, more than three-quarters (77%) took place at or near the victim's home; another 10.7% occurred at or near the home of a friend, neighbor, or relative, and 12.3% took place at some other location, such as a business, parking lot, school, or open area. (See Table 6.6.) By comparison, only about one out of five (19.7%) violent incidents involving strangers took place at or near the victim's home, and 75% took place at another location. As shown in Table 6.7, urban (6.9 per 1,000 population) and rural (6.7 per 1,000) individuals were more likely than those living in the suburbs (4.5 per 1,000) to have been a victim of domestic violence between 2003 and 2012 and were more likely to be victimized by an intimate partner, immediate family member, or acquaintance.

WEAPON USE. Table 6.8 provides a breakdown of weapon use during violent victimizations by intimate partners and other relatives between 2010 and 2014. In 2014 no weapon was used in 510,977 violent victimizations by intimate partners. This was 80.5% of the total 634,612 violent victimizations by intimate partners that year. A firearm was used in 17,831 of the victimizations, a knife in 34,220 of the victimizations, and another type of weapon in 60,826 of the victimizations. Overall, an identified weapon was used in 112,877 of the victimizations, or 17.8% of the total victimizations by intimate partners.

Trends in Intimate Partner Violence

As noted earlier, NCVS data indicate that in 2014 the majority (66.4%) of domestic violence victimizations involved intimate partners. In *Intimate Partner Violence: Attributes of Victimization, 1993–2011* (November 2013, http://www.bjs.gov/content/pub/pdf/ipvav9311.pdf), the most recent report on this topic as of September 2016, Shannan Catalano of the BJS uses NCVS data to describe trends between 1993 and 2011 in intimate partner victimizations via rape, sexual assault, robbery, aggravated assault, and simple assault.

Catalano observes an overall decrease in intimate partner violence between 1994 and 2011. Incidences of simple assault against female victims registered the biggest decline during this span, followed by incidences of serious violence against female victims. There were nearly 1.8 million female victims of intimate partner

TABLE 6.4

Percentage breakdown of violent victimizations, by degree of violence, victim's sex, and victim-offender relationship, 2003–12

Victim-offender relationship	Serious violent crime[a]		Simple assault	
	Male	Female	Male	Female
Total	100%	100%	100%	100%
Known	34.3%	65.0%	43.5%	68.7%
Domestic	10.0	37.0	9.4	33.6
Intimate partner[b]	5.8	26.6	4.5	25.3
Immediate family	2.7	6.5	3.2	5.4
Other relative	1.5	4.0	1.7	3.0
Well-known/casual acquaintance	24.3	28.0	34.1	35.1
Stranger	54.8%	28.6%	46.1%	25.4%
Average annual violent victimizations	1,151,980	1,042,090	2,382,070	2,047,370

[a]Includes rape or sexual assault, robbery, and aggravated assault.
[b]Includes current or former spouses, boyfriends, and girlfriends.
Note: Detail may not sum to total due to rounding. In a small percentage of victimizations, the victim-offender relationship was unknown or the number of offenders was unknown. These estimates are not shown.

SOURCE: Jennifer L. Truman and Rachel E. Morgan, "Table 3. Percent of Violent Victimization, by Victim–Offender Relationship and Victim's Sex, 2003–2012," in *Nonfatal Domestic Violence, 2003–2012*, U.S. Department of Justice, Office of Justice Programs, Bureau of Justice Statistics, April 2014, http://www.bjs.gov/content/pub/pdf/ndv0312.pdf (accessed June 17, 2016)

TABLE 6.5

Violent victimizations resulting in injury and medical treatment, by victim-offender relationship, types of injury, and treatment status, 2003–12

Type of injury and treatment	Domestic violence				Well-known/casual acquaintance	Stranger
	Total	Intimate partner[a]	Immediate family[b]	Other relative		
Injury	100%	100%	100%	100%	100%	100%
Not injured	55.4	51.9	62.6	63.5	78.3	78.7
Injured	44.6	48.1	37.4	36.5	21.7	21.3
Serious injuries[c]	8.9	11.1	4.1	4.2	3.8	4.4
Bruises or cuts	39.6	43.2	32.1	31.3	17.3	17.7
Other injuries	4.1	3.3	7.3	3.1	3.1	2.5
Treatment for injury[d]	100%	100%	100%	100%	100%	100%
No treatment	63.4	66.1	59.1	49.5	63.0	52.6
Any treatment	36.6	33.9	40.6	50.5	37.0	47.4
Treatment setting[e]	100%	100%	100%	100%	100%	100%
At the scene/home of victim, neighbor, or friend/other location	47.0	51.4	46.2	24.3	38.5	39.1
In doctor's office/hospital emergency room/overnight at hospital	53.0	48.6	53.8	75.7	61.5	60.9
Average annual violent victimizations	1,411,330	967,710	284,670	158,950	2,103,240	2,548,860

[a]Includes current or former spouses, boyfriends, and girlfriends.
[b]Includes parents, children, and siblings.
[c]Includes sexual violence injuries, gunshot wounds, knife wounds, internal injuries, unconsciousness, and broken bones.
[d]Includes only victims who were injured.
[e]Includes only victims who were injured and received treatment.
Note: Detail may not sum to total due to rounding. In a small percentage of victimizations, the victim-offender relationship was unknown or the number of offenders was unknown. These estimates are not shown.

SOURCE: Jennifer L. Truman and Rachel E. Morgan, "Table 6. Violent Victimization Resulting in Injury and Medical Treatment, by Victim–Offender Relationship, 2003–2012," in *Nonfatal Domestic Violence, 2003–2012*, U.S. Department of Justice, Office of Justice Programs, Bureau of Justice Statistics, April 2014, http://www.bjs.gov/content/pub/pdf/ndv0312.pdf (accessed June 17, 2016)

TABLE 6.6

Locations of violent victimizations, by victim-offender relationship, 2003–12

Location of crime	Domestic violence				Well-known/casual acquaintance	Stranger
	Total	Intimate partner[a]	Immediate family[b]	Other relative		
Total	100%	100%	100%	100%	100%	100%
At or near victim's home	77.0	78.6	77.7	66.0	29.5	19.7
At or near friend, neighbor, or relative's home	10.7	8.3	16.2	15.4	9.5	5.3
Other location[c]	12.3	13.1	6.2	18.6	61.0	75.0
Average annual violent victimizations	1,411,330	967,710	284,670	158,950	2,103,240	2,548,860

[a]Includes current or former spouses, boyfriends, and girlfriends.
[b]Includes parents, children, and siblings.
[c]Includes commercial places, parking lots or garages, schools, open areas, public transportation, and other locations.
Note: Detail may not sum to total due to rounding. In a small percentage of victimizations, the victim-offender relationship was unknown or the number of offenders was unknown. These estimates are not shown.

SOURCE: Jennifer L. Truman and Rachel E. Morgan, "Table 10. Location of Violent Victimization, by Victim–Offender Relationship, 2003–2012," in *Nonfatal Domestic Violence, 2003–2012*, U.S. Department of Justice, Office of Justice Programs, Bureau of Justice Statistics, April 2014, http://www.bjs.gov/content/pub/pdf/ndv0312.pdf (accessed June 17, 2016)

TABLE 6.7

Rates of violent victimizations, by setting and victim-offender relationship, 2003–12

Location of residence	Domestic violence				Well-known/casual acquaintance	Stranger
	Total	Intimate partner[a]	Immediate family[b]	Other relative		
Urban	6.9	5.1	1.2	0.6	8.8	14.2
Suburban	4.5	3.0	1.0	0.6	7.8	8.8
Rural	6.7	4.3	1.6	0.8	9.5	7.2

[a]Includes current or former spouses, boyfriends, and girlfriends.
[b]Includes parents, children, and siblings.
Note: Victimization rates are per 1,000 persons age 12 or older. In a small percentage of victimizations the victim-offender relationship was unknown or the number of offenders was unknown. These estimates are not shown.

SOURCE: Jennifer L. Truman and Rachel E. Morgan, "Table 12. Rate of Violent Victimization, by Household Location and Victim–Offender Relationship, 2003–2012," in *Nonfatal Domestic Violence, 2003–2012*, U.S. Department of Justice, Office of Justice Programs, Bureau of Justice Statistics, April 2014, http://www.bjs.gov/content/pub/pdf/ndv0312.pdf (accessed June 17, 2016)

violence in 1994, out of a total female population of 109.4 million in that age group. In other words, there were 16.1 female victims of intimate partner violence per 1,000 members of the population that year. By 2011 the number of female victims of intimate partner violence had fallen to 620,850 out of a total population of 131.2 million, or 4.7 out of 1,000 females 12 years of age or older. Although far fewer males become victims of intimate partner violence, the rate of male intimate partner violence victims also fell significantly between 1994 and 2011. Whereas three out of every 1,000 males aged 12 years and older were victims of intimate partner violence in 1994, by 2011 this proportion had fallen to 1.5 out of every 1,000.

Catalano also breaks down intimate partner violence into two categories: serious violence (which includes crimes such as rape and sexual assault, aggravated assault, and robbery) and simple assault. The rates of serious violence among female victims of intimate partner violence fell steadily between 1994, when there were 5.9 victims per 1,000 females aged 12 years and older,

and 2011, when there were 1.6 victims per 1,000 members of that population. Overall, this figure represents a decrease of nearly 370% over an 18-year period. For male intimate partner violence victims aged 12 years and older, the rate of serious violence also fell, from 1.1 per 1,000 individuals to 0.4 per 1,000. Among victims of both sexes, the rate of serious violence among victims of intimate partner violence aged 12 years and older fell from 3.6 per 1,000 individuals in 1993 to one per 1,000 in 2012. Rates of simple assault among victims of intimate partner violence also fell during this span, from 6.2 per 1,000 individuals in 1993 to 2.2 per 1,000 in 2012.

While the rate of serious incidents involving intimate partner violence clearly declined between 1994 and 2011, the proportion of intimate partner violence incidents that were categorized as acts of serious violence remained roughly constant. Catalano provides an overview of female victims of intimate partner violence between 1994 and 2011. Specifically, the proportion of female intimate partner violence victims who were victims of

TABLE 6.8

Violent victimizations, by type of violence, weapon use, and victim-offender relationship, 2010–14

Crime type	2010	2011	2012	2013	2014
Violent victimization	**4,935,983**	**5,812,523**	**6,842,593**	**6,126,423**	**5,359,570**
Intimates	**773,434**	**850,772**	**810,794**	**748,795**	**634,612**
No weapon	623,137	680,010	670,452	621,447	510,977
Firearm	75,669!	46,837	38,232	25,614!	17,831!
Knife	48,742	41,367	34,039	27,406!	34,220
Other type weapon	9,393!	39,969!	48,857!	54,323	60,826!
Type weapon unknown	10,802!	13,221!	11,468!	11,469!	6,392!
Do not know if offender had weapon	5,691!	29,368!	7,745!	8,535!	4,366!
Other relatives	**356,129**	**504,135**	**448,598**	**367,291**	**475,265**
No weapon	297,562	438,520	360,261	272,576	402,117
Firearm	9,709!	10,159!	—	8,052!	10,175!
Knife	15,399!	21,521!	57,474!	48,108!	24,433!
Other type weapon	20,015!	9,918!	26,513!	10,504!	31,605
Type weapon unknown	—	16,248!	—	3,924!	—
Do not know if offender had weapon	13,444!	7,768!	4,349!	24,127!	6,934!
Well-known/casual acquaintances	**1,573,294**	**1,779,618**	**2,263,252**	**2,445,099**	**1,709,366**
No weapon	1,273,099	1,465,315	1,842,368	2,021,057	1,335,869
Firearm	84,430	95,493	70,810	62,265!	52,499
Knife	72,817	85,920	83,082	96,945	149,548
Other type weapon	78,700	75,000	111,054	104,178	87,602
Type weapon unknown	16,866!	9,654!	35,538!	46,013	8,626!
Do not know if offender had weapon	47,382	48,236	120,400	114,641	75,223
Stranger	**1,812,303**	**2,146,307**	**2,710,114**	**2,098,170**	**2,166,129**
No weapon	1,069,015	1,319,518	1,608,556	1,321,121	1,176,131
Firearm	203,448	255,404	299,141	204,479	320,972
Knife	105,910	137,625	159,533	116,349	115,105
Other type weapon	180,725	152,224	232,515	157,625	229,188
Type weapon unknown	40,638!	26,797!	64,764	70,001	56,337
Do not know if offender had weapon	212,565	254,739	345,604	228,595	268,396
Do not know relationship	**288,667**	**240,956**	**371,910**	**288,795**	**223,847**
No weapon	201,207	167,474	282,846	209,335	143,076
Firearm	30,806	44,784	33,875!	29,261!	61,473!
Knife	20,090!	6,762!	6,424!	25,232!	2,292!
Other type weapon	11,955!	9,731!	21,316!	4,078!	9,033!
Type weapon unknown	6,084!	12,631!	6,637!	6,803!	3,398!
Do not know if offender had weapon	18,526!	9,575!	20,811!	14,086!	4,575!
Do not know number of offenders	**132,156**	**290,736**	**228,660**	**178,273**	**150,351**
No weapon	83,131	176,355	140,186	109,365	114,256
Firearm	10,941!	15,250!	18,659!	3,280!	3,163!
Knife	—	46,594!	—	7,098!	3,176!
Other type weapon	11,462!	11,143!	13,888!	5,762!	19,005!
Type weapon unknown	2,931!	10,168!	41,301!	45,601!	—
Do not know if offender had weapon	23,690!	31,225!	14,626!	7,166!	10,752!
Rape/sexual assault	**268,574**	**244,188**	**346,830**	**300,165**	**284,345**
Intimates	**109,205**	**44,155**	**64,412**	**107,860**	**70,110**
No weapon	63,818!	32,818	64,412	100,859	70,110
Firearm	43,747!	—	—	—	—
Knife	1,640!	—	—	3,281!	—
Other type weapon	—	2,925!	—	—	—
Do not know if offender had weapon	—	8,412!	—	3,720!	—
Other relatives	**12,921!**	**1,721!**	**3,458!**	**1,936!**	**2,909!**
No Weapon	12,921!	1,721!	3,458!	1,936!	2,909!
Well-known/casual acquaintances	**97,817**	**117,760**	**162,288**	**120,927**	**126,649**
No weapon	83,889	104,002	103,856	120,927	126,649
Firearm	7,328!	—	2,508!	—	—
Knife	2,895!	—	12,297!	—	—
Other type weapon	—	2,891!	38,761!	—	—
Do not know if offender had weapon	3,705!	10,866!	4,866!	—	—
Stranger	**43,167**	**72,807**	**59,126**	**57,136**	**69,054**
No weapon	25,566!	61,719	42,687	30,942!	34,562
Firearm	3,224!	2,609!	—	2,866!	4,531!
Knife	—	—	—	6,035!	—
Other type weapon	—	—	—	—	1,489!
Type weapon unknown	2,044!	—	—	—	—
Do not know if offender had weapon	12,333!	8,478!	16,439!	17,293!	28,472!

TABLE 6.8

Violent victimizations, by type of violence, weapon use, and victim-offender relationship, 2010–14 [CONTINUED]

Crime type	2010	2011	2012	2013	2014
Do not know relationship	**5,464!**	**4,835!**	**17,174!**	**9,305!**	**8,812!**
No weapon	—	4,835!	11,028!	7,702!	8,812!
Firearm	2,073!	—	—	—	—
Knife	—	—	3,317!	—	—
Type weapon unknown	3,391!	—	—	—	—
Do not know if offender had weapon	—	—	2,829!	1,603!	—
Do not know number of offenders	**—**	**2,911!**	**40,372!**	**3,000!**	**6,812!**
No weapon	—	2,911!	2,154!	3,000!	3,636!
Knife	—	—	—	—	3,176!
Type weapon unknown	—	—	38,218!	—	—
Robbery	**568,510**	**557,258**	**741,756**	**645,645**	**664,211**
Intimates	**58,642**	**56,876**	**80,712**	**112,621**	**71,347**
No weapon	43,983	37,128	58,621	99,838	54,596
Firearm	4,366!	3,657!	15,106!	3,723!	—
Knife	2,584!	6,781!	6,985!	4,882!	10,219!
Other type weapon	2,113!	—	—	4,177!	3,621!
Type weapon unknown	2,710!	1,482!	—	—	2,911!
Do not know if offender had weapon	2,886!	7,829!	—	—	—
Other relatives	**42,107!**	**57,801!**	**44,386**	**73,617**	**45,032**
No weapon	37,028!	40,351!	44,386	24,660!	38,047
Firearm	1,900!	—	—	6,270!	2,840!
Knife	—	—	—	35,961!	—
Other type weapon	—	—	—	—	4,146!
Type weapon unknown	—	14,836!	—	—	—
Do not know if offender had weapon	3,179!	2,615!	—	6,726!	—
Well-known/casual acquaintances	**117,023**	**105,243**	**94,606**	**142,313**	**194,805**
No weapon	75,593	61,082	30,824!	131,677	125,893
Firearm	2,874!	5,666!	25,954!	6,865!	12,481!
Knife	38,555!	23,617!	4,720!	—	51,125!
Other type weapon	—	4,169!	21,147!	—	5,306!
Type weapon unknown	—	—	—	3,771!	—
Do not know if offender had weapon	—	10,708!	11,961!	—	—
Stranger	**310,096**	**266,911**	**451,631**	**283,193**	**313,393**
No weapon	82,824	79,642	118,461	87,618	75,589
Firearm	117,978	91,629	145,598	77,757	114,022
Knife	35,199!	24,693!	76,111	46,604!	38,282
Other type weapon	8,088!	11,914!	26,637!	20,333!	32,905!
Type weapon unknown	10,583!	3,656!	14,683!	11,676!	6,334!
Do not know if offender had weapon	55,424	55,377	70,141	39,205	46,261
Do not know relationship	**40,642**	**58,156**	**47,842**	**20,855!**	**28,709!**
No weapon	6,622!	16,042!	13,440!	3,519!	20,650!
Firearm	13,521!	32,832!	22,158!	14,139!	8,059!
Knife	10,477!	2,098!	—	—	—
Other type weapon	—	—	5,079!	—	—
Type weapon unknown	—	2,165!	—	—	—
Do not know if offender had weapon	10,021!	5,019!	7,166!	3,197!	—
Do not know number of offenders	**—**	**12,271!**	**22,578!**	**13,046!**	**10,925!**
No weapon	—	—	10,902!	3,462!	1,926!
Firearm	—	9,335!	9,273!	—	—
Knife	—	2,935!	—	4,089!	—
Other type weapon	—	—	2,403!	—	5,339!
Type weapon unknown	—	—	—	2,283!	—
Do not know if offender had weapon	—	—	—	3,212!	3,660!
Aggravated Assault	**857,751**	**1,053,391**	**996,106**	**994,220**	**1,092,091**
Intimates	**100,933**	**161,627**	**125,115**	**140,336**	**124,430**
No weapon	13,488!	35,078!	14,610!	37,587!	21,913!
Firearm	27,555!	43,180	23,126!	21,891!	17,831!
Knife	44,518	34,586	27,054!	19,243!	24,001!
Other type weapon	7,281!	37,044!	48,857!	50,146	57,204!
Type weapon unknown	8,091!	11,739!	11,468!	11,469!	3,481!

serious violence fluctuated between 27.5% and 42% during this span. In 2011 more than one-third (34.8%) of female intimate partner violence victims suffered some act of serious violence.

FOCUS ON FEMALE VICTIMS. According to Catalano, between 2002 and 2011 two-thirds (66.6%) of female intimate partner violence victims were physically attacked by the offender; a comparable proportion of

TABLE 6.8

Violent victimizations, by type of violence, weapon use, and victim-offender relationship, 2010–14 [CONTINUED]

Crime type	2010	2011	2012	2013	2014
Other relatives	**56,223**	**46,858**	**92,992**	**28,357!**	**86,203**
No weapon	13,000!	3,847!	9,005!	—	26,975!
Firearm	7,809!	10,159!	—	1,782!	7,336!
Knife	15,399!	21,521!	57,474!	12,148!	24,433!
Other type weapon	20,015!	9,918!	26,513!	10,504!	27,459!
Type weapon unknown	—	1,412!		3,924!	
Well-known/casual acquaintances	**247,312**	**260,667**	**203,087**	**321,308**	**248,244**
No weapon	42,396	30,943!	7,990!	18,863!	18,881!
Firearm	74,229	89,827	42,348	55,400!	40,017
Knife	31,367!	62,303	66,064	96,945	98,423
Other type weapon	78,700	67,940	51,146	104,178	82,296
Type weapon unknown	16,866!	9,654!	35,538!	42,242!	8,626!
Do not know if offender had weapon	3,755!	—	—	3,680!	—
Stranger	**368,408**	**464,043**	**509,640**	**397,613**	**548,248**
No weapon	10,919!	22,056!	16,716!	14,430!	21,427!
Firearm	82,246	161,165	153,543	123,856	202,420
Knife	70,712	112,932	83,422	63,711	76,823
Other type weapon	172,637	140,310	205,878	137,292	194,795
Type weapon unknown	28,011!	23,141!	50,081	58,325!	50,003!
Do not know if offender had weapon	3,883!	4,439!	—	—	2,781!
Do not know relationship	**47,670**	**49,311**	**41,317**	**51,236**	**68,137!**
No weapon	4,418!	12,499!	3,618!	—	—
Firearm	15,211!	11,952!	11,717!	15,122!	53,414!
Knife	9,612!	4,664!	3,107!	25,232!	2,292!
Other type weapon	11,955!	9,731!	16,238!	4,078!	9,033!
Type weapon unknown	2,693!	10,466!	6,637!	6,803!	3,398!
Do not know if offender had weapon	3,781!	—	—	—	—
Do not know number of offenders	**37,205!**	**70,886**	**23,954!**	**55,369!**	**16,829!**
No weapon	3,166!	—	—	—	—
Firearm	10,941!	5,915!	9,387!	3,280!	3,163!
Knife	—	43,659!	—	3,010!	—
Other type weapon	11,462!	11,143!	11,485!	5,762!	13,666!
Type weapon unknown	2,931!	10,168!	3,083!	43,318!	—
Do not know if offender had weapon	8,704!	—	—	—	—
Simple assault	**3,241,148**	**3,957,686**	**4,757,902**	**4,186,394**	**3,318,923**
Intimates	**504,654**	**588,113**	**540,555**	**387,978**	**368,725**
No weapon	501,848	574,986	532,809	383,100	364,359
Do not know if offender had weapon	2,805!	13,127!	7,745!	4,815!	4,366!
Other relatives	**244,878**	**397,755**	**307,761**	**263,381**	**341,121**
No weapon	234,613	392,602	303,412	245,980	334,186
Do not know if offender had weapon	10,265!	5,154!	4,349!	17,401!	6,934!
Well-known/casual acquaintances	**1,111,143**	**1,295,949**	**1,803,271**	**1,860,551**	**1,139,669**
No weapon	1,071,221	1,269,288	1,699,697	1,749,590	1,064,446
Do not know if offender had weapon	39,922	26,661!	103,573	110,961	75,223
Stranger	**1,090,632**	**1,342,546**	**1,689,717**	**1,360,228**	**1,235,434**
No weapon	949,707	1,156,100	1,430,693	1,188,131	1,044,553
Do not know if offender had weapon	140,925	186,445	259,024	172,096	190,882
Do not know relationship	**194,890**	**128,654**	**265,577**	**207,399**	**118,189**
No weapon	190,167	124,099	254,761	198,114	113,614
Do not know if offender had weapon	4,724!	4,556!	10,817!	9,285!	4,575!
Do not know number of offenders	**94,952**	**204,669**	**141,756**	**106,857**	**115,785**
No weapon	79,965	173,444	127,130	102,903	108,693
Do not know if offender had weapon	14,986!	31,225!	14,626!	3,954!	7,092!

—Estimate is equal to 0 sample cases.
!Interpret data with caution, based on 10 or fewer sample cases or the coefficient of variation is greater than 50%.
Notes: Special tabulations from the NCVS Victimization Analysis Tool (NVAT). (NCVS is the National Crime Victimization Survey.) Detail may not sum to total due to rounding and/or missing data.

SOURCE: "Number of Violent Victimizations, Rape/Sexual Assaults, Robberies, Aggravated Assaults, and Simple Assaults by Victim-Offender Relationship and Weapon Category, 2010–2014," in *NCVS Victimization Analysis Tool (NVAT)*, U.S. Department of Justice, Office of Justice Programs, Bureau of Justice Statistics, June 10, 2016, http://www.bjs.gov/index.cfm?ty=nvat (accessed June 10, 2016)

male intimate partner violence victims (64.6%) also suffered physical attacks during this span. Female victims of intimate partner violence were far more likely to be threatened prior to a physical attack. More than half (51.8%) of female victims were threatened before being attacked by an intimate partner. By comparison, fewer than one-third (31.4%) of male victims of intimate part- ner violence were threatened prior to being physically attacked. In general, there is a strong correlation between being threatened and being physically attacked for female victims of intimate partner violence. Between 1994 and 2011 the percentage of female intimate partner violence victims who were physically attacked ranged from 60% to 72%, and the proportion of female victims who were threatened prior to a physical attack ranged between 39% and 63%.

Catalano also provides an overview of the types of physical attacks suffered by victims of intimate partner violence. Of the female victims of intimate partner vio- lence who were physically attacked between 2002 and 2011, 44.6% were struck, slapped, or knocked down; 36.1% were held, pushed, grabbed, tripped, or jumped; and 8.2% were sexually assaulted. Among male intimate partner violence victims who were physically attacked, 43.3% were hit, slapped, or knocked down, and 19.3% were struck by some sort of object. Less than 1% of male intimate partner violence victims who suffered physical attacks were sexually assaulted by their partner. Further- more, between 2002 and 2011 male victims of intimate partner violence (27%) were considerably more likely than female intimate partner violence victims (17.6%) to be victimized in a way that involved some sort of weapon.

In intimate partner violence situations, female vic- tims are more likely than male victims to suffer physical injury. Catalano notes that between 2002 and 2011 roughly half (49.7%) of female victims of intimate part- ner violence sustained injuries after being attacked; among male victims, 43.5% suffered injuries during this same period. Between 1994 and 2011 the proportion of female intimate partner violence victims who suffered injuries peaked between 2006 and 2007, when 60% of all female victims were physically injured. This rate fell in subsequent years, dropping to 42% in 2011.

According to Catalano, of the female victims who sustained physical injuries as a result of intimate partner violence between 2002 and 2011, nearly half (45.7%) suffered cuts, bruises, or other injuries, and 13% suffered serious injuries as a result of a physical attack. Between 2002 and 2011 nearly one out of five (18.2%) female victims of intimate partner violence received medical attention for injuries sustained in a physical attack; 8.3% received treatment at a hospital. By comparison, one out of 10 (10.8%) male victims of intimate partner violence received treatment for injuries during that span, with 4.4% receiving hospital care. Between 1994 and 2011 the proportion of female intimate partner victims who received medical treatment following an attack peaked in 2003, when more than a quarter (27%) received medical attention for their injuries.

The *NSCAW II Wave 3 Report: Wave 3 Tables* (June 2014, http://www.acf.hhs.gov/sites/default/files/opre/nscaw _wave_3_tables_june_2014_clean.pdf) by Cecilia Casa- nueva et al. is part of the second National Survey of Child and Adolescent Well-Being (NSCAW II), a longi- tudinal study (a study of the same group of people over time) created by the Office of Planning, Research, and Evaluation, a division of the Administration for Children and Families. NSCAW II is designed to provide a compre- hensive analysis of the efficacy and impact of the child welfare system. Casanueva et al. report that children who have become involved with the child welfare system often come from homes where domestic violence is prevalent. Table 6.9 provides an overview of NSCAW participants whose mothers demonstrated a need for domestic violence services between June 2011 and December 2012, when the Wave 3 data were collected. As Table 6.9 shows, 16.2% of all mothers involved in the study showed a need for social services related to domestic violence. African American mothers (19.8%) demonstrated the greatest need for these services, followed by Hispanic mothers (18.3%) and white mothers (13.5%).

NATIONAL INTIMATE PARTNER AND SEXUAL VIOLENCE SURVEY

The Centers for Disease Control and Prevention (CDC) is an agency within the U.S. Department of Health and Human Services. The CDC operates the National Center for Injury Prevention and Control, which is devoted to preventing violence and injuries. In 2010 the center, in collaboration with the Department of Justice's National Institute of Justice and the U.S. Department of Defense, conducted the National Intimate Partner and Sexual Violence Survey (NISVS), a com- prehensive survey that collected information from adults about their experiences of sexual violence, stalking, and intimate partner violence. The results are summarized by Michele C. Black et al. in *National Intimate Partner and Sexual Violence Survey: 2010 Summary Report* (November 2011, http://www.cdc.gov/ViolencePreven tion/pdf/NISVS_Report2010-a.pdf). This publication was the most comprehensive report on this topic as of September 2016.

According to Black et al., the survey was conducted by telephone using a nationally representative sample of 16,507 adults (9,086 women and 7,421 men) in the United States who were aged 18 years and older, spoke English and/or Spanish, and were not living in institu- tional settings such as prisons, military bases, nursing homes, or college dormitories. The researchers consid- ered intimate partners to be former or current "romantic or sexual partners." Intimate partners included couples who were cohabitating (living together) and not cohab- itating. In addition, opposite sex and same-sex couples were included.

TABLE 6.9

In-home mothers' need, referral to, and receipt of domestic violence services, by age and race and ethnicity, 2012

	Need for domestic violence services[a]	Referred to domestic violence services	Stayed in a shelter for battered women or received some other domestic violence services
	%	%	%
Total	16.2	3.8	1.3
Parent age (years)			
Under 20	9.2	3.0	0.0
20–29	17.3	3.0[b]	0.5
30–49	16.4	4.3[c]	1.7
50–59	6.0	0.8	0.6
60 and older	3.1	0.0	0.0
Parent race/ethnicity			
Black	19.8	3.6	1.3
White	13.5	4.0	1.2
Hispanic	18.3	2.8	1.2
Other	16.1	8.3	2.5

[a]Mothers were determined to be "in need of domestic violence services" if they met any one of three criteria: (1) caseworker report of a parent's need for domestic violence services at Wave 3, (2) a Conflicts Tactics Scale-2 (CTS-2) score indicating at least one incident of severe or less severe physical interpersonal violence suffered in the past 12 months, or (3) the mother's self-reported need ("a lot" or "somewhat") for domestic violence services in the past year, if she had not received any such services.
[b]Mothers 20 to 29 years old were significantly more likely to be referred for domestic violence services than mothers 50 to 59 years old.
[c]Mothers 30 to 49 years old were significantly more likely to be referred for domestic violence services than mothers 50 to 59 years old.
Note: The term "in-home mother" refers to the mothers of children living at home at Wave 3. Only permanent caregivers were asked about domestic violence services; responses here reflect only those of in-home mothers. Mothers who indicated that they had not ever received domestic violence services were included as not having received this service in the past 12 months. All analyses were on weighted NSCAW II Wave 3- data.

SOURCE: Adapted from Cecelia Casanueva et al., "Exhibit 22. In-Home Mothers' Need, Referral to, and Receipt of Domestic Violence Services in Past 12 Months (Wave 3)," in *NSCAW II Wave 3 Report: Wave 3 Tables*, U.S. Department of Health and Human Services, Administration for Children and Families, Office of Planning, Research, and Evaluation, June 5, 2014, http://www.acf.hhs.gov/sites/default/files/opre/nscaw_wave_3_tables_june_2014_clean.pdf (accessed June 17, 2016)

The NISVS provides a particularly comprehensive look at intimate partner violence because it covers not only physical and sexual violence but also other actions, such as psychological aggression, stalking, and control of reproductive or sexual health. Black et al. note that the survey included "a broad range of behaviorally specific questions to capture the full burden of physical, sexual, and psychological violence by an intimate partner, as well as stalking."

Terms and Definitions

The survey participants were asked about their lifetime experiences and previous 12-month experiences of being subjected to violent actions by their intimate partners. The assessed behaviors fell within five broad violence types:

- Sexual violence—rape (completed forced penetration, attempted penetration, and alcohol- or drug-facilitated completed penetration), being made to penetrate someone else, sexual coercion, unwanted sexual contact, and noncontact unwanted sexual experiences

- Physical violence—behaviors such as slapping, pushing, or shoving and being beaten, burned, or choked

- Psychological aggression—expressive aggression (such as name calling, insulting, or humiliating an intimate partner) and coercive control (behaviors intended to monitor and control or threaten an intimate partner)

- Stalking—a pattern of harassing or threatening tactics used by a perpetrator that is both unwanted and causes fear or safety concerns in the victim

- Control of reproductive or sexual health—behaviors such as refusing to wear a condom when requested to do so, trying to impregnate a partner who does not want to get pregnant, and trying to become pregnant by a partner who does not want a pregnancy to occur

In addition, survey participants provided demographic information about themselves and the intimate partners who acted violently against them. The participants were also asked detailed questions about the impacts on them of intimate partner violence and about the violent patterns of the perpetrators.

Rape, Physical Violence, and Stalking

As noted earlier, Black et al. define rape as including attempted and complete penetration. More specifically, the researchers provide the following examples of the actions that fall into this category for female and male victims:

- Female victims—unwanted vaginal, oral, or anal penetration through the use of threats of physical harm or through the use of physical force (such as being pinned or held down, or by the use of violence)

- Female victims—unwanted vaginal, oral, or anal penetration when the victims were drunk, high or otherwise drugged, or passed out and unable to consent

- Female victims—unwanted vaginal, oral, or anal penetration by a penis and unwanted vaginal or anal penetration by a male or female perpetrator using his or her fingers or an object

- Male victims—unwanted oral or anal penetration by a penis and unwanted anal penetration by a male or female perpetrator using his or her fingers or an object

FEMALE VICTIMS. Black et al. estimate that more than one-third (35.6%) of adult women in the United States have been victimized during their lifetime by an intimate partner using rape (9.4%), physical violence (32.9%), and/or stalking (10.7%). Overall, this sums to more than 42.4 million victims. In addition, 28.8% of women are believed to have experienced specific impacts from their lifetime experiences of intimate partner violence. (The effects and impacts of domestic violence are discussed in detail in Chapter 7.)

Nearly two-thirds (63.8%) of women who were victimized during their lifetime experienced only one of the three types of intimate partner violence. More than half (56.8%) experienced physical violence only, 4.4% experienced rape only, and 2.6% experienced stalking only. The remaining women were victimized by a combination of intimate partner violence types, including 12.5% who experienced rape, physical violence, and stalking during their lifetime.

Black et al. also provide lifetime prevalence percentages for rape, physical violence, and/or stalking broken down by the race and ethnicity of women victims. It should be noted that estimates are not available for races with small sample sizes. In descending order for each violence type, the percentages were:

- Rape, physical violence, and/or stalking—multiracial (53.8%), Native American or Alaskan Native (46%), non-Hispanic African American (43.7%), Hispanic (37.1%), non-Hispanic white (34.6%), and Asian or Pacific Islander (19.6%)

- Rape—multiracial (20.1%), non-Hispanic African American (12.2%), non-Hispanic white (9.2%), and Hispanic (8.4%)

- Physical violence—multiracial (50.4%), Native American or Alaskan Native (45.9%), non-Hispanic African American (40.9%), Hispanic (35.2%), and non-Hispanic white (31.7%)

- Stalking—multiracial (18.9%), non-Hispanic African American (14.6%), Hispanic (10.6%), and non-Hispanic white (10.4%)

MALE VICTIMS. According to Black et al., more than a quarter (32.3 million, or 28.5%) of the total U.S. adult male population have been victimized during their lifetime by an intimate partner using physical violence (28.2%) and/or stalking (2.1%). It should be noted that the sample size for rape was too small to provide a reliable national estimate. The 12-month prevalence among adult men for all three types of victimizations was 5%. The percentages by violence type were 4.7% for physical violence and 0.5% for stalking.

According to Black et al., men were much more likely than women to experience only one of the three victimization types during their lifetime. Nearly all the victimized men (92.1%) experienced physical violence only. Another 6.3% experienced physical violence and stalking. The percentage of victimized men who experienced other combinations of the three violence types could not be reliably calculated.

Among male victims of rape, physical violence, and/or stalking, nearly one out of seven (15%) were aged 11 to 17 years, and more than one-third (38.6%) were aged 18 to 24 years. Another 30.6% were aged 25 to 34 years. Overall, 84.2% of the male victims were 34 years old or younger when they first experienced intimate partner violence.

Black et al. break down the lifetime prevalence percentages for rape, physical violence, and/or stalking by the race and ethnicity of the male victims. It should be noted that estimates are not available for racial and ethnic groups with small sample sizes. In descending order for each violence type, the percentages were:

- Rape, physical violence, and/or stalking—Native American or Alaskan Native (45.3%), multiracial (39.3%), non-Hispanic African American (38.6%), non-Hispanic white (28.2%), and Hispanic (26.6%)

- Physical violence—Native American or Alaskan Native (45.3%), multiracial (38.8%), non-Hispanic African American (36.8%), non-Hispanic white (28.1%), Hispanic (26.5%), and Asian or Pacific Islander (8.4%)

- Stalking—non-Hispanic white (1.7%)

Sexual Violence

Within the category of sexual violence Black et al. include rape (as defined earlier) and other sexual acts described as follows:

- Being made to penetrate someone else—the perpetrator made or attempted to make the victim sexually penetrate someone without the victim's consent by threatening to physically harm the victim or using physical force against the victim (such as being pinned or held down, or by the use of violence). This includes being made to receive oral sex.

- Being made to penetrate someone else—the perpetrator made or attempted to make the victim sexually penetrate someone without the victim's consent, because the victim was drunk, high, drugged, or passed out and unable to consent. This includes being made to receive oral sex.

- Sexual coercion—unwanted sexual penetration of a victim who was coerced in a nonphysical way, such as through lies or emotional compulsion.

- Unwanted sexual contact—unwanted sexual experiences involving touch but not sexual penetration, such as being kissed in a sexual way or having sexual body parts fondled or grabbed.

- Noncontact unwanted sexual experiences—unwanted sexual experiences that do not involve any touching or penetration, including someone exposing their sexual body parts, flashing, or masturbating in front of the victim, someone making a victim show his or her body parts, someone making a victim look at or participate in sexual photos or movies, or someone harassing the victim in a public place in a way that made the victim feel unsafe.

FEMALE VICTIMS. As noted earlier, Black et al. estimate a 9.4% lifetime prevalence rate and a 0.6% 12-month prevalence rate for rape of adult women by intimate partners. The lifetime prevalence percentages by rape type were 6.6% for completed forced penetration, 2.5% for attempted forced penetration, and 3.4% for completed alcohol/drug-facilitated penetration. The percentages for lifetime prevalence of nonrape acts of sexual violence were 9.8% for sexual coercion, 6.4% for unwanted sexual contact, and 7.8% for noncontact unwanted sexual experiences. Sufficient data were available for the researchers to estimate 0.4% as the 12-month prevalence of completed forced penetration. The 12-month prevalence rates for specific types of nonrape sexual violence were 1.7% for sexual coercion, 0.5% for unwanted sexual contact, and 0.7% for noncontact unwanted sexual experiences.

MALE VICTIMS. According to Black et al., "too few men reported rape by an intimate partner to produce reliable prevalence estimates." However, estimated prevalence rates for overall nonrape sexual violence are 8% for lifetime prevalence and 2.5% for 12-month prevalence. In terms of specific sexually violent acts, sexual coercion had the highest lifetime prevalence at 4.2%, followed by noncontact unwanted sexual experiences (2.7%), unwanted sexual contact (2.6%), and being made to penetrate someone else (2.2%). The 12-month prevalence estimates were lower than the lifetime prevalence estimates, but again, sexual coercion was the most common type of nonrape sexual violence, at 1%. All the other types of sexual violence in this category had rates of less than 1%.

Physical Violence

Black et al. divide physical violence into two broad categories: slapping, pushing, or shoving and severe physical violence. The latter category includes actions that are particularly painful and/or injurious.

FEMALE VICTIMS. Overall, Black et al. indicate that an estimated 36.2 million women have been slapped, pushed, or shoved by an intimate partner during their lifetime. This represents 30.3% of all adult U.S. women. Nearly as many women (29 million, or 24.3% of the total U.S. women population) have experienced at least one form of severe physical violence. The lifetime prevalence rates for the five most commonly reported types of severe physical violence are: being slammed against something (17.2%), being hit with a fist or something hard (14.2%), being beaten (11.2%), being hurt by having hair pulled (10.4%), and being choked or suffocated (9.7%).

MALE VICTIMS. Black et al. estimate that 29.1 million men have been slapped, pushed, or shoved by an intimate partner during their lifetime. This represents 25.7% of all adult U.S. men. In addition, 15.6 million (13.8% of the total U.S. adult male population) men have experienced at least one form of severe physical violence. The lifetime prevalence rates for the five most commonly reported types of severe physical violence for male victims are: being hit with a fist or something hard (9.4%), being kicked (4.3%), being hurt by having hair pulled (2.9%), being attacked by a perpetrator armed with a knife or gun (2.8%), and being slammed against something (2.7%).

Stalking

As noted earlier, Black et al. define stalking as harassing or threatening actions that are unwanted and cause a victim to be afraid or otherwise concerned about his or her personal safety.

FEMALE VICTIMS. Black et al. estimate that 10.7% of U.S. adult women (or approximately 12.7 million women nationally) have been victimized by stalking by an intimate partner at some point during their lifetime. The most commonly experienced stalking actions reported by victims were: receiving unwanted phone calls or text messages (77.4%) and having a current or former intimate partner show up unwanted at their home, workplace, or school (64.8%). In addition, more than one-third (37.4%) of the women said that during their lifetime they had been watched or followed by a current or former intimate partner. The estimated 12-month prevalence rate for stalking of female victims was 2.8%. This equates to approximately 3.3 million women nationally.

MALE VICTIMS. According to Black et al., an estimated 2.4 million men have been the victims of stalking by an intimate partner at some point during their lifetime. This equates to 2.1% of the total U.S. adult male population. Male stalking victims most commonly reported that they experienced unwanted phone calls or text messages (83.7%), were approached by a current or former intimate partner or experienced that person showing up unwanted at their home, workplace, or school (52.1%), and/or experienced being watched or followed by a current or former intimate partner (52.1%).

Psychological Aggression

Although physical and sexual forms of domestic violence typically receive the most attention from researchers, psychological aggression is another focus point. Black et al. divide acts of psychological aggression into two broad categories: expressive aggression (such as name calling and insulting behavior) and coercive control (such as overly controlling behaviors).

FEMALE VICTIMS. Black et al. find that psychological aggression by intimate partners is quite prevalent. Nearly half (48.4%) of adult women in the United States are estimated to have experienced it during their lifetime. This equates to about 57.6 million women nationally. The lifetime prevalence rates for expressive aggression (40.3%) and coercive control (41.1%) were nearly equal. The most frequently reported forms of psychological aggression were being called names, such as ugly or stupid (64.3%), and having one's whereabouts and movements monitored and questioned in a demanding fashion (61.7%). In addition, 58% of the women surveyed said they had been insulted, made fun of, or humiliated by an intimate partner, whereas 57.9% reported witnessing an intimate partner so angry that he or she "seemed dangerous."

MALE VICTIMS. Overall, Black et al. note that an estimated 55.2 million men have at some point during their lifetime experienced psychological aggression by an intimate partner. This value represents 48.8% of all adult U.S. men. The lifetime prevalence rates were 31.9% for expressive aggression and 42.5% for coercive control. The most frequently reported forms of psychological aggression were having one's whereabouts and movements monitored and questioned in a demanding fashion (63.1%) and being called names, such as ugly or stupid (51.6%). In addition, 42.4% of the men surveyed said they had been told by an intimate partner that they were a loser, a failure, or not good enough, and 40.4% reported witnessing an intimate partner so angry that he or she "seemed dangerous."

HOMICIDE TRENDS AND DOMESTIC VIOLENCE

Another source of data regarding the prevalence of domestic violence is the Federal Bureau of Investigation (FBI), because the agency compiles Uniform Crime Reports (UCR) that track the number of certain crimes committed in the United States based on reports from local law enforcement agencies. Crimes that are not reported to the police are not included in the UCR counts. Selected UCR statistics are published annually by the FBI in the *Crime in the United States* series. In addition, the BJS uses UCR data in occasional reports on crime trends.

Fatal Domestic Violence Estimates

In *Crime in the United States*, the FBI focuses mostly on crime types, perpetrator characteristics, and agency actions, such as arrests; few data are available on the victim-offender relationships. However, the FBI does provide some limited information on the victim-offender relationships involved in homicides (murders). These data are useful in trying to establish the prevalence of fatal domestic violence.

The FBI indicates in *Crime in the United States, 2014* (September 28, 2015, https://www.fbi.gov/about-us/cjis/ucr/crime-in-the-u.s/2014/crime-in-the-u.s.-2014) that 11,961 murders were reported to law enforcement agencies in 2014. The victim-offender relationship was known for 6,521 of the murders, or 54.5% of the total. The data provide the following counts of people murdered by family members or intimate partners:

- Women murdered by husbands (539)
- Men murdered by wives (99)
- People murdered by other family members (1,073)
- Women murdered by boyfriends (414)
- Men murdered by girlfriends (151)

These 2,276 murders account for nearly 35% of the 6,521 homicides in 2014 in which the victim-offender relationship was known. It should be noted that the FBI specifies that the spousal categories include former spouses and common-law spouses (people whose spousal standing has been afforded by state laws that consider long-time cohabitating couples to have a spousal relationship). In addition, the FBI includes stepparents, stepchildren, and stepsiblings in its definition of family members. However, the FBI counts murders that occur within homosexual relationships as murders by acquaintances, rather than under the spousal or boyfriend/girlfriend categories. Thus, the number of homicides involving homosexual intimate partners is not specified. In 2014, 331 of the 6,521 homicides for which the victim-offender relationship was known were attributed to friends and 2,416 were attributed to acquaintances without further description of the relationships.

Homicide Trends

In *Homicide Trends in the United States, 1980–2008: Annual Rates for 2009 and 2010* (November 2011, http://bjs.ojp.usdoj.gov/content/pub/pdf/htus8008.pdf), the most comprehensive homicide trends report published by the BJS as of September 2016, Alexia Cooper and Erica L. Smith of the BJS discuss data obtained from the FBI's Supplementary Homicide Reports, which are compiled as part of the UCR program. The Supplementary Homicide Reports include some detailed information about homicide circumstances and victim-offender relationships. Cooper and Smith use the data to describe homicide trends between 1980 and 2008. They note that the victim-offender relationship was known in 63.1% of the homicides. All of the following discussion and related graphics present statistics for this subset of murders.

VICTIM-OFFENDER TRENDS. Overall, 10% of the homicides in which the victim-offender relationship was known involved spousal murder, 12.4% were homicides between other family members, and 6.3% involved girlfriend/boyfriend murder. Thus, 28.7% of the homicides during this period could be classified as domestic violence murders.

According to Cooper and Smith, between 1980 and 2008 females (41.5%) were nearly six times more likely than males (7.1%) to be the victims of intimate homicides. The distinction was less pronounced in murders involving other family members. In these cases females (16.7%) were only slightly more likely than males (10.9%) to be the victims. However, the predominance of female victims in these murder types stands in stark contrast to the gender breakdown in homicides that do not involve intimate partners or family members. Male victims outnumbered female victims in murders involving strangers (25.5% male victims compared with 11.9% female victims) and in cases where the perpetrators were acquaintances or otherwise known (56.4% male victims compared with 29.9% female victims). Thus, only in cases in which homicides were committed by intimate partners and other family members were females more often the victims than males.

Cooper and Smith also provide demographic data for the victims and perpetrators of murders involving intimate partners (spouses, former spouses, boyfriends, or girlfriends) and family members. In intimate homicides nearly half of the victims (48.5%) and offenders (47%) were in the age group 18 to 34 years. For murders involving family members, nearly one-third (32.8%) of the victims were aged 18 to 34 years; 50.5% of the perpetrators fell into this age group. Overall, victims of intimate partner homicide were predominantly female (63.7%) rather than male (36.3%), and male murderers (70.3%) were far more common than female murderers (29.7%) in these cases. The sex differences were less stark among victims of interfamilial (within the family) homicide, in that 54.7% of the victims were male and 45.3% of the victims were female. Again, males predominated among perpetrators (74.4%), compared with females (25.6%).

Between 1980 and 2008 whites accounted for slightly more than half of the parties involved in intimate homicides (55% of the victims and 54.2% of the offenders). African Americans made up 42.7% of the victims and 43.5% of the perpetrators, whereas other races accounted for 2.4% of the victims and 2.3% of the offenders. In interfamilial homicides whites also accounted for the majority of the victims and perpetrators (59.2% each). By comparison, African Americans made up 38.2% of the victims and 38.3% of the perpetrators, and other races accounted for 2% of the victims and 2.5% of the murderers.

INTIMATE PARTNER HOMICIDES. Of all homicide victims aged 12 years and older who were murdered between 1980 and 2008, 16% were killed by their intimate partners. Cooper and Smith note that in 1980 the majority (69.1%) of intimate homicides involved spousal murder. However, this percentage fell over time as boyfriend/girlfriend homicides became more prevalent. In 2008 fewer than half (46.7%) of the intimate homicides were spousal murders, whereas boyfriend/girlfriend murders accounted for 48.6% of the total, up from 26.8% in 1980. The changes over time in the victim-offender relationship of intimate homicides reflect the changes described in Chapter 1 for the makeup of intimate couples (i.e., the trend away from marriage and toward other arrangements, such as cohabitation).

Far more females than males were murdered by intimate partners between 1980 and 2008. The percentage of males killed in intimate homicides declined from 10.4% in 1980 to 4.9% in 2008, a decrease of 53%. The percentage of females murdered by intimate partners dropped from 43% in 1980 to 38% in 1995. However, the percentage rose to 45% by 2008. Overall, in 1980 females were about four times more likely than males to be the victims of intimate homicide. By 2008 females were approximately nine times more likely than males to be the victims of intimate homicide.

White females were slightly more likely than African American females to be murdered by an intimate partner between 1980 and 2008. The two cohorts were roughly equal during the early 1980s, but white females predominated over the remainder of the period. On average, white women accounted for 44% of the victims in intimate homicides between 1980 and 2008. Intimate homicides of African American women declined from 43% in 1980 to 33% in 1995, but then climbed back up to 43% by 2008. In 1980 the percentage of African American male murder victims killed by an intimate partner was 13%. This value declined through 2008, when it was about 5%, the same percentage as for white males.

Guns were the most commonly used weapons on all intimate homicide victims between 1980 and 2008, except for boyfriends murdered by their girlfriends and people murdered by a same-sex intimate partner. These homicides more frequently involved knives than guns. Guns were the murder weapons in a vast majority of the homicides in which ex-husbands were killed by ex-wives (83.6%), ex-wives were killed by ex-husbands (75%), wives were killed by husbands (66.7%), and husbands were killed by wives (66.1%).

INTERFAMILIAL HOMICIDES. Cooper and Smith also provide data on interfamilial homicides committed by various family members. It should be noted that spouses and ex-spouses are included in the same category; thus, there is some overlap between these data and the statistics presented earlier for intimate partner murders. Overall, spouses and ex-spouses were the perpetrators in just over half (52%) of interfamilial homicides in 1980. By 2008 this percentage had fallen to 37%. Parental murders of children made up 15% of the total in 1980 and climbed to 25% in 2008. Likewise, homicides in which children killed their parents increased from 10% in 1980 to 13% in 2008. The percentages of murders committed by siblings also rose, from 15% in 1980 to 18% in 2008. The rate of interfamilial homicides in which other family members were the perpetrators changed little during this period.

Cooper and Smith make the following general observations regarding interfamilial homicides between 1980 and 2008:

- Fathers were more likely than mothers to be murdered by one of their own children

- Sons aged 16 to 19 years old were most often the offenders when children killed their parents

- Brothers were more likely than sisters to be murdered by a sibling, and the perpetrators were usually brothers

- Approximately half of the brothers who murdered brothers were aged 16 to 30 years

- Sisters murdered by siblings were most often killed by brothers

Additional BJS Homicide Data

Although Cooper and Smith's findings represented the most extensive compilation of U.S. homicide statistics as of September 2016, the BJS has produced subsequent reports offering additional data concerning spousal and interfamilial homicides. In *Intimate Partner Violence: Attributes of Victimization, 1993–2011*, Catalano provides an overview of homicides committed by intimate partners between 1993 and 2010. Catalano notes that the percentage of female homicide victims who were killed by intimate partners rose steadily between 2008 and 2010. In 2008, 36.4% of female homicide victims were murdered by an intimate partner. In 2010 this figure

rose to 39.3%. The percentage of male homicide victims who were killed by intimate partners rose from 2.7% in 2008 to 3% in 2009, before dropping to 2.8% in 2010. Overall, the total number of female homicide victims fell during this period, from 3,282 in 2008 to 3,032 in 2010. The number of male homicide victims also declined during this span, dropping from 12,296 in 2008 to 10,878 in 2010.

NATIONAL VIOLENCE AGAINST WOMEN SURVEY

As a joint effort of the Department of Justice's National Institute of Justice and the CDC, the National Violence against Women Survey (NVAWS) collected data about intimate and nonintimate partner violence in 1995–96. The NVAWS collected information from interviews with 8,000 men and 8,000 women to assess their experiences as victims of various types of violence, including domestic violence. The NVAWS asked survey respondents about physical assaults and rape, but excluded other sexual assaults, murders, and robberies.

Patricia Tjaden and Nancy Thoennes of the Center for Policy Research in Denver, Colorado, find in *Extent, Nature, and Consequences of Intimate Partner Violence: Findings from the National Violence against Women Survey* (July 2000, http://www.ncjrs.gov/pdffiles1/nij/181867.pdf) that intimate violence is pervasive in American society. They estimate that in 1998, 22.3 million (22.1%) women had been physically assaulted by intimates during the course of their lifetime, whereas 6.9 million (7.4%) men had been physically assaulted by intimates during the course of their lifetime. Women were also more likely to become victims of rape, stalking, and physical assault by intimates than their male counterparts at some point during their lifetime. Furthermore, women physically assaulted by their partners averaged 6.9 assaults by the same person, as opposed to men, who averaged 4.4 assaults by the same person.

Tjaden and Thoennes conclude that most partner abuse and violence is not reported to the police. Women reported 17.2% of rapes, 26.7% of physical assaults, and 51.9% of stalking incidents to police, whereas men reported 13.5% of physical assaults and 36.2% of stalking incidents. Many victims said they thought the police would not or could not do anything on their behalf. These expressions of helplessness and hopelessness (feeling that others in a position to assist would be unwilling or unable to do so) is a common characteristic shared by many victims of intimate partner violence.

According to Tjaden and Thoennes, in *Full Report of the Prevalence, Incidence, and Consequence of Violence against Women* (November 2000, https://www.ncjrs.gov/pdffiles1/nij/183781.pdf), 22.1% of women surveyed reported experiencing intimate partner violence; by comparison, 7.4% of men interviewed reported being victims of intimate partner violence. Overall, intimate partner violence accounted for nearly two-thirds (64%) of all violent acts committed against women aged 18 years and older. Tjaden and Thoennes note that women who were raped or assaulted by an intimate partner were considerably more likely to report sustaining an injury than women who were raped or assaulted by another category of assailant.

Subsequent studies conducted by the CDC reveal that domestic violence in the United States is even more prevalent than originally reported in the NVAWS. For example, Matthew J. Breiding et al. of the CDC's National Center for Injury Prevention and Control present in "Prevalence and Characteristics of Sexual Violence, Stalking, and Intimate Partner Violence Victimization—National Intimate Partner and Sexual Violence Survey, United States, 2011" (*Morbidity and Mortality Weekly Report*, vol. 63, no. 8, September 5, 2014) the results of a 2011 telephone survey that was conducted with more than 14,000 adult women and men. In 2011 more than 38 million adult women, or nearly one-third (31.5%) of all women in the United States, had experienced some form of intimate partner physical violence during their lifetime. This figure represents a substantial increase over the 22.1% of adult women who reported experiencing lifetime intimate partner physical violence in the original NVAWS report. In addition, Breiding et al. report that more than a quarter (27.5%) of men in the United States reported experiencing intimate partner physical violence at some point during their lifetime. This percentage was nearly four times greater than the 7.4% reported by Tjaden and Thoennes. Although Breiding et al. do not offer an explanation for the steep rise in intimate partner physical violence among men, it is possible that greater awareness of the impact of domestic violence on men has resulted in a greater willingness to report incidents of intimate partner physical violence by male victims.

Violence Statistics in Same-Sex Relationships

Intimate partner violence is also a serious problem among same-sex couples in the United States. In *The National Intimate Partner and Sexual Violence Survey (NISVS): 2010 Findings on Victimization by Sexual Orientation* (January 2013, https://www.cdc.gov/violence prevention/pdf/nisvs_sofindings.pdf), Mikel L. Walters, Jieru Chen, and Matthew J. Breiding report that in 2010 lesbian and bisexual women were considerably more likely to have experienced intimate partner violence during their lifetime than heterosexual women. According to the researchers, more than half (56.9%) of bisexual women and four out of 10 (40.4%) lesbian women reported experiencing intimate partner physical violence during their lifetime. By comparison, less than one-third (32.3%) of heterosexual women had been victims of intimate partner physical violence during their lifetime. Among males surveyed by Walters, Chen, and Breiding, bisexual men (37.3%) were the most likely to have experienced intimate partner physical violence during their lifetime in 2010, followed by heterosexual men (28.7%) and gay men (25.2%).

CHAPTER 7

CAUSES, EFFECTS, AND PREVENTION OF DOMESTIC VIOLENCE

THEORIES ON THE CAUSES OF DOMESTIC VIOLENCE

It should be noted that many theories have been put forward to explain why domestic violence occurs. Each theory has its champions and critics. People who support certain theories can cite studies that include empirical research (research based on observation and measurement) as supporting evidence. In reality, no single theory can explain what causes people to act violently in certain situations. In fact, there can be considerable overlap between theories in certain elements, such as the idea that society at large helps perpetuate violent behaviors. Because males have historically been the primary perpetrators of domestic violence, most theories tend to focus on male attitudes and behaviors. In addition, most theories focus on intimate partner violence, which as is noted in previous chapters is domestic violence in which the offender is a former or current spouse, boyfriend, or girlfriend of the victim. Some of the most common types of theories are briefly described in this chapter.

Resource Theories

According to resource theories of domestic violence, the more resources (social, personal, and economic) a person can command, the more power he or she can potentially call on. The individual who is rich in terms of these resources has less need to use force in an open manner. By contrast, a person with little education, low job prestige and income, or poor interpersonal skills may use violence to compensate for a real or perceived lack of resources and to maintain dominance.

Learned Behavior Theories

Theories based on learned behavior view domestic violence as behavior that may be learned early in life by children who experience domestic violence in their home and consider it to be "normal." As these children grow up, they may receive societal feedback that seems to support the notion that violent behavior within relationships is acceptable. In addition, people who engage in domestic violence may learn that it achieves the desired results and has no negative consequences to them, thus, reinforcing its usefulness in their mind.

Feminist Theories

Feminist theories of violence against women emphasize that patriarchal structures of gender-based inequalities of power in society are at the root of the problem. That is, the violence, rather than being an individual psychological problem, is instead an expression of male domination of females. Pointing to history, some feminist researchers see wife abuse as a natural consequence of women's second-class status in society. In the feminist view, violence against women includes a variety of control tactics that are meant to control women.

Psychological and Personality Theories

Some analysts believe that perpetrator psychological and personality disorders contribute to domestic violence behaviors. In *Domestic Violence* (January 2007, http://www.popcenter.org/problems/pdfs/domestic_violence.pdf), Rana Sampson notes that possible disorders and problems include posttraumatic stress, poor impulse control, low self-esteem, and substance abuse.

Control and Power Motivations

Many theories posit the desire for control and power in a relationship as a major motivation for people who use violence against their intimate partners. Evan Stark argues in *Coercive Control: The Entrapment of Women in Personal Life* (2007) that intimate partner violence is best understood as part of men's attempts to destroy women's autonomy and assert patriarchal power in relationships and that physical violence must be seen as one aspect of a power dynamic that also includes economic and emotional measures of control. Control motivations often feature prominently in the domestic violence definitions that are crafted by government agencies and nonprofit organizations. For example, in "Domestic Violence" (October 6, 2015, http://www.justice.gov/ovw/domestic-violence), the Office on Violence against Women, which is part of the U.S. Department of Justice, notes, "We define domestic violence as a pattern of abusive behavior in any relationship that is used by one partner to gain or maintain power and control over another intimate partner."

Champions of control theories as the cause of domestic violence sometimes stress the role of societal beliefs and practices as a contributing factor. These people believe that society in some ways condones and even fosters violence against certain classes of people, including women and children. The National Coalition against Domestic Violence (NCADV) explains in "What Is Domestic Violence?" (2016, http://www.ncadv.org/need-help/what-is-domestic-violence) that domestic violence "is the willful intimidation, physical assault, battery, sexual assault, and/or other abusive behavior as part of a systematic pattern of power and control perpetrated by one intimate partner against another." Describing domestic violence as "an epidemic affecting individuals in every community, regardless of age, economic status, sexual orientation, gender, race, religion, or nationality," the NCADV further notes that such violence "is often accompanied by emotionally abusive and controlling behavior that is only a fraction of a systematic pattern of dominance and control."

RISK FACTORS FOR DOMESTIC VIOLENCE

The risk factors for domestic violence are gleaned from empirical studies conducted by researchers who examine demographic or relationship factors associated with domestic violence cases to compare prevalence rates between different population subsets. Researchers do differ in their definitions of domestic violence and in the types of cases or victims that they assess. Nevertheless, their studies give valuable clues about what types of victims are most at risk for experiencing domestic violence.

In "Making Sociological Sense out of Trends in Intimate Partner Violence" (*Violence against Women*, vol. 10, no. 6, June 2004), Joseph H. Michalski of the University of Western Ontario indicates that key risk factors of domestic violence include:

- Social isolation of the couple

- Separate peer support networks

- Inequality between partners

- Lack of relational distance, or a high degree of intimacy within a couple

- The centralization of authority—in other words, patriarchal dominance within a family

- Exposure to violence and violent networks

Sarah Romans et al. of the University of Toronto find in "Who Is Most at Risk for Intimate Partner Violence?: A Canadian Population-Based Study" (*Journal of Interpersonal Violence*, vol. 22, no. 12, December 2007) that risk factors for intimate partner violence include a younger age; being divorced, separated, or single; having children living in the household; and having poor physical health. A lower income or minority status puts women, but not men, at a higher risk for intimate partner violence. Still, Romans et al. explain that classification is not exclusive. Just about anyone, rich or poor, male or female, may be a victim of domestic violence.

Some studies have assessed the relationship between socioeconomic status and domestic violence prevalence. Deborah N. Pearlman et al. of Brown University find in "Neighborhood Environment, Racial Position, and Risk of Police-Reported Domestic Violence: A Contextual Analysis" (*Public Health Reports*, vol. 118, no. 1, January–February 2003) a complex but strong relationship between poverty and domestic violence and speculate that one explanation for the increased risk of domestic violence in poorer neighborhoods might be differences in law enforcement availability and practices; that is, economically deprived communities might have less police notification, attention, and documentation.

Risk Factors for Fatal Domestic Violence

In "How Can Practitioners Help an Abused Woman Lower Her Risk of Death?" (*National Institute of Justice Journal*, no. 250, November 2003), Carolyn Rebecca Block of the Illinois Criminal Justice Information Authority investigates what factors present in abusive relationships might indicate that a threat of violence will escalate to homicide. She finds that certain types of past violence directed against female intimates indicate an increased risk of homicide, especially choking. She also finds that recently abused women are more likely to be killed. Half of women who were killed in 1995 and 1996 by their partners had experienced violence in the previous 30 days before the survey. Increasingly, frequent violent incidents pose a higher risk of homicide.

Jacquelyn C. Campbell et al. evaluate in "Intimate Partner Homicide: Review and Implications of Research and Policy" (*Trauma, Violence, and Abuse*, vol. 8, no. 3, July 2007) the risk factors among abused women for being killed by their intimate partners. The researchers find that prior domestic violence is a key risk factor in cases of intimate partner homicide. In addition, Campbell et al. find that abused women whose abusers owned guns and who had threatened to kill them were also at a high risk of being killed by their intimate partners. Other high-risk factors for homicide include death threats, attempts to choke, the presence of a stepchild in the home, and marital rape.

In "Intimate Partner Homicide: Risk Assessment and Prospects for Prediction" (*Journal of Family Violence*, vol. 26, no. 3, April 2011), Angela W. Eke et al. examine select characteristics found in male perpetrators of intimate partner homicide. In a study of 146 men who had either killed or attempted to kill an intimate partner, the researchers find that only a quarter (26%) were married to the victim. Of the men surveyed, 42% had a prior criminal record, 15% had a history of psychiatric problems, and 18% had both criminal records and a psychiatric history. According to Eke et al., nearly one out of 10 (9%) of the subjects studied had previously been arrested on domestic violence charges.

Brynn E. Sheehan et al. attempt to identify in "Intimate Partner Homicide: New Insights for Understanding Lethality and Risks" (*Violence against Women*, vol. 21, no. 2, February 2015) potential predictors of intimate partner homicide through interviews with individuals who have lost family members or friends in fatal domestic violence situations. In these interviews, the researchers identify a pattern that shows dramatic behavioral changes among perpetrators prior to committing intimate partner homicide, in particular an increased sense of losing control over the victim. Sheehan et al. suggest that by learning to identify and categorize these shifts in behavior many cases of intimate partner homicide might be avoided.

Substance Abuse as a Risk Factor

Although researchers generally do not consider alcohol and drug use to be the cause of violence, they find that it can contribute to, accelerate, or increase aggression. A variety of data sources establish a correlation (a complementary or parallel relationship) between substance abuse and violence, but a correlation does not establish a causation.

According to the National Institute on Alcohol Abuse and Alcoholism, in "Model 8: Alcohol and Intimate Partner Violence" (March 2005, http://pubs.niaaa.nih.gov/publications/Social/Module8IntimatePartnerViolence/Module8.html), "Alcohol is not a clearly identified direct cause of [intimate partner violence], though it clearly is a correlate and may be a contributing factor." Substance abuse may promote or provoke domestic violence, but both may also be influenced by other factors, such as environmental, biological, and situational stressors. Based on available research, it remains unclear whether substance abuse is a key factor in most domestic violence incidents. Jennifer M. Reingle et al. note in "On the Pervasiveness of Event-Specific Alcohol Use, General Substance Use, and Mental Health Problems as Risk Factors for Intimate Partner Violence" (*Journal of Interpersonal Violence*, vol. 29, no. 16, November 2014) that whereas alcohol and marijuana abuse are often associated with higher rates of intimate

partner violence, other factors, notably mental health issues such as depression and personality disorders, are also prevalent in domestic violence situations.

Although anecdotal evidence suggests that alcohol and drugs appear to be linked to violence and abuse, in controlled studies the connection is not as clear. Richard J. Gelles and Mary M. Cavanaugh suggest in "Association Is Not Causation: Alcohol and Other Drugs Do Not Cause Violence" (Donileen R. Loseke, Richard J. Gelles, and Mary M. Cavanaugh, eds., *Current Controversies on Family Violence*, 2005) that substance abuse is not a cause of family violence; rather, it is often used as an excuse for family violence. Gelles and Cavanaugh argue that although substantial evidence has linked alcohol and drug use to violence, there is little scientific evidence that alcohol or other drugs, such as cocaine, have pharmacological properties that produce violent and abusive behavior. The researchers maintain that alcoholism may be associated with intimate violence but that it is not a primary cause of the violence. They cite experiments using college students as subjects that have found that when the students thought they were consuming alcohol, they acted more aggressively than if they were told they had been given nonalcoholic drinks. According to Gelles and Cavanaugh, it is the expectation of the effects of alcohol that influences behavior, not the actual liquor consumed.

In "Risky Mix: Drinking, Drug Use, and Homicide" (*National Institute of Justice Journal*, no. 250, November 2003), a study of patterns of alcohol and drug use in murders and attempted murders of women by their partners, Phyllis Sharps et al. show a relationship between substance use and violence. They find that in the year before the violent incident, female victims used alcohol and drugs less frequently and consumed smaller amounts than did their male partners. Sharps et al. also note that during the homicide or attempted homicide 31.3% of perpetrators consumed alcohol, 12.6% used drugs, and 26.2% used both. Nearly three out of 10 (29.9%) homicide or attempted homicide perpetrators used neither alcohol nor drugs. In contrast, perpetrators who abused their partners without attempting to kill them consumed alcohol 21% of the time, drugs 6.7% of the time, and both 5.8% of the time. Nearly two-thirds (65.8%) of perpetrators who abused their partners without attempting to kill them used neither alcohol nor drugs. Sharps et al. conclude that increased substance use results in more serious violence. Martie P. Thompson and J. B. Kingree of Clemson University agree. They find in "The Roles of Victim and Perpetrator Alcohol Use in Intimate Partner Violence Outcomes" (*Journal of Interpersonal Violence*, vol. 21, no. 2, February 2006) that alcohol use among male batterers led to a significant increase in the likelihood that their partners would suffer injury in a violent incident. Jill T. Messing, Natasha S. Mendoza, and Jacquelyn C. Campbell observe similar findings in "Alcohol Use and Latent Profiles of Intimate Partner Violence" (*Journal of Social Work Practice in the Addictions*, vol. 16, nos. 1–2, January–June 2016), noting that alcohol abuse is associated with greater severity and frequency of violence, stalking, and potential for future homicide.

Although most studies focus on substance abuse by the offenders in domestic violence cases, research also finds that women with substance abuse problems are at higher risk of being victimized by their intimate partners. In "Working at the Intersection of Domestic Violence, Substance Abuse and Mental Health: Creating Trauma-Informed Services and Organizations" (March 29, 2012, http://www.nationalcenterdvtraumamh.org/wp-content/uploads/2012/01/March-29-Mental-Health-Pre-Con-Flyer .pdf), Carole Warshaw of the National Center on Domestic Violence, Trauma, and Mental Health cites studies showing that women who are treated for substance abuse problems in outpatient and inpatient settings are at higher risk than other women for domestic violence. According to Warshaw, batterers take advantage of, or even exacerbate, substance abuse issues in their female partners to better exert control over them.

Childhood and Youth Victimization as a Risk Factor

Research demonstrates a relationship between having experienced violence as a child or youth and being further victimized or becoming an abuser later in life.

Shelby A. Kaura and Craig M. Allen of Iowa State University note in "Dissatisfaction with Relationship Power and Dating Violence Perpetration by Men and Women" (*Journal of Interpersonal Violence*, vol. 19, no. 5, May 2004), a study of 352 male and 296 female undergraduate college students, that witnessing parental violence was the strongest predictor of perpetrating dating violence. The National Institute of Justice finds in *Violence against Women: Identifying Risk Factors* (November 2004, https://www.ncjrs.gov/pdffiles1/nij/197019.pdf) exceedingly high rates of abuse during college, especially of women who had been victimized in childhood or adolescence. During their first year of college, 23% of women who had not been victimized in the past were victimized physically, sexually, or both. By contrast, 32% of women who had been victimized in childhood, 42% of women who had been victimized in adolescence, and 66% of women who had been victimized in both childhood and adolescence were abused during their first year of college.

The National Institute of Justice also looks at whether adults who experienced sexual abuse or domestic violence had been abused in childhood or adolescence. More than a quarter (28%) of adults who had not been abused before reaching adulthood were sexually abused as adults, whereas 75% of those who had been abused in childhood and adolescence were sexually abused as adults. Sixty percent of women who had not been abused in childhood or adolescence experienced some domestic violence in adulthood, whereas 97% of women who had been sexually abused in childhood and adolescence experienced some domestic violence in adulthood.

DATING VIOLENCE IN ADOLESCENCE. Dating violence encompasses physical, sexual, or psychological violence in a dating relationship. Experiencing dating violence puts victims at a greater risk for engaging in risky sexual behavior, anorexia nervosa (intense fear of becoming fat even when dangerously underweight) or bulimia (recurrent episodes of binge eating followed by purging to prevent weight gain), substance abuse, and suicide. It can also be an indicator that an adolescent is at risk for victimization in intimate relationships in adulthood.

Carl D. Maas et al. explore in "Childhood Predictors of Teen Dating Violence Victimization" (*Violence and Victims*, vol. 25, no. 2, 2010) the relationship between child maltreatment and domestic violence and teen dating violence. The researchers examined data from the Raising Healthy Children project, a longitudinal study (a study of the same group of people over time) of students in a suburban school district in the Pacific Northwest. They find a strong association between child maltreatment and dating violence victimization for female adolescents. In addition, witnessing intimate partner violence in childhood also puts girls at greater risk for dating violence. However, Maas et al. also note that strong bonds between parents and children provide a protective effect against teen dating violence victimization.

The Centers for Disease Control and Prevention (CDC) in its Youth Risk Behavior Survey questions students in grades nine to 12 on their experiences of dating violence and forced sexual intercourse. In 2015 about one out of 10 (9.6%) students said they had been physically hurt on purpose by their boyfriend or girlfriend during the past year. (See Table 7.1.) Female students (11.7%) were considerably more likely to say they had experienced dating violence than were male students (7.4%). Students in grades 11 and 12 had higher rates of dating violence than did students in grades nine and 10, possibly because older students are more likely to go on dates. The overall rates by race and ethnicity were 10.5% for non-Hispanic African American students, 9.7% for Hispanic students, and 9% for non-Hispanic white students. Students were also asked if they had ever been "physically forced" to engage in sexual activity. As shown in Table 7.1, 10.6% had experienced this type of abuse in 2015. The rate for female students (15.6%) was nearly three times higher than the rate for male students (5.4%). Younger female students were more likely than older female students to have experienced an incident of

TABLE 7.1

Percentage of high school students who experienced dating violence and sexual dating violence, by sex, race and Hispanic origin, and grade, 2015

Category	Physical dating violence			Sexual dating violence		
	Female	**Male**	**Total**	**Female**	**Male**	**Total**
	%	%	%	%	%	%
Race/ethnicity						
White*	11.9	5.9	9.0	16.6	3.5	10.1
Black*	12.2	9.0	10.5	11.7	8.0	10.0
Hispanic	11.4	8.0	9.7	14.2	7.0	10.6
Grade						
9	11.1	5.3	8.1	17.6	4.5	10.8
10	10.9	8.2	9.6	15.8	7.4	11.8
11	11.6	7.9	10.1	14.9	5.1	10.3
12	12.9	8.2	10.5	13.9	4.6	9.2
Total	**11.7**	**7.4**	**9.6**	**15.6**	**5.4**	**10.6**

*Non-Hispanic.

Notes: Refers to high school students who experienced physical dating violence one or more times during the 12 months before the survey. Among the 68.6% of students nationwide who dated or went out with someone during the 12 months before the survey, being physically hurt on purpose (counting being hit, slammed into something, or injured with an object or weapon) by someone they were dating or going out with. Among the 69.1% of students nationwide who dated or went out with someone during the 12 months before the survey, being forced to do sexual things (counting kissing, touching, or being physically forced to have sexual intercourse) they did not want to do by someone they were dating or going out with. The prevalence of dating or going out with someone during the 12 months before the survey varies slightly for physical dating violence and sexual dating violence because of di erences in the number of usable responses to each question.

SOURCE: Adapted from Laura Kann et al., "Table 21. Percentage of High School Students Who Experienced Physical Dating Violence and Sexual Dating Violence, by Sex, Race/Ethnicity, and Grade—United States, Youth Risk Behavior Survey, 2015," in "Youth Risk Behavior Surveillance—United States, 2015," *MMWR*, vol. 65, no. 6, June 10, 2016, http://www.cdc.gov/healthyyouth/data/yrbs/pdf/2015/ss6506_updated.pdf (accessed June 10, 2016)

sexual dating violence. The overall rates by race and ethnicity were 10.6% for Hispanic students, 10.1% for non-Hispanic white students, and 10% for non-Hispanic African American students.

EFFECTS OF DOMESTIC VIOLENCE

There are often urgent and long-term physical and mental health consequences of domestic violence. Short-term physical consequences include mild to moderate injuries, such as broken bones, bruises, and cuts. More serious medical problems include sexually transmitted diseases, miscarriages, premature labor, and injury to unborn children, as well as damage to the central nervous system sustained as a result of blows to the head, including traumatic brain injuries, chronic headaches, and loss of vision and hearing. The medical consequences of abuse may go unreported because women are reluctant to disclose abuse as the cause of their injuries, and health professionals are uncomfortable inquiring about it.

Kristie A. Thomas et al. explain in "Intersections of Harm and Health: A Qualitative Study of Intimate Partner Violence in Women's Lives" (*Violence against Women*, vol. 14, no. 11, November 2008) that on the one hand intimate partner violence produces adverse health effects in victims, in addition to worsening already compromised health. On the other hand, ill health increases women's dependence on the abuser. The researchers conducted qualitative interviews with female volunteers from eight Philadelphia, Pennsylvania, social service agencies. They find that there was a high correlation between intimate partner violence and adverse health effects, including headaches, high blood pressure, drug and alcohol abuse, chronic pain, and embarrassing scars. Thomas et al. conclude that "the pathways linking [intimate partner violence] and health are often bidirectional and cyclical, ultimately resulting in compromised health quality over the long term."

Abused women are also at risk for health problems that are not directly caused by the abuse. In "Intimate Partner Violence and Physical Health Consequences" (*Archives of Internal Medicine*, vol. 162, no. 10, May 27, 2002), Jacquelyn Campbell et al. compare the physical health problems of abused women to a control group of women who had never suffered abuse. The researchers find that abused women suffered 50% to 70% more gynecological, central nervous system, and stress-related problems. Examples of stress-related problems included chronic fear, headaches, back pain, gastrointestinal disorders, appetite loss, and increased incidence of viral infections such as colds. Although women who most recently suffered physical abuse reported the most health problems, Campbell et al. find evidence that abused women remain less healthy over time. Other scholars have identified a range of both mental and physical health issues suffered by female victims of intimate partner violence. Laura E. Watkins et al. observe in "The Longitudinal Impact of Intimate Partner Aggression and Relationship Status on Women's Physical Health and Depression Symptoms" (*Journal of Family Psychology*, vol. 28, no. 5, October 2014) that the presence of both physical and psychological health problems was particularly prevalent among younger women who remained in relationships with abusive partners.

Post-traumatic Stress Disorder

Women who have been abused are at risk for developing post-traumatic stress disorder (PTSD). According to the National Institutes of Health, in "Post-traumatic Stress Disorder" (February 2016, http://www.nimh.nih.gov/health/topics/post-traumatic-stress-disorder-ptsd/index.shtml), PTSD symptoms include startling easily, emotional numbness (especially in relationships), irritability or aggressiveness, avoidance of situations that are similar to the traumatic event, and reliving the trauma in flashbacks and nightmares.

The development of PTSD may lead to some of the adverse health outcomes associated with intimate partner violence. Studies such as Mary Ann Dutton et al.'s "Intimate Partner Violence, PTSD, and Adverse Health Outcomes" (*Journal of Interpersonal Violence*, vol. 21, no. 7, July 2006) and Stephanie J. Woods's "Intimate Partner Violence and Post-traumatic Stress Disorder Symptoms in Women: What We Know and Need to Know" (*Journal of Interpersonal Violence*, vol. 20, no. 4, April 2005) show that victims of intimate partner violence have up to five times a greater likelihood of having or developing PTSD, as well as a host of other mental health problems such as depression and substance abuse. Some researchers estimate that between 31% and 84% of all battered women develop PTSD. The more severe the violence, the higher the likelihood that a woman will develop the disorder.

According to Dutton et al., PTSD "appears to be a linchpin in the relationship between exposure to violence and negative health outcomes." The researchers postulate that PTSD, which has been shown to lead to negative health behaviors, has consequences on battered women's health. These consequences may result from not adhering to a doctor's instructions or from specific coping strategies to deal with PTSD. In addition, biological responses to PTSD may contribute to an increase in blood pressure or a suppression of the immune system.

Researchers find that women exhibit a range of psychological responses to the traumatic impact of intimate partner violence. In "Impact of Intimate Partner Violence on Women's Mental Health" (*Journal of Family Violence*, vol. 29, no. 7, October 2014), Gunnur Karakurt, Douglas Smith, and Jason Whiting assess the mental health status of women living in domestic abuse shelters. According to the researchers, women seeking mental health services for domestic violence can be divided into three basic categories. Whereas one segment of female domestic violence victims expresses a readiness to sever their relationship with their abuser, some women become primarily fixated on the psychological damage they have incurred as a result of abuse, and the remaining victims express feelings of guilt for their perceived role in causing the domestic violence situation to arise in the first place.

As is discussed in Chapter 3, children living in domestic violence situations also suffer a range of negative outcomes. In the long term, domestic violence can have a profound impact on the psychological well-being of children who have been exposed to abusive situations. In many cases, these negative effects stem from a child's fundamental inability to comprehend domestic violence. Victoria Thornton of the Brighton General Hospital in England indicates in "Understanding the Emotional Impact of Domestic Violence on Young Children" (*Educational and Child Psychology*, vol. 31, no. 1, March 2014) that small children lack the intellectual and emotional tools to process their feelings in the aftermath of an abusive situation. According to Thornton, the failure to express these feelings adequately can often lead to long-term emotional struggles.

PREVENTING DOMESTIC VIOLENCE

The United States has a two-pronged approach to preventing domestic violence. One prong is the criminal justice system, which investigates and prosecutes people who violate criminal laws, including laws against domestic violence. Chapter 1 describes federal and state legislation that establishes the legal basis for dealing with abusers. Additional information about the role of the criminal justice system is presented in Chapter 9. This chapter will focus on preventive measures of other forms, including those facilitated by government agencies that are devoted to public health and welfare and private organizations that work to prevent domestic violence in society. Some of the key elements of prevention include increasing public awareness about domestic violence (e.g., through education campaigns) and providing victim services, such as domestic violence hotlines and emergency shelters for victims.

INCREASING PUBLIC AWARENESS

As noted earlier, domestic violence was historically considered to be a private matter settled within families. The secrecy surrounding this type of violence made it easier for society at large to believe that domestic violence was not particularly common or problematic. Greater public awareness has been achieved in part through the higher priority paid to domestic violence cases in the legal and criminal justice system. This has opened many cases to the public eye through media coverage, particularly when the victims or perpetrators are celebrities, such as movie stars or famous sports figures. Since the 1990s dozens of domestic violence accusations involving celebrities have received media coverage. In most cases, the charges are dropped by the alleged victims and never reach a courtroom. Famous people involved in these cases include the boxer Floyd Mayweather Jr. (1977–); the actor Charlie Sheen (1965–); and the singers Chris Brown (1989–), Rihanna (1988–), Whitney Houston (1963–2012), and Bobby Brown (1969–).

In recent years the National Football League (NFL) has come under particularly intense scrutiny for the high number of domestic violence incidents involving its players. Michael Martinez reports in "NFL's Past Penalties for Domestic Violence 'a Different Story'" (CNN.com, September 16, 2014) that between 2000 and 2014, 85 NFL players were arrested on domestic violence charges. The most controversial domestic violence case involving an NFL player occurred in February 2014, when the Baltimore Ravens running back Ray Rice (1987—) was arrested for assaulting his girlfriend, Janay Palmer, at an

Atlantic City casino. The incident gained national attention days later, when the celebrity news outlet TMZ aired video footage that showed Rice dragging an unconscious Palmer out of an elevator. The NFL's decision to suspend Rice for two games sparked further outrage among a number of women's groups and antidomestic violence organizations, who decried the punishment as inadequate. In the face of mounting criticism, the league announced in August 2014 harsher rules governing domestic violence incidents involving its players and increasing the penalty for a first offense to a six-game suspension. On September 8, 2014, less than two weeks after the NFL introduced its new code of conduct, TMZ released additional video footage from inside the casino elevator, which clearly showed Rice punching Palmer in the face. That same day the Baltimore Ravens terminated Rice's contract and the league suspended him indefinitely (the suspension was later overturned in court).

Despite these actions, the NFL remained a target of criticism in the media for its overall handling of the Rice case, as well as for the apparent inconsistency of its rules concerning players with a history of domestic violence. In "Domestic Violence Is a Recurring Quandary for the N.F.L." (NYTimes.com, November 10, 2015), Ken Belson notes that the league once again came under fire in 2015 after the Dallas Cowboys defensive end Greg Hardy (1988–), who had been convicted of assault against his girlfriend Nicole Holder the previous year, was able to get a 10-game suspension reduced to only four games. Although Hardy was ultimately acquitted of the charges after reaching an out-of-court settlement with Holder, his return to action prompted harsh criticism even among people within the NFL, with the Hall-of-Fame quarterback and Fox NFL Sunday analyst Terry Bradshaw (1948–) vehemently condemning both Hardy and Cowboys owner Jerry Jones (1942–) on the air in October 2015.

Meanwhile, the league once again found itself confronting a domestic abuse scandal in February 2016, when the Cleveland Browns quarterback Johnny Manziel (1992–) became the subject of a criminal investigation following an incident in which he physically attacked his ex-girlfriend, Colleen Crowley (1992–). The news of Manziel's case came at the same time that the NFL introduced new rules that prohibited college prospects with a history of domestic violence from participating in the league's annual scouting combine. Even with this measure, as of September 2016 it remained to be seen whether or not the NFL would implement additional statutes aimed at curbing domestic abuse cases involving its players.

Public Health Campaigns

The CDC provides in *Breaking the Silence—Public Health's Role in Intimate Partner Violence Prevention* (May 17, 2012, http://www.cdc.gov/cdcgrandrounds/archives/2012/june2012.htm) information about programs and activities that are facilitated by the agency to aid in the prevention of intimate partner violence. Besides data collection and research projects, the CDC operates three key programs: Domestic Violence Prevention Enhancement and Leadership through Alliances, Focusing on Outcomes for Communities United with States, and Dating Matters: Strategies to Promote Healthy Teen Relationships.

In the fact sheet "Affordable Care Act Rules on Expanding Access to Preventive Services for Women" (June 28, 2013, http://www.hhs.gov/healthcare/facts/factsheets/2011/08/womensprevention08012011a.html), the U.S. Department of Health and Human Services (HHS) notes that under the Patient Protection and Affordable Care Act of 2010 medical insurance plans that were initiated or renewed after August 2012 must cover interpersonal and domestic violence screening and counseling services for all adolescent and adult women at no charge to them. The Affordable Care Act includes major reforms to the nation's health care system including greatly expanded preventive programs. According to the HHS, the new screening and counseling requirement should aid in the detection and treatment of abused women.

Victim Services

One of the most common victim services is the operation of domestic violence hotlines by government entities and private organizations. For example, the National Domestic Violence Hotline (2016, http://www.thehotline.org) was established in 1996 as part of the Violence Against Women Act of 1994. The hotline is available 24 hours a day, seven days a week. The operators who answer the phone can provide informational materials on battering intervention, the criminal justice system, sexual assault, and other issues, as well as crisis intervention and safety planning. Referrals to local service providers are also available. According to the National Domestic Violence Hotline, between 1996 and 2016 the hotline provided assistance to more than 4 million people seeking help for domestic violence and dating violence issues.

A new innovation in victim services technology is the availability of application (app) software for mobile computerized devices such as smartphones and tablets. For example, in August 2012 the communications corporation Verizon Wireless introduced the HopeLine app. The company notes in "HopeLine from Verizon Introduces Mobile App for Android Smartphones and Tablets" (August 2, 2012, http://news.verizonwireless.com/news/2012/08/pr2012-08-02c.html) that the app allows users to connect directly to resources, such as the National Domestic Violence Hotline. In addition, the app provides access to an online community through which people can share stories, photos, and videos and learn about domestic violence services.

There are thousands of victim service agencies around the country that help domestic violence victims. The "Directory of Crime Victim Services" (2016, http://ovc.ncjrs.gov/findvictimservices/), operated by the Department of Justice's Office for Victims of Crime, includes an extensive online directory of more than 10,000 programs. Online visitors can search for crime victim services in a particular state. For example, a search for resources in California yields more than 600 services available to domestic violence victims. The directory also lists resources that are located in some other countries and services that are provided through the U.S. military.

Besides law enforcement and other criminal justice agencies, the directory includes government and private agencies that offer the following types of services to domestic violence victims:

- In-person information about and referrals to available services and support organizations

- Assistance in filing crime victim compensation claims with appropriate agencies

- Support, assistance, and advocacy as victims navigate the criminal justice process, including postsentencing services and support

- Crisis counseling, including in-person crisis intervention, hotline counseling, emotional support, and guidance, provided by advocates, counselors, mental health professionals, or peers

- Emergency financial assistance, including cash outlays for needs such as transportation, food, clothing, and emergency housing

- Emergency assistance in certain legal matters, such as filing of temporary restraining orders, injunctions, and other protective orders

- Follow-up contact via telephone, in-person meetings, or written communications to offer emotional support and check on a victim's progress

- Coordination and provision of supportive group activities, including social support services

- Personal advocacy services, such as accompanying victims to the hospital; intervening with employers, creditors, and others on behalf of victims; and assisting in filing insurance claims and for programs, such as public assistance, workers' compensation, or unemployment benefits, as appropriate

- Safety planning for stalking victims to help reduce the chances of physical or emotional harm from stalkers

- Shelters and safe houses that offer short- and long-term housing and related support services for victims and families after a victimization

- Professional, psychological, psychiatric, or other therapy or counseling-related evaluation and treatment for individuals, couples, and family members affected by victimization

- Transportation services to and from victim service agencies

Table 7.2 provides an overall breakdown of violent victimizations between 2005 and 2014. Most victims of intimate partner violence do not end up receiving victim services. For example, of the 634,612 victims of intimate partner violence in 2014, only 179,220 (28.2%) received victim services following the incident. Although this pattern has generally also proven true for victims of rape and sexual assault, in recent years the proportion of rape and sexual assault victims who received victim services has seen a sudden rise. In 2006, 157,698 individuals were raped or sexually assaulted by an intimate partner; of these, 65,485 (41.5%) received victim services. (See Table 7.3.) Of the 70,110 cases of intimate partner rape and sexual assault that were recorded in 2014, more than four out of five victims (57,108, or 81.5%) went on to receive victim services.

Table 7.4 provides a breakdown of victims who received medical treatment for injuries related to domestic violence incidents between 2005 and 2014. Of the 634,612 victims of intimate partner violence in 2014, 339,261 (53.5%) reported no injury following the incident, 167,096 (26.3%) were injured but not treated, and 91,007 (14.3%) were treated for an injury. Victims of rape and sexual assault are far more likely to sustain injuries than other victims of intimate partner violence. Of the 70,110 victims who were raped or sexually assaulted by an intimate partner in 2014, nearly two-thirds (46,131, or 65.8%) were reported as sustaining injuries; however, only 3,097 victims (6.7% of those injured; 4.4% of victims of this type of violence) received some form of medical treatment. (See Table 7.5.)

Why Do Abused Women Stay?

One complicated issue for people who are devoted to preventing domestic violence is that victims sometimes choose to stay in violent relationships. This begs the question: Why do victims stay? Some authors and advocates believe this question implies that there is something wrong with the victims for staying, rather than placing the blame where it belongs: on the abusers. Ola W. Barnett of Pepperdine University argues in "Why Battered Women Do Not Leave, Part 1: External Inhibiting Factors within Society" (*Trauma, Violence, and Abuse*, vol. 1, no. 4, October 2000) that better questions might be: "Why does he beat her?" or "Why does society let him get away with it?" or "What can be done to stop him?" Nevertheless, researchers have focused their efforts on determining the motivations that drive victims, particularly women, to stay in abusive relationships.

WOMEN'S REASONS TO STAY. Women stay in abusive relationships for a variety of reasons. A major reason women stay is their economic dependency on their batterer.

TABLE 7.2

Violent victimizations, by victim-offender relationship, type of victimization, and victim services status, 2005–14

Crime type	2005	2006	2007	2008	2009	2010	2011	2012	2013	2014
Violent victimization	6,947,795	8,430,430	6,814,183	6,393,471	5,669,237	4,935,983	5,812,523	6,842,593	6,126,423	5,359,570
Intimates	816,006	1,305,249	905,810	1,103,332	1,039,650	773,434	850,772	810,794	748,795	634,612
Services received from victim service agencies	198,909	281,045	261,604	240,625	217,766	179,200	136,650	227,300	232,398	179,220
No services received from victim service agencies	613,323	1,024,205	641,433	862,767	816,060	588,985	687,562	571,060	498,573	455,392
Other relatives	426,284	558,407	501,907	454,683	343,020	356,129	504,135	448,598	367,291	475,265
Services received from victim service agencies	44,074	72,067	42,288	103,397!	32,192!	65,493	98,815	48,375	67,048	96,392
No services received from victim service agencies	382,211	472,819	456,386	347,182	259,374	286,381	401,192	395,057	297,435	377,444
Well-known/casual acquaintances	2,356,241	2,661,522	1,997,175	1,781,331	1,756,014	1,573,294	1,779,618	2,263,252	2,445,099	1,709,366
Services received from victim service agencies	241,004	131,423	185,473	117,579	116,849	125,725	127,146	214,089	134,315	188,776
No services received from victim service agencies	2,108,625	2,525,332	1,806,263	1,651,546	1,639,164	1,445,512	1,628,526	2,039,402	2,305,288	1,504,159
Stranger	2,829,598	3,184,058	2,706,132	2,154,770	2,165,849	1,812,303	2,146,307	2,710,114	2,098,170	2,166,129
Services received from victim service agencies	131,079	162,685	116,067	74,153	86,549	35,277!	103,639	57,636	96,072	64,452
No services received from victim service agencies	2,692,957	3,014,495	2,590,066	2,063,254	2,065,653	1,762,695	2,031,405	2,603,245	1,980,395	2,093,726
Do not know relationship	361,855	506,652	448,275	486,084	217,989	288,667	240,956	371,910	288,795	223,847
Services received from victim service agencies	25,115!	27,612!	3,584!	37,101!	12,176!	13,638!	19,326!	10,053!	46,945!	29,482!
No services received from victim service agencies	321,009	465,480	422,566	431,443	194,488	259,214	216,374	355,561	235,677	184,662
Do not know number of offenders	157,809	214,541	254,885	413,292	139,707	132,156	290,736	228,660	178,273	150,351
Services received from victim service agencies	32,778!	11,162!	14,767!	4,017!	—	6,019!	12,648!	3,501!	7,850!	6,696!
No services received from victim service agencies	114,015	197,311	237,461	395,569	122,292	121,178	211,167	219,040	167,423	131,584
Serious violent victimization	2,258,400	3,149,814	2,242,721	1,998,691	1,969,921	1,694,835	1,854,837	2,084,691	1,940,030	2,040,647
Intimates	311,475	535,611	305,986	398,306	250,475	268,780	262,658	270,239	360,817	265,887
Services received from victim service agencies	111,033	139,378	90,492	72,473	41,680	70,495	39,075	84,628	120,217	85,320
No services received from victim service agencies	196,667	396,232	213,720	325,833	206,303	196,350	223,584	184,010	230,685	180,567
Other relatives	113,790	254,037	283,009	185,741	94,760	111,251	106,379	140,837	103,910	134,144
Services received from victim service agencies	20,661!	36,642!	24,463!	16,954!	17,510!	28,605!	18,680!	11,301!	36,005!	21,986!
No services received from victim service agencies	93,129	206,527	258,547	168,788	42,471!	78,390	85,212	129,535	67,905	112,158
Well-known/casual aquaintances	529,824	853,719	501,995	445,012	648,287	462,152	483,669	459,981	584,548	569,697
Services received from victim service agencies	95,781	39,682	46,336!	44,434	105,049!	64,259	50,095!	54,989	69,405!	93,778
No services received from victim service agencies	430,924	812,654	453,421	397,060	543,238	395,836	428,680	400,312	515,143	470,362
Stranger	1,096,475	1,259,605	937,792	709,102	821,534	721,671	803,761	1,020,398	737,943	930,694
Services received from victim service agencies	47,325	105,035	56,320	43,811	22,941!	15,721!	60,819	35,605	37,590	23,438!
No services received from victim service agencies	1,049,150	1,154,570	881,472	652,925	784,946	695,423	735,299	974,289	681,430	905,614
Do not know relationship	152,888	176,216	141,219	157,134	121,315	93,777	112,302	106,332	81,396	105,658
Services received from victim service agencies	17,833!	18,083!	—	12,718!	5,160!	2,933!	15,158!	10,053!	2,340!	23,080!
No services received from victim service agencies	122,424	147,597	136,759	134,800	111,904	85,362	95,622	93,411	72,883	79,181
Do not know number of offenders	53,948	70,626	71,720	103,401	33,550!	37,205!	86,067	86,904	71,416	34,566
Services received from victim service agencies	6,828!	7,277!	11,314!	4,017!	—	2,118!	8,289!	3,501!	—	3,636!
No services received from victim service agencies	42,286	57,281	60,406	99,385	33,550!	30,127!	72,513	79,209	68,416!	24,714!

TABLE 7.2

Violent victimizations, by victim-offender relationship, type of victimization, and victim services status, 2005–14 [CONTINUED]

Crime type	2005	2006	2007	2008	2009	2010	2011	2012	2013	2014
Simple assault	4,689,395	5,280,616	4,571,462	4,394,774	3,699,316	3,241,148	3,957,686	4,757,902	4,186,394	3,318,923
Intimates	504,532	769,639	598,824	705,086	789,175	504,654	588,113	540,555	387,978	368,725
Services received from victim service agencies	87,876	141,666	171,111	168,152	176,086	108,705	97,575	142,671	112,181	93,899
No services received from victim service agencies	416,656	627,972	427,713	536,934	609,757	392,635	463,978	387,049	267,888	274,825
Other relatives	312,494	304,370	218,897	268,862	248,260	244,878	397,755	307,761	263,381	341,121
Services received from victim service agencies	23,413!	35,426	17,826!	86,443!	14,682!	36,888!	80,135!	37,074	31,043	74,406
No services received from victim service agencies	289,082	266,292	198,339	178,394	216,903	207,990	315,979	265,522	229,530	265,286
Well-known/casual acquaintances	1,826,417	1,807,803	1,495,180	1,336,318	1,107,727	1,111,143	1,295,949	1,803,271	1,860,551	1,139,669
Services received from victim service agencies	145,223	91,741	139,138	73,146	11,800!	61,467	77,052	159,100	64,910	94,998
No services received from victim service agencies	1,677,701	1,712,678	1,352,843	1,254,486	1,095,927	1,049,676	1,199,846	1,639,089	1,790,145	1,033,797
Stranger	1,733,123	1,924,453	1,768,340	1,445,668	1,344,315	1,090,632	1,342,546	1,689,717	1,360,228	1,235,434
Services received from victim service agencies	83,754	57,651	59,747	30,342!	63,608!	19,556!	42,820	22,031!	58,482	41,014!
No services received from victim service agencies	1,643,807	1,859,925	1,708,593	1,410,329	1,280,707	1,067,272	1,296,106	1,628,957	1,298,965	1,188,112
Do not know relationship	208,968	330,436	307,055	328,949	96,674	194,890	128,654	265,577	207,399	118,189
Services received from victim service agencies	7,282!	9,529!	13,584!	24,382!	7,016!	10,704!	4,168!	—	44,605!	6,402!
No services received from victim service agencies	198,584	317,883	285,807	296,643	82,584	173,852	120,752	262,151	162,794	105,481
Do not know number of offenders	103,861	143,915	183,165	309,891	106,156	94,952	204,669	141,756	106,857	115,785
Services received from victim service agencies	25,950!	3,885!	3,453!	—	—	3,901!	4,359!	—	7,850!	3,060!
No services received from victim service agencies	71,729	140,030	177,055	296,185	88,742	91,051	138,654	139,831	99,007	106,870

—Estimate is equal to 0 sample cases.

!Interpret data with caution, based on 10 or fewer sample cases or the coefficient of variation is greater than 50%.

Notes: Special tabulations from the NCVS Victimization Analysis Tool (NVAT). Detail may not sum to total due to rounding and/or missing data. Due to methodological changes in the 2006 NCVS, use caution when comparing 2006 criminal victimization estimates to other years.

SOURCE: "Number of Violent Victimizations, Serious Violent Victimizations, and Simple Assaults by Victim-Offender Relationship and Victim Services, 2005–2014," in NCVS Victimization Analysis Tool (NVAT), U.S. Department of Justice, Office of Justice Programs, Bureau of Justice Statistics, June 10, 2016, http://www.bjs.gov/index.cfm?ty=nvat (accessed June 10, 2016)

TABLE 7.3

Rapes and sexual assaults, by victim-offender relationship and victim services status, 2005–14

Crime type	2005	2006	2007	2008	2009	2010	2011	2012	2013	2014
Rape/sexual assault	207,760	463,598	248,277	349,691	305,574	268,574	244,188	346,830	300,165	284,345
Intimates	66,750	157,698	55,110	103,675	43,198	109,205	44,155	64,412	107,860	70,110
Services received from victim service agencies	8,208	65,485	17,767	43,444	10,297	44,809	8,240	39,638	32,494	57,108
No services received from victim service agencies	58,542	92,213	37,343	60,231	32,901	64,396	35,915	24,774	70,912	13,002
Other relatives	11,853	7,397	6,529	24,670	34,779	12,921	1,721	3,458	1,936	2,909
Services received from victim service agencies	—	—	—	5,219	—	12,921	—	3,458	—	—
No services received from victim service agencies	11,853	7,397	6,529	19,451	—	—	1,721	—	1,936	2,909
Well-known/casual acquaintances	60,813	152,255	81,968	90,611	187,848	97,817	117,760	162,288	120,927	126,649
Services received from victim service agencies	25,103	3,440	14,700	10,590	8,787	39,914	29,515	29,061	18,094	28,714
No services received from victim service agencies	35,711	148,815	65,029	80,022	179,061	57,902	88,245	133,228	102,833	97,935
Stranger	59,982	134,929	77,477	76,907	36,586	43,167	72,807	59,126	57,136	69,054
Services received from victim service agencies	9,103	24,969	19,158	3,108	—	3,560	15,240	3,103	7,329	4,461
No services received from victim service agencies	50,879	109,960	58,318	73,798	36,586	39,607	57,567	52,246	49,808	64,593
Do not know relationship	5,375	11,320	13,823	9,346	3,163	5,464	4,835	17,174	9,305	8,812
Services received from victim service agencies	—	—	—	2,892	—	—	—	—	—	—
No services received from victim service agencies	5,375	11,320	13,823	6,454	3,163	5,464	4,835	17,174	9,305	8,812
Do not know number of offenders	2,987	—	13,370	44,483	—	—	2,911	40,372	3,000	6,812
Services received from victim service agencies	—	—	8,042	4,017	—	—	2,911	—	—	3,636
No services received from victim service agencies	2,987	—	5,329	40,466	—	—	—	40,372	—	—

—Estimate is equal to 0 sample cases.

Notes: Special tabulations from the National Crime Victimization Survey (NCVS) Victimization Analysis Tool (NVAT). Detail may not sum to total due to rounding and/or missing data. Due to methodological changes in the 2006 NCVS, use caution when comparing 2006 criminal victimization estimates to other years. No unique link for individual data sets.

SOURCE: "Number of Rape/Sexual Assaults by Victim-Offender Relationship and Victim Services, 2005–2014," in *NCVS Victimization Analysis Tool (NVAT)*, U.S. Department of Justice, Office of Justice Programs, Bureau of Justice Statistics, June 10, 2016, http://www.bjs.gov/index.cfm?ty=nvat (accessed June 10, 2016)

Many women feel they are better off with a violent husband than facing the challenge of raising children on their own. Some harbor deep feelings for their abusive partner and believe that over time they can change their partner's behavior. Others mistakenly interpret their abuser's efforts to control their life as expressions of love. Some frequently reported practical considerations include:

- The women have at least one dependent child who must be cared for

- The women are unemployed

- The women lack a support system, for example, their parents are distant, unable, or unwilling to help

- The women may fear losing mutual friends and the support of family, especially in-laws

- The women have no property that is solely their own

- The women lack access to cash, credit, or other financial resources

- If the women leave, then they risk being charged with desertion and losing their children and joint assets

- The women may face a decline in living standards for themselves and their children, and the children, especially older ones, may resent this reduced living standard

- The women and/or their children may be in poor health

In "'We Don't Have Time for Social Change': Cultural Compromise and the Battered Woman Syndrome" (*Gender and Society*, vol. 17, no. 5, October 2003), Bess Rothenberg of Clemson University argues that women are victimized and coerced into staying in violent relationships by a combination of different forces. According to Rothenberg, women are victimized first and foremost by violent abusers; second, by a society that sanctions the right of men to hit women and socializes women into staying in abusive relationships; third, by representatives of institutions who are in a position to help but who instead ignore the plight of battered women (e.g., doctors, police, the criminal justice system, clergy, and therapists); and fourth, by the everyday realities of being a woman in a patriarchal system that expects women to raise children and denies them access to education, job skills, and good employment.

Similarly, April L. Few and Karen H. Rosen examine in "Victims of Chronic Dating Violence: How Women's Vulnerabilities Link to Their Decisions to Stay" (*Family Relations*, vol. 54, no. 2, April 2005) why women stay in abusive dating relationships and describe a combination of "relational" and "situational" vulnerabilities that work together to influence a woman's decision to stay. They define relational vulnerabilities as one's beliefs about what behaviors and interactions are normal in an intimate relationship. Situational vulnerabilities refer to

TABLE 7.4

Violent victimizations, by victim-offender relationship, type of victimization, and injury and medical treatment status, 2005–14

Crime type	2005	2006	2007	2008	2009	2010	2011	2012	2013	2014
Violent victimization	6,947,795	8,430,430	6,814,183	6,393,471	5,669,237	4,935,983	5,812,523	6,842,593	6,126,423	5,359,570
Intimates	816,006	1,305,249	905,810	1,103,392	1,039,650	773,434	850,772	810,794	748,795	634,612
Not injured	375,134	481,470	490,532	655,364	604,905	431,806	569,855	486,920	285,452	339,261
Not treated for injury	261,570	660,217	309,492	297,608	332,745	175,653	188,499	193,699	314,832	167,096
Treated at scene, home, medical office, or other location	179,302	163,563	105,786	150,420	102,000	165,974	92,418	130,175	146,291	91,007
Other relatives	426,284	558,407	501,907	454,603	343,020	356,129	504,135	448,598	367,291	475,265
Not injured	306,988	353,011	268,267	328,052	237,219	250,478	298,142	276,341	249,599	317,694
Not treated for injury	83,376	115,123	70,124	63,489	64,647	58,292	91,563	81,466	95,325	84,433
Treated at scene, home, medical office, or other location	35,920!	90,273	163,516	63,061	41,155	44,510	114,430	90,791	22,367!	73,138
Well-known/casual acquaintances	2,356,241	2,661,522	1,997,175	1,781,331	1,756,014	1,573,294	1,779,618	2,263,252	2,445,099	1,709,366
Not injured	1,914,564	1,965,928	1,579,088	1,428,360	1,362,438	1,264,429	1,318,565	1,852,448	1,896,394	1,252,059
Not treated for injury	282,976	493,327	285,173	222,771	272,537	156,346	286,207	250,193	328,423	212,496
Treated at scene, home, medical office, or other location	158,702	202,267	132,914	130,199	121,039	152,519	174,846	160,611	217,077	244,810
Stranger	2,829,598	3,184,058	2,706,132	2,154,770	2,165,849	1,812,303	2,146,307	2,710,114	2,098,170	2,166,129
Not injured	2,208,657	2,469,966	2,105,304	1,756,549	1,712,201	1,357,845	1,730,944	2,163,554	1,674,591	1,740,641
Not treated for injury	320,075	348,710	279,204	206,093	238,183	256,033	200,459	308,346	223,769	218,694
Treated at scene, home, medical office, or other location	300,867	365,383	321,625	192,127	215,465	198,425	214,904	238,215	199,810	206,794
Do not know relationship	361,855	506,652	448,275	486,084	217,989	288,667	240,956	371,910	288,795	223,847
Not injured	257,243	428,649	385,545	424,444	142,937	237,558	196,770	315,250	254,915	193,696
Not treated for injury	47,706!	45,161	36,893	24,660!	14,872!	28,656!	26,105!	28,506!	16,828!	13,359!
Treated at scene, home, medical office, or other location	52,703	30,369!	22,704!	33,038!	52,702	22,453!	12,511!	21,667!	17,052!	12,625!
Do not know number of offenders	157,809	214,541	254,885	413,292	139,707	132,156	290,736	228,660	178,273	150,351
Not injured	125,995	177,667	225,608	349,711	125,462	104,039	247,597	170,724	161,512	140,267
Not treated for injury	14,431!	8,705!	18,159!	63,581!	8,072!	20,810!	8,313!	10,495!	3,698!	1,752!
Treated at scene, home, medical office, or other location	17,383!	28,169!	11,118!	—	6,173!	7,307!	34,825!	47,441!	9,635!	8,333!
Serious violent victimization	2,258,400	3,149,814	2,242,721	1,998,697	1,969,921	1,694,835	1,854,837	2,084,691	1,940,030	2,040,647
Intimates	311,475	535,611	306,986	398,306	250,475	268,780	262,658	270,239	360,817	265,887
Not injured	54,779	208,383	134,990	141,140	91,069	88,514	121,745	99,847	89,954	117,981
Not treated for injury	122,331	255,036	114,718	153,410	120,419	60,756	86,733	98,807	179,164	61,620
Treated at scene, home, medical office, or other location	134,365	72,191	57,278	103,756	38,987	119,510	54,181	71,585	89,478	51,561
Other relatives	113,790	254,037	283,009	185,741	94,760	111,251	106,379	140,837	103,910	134,144
Not injured	91,533	166,455	129,647	149,780	58,370!	71,161	90,692	81,385	46,442	60,456
Not treated for injury	12,860!	39,476!	11,663!	3,387!	16,031!	15,904!	5,236!	20,639!	45,449!	29,853
Treated at scene, home, medical office, or other location	9,396!	48,107!	141,699!	32,574!	20,359!	24,186!	10,451!	38,813	12,019!	43,835
Well-known/casual acquaintances	529,824	853,719	501,995	445,012	648,287	462,152	483,669	459,981	584,548	569,697
Not injured	372,879	570,711	376,762	317,454	414,712	306,304	270,341	339,562	399,871	367,846
Not treated for injury	55,283	179,336	77,365	67,720	148,821	53,336	112,256	68,260	75,486	117,032
Treated at scene, home, medical office, or other location	101,662	103,673	47,868	59,839	84,753	102,512	101,073	52,159	109,191	84,819
Stranger	1,096,475	1,259,605	937,792	709,102	821,534	721,671	803,761	1,020,398	737,943	930,694
Not injured	785,121	889,925	637,897	467,249	555,738	470,259	562,860	697,624	549,149	696,695
Not treated for injury	154,334	128,185	111,082	117,115	100,838	126,390	77,395	167,838	79,729	81,732
Treated at scene, home, medical office, or other location	157,019	241,495	188,813	124,738	164,958	125,022	163,506	154,935	109,065	152,267
Do not know relationship	152,888	176,216	141,219	157,134	121,315	93,777	112,302	106,332	81,396	105,658
Not injured	98,441	130,760	122,526	107,932	77,237	69,490	71,062	68,025	57,056	75,507
Not treated for injury	22,607!	25,593!	15,561!	18,277!	—	9,993!	23,158!	10,153!	9,758!	13,359!
Treated at scene, home, medical office, or other location	31,840!	19,863!	—	30,926!	39,301!	14,294!	12,511!	21,667!	14,582!	12,625!

TABLE 7.4

Violent victimizations, by victim-offender relationship, type of victimization, and injury and medical treatment status, 2005–14 [CONTINUED]

Crime type	2005	2006	2007	2008	2009	2010	2011	2012	2013	2014
Do not know number of offenders	53,948	70,626	71,720	103,401	33,550!	37,205!	86,067	86,904	71,416	34,566
Not injured	30,849!	37,186!	45,859	51,918	21,446!	20,950!	48,331	36,075	58,353!	29,695!
Not treated for injury	5,716!	8,705!	14,744!	51,483!	5,931!	8,948!	2,911!	3,388!	—	—
Treated at scene, home, medical office, or other location	17,383!	24,734!	11,118!	—	6,173!	7,307!	34,825!	47,441!	9,635!	4,870!
Simple assault	4,689,395	5,280,616	4,571,462	4,394,774	3,699,316	3,241,148	3,957,686	4,757,902	4,186,394	3,318,923
Intimates	504,532	769,639	598,824	705,086	769,175	504,654	588,113	540,555	387,978	368,725
Not injured	320,356	273,087	355,542	514,224	513,836	343,292	448,110	387,073	195,498	221,280
Not treated for injury	139,239	405,180	194,774	144,197	212,326	114,897	101,767	94,892	135,667	105,477
Treated at scene, home, medical office, or other location	44,937	91,371	48,508	46,664	63,013	46,465	38,237	58,590	56,813	39,446
Other relatives	312,494	304,370	218,897	268,862	248,260	244,878	397,755	307,761	263,381	341,121
Not injured	215,455	186,557	138,619	178,272	178,848	179,318	207,450	194,956	203,157	257,238
Not treated for injury	70,516	75,647	58,461	60,102	48,616	42,387	86,327	60,827	49,876	54,580
Treated at scene, home, medical office, or other location	26,524!	42,166!	21,817!	30,487!	20,796!	20,324!	103,979	51,978!	10,348!	29,303!
Well-known/casual acquaintances	1,826,417	1,807,803	1,495,180	1,336,318	1,107,727	1,111,143	1,295,949	1,803,271	1,860,551	1,139,669
Not injured	1,541,684	1,395,218	1,202,326	1,110,907	947,725	958,126	1,048,225	1,512,885	1,496,523	884,213
Not treated for injury	227,693	313,991	207,808	155,051	123,716	103,010	173,951	181,933	252,937	95,464
Treated at scene, home, medical office, or other location	57,040	98,594	85,046	70,360	36,286!	50,007	73,773	108,452	107,886	159,991
Stranger	1,733,123	1,924,453	1,768,340	1,445,668	1,344,315	1,090,632	1,342,546	1,689,717	1,360,228	1,235,434
Not injured	1,423,536	1,580,041	1,467,407	1,289,299	1,156,463	887,586	1,168,083	1,465,930	1,125,442	1,043,946
Not treated for injury	165,740	220,525	168,121	38,979	137,346	129,642	123,064	140,508	144,041	136,962
Treated at scene, home, medical office, or other location	143,847	123,888	132,812	67,390	50,507	73,403	51,398	83,279	90,745	54,527
Do not know relationship	208,968	330,436	307,055	328,949	96,674	194,890	128,654	265,577	207,399	118,189
Not injured	158,802	297,889	263,019	316,512	65,700	168,068	125,708	247,225	197,859	118,189
Not treated for injury	25,099!	19,568!	21,332!	6,383!	14,872!	18,663!	2,947!	18,353!	7,071!	—
Treated at scene, home, medical office, or other location	20,864!	10,506!	22,704!	2,111!	13,401!	8,160!	—	—	2,469!	—
Do not know number of offenders	103,861	143,915	183,165	309,891	106,156	94,952	204,669	141,756	106,857	115,785
Not injured	95,145	140,481	179,749	297,793	104,016	83,090	199,267	134,649	103,159	110,571
Not treated for injury	8,715!	—	3,415!	12,098!	2,140!	11,862!	5,402!	7,106!	3,698!	1,752!
Treated at scene, home, medical office, or other location	—	3,434!	—	—	—	—	—	—	—	3,462!

—Estimate is equal to 0 sample cases.

!Interpret data with caution, based on 10 or fewer sample cases or the coefficient of variation is greater than 50%.

Notes: Special tabulations from the NCVS Victimization Analysis Tool (NVAT). (NCVS is National Crime Victimization Survey.) Detail may not sum to total due to rounding and/or missing data. Due to methodological changes in the 2006 NCVS, use caution when comparing 2006 criminal victimization estimates to other years.

SOURCE: "Number of Violent Victimizations, Serious Violent Victimizations, and Simple Assaults by Victim-Offender Relationship and Medical Treatment for Physical Injuries, 2005–2014," in NCVS Victimization Analysis Tool (NVAT), U.S. Department of Justice, Office of Justice Programs, Bureau of Justice Statistics, June 10, 2016, http://www.bjs.gov/index.cfm?ty=nvat (accessed June 10, 2016)

TABLE 7.5

Rapes and sexual assaults, by victim–offender relationship and injury and medical treatment status, 2005–14

Crime type	2005	2006	2007	2008	2009	2010	2011	2012	2013	2014
Rape/sexual assault	207,760	463,598	248,277	349,691	305,574	268,574	244,188	346,830	300,165	284,345
Intimates	66,750	157,698	55,110	103,675	43,198	109,205	44,155	64,412	107,860	70,110
Not injured	10,965	11,419	13,251	14,811	28,067	9,533	15,524	18,020	19,017	23,979
Not treated for injury	27,882	123,119	28,676	81,291	6,427	14,190	27,169	39,417	73,653	43,034
Treated at scene, home, medical office, or other location	27,904	23,160	13,183	7,573	8,703	85,482	1,463	6,975	15,190	3,097
Other relatives	11,853	7,397	6,529	24,670	34,779	12,921	1,721	3,458	1,936	2,909
Not injured	4,604	—	6,529	19,451	34,779	10,866	1,721	3,458	—	—
Not treated for injury	7,249	7,397	—	—	—	2,055	—	—	1,936	2,909
Treated at scene, home, medical office, or other location	—	—	—	5,219	—	—	—	—	—	—
Well-known/casual acquaintances	60,813	152,255	81,968	90,611	187,848	97,817	117,760	162,288	120,927	126,649
Not injured	21,327	98,347	47,503	57,720	110,808	66,428	62,622	120,667	80,495	64,213
Not treated for injury	17,443	33,010	28,396	23,598	69,942	19,271	55,138	27,096	24,314	34,648
Treated at scene, home, medical office, or other location	22,043	20,898	6,069	9,294	7,098	12,118	—	14,526	16,118	27,787
Stranger	59,982	134,929	77,477	76,907	36,586	43,167	72,807	59,126	57,136	69,054
Not injured	30,975	100,622	37,532	34,516	22,140	26,102	37,162	50,697	39,499	51,008
Not treated for injury	15,230	14,582	17,738	31,717	3,974	11,443	16,965	8,429	14,587	3,122
Treated at scene, home, medical office, or other location	13,777	19,724	22,206	10,673	10,472	5,623	18,680	—	3,050	14,923
Do not know relationship	5,375	11,320	13,823	9,346	3,163	5,464	4,835	17,174	9,305	8,812
Not injured	5,375	3,797	13,823	6,454	3,163	5,464	1,572	6,817	5,244	5,604
Not treated for injury	—	7,523	—	—	—	—	—	2,829	—	3,208
Treated at scene, home, medical office, or other location	—	—	—	2,892	—	—	3,263	7,528	4,061	—
Do not know number of offenders	2,987	—	13,370	44,483	—	—	2,911	40,372	3,000	6,812
Not injured	—	—	—	4,378	—	—	—	2,154	—	—
Not treated for injury	2,987	—	5,329	40,105	—	—	2,911	—	3,000	6,812
Treated at scene, home, medical office, or other location	—	—	8,042	—	—	—	—	38,218	—	—

—Estimate is equal to 0 sample cases.

Notes: Special tabulations from the National Crime Victimization Survey (NCVS) Victimization Analysis Tool (NVAT). Detail may not sum to total due to rounding and/or missing data. Due to methodological changes in the 2006 NCVS, use caution when comparing 2006 criminal victimization estimates to other years. No unique link for individual data sets.

SOURCE: "Number of Rape/Sexual Assaults by Victim-Offender Relationship and Medical Treatment for Physical Injuries, 2005–2014," in *NCVS Victimization Analysis Tool (NVAT)*, U.S. Department of Justice, Office of Justice Programs, Bureau of Justice Statistics, June 10, 2016, http://www.bjs.gov/index.cfm?ty=nvat (accessed June 10, 2016) the degree to which a woman was experiencing stress at the beginning of the abusive relationship (either as a consequence of life changes or as a consequence of feeling like one is getting too old for marriage or parenthood). Few and Rosen find that an accumulation of vulnerabilities, combined with lacking protective factors such as a high self-esteem, a social support system, and healthy coping skills, made it more likely that a woman would stay in a chronically abusive dating relationship.

Barnett outlines in "Why Battered Women Do Not Leave, Part 2: External Inhibiting Factors—Social Support and Internal Inhibiting Factors" (*Trauma, Violence, and Abuse*, vol. 2, no. 1, January 2001) several internalized socialization beliefs (normal, learned beliefs about how society and relationships work) as well as psychological factors induced by trauma that serve as obstacles to battered women leaving their abuser. Barnett emphasizes that many of these beliefs are detrimental to all women, but battered women are particularly vulnerable. For example, some women turn to romantic relationships for a sense of self-worth. When an adult woman values her ability to form a relationship with a male partner over other characteristics, losing the relationship may seem worse than staying and enduring the abuse. Battered women tend to hold some distorted beliefs that keep them in abusive relationships. Common distorted thought patterns among battered women include a belief that violence is commonplace and not abusive, a belief that they caused the abuse, a lack of recognition that children are harmed more by witnessing intimate partner violence than by living with a single parent, and a belief that they can and should help the abuser to change.

In "The Role of Female Behavior and Attributions in Predicting Behavioral Responses to Hypothetical Male Aggression" (*Violence against Women*, vol. 16, no. 6, June 2010), Deborah L. Rhatigan and Alison M. Nathanson of the University of Tennessee, Knoxville, studied whether college women sometimes attribute abusive behavior to positive attributes and therefore choose to stay with their partner. The researchers asked 293 college women to read descriptions of scenes that involved conflict and abusive behavior. The women were then asked to describe the motives of the abuser and state whether or not they would leave him. Rhatigan and Nathanson find that some women interpreted male abuse as evidence of loving feelings. Women who made these "positive" attributions had lower scores of self-esteem, and they were much less likely to say that they would leave the relationship than women who attributed the behavior to negative motives.

Lenore E. Walker claims in *The Battered Woman* (1979) that abused women suffer from a constellation of symptoms—the so-called battered-woman syndrome—that keeps them from leaving abusive partners. She argues that a psychological condition known as "learned helplessness" plays a significant role in keeping women in abusive relationships. Although Walker believes, as do other multiple-victimization theorists, that women are victims of a patriarchal society and institutions that fail to advocate for abused women, she also emphasizes the psychological problems women develop in response to abuse.

The concept of learned helplessness was first articulated by Martin E. P. Seligman during the 1970s. In *Helplessness: On Depression, Development, and Death* (1992), Seligman describes how he conducted an experiment in which he taught dogs to fear the sound of a bell. He did so by restraining dogs, ringing the bell, and then subjecting the dogs to a painful (but not dangerous) shock. This process was repeated several times.

Next, to test the effectiveness of the training, Seligman placed the dogs in a cage that had an electrified floor on one side, an unelectrified floor on the other side, and a wall that separated the two parts of the cage. The wall was low enough that the dogs could jump over it if they wished. Seligman placed the dogs on the electrified floor, rang the bell, and administered shocks through the floor. He expected that the dogs would jump over the wall to the unelectrified floor. However, most of the dogs did not. Seligman theorized this was because their earlier experience, where they had been shocked with no possibility of escape, had taught them that they were helpless.

In *The Battered Woman*, Walker contends that battered women have learned through their life experiences that they are helpless to escape or avoid violence. These battered women are conditioned to believe that they cannot predict their safety and that nothing can be done to fundamentally change their situation. They become passive, submissive, depressed, overwhelmingly fearful, and psychologically paralyzed. Walker emphasizes that although they do not respond with total helplessness, they narrow their choices, choosing the ones that seem to have the greatest likelihood of success.

Victimized women may also fear that attempting to end an abusive relationship will lead to even worse violence. Research shows this fear of reprisal is well founded. Walker explains in *Terrifying Love: Why Battered Women Kill and How Society Responds* (1989) that batterers often panic when they think women are going to end the relationship. In the personal stories women told Walker, they repeatedly related that after calling the police or asking for a divorce, their partners' violence escalated.

Walker observes that in an abusive relationship it is often the man who is desperately dependent on the relationship. Battered women are likely to feel that the batterer's sanity and emotional stability are their responsibility, that they are their partner's only link to the normal world. Walker indicates that almost 10% of abandoned batterers committed suicide when their partners left them.

In the early 21st century scholars have begun examining the ways that everyday technology can perpetuate passive behavior in domestic abuse situations. Caitlin Halligan, David Knox, and Jason Brinkley reveal in "Trapped: Technology as a Barrier to Leaving an Abusive Relationship" (*College Student Journal*, vol. 47, no. 4, December 2013) that texting, social media, and other forms of electronic communication can actually impede victims in their efforts to leave an abusive partner. The researchers note that the ease and frequency with which partners remain in contact via technology can make it more difficult for victims to separate themselves psychologically from their abuser. By breaking down traditional boundaries of privacy, Halligan, Knox, and Brinkley suggest, social media and text messaging can undermine victims struggling to escape patterns of abuse.

WHAT CAN A WOMAN DO?

In "Understanding Women's Responses to Domestic Violence" (*Qualitative Social Work*, vol. 2, no. 3, September 2003), Kate Cavanagh of the University of Glasgow gathers qualitative data from interviews with the female partners of violent men to illustrate that battered women try to end the violence in their relationship in many ways, even if they stay. She finds that women worked to stop the violence by talking with their partner about the violence, developing strategies for avoiding the violence (e.g., being affectionate or feigning agreement with the abuser), challenging the violence (e.g., fighting back, orally or physically), telling other people about the violence, and leaving (usually temporarily) the relationship. Cavanagh argues that abused women almost always actively fight the abuse: "At some points in time the struggle to change took second place to the struggle to survive but not even women subjected to the extremes of abuse totally 'gave up.'"

For their landmark book *Intimate Violence* (1988), Richard J. Gelles and Murray A. Straus interviewed 192 women who suffered minor violence and 140 women who suffered severe violence and asked which long-range strategies they used to avoid violence. Fifty-three percent of the minor-violence victims and 69% of the severe-violence victims learned to avoid issues they thought would anger their partner. Others learned to read a change in their partner's facial expressions or body language as one of the first signs of impending abuse. Avoidance worked for about 68% of those women who suffered minor abuse, but this tactic was successful for less than one-third of the more severely abused victims.

Gelles and Straus find that 70% of battered women had left their spouse in the year preceding the interview. However, only about half of those who left reported that this was a "very effective" method of ending the abuse. In fact, for one out of eight women it only made things worse. Batterers put incredible pressure on their partner to return. Often, when the women returned they were abused more severely than before, as revenge or because the men learned that, once again, they could get away with this behavior. Women who returned also risked losing the aid of personal and public support systems because these people perceived that their help or advice was useless or ignored.

Silke Meyer of the University of Queensland notes in "Seeking Help to Protect the Children?: The Influence of Children on Women's Decisions to Seek Help When Experiencing Intimate Partner Violence" (*Journal of Family Violence*, vol. 25, no. 8, November 2010) that the single biggest predictor of a battered woman leaving an abusive relationship was whether the woman perceived that her children would have to witness violence if she stayed. In fact, the presence of children was the key predictor of the woman's likelihood of reporting abuse to the police; no other victim characteristic examined, including education, household income, marriage, or language spoken in the home, made her more likely to do so. Interestingly, pregnancy had no effect on help-seeking behaviors of any kind. Silke points out that the reasons why children's presence increased help-seeking have yet to be examined.

By contrast, Hee Yun Lee, Eonju Park, and Elizabeth Lightfoot of the University of Minnesota find in "When Does a Battered Woman Seek Help from the Police? The Role of Battered Women's Functionality" (*Journal of Family Violence*, vol. 25, no. 2, April 2010) that most victims of intimate partner violence seek help from the police at least once after a violent incident. The researchers conducted a telephone survey of 111 women in four cities who were recruited through social service agencies that provide services to victims of domestic violence. Lee, Park, and Lightfoot note that certain women were more likely to seek help from the police, including those who were more severely injured and those who were participating in social functions such as child-rearing and relationships with family and friends. In addition, battered women who were in shorter term relationships were more likely than women who were in longer term relationships to seek help from the police.

Just Say "No"

Many researchers believe there is real truth to the statement that men abuse because they can. A wife who will not permit herself to be beaten from the first act of minor abuse, such as a slap or push, is the most successful in stopping it. Gelles and Straus note in *Intimate Violence* that simply eliciting a promise to stop was by far the most effective strategy women could undertake, especially in cases of minor violence. Threatening to divorce or leave the home worked in about 40% of the minor-abuse cases, but this strategy worked in less than 5% of the severe-abuse situations. Physically fighting back was the least successful method. It worked in less than 2% of the minor-abuse cases and in less than 1% of the severe-abuse cases.

CHAPTER 8
RAPE AND STALKING

One of the difficulties inherent in the analysis of rape and stalking data is that neither of these crimes has a recognized standard definition. In its narrowest definition, rape includes only sexual acts that involve penetration of female victims by male perpetrators. Broader definitions include a wider variety of sexual acts committed against both female and male victims. Likewise, stalking encompasses various behaviors that are considered to be harassing and threatening, but do not involve direct violent contact. Law enforcement agencies use specific legal definitions for rape and stalking that are spelled out in criminal codes. For example, the Federal Bureau of Investigation (FBI) compiles rape data as part of its Uniform Crime Reports program, but only offenses known to police are included, and offenders are not categorized by their relationships to the victims. National victim surveys are far more informative for assessing the prevalence of rape and stalking because the surveys typically include incidents not reported to law enforcement and provide data about victim-offender relationships.

RAPE

Rape is an act of sexual violence by one person against another. It is an act of power that aims to hurt at the most intimate level. Rape is a violation, whether it occurs at the hands of a stranger or within the home at the hands of an abusive husband or partner.

National Crime Victimization Survey

The National Crime Victimization Survey (NCVS) is an annual survey overseen by the Bureau of Justice Statistics (BJS) within the U.S. Department of Justice (DOJ). The NCVS includes a nationally representative sample of people aged 12 years and older who are asked about their experiences of being victimized by certain crimes within the previous six months. The victimizations include both those reported and not reported to the police. The BJS publishes summary results in its annual *Criminal Victimization* series. The agency also operates a searchable database of historical NCVS results that is accessible online using the NCVS Victimization Analysis Tool (http://www.bjs.gov/index.cfm?ty=nvat). The NCVS crime set includes rape and sexual assault as defined as follows:

- Rape—forced sexual intercourse including both psychological coercion as well as physical force. Forced sexual intercourse means vaginal, anal, or oral penetration by the offender. This category also includes incidents where the penetration is from a foreign object such as a bottle. Includes attempted rapes, male as well as female victims, and both heterosexual and homosexual rape. Attempted rape includes verbal threats of rape.

- Sexual assault—a wide range of victimizations, separate from rape or attempted rape. These crimes include attacks or attempted attacks generally involving unwanted sexual contact between victim and offender. Sexual assaults may or may not involve force and include things such as grabbing or fondling. Sexual assault also includes verbal threats.

The BJS considers domestic violence as violence involving intimate partners or family members. In terms of victim-offender relationships, the following specific terms are used:

- Intimate partners—spouses or ex-spouses, boyfriends or ex-boyfriends, and girlfriends or ex-girlfriends

- Other relatives—parents or stepparents, children or stepchildren, brothers or sisters, and other relatives

As Table 8.1 shows, of the nearly 5.4 million violent victimizations reported in 2014, 11.8% (634,612) were committed by intimate partners. Roughly two-thirds (407,236, or 64.2%) of these victimizations were committed by non-Hispanic white offenders. Table 8.2 provides a breakdown of victim-offender relationships in rapes and sexual assaults based on NCVS data between

TABLE 8.1

Violent victimizations, by victim-offender relationship and race and Hispanic origin, 2005–14

Crime type	2005	2006	2007	2008	2009	2010	2011	2012	2013	2014
Violent victimization	6,947,795	8,430,430	6,814,183	6,393,471	5,669,237	4,935,983	5,812,523	6,842,593	6,126,423	5,359,570
Intimates	816,006	1,305,249	905,810	1,103,392	1,039,650	773,434	850,772	810,794	748,795	634,612
Non-Hispanic white	521,230	807,541	643,732	873,903	701,481	539,133	643,683	532,320	465,387	407,236
Non-Hispanic black	71,847	203,988	171,848	85,930	188,423	140,101	82,599	164,701	86,938	50,022
Non-Hispanic other	106,602!	155,440	39,653!	40,309!	26,786!	43,416	36,578	34,983!	110,320	45,664!
Hispanic	116,328	138,281	50,577!	103,249	122,960	50,783	87,913	78,789	86,151	131,691
Other relatives	426,284	558,407	501,907	454,603	343,020	356,129	504,135	448,598	367,291	475,265
Non-Hispanic white	310,765	380,022	289,403	309,530	265,041	224,169	409,105	304,999	239,986	349,388
Non-Hispanic black	51,255	77,783	153,199!	36,454!	35,018!	39,250	39,846	61,253	64,651	54,562
Non-Hispanic other	11,163!	52,070!	30,745!	88,976!	7,251!	35,784	19,274!	9,207!	23,737!	42,160
Hispanic	53,101	48,532	28,559!	19,643!	35,711!	56,926	35,910	73,139	38,917	29,155!
Well-known/casual acquaintances	2,356,241	2,661,522	1,997,175	1,781,331	1,756,014	1,573,294	1,779,618	2,263,252	2,445,099	1,709,366
Non-Hispanic white	1,727,646	1,772,900	1,308,500	1,344,869	1,224,250	1,159,011	1,068,410	1,526,150	1,676,573	1,230,049
Non-Hispanic black	313,915	402,315	307,177	199,191	228,098	183,406	394,577	336,063	259,631	210,507
Non-Hispanic other	155,067	162,550	142,809	78,821	86,337	69,431	103,095	126,662	195,278	114,313
Hispanic	159,612	323,757	238,689	158,449	217,328	161,447	213,535	274,377	313,617	154,498
Stranger	2,829,598	3,184,058	2,706,132	2,154,770	2,165,849	1,812,303	2,146,307	2,710,114	2,098,170	2,166,129
Non-Hispanic white	1,865,080	2,106,015	1,906,041	1,349,137	1,337,225	978,639	1,262,227	1,728,361	1,254,197	1,322,750
Non-Hispanic black	382,718	466,592	298,268	389,123	397,169	373,781	219,494	325,040	246,095	363,435
Non-Hispanic other	160,363	251,312	178,119	126,042	107,092	192,548	199,749	186,574	112,676	181,077
Hispanic	421,438	360,139	323,704	290,468	324,363	267,335	464,837	470,139	485,202	298,867
Do not know relationship	361,855	506,652	448,275	486,084	217,989	288,667	240,956	371,910	288,795	223,847
Non-Hispanic white	232,847	320,317	265,417	332,029	92,498	184,135	119,802	113,096	121,662	111,434
Non-Hispanic black	74,773	89,748	58,295	58,562	41,381!	46,771!	52,107	177,858	85,424	30,596!
Non-Hispanic other	18,818!	23,797!	22,536!	24,801!	4,264!	9,006!	3,865!	27,664!	12,184!	40,111!
Hispanic	35,418!	72,790	102,027	70,693	79,845	48,755	65,183	53,291	69,525!	41,707
Do not know number of offenders	157,809	214,541	254,885	413,292	139,707	132,156	290,736	228,660	178,273	150,351
Non-Hispanic white	93,585	99,506	193,512	289,663	113,520	97,084	216,502	146,489	74,722	96,604
Non-Hispanic black	18,129!	53,746!	9,105!	53,841	11,128!	3,501!	23,551!	26,258!	72,323!	29,406!
Non-Hispanic other	10,296!	—	24,030!	10,764!	9,673!	13,017!	22,626!	33,227!	8,968!	10,883!
Hispanic	35,799!	61,290!	28,238!	59,024!	5,386!	18,555!	28,057!	22,686!	22,260!	13,458!

—Estimate is equal to 0 sample cases.

!Interpret data with caution, based on 10 or fewer sample cases or the coefficient of variation is greater than 50%.

Notes: Special tabulations from the NCVS Victimization Analysis Tool (NVAT). (NCVS is National Crime Victimization Survey.) Detail may not sum to total due to rounding and/or missing data. The collection of racial and ethnic categories in 2003 changed from that of previous years. Due to methodological changes in the 2006 NCVS, use caution when comparing 2006 criminal victimization estimates to other years.

SOURCE: "Number of Violent Victimizations by Victim-Offender Relationship and Race/Hispanic Origin, 2005–2014," in *NCVS Victimization Analysis Tool (NVAT)*, U.S. Department of Justice, Office of Justice Programs, Bureau of Justice Statistics, June 10, 2016, http://www.bjs.gov/index.cfm?ty=nvat (accessed June 13, 2016)

TABLE 8.2

Rapes and sexual assaults, by victim-offender relationship, 2010–14

Crime type	2010	2011	2012	2013	2014
Rape/sexual assault	268,574	244,188	346,830	300,165	284,345
Intimates	109,205	44,155	64,412	107,860	70,110
Other relatives	12,921	1,721	3,458	1,936	2,909
Well-known/casual acquaintances	97,817	117,760	162,288	120,927	126,649
Stranger	43,167	72,807	59,126	57,136	69,054
Do not know relationship	5,464	4,835	17,174	9,305	8,812
Do not know number of offenders	—	2,911	40,372	3,000	6,812

—Estimate is equal to 0 sample cases.
Notes: Special tabulations from the National Crime Victimization Survey (NCVS) Victimization Analysis Tool (NVAT). Detail may not sum to total due to rounding and/or missing data. No unique link for individual data sets.

SOURCE: "Number of Rape/Sexual Assaults by Victim-Offender Relationship, 2010–2014," in *NCVS Victimization Analysis Tool (NVAT)*, U.S. Department of Justice, Office of Justice Programs, Bureau of Justice Statistics, June 10, 2016, http://www.bjs.gov/index.cfm?ty=nvat (accessed June 13, 2016)

2010 and 2014. There were 284,345 rapes and sexual assaults in 2014. Well-known and casual acquaintances committed the largest number (126,649) of the victimizations in 2014 and made up 44.5% of the total. Intimate partners committed the second-largest group of victimizations (70,110, or 24.7% of the total). Of the 70,110 incidences of intimate partner rape and sexual assault in 2014, nearly two-thirds (46,202, or 65.9%) were committed by Hispanic offenders, while 29.1% (20,412) were committed by non-Hispanic white offenders. (See Table 8.3.) By contrast, of the 126,649 rape and sexual assault victimizations perpetrated by well-known and casual acquaintances in 2014, nearly three-quarters (71.6%, or 90,681) were committed by non-Hispanic white perpetrators.

Table 8.4 provides a breakdown of weapon use during rapes and sexual assaults between 2010 and 2014. No record of weapon use exists for cases of rape and sexual assault involving intimate partners or other relatives in 2014. Of the 69,054 rapes and sexual assaults committed by strangers that year, 6,020 (8.7%) involved the use of some sort of weapon.

VICTIMIZATIONS NOT REPORTED TO THE POLICE. In *Criminal Victimization, 2014* (August 2015, http://www.bjs.gov/content/pub/pdf/cv14.pdf), Jennifer L. Truman and Lynn Langton of the BJS examine data to determine which types of crimes were the least likely to be reported by victims to the police in 2005, 2013, and 2014. On average slightly fewer than half (46%) of all violent crimes were reported to the police in 2014. The rate at which crimes were reported varied considerably among types of violent crimes. For example, about one-third (33.6%) of all rape and sexual assault cases were reported to the police in 2014. By comparison, more than half (57.9%) of all cases of intimate partner violence were reported to the police in 2014.

National Intimate Partner and Sexual Violence Survey

As is noted in Chapter 6, the National Intimate Partner and Sexual Violence Survey (NISVS) was conducted in 2010 and included a representative sample of 16,507 adults (9,086 women and 7,421 men) in the United States who were aged 18 years and older. The survey was overseen by the Centers for Disease Control and Prevention, an agency within the U.S. Department of Health and Human Services. The surveyors asked about physical and sexual victimizations, psychological aggression, stalking, and control of reproductive or sexual health. Michele C. Black et al. summarize the survey results in *National Intimate Partner and Sexual Violence Survey: 2010 Summary Report* (November 2011, http://www.cdc.gov/ViolencePrevention/pdf/NISVS_Report2010-a.pdf). Sexually violent experiences were divided into the following categories:

- Noncontact unwanted sexual experiences
- Unwanted sexual contact
- Sexual coercion
- Being made to penetrate someone else (males only)
- Rape (i.e., completed forced penetration, attempted penetration, and alcohol/drug-facilitated completed penetration; specific actions that were classified as rape are described in Chapter 6)

Black et al. note that the NISVS was different from many other surveys about sexual victimization because it questioned men about being made to penetrate someone else. They indicate that "being made to penetrate is a form of sexual victimization distinct from rape that is particularly unique to males and, to our knowledge, has not been explicitly measured in previous national studies."

Rape and Sexual Assault Demographics

Table 8.5 provides a breakdown by race and age of rape and sexual assault victims between 2010 and 2014. In 2014 there were 284,345 cases of rape and sexual assault in the United States. The highest number of rapes and sexual assaults occurred among victims aged 25 to 34

TABLE 8.3

Rapes and sexual assaults, by victim-offender relationship and race and Hispanic origin, 2005–14

Crime type	2005	2006	2007	2008	2009	2010	2011	2012	2013	2014
Rape/sexual assault	**207,760**	**463,598**	**248,277**	**349,691**	**305,574**	**268,574**	**244,188**	**346,830**	**300,165**	**284,345**
Intimates	**66,750**	**157,698**	**55,110**	**103,675**	**43,198**	**109,205**	**44,155**	**64,412**	**107,860**	**70,110**
Non-Hispanic white	30,835	114,688	55,110	91,857	19,537	105,541	23,708	53,044	74,151	20,412
Non-Hispanic black	23,937	36,866	—	8,416	20,623	—	2,925	1,289	12,101	3,496
Non-Hispanic other	2,839	3,182	—	3,402	3,038	3,664	—	6,975	21,608	—
Hispanic	9,139	2,962	—	—	—	—	17,521	3,104	—	46,202
Other relatives	**11,853**	**7,397**	**6,529**	**24,670**	**34,779**	**12,921**	**1,721**	**3,458**	**1,936**	**2,909**
Non-Hispanic white	4,604	—	2,070	22,183	34,779	—	—	3,458	1,936	—
Non-Hispanic black	7,249	2,681	—	2,487	—	4,786	—	—	—	2,909
Non-Hispanic other	—	—	4,459	—	—	4,025	1,721	—	—	—
Hispanic	—	4,716	—	—	—	4,110	—	—	—	—
Well-known/casual acquaintances	**60,813**	**152,255**	**81,968**	**90,611**	**187,848**	**97,817**	**117,760**	**162,288**	**120,927**	**126,649**
Non-Hispanic white	35,658	106,876	44,870	59,080	170,738	66,041	84,835	66,034	93,938	90,681
Non-Hispanic black	14,904	27,346	6,609	9,340	13,297	24,410	17,031	14,139	7,480	7,377
Non-Hispanic other	5,628	8,645	23,922	8,891	—	2,895	1,190	68,928	9,205	2,534
Hispanic	4,624	9,388	6,567	13,301	3,813	4,470	14,703	13,187	10,304	26,057
Stranger	**59,982**	**134,929**	**77,477**	**76,907**	**36,586**	**43,167**	**72,807**	**59,126**	**57,136**	**69,054**
Non-Hispanic white	32,396	103,587	65,154	40,242	23,430	19,971	45,782	45,192	38,737	25,637
Non-Hispanic black	5,574	20,831	9,064	27,757	4,881	3,578	12,745	3,849	3,445	33,151
Non-Hispanic other	—	3,814	—	4,153	—	—	—	3,103	2,219	6,020
Hispanic	22,011	6,697	3,258	4,754	8,274	19,618	14,280	6,982	12,736	4,246
Do not know relationship	**5,375**	**11,320**	**13,823**	**9,346**	**3,163**	**5,464**	**4,835**	**17,174**	**9,305**	**8,812**
Non-Hispanic white	5,375	7,343	13,823	6,935	—	3,391	1,572	10,357	5,244	6,544
Non-Hispanic Black	—	—	—	2,411	—	—	3,263	—	—	2,267
Hispanic	—	3,976	—	—	3,163	2,073	—	6,817	4,061	—
Do not know number of offenders	**2,987**	**—**	**13,370**	**44,483**	**—**	**—**	**2,911**	**40,372**	**3,000**	**6,812**
Non-Hispanic white	2,987	—	8,042	1,967	—	—	2,911	40,372	—	3,636
Non-Hispanic black	—	—	—	6,427	—	—	—	—	3,000	3,176
Non-Hispanic other	—	—	5,329	—	—	—	—	—	—	—
Hispanic	—	—	—	36,088	—	—	—	—	—	—

—Estimate is equal to 0 sample cases.

Notes: Special tabulations from the National Crime Victimization Survey (NCVS) Victimization Analysis Tool (NVAT). Detail may not sum to total due to rounding and/or missing data. The collection of racial and ethnic categories in 2003 changed from that of previous years. No unique link for individual data sets. Due to methodological changes in the 2006 NCVS, use caution when comparing 2006 criminal victimization estimates to other years.

SOURCE: "Number of Rape/Sexual Assaults by Victim-Offender Relationship and Race/Hispanic Origin, 2005–2014," in *NCVS Victimization Analysis Tool (NVAT)*, U.S. Department of Justice, Office of Justice Programs, Bureau of Justice Statistics, June 10, 2016, http://www.bjs.gov/index.cfm?ty=nvat (accessed June 13, 2016)

TABLE 8.4

Rapes and sexual assaults, by victim-offender relationship and weapon use, 2010–14

Crime type	2010	2011	2012	2013	2014
Rape/sexual assault	268,574	244,188	346,830	300,165	284,345
Intimates	109,205	44,155	64,412	107,860	70,110
Yes, offender had weapon	45,387	2,925	—	3,281	—
No, offender did not have weapon	63,818	32,818	64,412	100,859	70,110
Do not know if offender had weapon	—	8,412	—	3,720	—
Other relatives	12,921	1,721	3,458	1,936	2,909
No, offender did not have weapon	12,921	1,721	3,458	1,936	2,909
Well-known/casual acquaintances	97,817	117,760	162,288	120,927	126,649
Yes, offender had weapon	10,223	2,891	53,566	—	—
No, offender did not have weapon	83,889	104,002	103,856	120,927	126,649
Do not know if offender had weapon	3,705	10,866	4,866	—	—
Stranger	43,167	72,807	59,126	57,136	69,054
Yes, offender had weapon	5,268	2,609	—	8,901	6,020
No, offender did not have weapon	25,566	61,719	42,687	30,942	34,562
Do not know if offender had weapon	12,333	8,478	16,439	17,293	28,472
Do not know relationship	5,464	4,835	17,174	9,305	8,812
Yes, offender had weapon	5,464	—	3,317	—	—
No, offender did not have weapon	—	4,835	11,028	7,702	8,812
Do not know if offender had weapon	—	—	2,829	1,603	—
Do not know number of offenders	—	2,911	40,372	3,000	6,812
Yes, offender had weapon	—	—	38,218	—	3,176
No, offender did not have weapon	—	2,911	2,154	3,000	3,636

—Estimate is equal to 0 sample cases.

Notes: Special tabulations from the National Crime Victimization Survey (NCVS) Victimization Analysis Tool (NVAT). Detail may not sum to total due to rounding and/or missing data. No unique link for individual data sets.

SOURCE: "Number of Rape/Sexual Assaults by Victim-Offender Relationship and Weapon Use, 2010–2014," in *NCVS Victimization Analysis Tool (NVAT)*, U.S. Department of Justice, Office of Justice Programs, Bureau of Justice Statistics, June 10, 2016, http://www.bjs.gov/index.cfm?ty=nvat (accessed June 13, 2016)

years old, who accounted for nearly one-third (93,125, or 32.8%) of all cases that year. Individuals between the ages of 35 and 49 accounted for 72,409 (25.5%) of all rape and sexual assault victims in 2014; individuals between the ages of 21 and 24 accounted for 68,739 (24.1%) victims; individuals between the ages of 50 and 64 accounted for 17,295 (6.1%) victims; and individuals between the ages of 18 and 20 accounted for 14,870 (5.2%) victims. Of the 284,345 victims of rape and sexual assault in 2014, 256,313 (90.1%) were female and 28,032 (9.9%) were male. (See Table 8.6.)

Of the 284,345 cases of rape and sexual assault recorded in the NCVS Victimization Analysis Tool in 2014, 107,650 (37.9%) occurred in areas with populations of fewer than 100,000 residents. (See Table 8.7.) A breakdown of rapes and sexual assaults in 2014 by region and victim's age is presented in Table 8.8. Of the 14,870 cases of rape and sexual assault involving victims between the ages of 18 and 20 that year, 11,344 (76.3%) occurred in the Northeast. By contrast, of the 72,409 rapes and sexual assaults involving victims aged 35 to 49 years, fewer than one out of 10 (6,180, or 8.5%) occurred in the Northeast, 24,136 (33.3%) occurred in the South, 21,094 (29.1%) occurred in the West, and 20,999 (29%) occurred in the Midwest in 2014.

National Violence against Women Survey

The National Violence against Women Survey (NVAWS) was conducted in 1995 and 1996 and included 16,000 adult participants split evenly between men and women. Although the survey is much older than those already described, the NVAWS results are of particular note because they provide information about victim attitudes and reactions after the violent experiences.

In *Extent, Nature, and Consequences of Rape Victimization: Findings from the National Violence against Women Survey* (January 2006, http://www.ncjrs.gov/pdffiles1/nij/210346.pdf), the most recent report of its kind as of September 2016, Patricia Tjaden and Nancy Thoennes of the Center for Policy Research in Denver, Colorado, use NVAWS data to estimate that 302,091 women are raped each year and that 17.7 million women have been raped during their lifetime, compared with 92,748 men who are raped each year and 2.8 million men who have been raped during their lifetime. Native American or Alaskan Native women were estimated to have the highest rate of having been raped during their lifetime (34.1%), followed by African American women (18.8%), non-Hispanic white women (17.9%), Hispanic women (11.9%), and Asian or Pacific Islander women (6.8%).

TABLE 8.5

Rapes and sexual assaults, by victim's age and race and Hispanic origin, 2010–14

Crime type	2010	2011	2012	2013	2014
Rape/sexual assault	**268,574**	**244,188**	**346,830**	**300,165**	**284,345**
12 to 14	32,781	3,961	26,606	8,103	6,180
Non-Hispanic white	9,832	3,961	19,512	3,640	3,913
Non-Hispanic black	18,491	—	—	—	—
Hispanic	4,458	—	7,094	4,463	2,267
15 to 17	20,531	20,995	12,060	18,266	9,114
Non-Hispanic white	12,218	13,792	—	15,845	4,584
Non-Hispanic black	3,843	4,032	3,656	—	—
Non-Hispanic other	—	—	4,904	—	4,531
Hispanic	4,470	3,171	3,500	2,421	—
18 to 20	13,790	44,029	62,079	46,053	14,870
Non-Hispanic white	10,126	25,943	46,111	20,837	6,191
Non-Hispanic black	—	12,740	2,629	5,834	—
Non-Hispanic other	3,664	—	10,420	11,726	—
Hispanic	—	5,347	2,920	7,656	8,679
21 to 24	68,769	28,419	16,344	21,905	68,739
Non-Hispanic white	65,473	14,323	12,395	21,905	29,963
Non-Hispanic black	—	9,074	—	—	23,052
Hispanic	3,296	5,022	3,950	—	15,724
25 to 34	53,734	41,496	70,615	59,975	93,125
Non-Hispanic white	30,649	30,863	63,783	31,148	44,328
Non-Hispanic black	7,566	3,263	2,116	5,226	11,215
Non-Hispanic other	4,025	—	—	14,078	4,023
Hispanic	11,495	7,370	4,716	9,523	33,559
35 to 49	74,763	46,755	129,993	63,082	72,409
Non-Hispanic white	62,440	33,431	54,254	56,801	56,611
Non-Hispanic black	2,875	6,856	5,739	—	9,373
Non-Hispanic other	2,895	—	63,682	6,281	—
Hispanic	6,553	6,468	6,318	—	6,424
50 to 64	—	23,959	21,788	77,258	17,295
Non-Hispanic white	—	6,869	15,058	58,307	1,321
Non-Hispanic black	—	—	5,137	11,966	6,468
Non-Hispanic other	—	1,190	—	3,946	—
Hispanic	—	15,900	1,593	3,039	9,505
65 or older	4,206	34,573	7,344	5,522	2,612
Non-Hispanic white	4,206	29,625	7,344	5,522	—
Hispanic	—	4,948	—	—	2,612

—Estimate is equal to 0 sample cases.
Notes: Special tabulations from the National Crime Victimization Survey (NCVS) Victimization Analysis Tool (NVAT). Detail may not sum to total due to rounding and/or missing data. The collection of racial and ethnic categories in 2003 changed from that of previous years. No unique link for individual data sets.

SOURCE: "Number of Rape/Sexual Assaults by Age and Race/Hispanic Origin, 2010–2014," in *NCVS Victimization Analysis Tool (NVAT)*, U.S. Department of Justice, Office of Justice Programs, Bureau of Justice Statistics, June 10, 2016, http://www.bjs.gov/index.cfm?ty=nvat (accessed June 13, 2016)

TABLE 8.6

Rapes and sexual assaults, by victim's sex and race and Hispanic origin, 2010–14

Crime type	2010	2011	2012	2013	2014
Rape/sexual assault	**268,574**	**244,188**	**346,830**	**300,165**	**284,345**
Male	15,020	34,804	131,259	34,057	28,032
Non-Hispanic white	12,947	13,243	54,093	23,776	16,421
Non-Hispanic black	—	5,344	3,849	7,282	10,122
Non-Hispanic other	—	—	63,682	3,000	1,489
Hispanic	2,073	16,217	9,635	—	—
Female	253,555	209,384	215,570	266,107	256,313
Non-Hispanic white	181,998	145,565	164,363	190,230	130,490
Non-Hispanic black	32,774	30,620	15,428	15,744	39,987
Non-Hispanic other	10,584	1,190	15,324	33,032	7,065
Hispanic	28,199	32,008	20,455	27,101	78,772

—Estimate is equal to 0 sample cases.
Notes: Special tabulations from the National Crime Victimization Survey (NCVS) Victimization Analysis Tool (NVAT). Detail may not sum to total due to rounding and/or missing data. The collection of racial and ethnic categories in 2003 changed from that of previous years. No unique link for individual data sets.

SOURCE: "Number of Rape/Sexual Assaults by Sex and Race/Hispanic Origin, 2010–2014," in *NCVS Victimization Analysis Tool (NVAT)*, U.S. Department of Justice, Office of Justice Programs, Bureau of Justice Statistics, June 10, 2016, http://www.bjs.gov/index.cfm?ty=nvat (accessed June 13, 2016)

TABLE 8.7

Rapes and sexual assaults, by victim's age and population size, 2010–14

Crime type	2010	2011	2012	2013	2014
Rape/sexual assault	268,574	244,188	346,830	300,165	284,345
12 to 14	32,781	3,961	26,606	8,103	6,180
Not a place	—	—	3,458	—	3,913
Under 100,000	9,654	3,961	23,148	8,103	2,267
250,000–499,999	4,636	—	—	—	—
1 million or more	18,491	—	—	—	—
15 to 17	20,531	20,995	12,060	18,266	9,114
Not a place	6,187	—	—	3,036	—
Under 100,000	9,874	20,995	4,904	7,546	9,114
100,000–249,999	4,470	—	—	5,263	—
500,000–999,999	—	—	3,656	—	—
1 million or more	—	—	3,500	2,421	—
18 to 20	13,790	44,029	62,079	46,053	14,870
Not a place	7,051	11,204	12,373	8,310	2,664
Under 100,000	6,739	28,146	27,320	26,437	3,486
100,000–249,999	—	3,006	8,121	—	—
250,000–499,999	—	—	11,289	2,219	8,719
500,000–999,999	—	1,674	—	9,087	—
1 million or more	—	—	2,976	—	—
21 to 24	68,769	28,419	16,344	21,905	68,739
Not a place	5,116	—	—	4,489	27,229
Under 100,000	60,004	20,855	9,247	8,312	19,746
100,000–249,999	3,649	3,725	—	—	4,650
250,000–499,999	—	—	7,097	—	15,724
500,000–999,999	—	3,839	—	4,454	1,391
1 million or more	—	—	—	4,650	—
25 to 34	53,734	41,496	70,615	59,975	93,125
Not a place	5,857	11,747	—	5,659	1,973
Under 100,000	18,613	11,148	50,131	24,051	27,150
100,000–249,999	14,813	15,274	5,056	9,321	7,074
250,000–499,999	—	—	8,913	11,123	34,816
500,000–999,999	7,265	1,721	—	9,821	3,776
1 million or more	7,186	1,607	6,515	—	18,337
35 to 49	74,763	46,755	129,993	63,082	72,409
Not a place	—	11,984	—	9,864	2,972
Under 100,000	62,275	30,841	70,890	44,184	44,566
100,000–249,999	3,705	3,930	9,280	9,035	3,336
250,000–499,999	—	—	38,761	—	15,514
500,000–999,999	—	—	8,826	—	6,022
1 million or more	8,782	—	2,237	—	—
50 to 64	—	23,959	21,788	77,258	17,295
Not a place	—	—	2,958	6,389	—
Under 100,000	—	5,287	13,389	55,879	1,321
100,000–249,999	—	11,184	—	6,311	9,505
250,000–499,999	—	—	—	1,804	—
500,000–999,999	—	—	1,593	3,837	6,468
1 million or more	—	7,488	3,849	3,038	—
65 or older	4,206	34,573	7,344	5,522	2,612
Not a place	—	2,818	—	—	—
Under 100,000	2,987	26,807	5,858	5,522	—
100,000–249,999	1,219	—	—	—	—
250,000–499,999	—	—	1,487	—	—
1 million or more	—	4,948	—	—	2,612

—Estimate is equal to 0 sample cases.

Notes: Special tabulations from the National Crime Victimization Survey (NCVS) Victimization Analysis Tool (NVAT). Detail may not sum to total due to rounding and/or missing data. No unique link for individual data sets.

SOURCE: "Number of Rape/Sexual Assaults by Age and Population Size, 2010–2014," in *NCVS Victimization Analysis Tool (NVAT)*, U.S. Department of Justice, Office of Justice Programs, Bureau of Justice Statistics, June 10, 2016, http://www.bjs.gov/index.cfm?ty=nvat (accessed June 13, 2016)

Tjaden and Thoennes find that most female victims of rape had been raped by a current or former intimate partner. Just over one out of five (21.5%) had been raped by a date or former date, 20.2% by a spouse or former spouse, and 4.3% by a cohabitating partner or former partner. Male victims tended to be raped by acquaintances (40.3%). Only 4.1% of males had been raped by a spouse or former spouse, 3.7% by a current or former cohabitating partner, and 2.7% by a date or former date.

In fact, Tjaden and Thoennes note that 7.7% of all women, but only 0.4% of all men, had ever been raped by a current or former intimate partner.

JUSTICE SYSTEM OUTCOMES. Tjaden and Thoennes find that the overwhelming majority of rapes went unreported to the police and that women raped by intimate partners were less likely to report rapes to the police than were women raped by nonintimate partners. Only 18% of

TABLE 8.8

Rapes and sexual assaults, by victim's age and geographical region, 2010–14

Crime type	2010	2011	2012	2013	2014
Rape/sexual assault	268,574	244,188	346,830	300,165	284,345
12 to 14	32,781	3,961	26,606	8,103	6,180
Northeast	18,491	—	3,458	—	—
Midwest	—	—	12,292	3,640	3,913
South	4,458	—	7,539	—	—
West	9,832	3,961	3,317	4,463	2,267
15 to 17	20,531	20,995	12,060	18,266	9,114
Northeast	—	—	3,500	3,036	—
Midwest	—	13,792	3,656	9,353	—
South	15,519	7,202	4,904	3,456	—
West	5,012	—	—	2,421	9,114
18 to 20	13,790	44,029	62,079	46,053	14,870
Northeast	—	13,747	—	5,834	11,344
Midwest	10,126	16,228	29,243	17,347	3,526
South	3,664	3,560	13,366	20,653	—
West	—	10,494	19,470	2,219	—
21 to 24	68,769	28,419	16,344	21,905	68,739
Northeast	16,610	—	—	8,295	9,054
Midwest	43,747	9,719	2,068	—	—
South	5,116	16,995	7,097	4,454	31,450
West	3,296	1,705	7,179	9,156	28,235
25 to 34	53,734	41,496	70,615	59,975	93,125
Northeast	7,613	5,226	6,091	7,423	25,588
Midwest	3,391	11,088	11,115	15,025	38,599
South	10,458	10,562	3,254	13,927	19,761
West	32,272	14,620	50,155	23,601	9,176
35 to 49	74,763	46,755	129,993	63,082	72,409
Northeast	6,896	9,677	5,468	18,688	6,180
Midwest	8,764	5,910	36,667	6,510	20,999
South	2,875	25,347	13,631	37,884	24,136
West	56,227	5,821	74,227	—	21,094
50 to 64	—	23,959	21,788	77,258	17,295
Northeast	—	3,989	6,807	33,608	—
Midwest	—	—	2,555	7,247	2,909
South	—	18,461	4,109	17,815	13,065
West	—	1,509	8,317	18,588	1,321
65 or older	4,206	34,573	7,344	5,522	2,612
Northeast	2,987	2,818	—	2,670	—
Midwest	—	26,807	5,858	—	—
South	—	4,948	—	—	—
West	1,219	—	1,487	2,852	2,612

—Estimate is equal to 0 sample cases.
Notes: Special tabulations from the National Crime Victimization Survey (NCVS) Victimization Analysis Tool (NVAT). Detail may not sum to total due to rounding and/or missing data. No unique link for individual data sets.

SOURCE: "Number of Rape/Sexual Assaults by Age and Region, 2010–2014," in *NCVS Victimization Analysis Tool (NVAT)*, U.S. Department of Justice, Office of Justice Programs, Bureau of Justice Statistics, June 10, 2016, http://www.bjs.gov/index.cfm?ty=nvat (accessed June 13, 2016)

women raped by intimates reported the rape, compared with 20.9% of women raped by nonintimates. Of the women who did not report the rape to the police, 22.1% said they were too afraid of the rapist, 18.1% said they were too ashamed, 17.7% said it was a minor incident, 12.6% said the police could not do anything, and 11.9% said the police would not believe them. Almost one out of 10 (8.6%) said it was because the perpetrator was a husband, family member, or friend.

When women did call the police, the police took a report 75.9% of the time, and in 9.9% of the cases the police did nothing. In 43.3% of the reported cases the perpetrator was arrested or detained. The perpetrator was prosecuted in 37% of reported cases, and 46.2% of those prosecutions resulted in a conviction. Of those convicted rapists, 24% did not go to jail.

MARITAL RAPE

Historically, wives were considered to be the property of the husband, and therefore rape of a wife was viewed as impossible. No husband still living with his wife was prosecuted for marital rape in the United States until 1978, and at that time marital rape was a crime in only five states, as reported by Jennifer A. Bennice and Patricia A. Resick of the University of Missouri, St. Louis, in "Marital Rape: History, Research, and Practice" (*Trauma, Violence, and Abuse*, vol. 4, no. 3, July 2003). By 1993 marital rape under some conditions was recognized in all 50 states.

ACQUAINTANCE RAPE

As shown in Table 8.2, NCVS data indicate that 126,649 rapes and sexual assaults in 2014 were by well-known or casual acquaintances of the victims. This number accounts for nearly half (44.5%) of the 284,345 total rapes and sexual assaults for that year.

Date Rape

As noted earlier, intimate partners are commonly defined as current or former spouses, boyfriends or ex-boyfriends, and girlfriends or ex-girlfriends. Although a spousal relationship has a legal definition, the distinction between a boyfriend/girlfriend and a dating acquaintance is far less clear-cut. However, in general, date rape is considered to be a form of acquaintance rape (as opposed to intimate partner rape), especially if the perpetrator and victim have not known one another for long and the abuse begins early in the relationship. Date rape is typically discussed by researchers in association with older teenagers and young people in their 20s.

HIGH SCHOOL RAPE. As Figure 8.1 shows, in 2015 more than one out of 10 (10.3%) high school girls reported that they had been forced to have sexual intercourse at some point during their lifetime; by comparison, 3.1% of high school boys reported ever having been forced to engage in sexual intercourse. Female non-Hispanic African American high school students (10.3%) reported the highest rate of forced sexual inter-

course, followed by female Hispanic high school students (10.1%) and female non-Hispanic white high school students (9.9%). (See Table 8.9.) Between 2001 and 2015 the proportion of all high school students who had been forced to have sexual intercourse at some point during their lifetime peaked in 2003, when it topped 9%; that figure fluctuated over the next decade, before dropping to 6.7% in 2015. (See Figure 8.2.)

Among reporting states in 2015, Arkansas (11.7%) and Mississippi (11.4%) had the highest rates of high school students who had ever been forced to have sexual intercourse; South Dakota (5.1%) had the lowest percentage of high school students who had ever been forced to have sexual intercourse. (See Table 8.10.) Arkansas (16.4%) and Kentucky (14.1%) reported the highest percentages of female high school students who had ever been forced to engage in sexual intercourse, whereas Mississippi (8.7%) and Alabama (7.8%) had the highest proportions of male high school students who had ever been forced to have sex. Among large urban school districts, Duval County, Florida (12.6%; greater Jacksonville), reported the highest percentage of high school students who had ever been forced to have sex, followed by Cleveland, Ohio (12%), and Dekalb County, Georgia (11.9%; suburban Atlanta).

FIGURE 8.1

Percentage of high school students who have ever been physically forced to have sexual intercourse, by race and Hispanic origin, grade, and sex, 2015

*When they did not want to
All Hispanic students are included in the Hispanic category. All other races are non-Hispanic.
Note: This graph contains weighted results.

SOURCE: "Percentage of High School Students Who Were Ever Physically Forced to Have Sexual Intercourse, by Sex, Grade, and Race/Ethnicity, 2015," in "Behaviors That Contribute to Unintentional Injuries," *Youth Risk Behavior Surveillance System (YRBSS): 2015,* Centers for Disease Control and Prevention, Division of Adolescent and School Health, 2015, http://www.cdc.gov/healthyyouth/data/yrbs/slides/2015/injury_slides_yrbs.pptx (accessed June 17, 2016)

TABLE 8.9

Percentage of high school students who have ever been forced to have sexual intercourse, by sex, grade, and race and Hispanic origin, 2015

Category	Female %	Male %	Total %
Race/ethnicity			
White*	9.9	2.0	6.0
Black*	10.3	4.4	7.3
Hispanic	10.1	4.0	7.0
Grade			
9	9.4	2.1	5.6
10	7.9	3.9	5.9
11	12.0	2.8	7.6
12	11.9	3.5	7.6
Total	**10.3**	**3.1**	**6.7**

*Non-Hispanic.
Note: Refers to high school students who were ever physically forced to have sexual intercourse when they didn't want to.

SOURCE: Adapted from Laura Kann et al., "Table 19. Percentage of High School Students Who Were Ever Physically Forced to Have Sexual Intercourse, by Sex, Race/Ethnicity, and Grade—United States, Youth Risk Behavior Survey, 2015," in "Youth Risk Behavior Surveillance—United States, 2015," *MMWR*, vol. 65, no. 6, June 10, 2016, http://www.cdc.gov/healthyyouth/data/yrbs/pdf/2015/ss6506_updated.pdf (accessed June 13, 2016)

FIGURE 8.2

Percentage of high school students who have ever been physically forced to have sexual intercourse, 2001–15

Note: This graph contains weighted results.

SOURCE: "Percentage of High School Students Who Were Ever Physically Forced to Have Sexual Intercourse, 2001–2015," in "Behaviors That Contribute to Unintentional Injuries," *Youth Risk Behavior Surveillance System (YRBSS): 2015*, Centers for Disease Control and Prevention, Division of Adolescent and School Health, 2015, http://www.cdc.gov/healthyyouth/data/yrbs/slides/2015/injury_slides_yrbs.pptx (accessed June 17, 2016)

Dating violence is not limited to forced sexual intercourse. As Figure 8.3 reveals, in 2015 nearly one out of 10 (9.6%) high school students had experienced physical dating violence during their lifetime. In 2015 Arkansas, California, Hawaii, Idaho, Indiana, New Hampshire, New York, and Michigan had the highest percentages of high school students who had experienced sexual dating violence during the past year. (See Figure 8.4.) That year, female high school students (15.6%) were nearly three times more likely than male high school students (5.4%) to have experienced sexual dating violence during the previous 12 months. (See Figure 8.5.)

Table 8.11 provides an overview of high school students who had ever experienced either physical dating violence or sexual dating violence in 2015, by sex, state, and urban school district. Arkansas (14.6%) had the highest rate of high school students who had ever experienced physical dating violence that year, while New York (14.7%) reported the highest rate of high school students who had ever experienced sexual dating violence. (See Table 8.11.)

As Table 8.12 shows, sexual harassment among students also poses a problem for public school administrators in the United States. During the 2013–14 school year, 1.4% of all U.S. public schools reported experiencing incidents of sexual harassment involving students. This figure represents a notable decline from the 2003–04 school year, when 4% of all U.S. public schools reported incidents of students having been sexually harassed.

COLLEGE RAPE. Table 8.13 offers a breakdown of the number of sexual offenses that occurred at U.S. colleges and universities between 2001 and 2013. There were a total of 4,964 incidents involving forced sexual activity at degree-granting postsecondary institutions in 2013. This figure was more than double the 2,201 forcible sex offenses recorded in 2001, while representing an increase of 23.6% over the 4,017 forcible sex offenses recorded in 2012. Nearly three-quarters (3,627, or 73.1%) of forcible sex offenses in 2013 occurred in residence halls.

Table 8.14 shows rates of forced sexual activity at U.S. postsecondary institutions between 2001 and 2013. Incidents involving forced sexual activity at colleges and universities reached their highest level in 2013, when there were more than 3.3 incidents per 10,000 students attending degree-granting institutions. The rate was higher at institutions with residence halls, where there were 4.6 incidents of forced sexual activity per 10,000 students.

Sofi Sinozich and Lynn Langton of the BJS report in *Rape and Sexual Assault Victimization among College-Age Females, 1995–2013* (December 2014, http://www.bjs.gov/content/pub/pdf/rsavcaf9513.pdf) that rates of rape and sexual assault among women aged 18 to 24 years vary according to college-enrollment status. Between 1997 and 2011 rates of rape and sexual assault were generally higher among young women who were not enrolled in a postsecondary institution. (See Figure 8.6.) By 2012, however, the rate of rape and sexual assault among young women attending college was higher than that of women not attending college, while

TABLE 8.10

Percentage of high school students who have ever been forced to have sexual intercourse, by sex, state, and select metropolitan areas, 2015

Site	Female %	Male %	Total %
State surveys			
Alabama	12.9	7.8	10.4
Alaska	11.3	4.0	7.5
Arizona	11.9	6.0	9.0
Arkansas	16.4	7.1	11.7
California	7.8	4.3	6.0
Connecticut	9.3	6.2	7.8
Delaware	8.6	4.4	6.6
Florida	8.3	4.2	6.4
Hawaii	10.9	6.5	8.8
Idaho	9.0	4.4	6.7
Illinois	11.5	6.4	8.9
Indiana	13.4	6.4	10.0
Kentucky	14.1	6.5	10.3
Maine	10.0	4.2	7.1
Maryland	9.9	6.2	8.1
Massachusetts	7.6	3.3	5.5
Michigan	12.2	4.4	8.3
Mississippi	13.9	8.7	11.4
Missouri	11.9	4.7	8.4
Montana	12.7	5.0	8.7
Nebraska	11.4	5.4	8.3
Nevada	11.1	5.6	8.4
New Hampshire	9.8	3.0	6.3
New Mexico	10.6	4.1	7.3
New York	—NA	—	—
North Carolina	8.8	4.4	6.6
North Dakota	9.8	3.0	6.3
Oklahoma	10.1	3.2	6.7
Pennsylvania	9.5	3.4	6.4
Rhode Island	9.8	6.4	8.1
South Carolina	8.4	6.0	7.2
South Dakota	6.1	4.2	5.1
Tennessee	—	—	—
Vermont	10.2	3.1	6.6
Virginia	—	—	—
West Virginia	12.7	7.5	10.0
Wyoming	13.2	6.8	10.1
Median	10.4	4.8	7.9
Range	(6.1–16.4)	(3.0–8.7)	(5.1–11.7)
Large urban school district surveys			
Baltimore, MD	9.9	10.7	10.6
Boston, MA	8.9	6.1	7.6
Broward County, FL	9.9	7.7	8.9
Cleveland, OH	14.8	8.5	12.0
DeKalb County, GA	13.1	10.6	11.9
Detroit, MI	11.4	9.5	10.6
District of Columbia	9.7	6.3	8.2
Duval County, FL	14.3	10.2	12.6
Ft. Worth, TX	7.5	3.5	5.5
Houston, TX	11.0	8.3	9.6
Los Angeles, CA	6.8	6.0	6.5
Miami-Dade County, FL	7.1	4.7	6.0
New York City, NY	—	—	—
Oakland, CA	—	—	—
Orange County, FL	8.4	4.4	6.4
Palm Beach County, FL	11.8	8.6	10.5
Philadelphia, PA	11.2	4.9	8.0
San Diego, CA	8.8	5.9	7.4
San Francisco, CA	9.2	5.7	7.6
Median	9.9	6.3	8.2
Range	(6.8–14.8)	(3.5–10.7)	(5.5–12.6)

TABLE 8.10

Percentage of high school students who have ever been forced to have sexual intercourse, by sex, state, and select metropolitan areas, 2015 [CONTINUED]

NA = not available.
Note: Refers to students who did not want to be forced to have sexual intercourse.

SOURCE: Adapted from Laura Kann et al., "Table 20. Percentage of High School Students Who Were Ever Physically Forced to Have Sexual Intercourse, by Sex–Selected U.S. Sites, Youth Risk Behavior Survey, 2015," in "Youth Risk Behavior Surveillance—United States, 2015," *MMWR*, vol. 65, no. 6, June 10, 2016, http://www.cdc.gov/healthyyouth/data/yrbs/pdf/2015/ss6506_updated.pdf (accessed June 13, 2016)

experienced completed rape, compared with 33% of those who were enrolled. (See Figure 8.7.) Overall, the rate of college-enrolled women aged 18 to 24 years who were victims of rape, sexual assault, or the threat of rape or sexual assault between 1995 and 2013 was 6.1 per 1,000 students. (See Table 8.15.) By comparison, 7.6 per 1,000 women aged 18 to 24 years not attending postsecondary institutions experienced rape, sexual assault, or the threat of rape or sexual assault during that span.

Among college-enrolled individuals aged 18 to 24 years who were victims of rape and sexual assault between 1995 and 2013, 83% were female students and 17% were male students. (See Table 8.16.) Among nonstudent victims of rape and sexual assault aged 18 to 24 years during that span, 96% were women and 4% were men. Between 1995 and 2013 the average annual number of female victims of rape and sexual assault who were not enrolled in college (65,668) was more than twice the average annual number of college-enrolled female victims (31,302). Between 1995 and 2013, 50% of all rapes and sexual assaults involving 18- to 24-year-olds not enrolled in college occurred at or near the victim's home. (See Table 8.17.) By comparison, only 38% of rapes and sexual assaults involving college-enrolled young people aged 18 to 24 years took place at or near the victim's home.

Among female students and nonstudents aged 18 to 24 years who were victims of rape and sexual assault between 1995 and 2013, most were victimized by someone they knew. As Table 8.18 shows, female nonstudent victims (34%) were more likely to have been raped and sexually assaulted by an intimate partner than female student victims (24%). In contrast, 50% of female student victims were raped and sexually assaulted by an acquaintance or someone they knew well, compared with 37% of female nonstudent victims.

Among women aged 18 to 24 years who were victims of rape and sexual assault between 1995 and 2013, those not enrolled in postsecondary institutions (32%) were more likely than college students (20%) to have reported the crime. (See Table 8.19.) Table 8.20 provides

in 2013 the rates for both groups were roughly the same. Among women aged 18 to 24 years who were victims of rape or sexual assault between 1995 and 2013, 40% of those not enrolled in postsecondary institutions

FIGURE 8.3

Percentage of high school students who experienced physical dating violence in the past year, by race and Hispanic origin, grade, and sex, 2015

Note: This graph contains weighted results. Experienced physical dating violence one or more times during the 12 months before the survey, including being hit, slammed into something, or injured with an object or weapon on purpose by someone they were dating or going out with among students who dated or went out with someone during the 12 months before the survey. All Hispanic students are included in the Hispanic category. All other races are non-Hispanic.

SOURCE: "Percentage of High School Students Who Experienced Physical Dating Violence, by Sex, Grade, and Race/Ethnicity, 2015," in "Behaviors That Contribute to Unintentional Injuries," *Youth Risk Behavior Surveillance System (YRBSS): 2015*, Centers for Disease Control and Prevention, Division of Adolescent and School Health, 2015, http://www.cdc.gov/healthyyouth/data/yrbs/slides/2015/injury_slides_yrbs.pptx (accessed June 17, 2016)

a breakdown of rape and sexual assault rates among women aged 18 to 24 years between 1995 and 2013, by select characteristics. The rate of rape and sexual assault victimizations involving college-enrolled women aged 18 to 24 years was highest among those living in urban settings, whereas the rate of victimizations involving young women not enrolled in college was highest among those residing in rural areas. Non-Hispanic white non-students aged 18 to 24 years (9.2 per 1,000 women not enrolled in postsecondary institutions) had the highest rate of rape and sexual assault victimizations between 1995 and 2013, followed by non-Hispanic white students (6.7 per 1,000 college-enrolled women), non-Hispanic African American students (6.4 per 1,000), and non-Hispanic African American nonstudents (6.2 per 1,000).

FRATERNITIES AND ATHLETICS. The relationship between athletics, fraternities, and rape is a persistent problem at the nations' colleges and universities. Several studies find that peer support of violence and social ties with abusive peers are predictors of abuse against women. In addition, training for violent occupations such as athletics and the military can "spill over" into personal life. Athletic training is sex-segregated, promotes hostile attitudes toward rivals, and rewards athletes for physically dominating others. Todd W. Crosset et al. report in "Male Student-Athletes and Violence against

Women: A Survey of Campus Judicial Affairs Offices" (*Violence against Women*, vol. 2, no. 2, June 1996) on data that they gathered from the judicial affairs offices of the 10 Division I schools with the largest athletic programs. Although male student athletes made up just 3% of the student population, they accounted for 35% of the reported perpetrators.

In "Dating Aggression, Sexual Coercion, and Aggression-Supporting Attitudes among College Men as a Function of Participation in Aggressive High School Sports" (*Violence against Women*, vol. 12, no. 5, May 2006), Gordon B. Forbes et al. indicate that participation in aggressive male sports in high school is a risk factor in perpetrating dating violence in college. In a study of 147 men, the researchers find that men who had been involved in aggressive sports in high school engaged in more psychological and physical aggression and sexual coercion in their dating relationships. They were also more accepting of violence, caused their sexual partners more physical injury, and were more hostile toward women. According to Forbes et al., the results indicate "that participation in aggressive high school sports is one of the multiple developmental pathways leading to relationship violence."

DATE RAPE DRUGS. Some drugs are known as date rape drugs because they are used by perpetrators to

FIGURE 8.4

Percentage of high school students who experienced sexual dating violence in the past year, by state, 2015

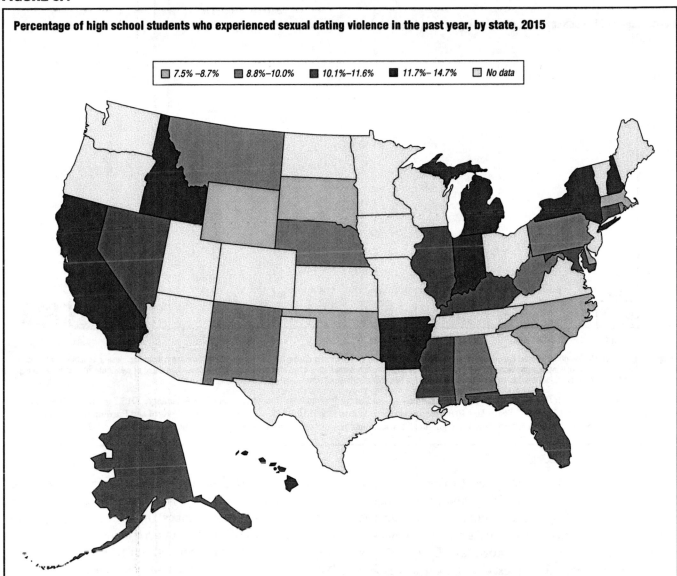

☐ 7.5%–8.7%   ▨ 8.8%–10.0%   ▩ 10.1%–11.6%   ■ 11.7%–14.7%   ☐ No data

Note: Experience of sexual dating violence one or more times during the 12 months before the survey, counting kissing, touching, or being physically forced to have sexual intercourse when they did not want to by someone they were dating or going out with among students who dated or went out with someone during the 12 months before the survey.

SOURCE: "Percentage of High School Students Who Experienced Sexual Dating Violence," in "Behaviors That Contribute to Unintentional Injuries," *Youth Risk Behavior Surveillance System (YRBSS): 2015*, Centers for Disease Control and Prevention, Division of Adolescent and School Health, 2015, http://www.cdc.gov/healthyyouth/data/yrbs/slides/2015/injury_slides_yrbs.pptx (accessed June 17, 2016)

render victims incapable of resisting sexual attacks. One such date rape drug is Rohypnol, which is a hypnotic sedative 10 times more powerful than Valium. Rohypnol has been used to obtain nonconsensual sex from many women. When mixed in a drink, it causes memory impairment, confusion, and drowsiness. A woman may be completely unaware of a sexual assault until she wakes up the following morning. The only way to determine if a victim has been given Rohypnol is to test for the drug within two or three days of the rape, and few hospital emergency departments routinely screen for this drug. Health educators, high school guidance counselors, resident advisers at colleges, and scores of newspaper and magazine articles

advise women not to accept drinks at parties or to leave drinks sitting unattended.

Rohypnol is legally prescribed outside of the United States for short-term treatment of severe sleep disorders, but it is neither manufactured nor approved for sale in the United States. In addition, its use (as is the use of other controlled substances) to facilitate a violent act, such as a rape, is against the law. The importation of the drug was banned in March 1996, and the U.S. Customs and Border Protection began seizing quantities of Rohypnol at U.S. borders. In response to reported abuse, the manufacturers reformulated the drug as green tablets that can be detected in clear liquids and are visible in the bottom of a cup.

FIGURE 8.5

Percentage of high school students who experienced sexual dating violence in the past year, by race and Hispanic origin, grade, and sex, 2015

Note: This graph contains weighted results. Experience of sexual dating violence one or more times during the 12 months before the survey, including kissing, touching, or being physically forced to have sexual intercourse when they did not want to by someone they were dating or going out with among students who dated or went out with someone during the 12 months before the survey. All Hispanic students are included in the Hispanic category. All other races are non-Hispanic.

SOURCE: "Percentage of High School Students Who Experienced Sexual Dating Violence, by Sex, Grade, and Race/Ethnicity, 2015," in "Behaviors That Contribute to Unintentional Injuries," *Youth Risk Behavior Surveillance System (YRBSS): 2015*, Centers for Disease Control and Prevention, Division of Adolescent and School Health, 2015, http://www.cdc.gov/healthyyouth/data/yrbs/slides/2015/injury_slides_yrbs.pptx (accessed June 17, 2016)

Three other drugs are also used as date rape pills. Gamma hydroxybutyric acid (also known as "liquid ecstasy") enhances the effects of alcohol, which reduces the drinker's inhibitions. It also causes a form of amnesia. Ketamine hydrochloride (also known as "Special K") is an animal tranquilizer that is used to impair a person's natural resistance impulses. Another dangerous date rape drug is a combination of ecstasy and Viagra (a prescription drug that is used to treat erectile dysfunction); this combination is dubbed "sextasy." According to media reports, the drugs are taken together by male teens because Viagra offsets impotence, which is a potential side effect of ecstasy use. Public health officials are alarmed by this off-label use of Viagra and fear that it may contribute to increased rates of sexually transmitted diseases and sexual assault.

In preparing *Drug-Facilitated, Incapacitated, and Forcible Rape: A National Study* (July 2007, http://www.ncjrs.gov/pdffiles1/nij/grants/219181.pdf), Dean G. Kirkpatrick et al. interviewed 5,000 women between the ages of 18 and 86, 2,000 of whom were currently attending college. The researchers reveal that 18% of all women had been raped during their lifetime and that 11.5% of college women had been raped during their lifetime. They also indicate that more college women than women in the general population had experienced either drug-assisted rapes (in which the perpetrator purposely administered drugs or alcohol to assault the victim) or drug-facilitated rapes (in which the perpetrator took advantage of the victim's voluntary intoxication to assault her). During their lifetime, 6.4% of college women and 5% of women in the general population had experienced these types of rape.

Combating Sexual Violence on Campus

In recent years advocacy groups and government agencies have become increasingly active in confronting the problem of sexual violence at the nation's postsecondary institutions. One specific area of reform has focused on improving the ways that colleges and universities report incidents of rape and sexual assault. Claire Groden reports in "Campus Rape Victims Find a Voice" (Time.com, August 8, 2013) that rape and sexual assault is "notoriously underreported" at American institutions of higher learning. According to Groden, between one-fifth and one-quarter of all female college students experience sexual assault, rape, or attempted rape at some point before completing their degree. However, statistics provided by most colleges and universities fail to reflect this reality. For example, Groden notes that in 2011 the University of Southern California reported a total of only 15 cases of rape or sexual assault, despite having a student body of 40,000.

TABLE 8.11

Percentage of high school students who have ever experienced physical dating violence and sexual dating violence, by sex, state, and select metropolitan areas, 2015

Site	Physical dating violence			Sexual dating violence		
	Female	Male	Total	Female	Male	Total
	%	%	%	%	%	%
State surveys						
Alabama	13.9	8.4	11.4	13.4	6.1	10.0
Alaska	10.5	8.2	9.5	14.9	5.2	10.1
Arizona	—NA	—	—	—	—	—
Arkansas	18.2	10.5	14.6	16.0	7.1	11.8
California	11.7	7.4	9.7	18.1	5.3	11.8
Connecticut	8.7	6.8	8.0	16.4	6.4	11.5
Delaware	9.8	7.2	8.6	9.8	5.7	7.9
Florida	11.2	10.5	11.0	13.8	8.5	11.3
Hawaii	10.7	8.1	9.8	15.4	8.9	12.7
Idaho	12.6	5.1	8.9	21.6	3.2	12.4
Illinois	12.7	9.7	11.3	15.0	6.9	11.1
Indiana	11.9	7.7	10.0	16.4	8.6	12.6
Kentucky	12.1	5.3	8.9	13.8	6.1	10.1
Maine	9.9	6.4	8.3	—	—	—
Maryland	11.2	8.5	10.1	13.1	6.9	10.3
Massachusetts	9.3	4.1	6.7	11.2	3.7	7.5
Michigan	9.2	6.8	8.2	17.5	5.9	11.9
Mississippi	12.3	8.2	10.6	14.8	7.7	11.4
Missouri	10.2	12.9	11.7	—	—	—
Montana	10.8	5.5	8.2	14.4	5.6	10.0
Nebraska	11.7	3.7	8.1	13.8	3.2	8.8
Nevada	10.5	8.8	9.6	14.4	8.5	11.5
New Hampshire	9.5	6.1	7.8	17.3	6.0	11.7
New Mexico	9.6	7.6	8.6	12.7	5.8	9.2
New York	11.9	10.3	11.5	16.6	11.9	14.7
North Carolina	9.2	7.3	8.3	11.1	4.4	7.8
North Dakota	9.6	5.6	7.6	—	—	—
Oklahoma	8.9	5.3	7.2	13.1	3.9	8.6
Pennsylvania	9.4	5.0	7.2	14.2	4.3	9.3
Rhode Island	9.5	7.9	8.8	12.8	5.9	9.6
South Carolina	8.4	7.7	8.0	9.8	5.3	7.6
South Dakota	9.8	7.8	8.8	10.1	6.2	8.1
Tennessee	12.9	9.5	11.2	—	—	—
Vermont	10.7	7.2	9.1	—	—	—
Virginia	12.3	9.5	10.9	—	—	—
West Virginia	11.2	8.7	10.1	11.7	6.1	9.0
Wyoming	9.9	8.1	9.1	10.7	5.1	8.0
Median	10.6	7.7	9.0	14.0	5.9	10.1
Range	(8.4–18.2)	(3.7–12.9)	(6.7–14.6)	(9.8–21.6)	(3.2–11.9)	(7.5–14.7)
Large urban school district surveys						
Baltimore, MD	10.0	12.1	11.8	11.5	12.1	12.1
Boston, MA	7.0	5.5	6.4	8.3	5.1	6.8
Broward County, FL	10.6	7.5	9.2	14.4	6.6	10.5
Cleveland, OH	11.6	12.5	12.7	8.3	11.9	10.7
DeKalb County, GA	11.1	7.7	9.4	10.3	7.9	9.1
Detroit, MI	12.2	8.6	10.8	8.2	9.0	8.8
District of Columbia	11.8	8.4	10.3	8.3	6.5	7.7
Duval County, FL	12.3	11.3	12.4	17.3	10.0	14.4
Ft. Worth, TX	10.4	6.2	8.3	10.0	7.1	8.6
Houston, TX	11.7	8.1	10.1	11.1	5.9	8.8
Los Angeles, CA	6.6	7.5	7.2	10.8	6.3	8.6
Miami-Dade County, FL	7.6	7.0	7.4	9.5	6.8	8.2
New York City, NY	12.5	11.1	12.0	13.6	8.6	11.4
Oakland, CA	13.4	9.7	11.6	12.4	8.7	10.8
Orange County, FL	8.9	9.0	9.0	16.3	6.9	11.4
Palm Beach County, FL	10.8	8.5	10.2	13.1	8.7	11.6
Philadelphia, PA	13.6	7.7	10.8	14.4	6.4	10.6
San Diego, CA	9.1	6.4	7.8	16.0	5.9	10.7
San Francisco, CA	7.5	5.6	6.6	12.1	4.7	8.3
Median	10.8	8.1	10.1	11.5	6.9	10.5
Range	(6.6–13.6)	(5.5–12.5)	(6.4–12.7)	(8.2–17.3)	(4.7–12.1)	(6.8–14.4)

By early 2013 the federal government began taking more aggressive measures to hold colleges and universities accountable. The Violence against Women Reauthorization Act, which was signed into law in March 2013, includes a stipulation known as the Campus Sexual Violence Act provision, which requires all institutions participating in federal financial aid programs to provide detailed reporting of all on-campus incidences of rape,

TABLE 8.11

Percentage of high school students who have ever experienced physical dating violence and sexual dating violence, by sex, state, and select metropolitan areas, 2015 [CONTINUED]

NA = not available.

Notes: Experiences occurred one or more times during the 12 months before the survey, among students who dated or went out with someone during the 12 months before the survey. Being physically hurt on purpose (counting being hit, slammed into something, or injured with an object or weapon) by someone they were dating or going out with. Being forced to do sexual things (counting kissing, touching, or being physically forced to have sexual intercourse) they did not want to do by someone they were dating or going out with.

SOURCE: Adapted from Laura Kann et al., "Table 22. Percentage of High School Students Who Experienced Physical Dating Violence, and Sexual Dating Violence, by Sex—Selected U.S. Sites, Youth Risk Behavior Survey, 2015," in "Youth Risk Behavior Surveillance—United States, 2015," *MMWR*, vol. 65, no. 6, June 10, 2016, http://www.cdc.gov/healthyyouth/data/yrbs/pdf/2015/ss6506_updated.pdf (accessed June 13, 2016)

sexual assault, domestic violence, and stalking. Furthermore, Groden notes that at the beginning of the 2013–14 academic year, nearly 30 schools, including Dartmouth College, the University of Southern California, and Princeton University, were under federal investigation for violations related to the underreporting of sexual violence on campus. In "Biden and Obama Rewrite the Rulebook on College Sexual Assaults" (Washington-Post.com, July 3, 2016), Juliet Eilperin indicates that by July 2016 the number of institutions under investigation had grown to 198 colleges and universities nationwide.

In January 2014 President Barack Obama (1961–) announced the formation of the White House Task Force to Protect Students from Sexual Assault, a new agency designed to provide support for victims of on-campus sexual violence. The initial findings of the task force were published in *Not Alone: The First Report of the White House Task Force to Protect Students from Sexual Assault* (April 2014, https://www.notalone.gov/assets/report.pdf). Among the task force's key recommendations is a requirement that schools conduct an "evidence-based survey" on sexual violence by 2016. To help institutions achieve this goal, the BJS launched the College Experiences Survey (CES) Pilot Test, a preliminary survey designed to develop a methodology for collecting and evaluating data relating to sexual violence on campus. Funded by the DOJ's Office on Violence against Women and conducted in collaboration with RTI International, the CES Pilot Test took place at nine institutions during the spring semester of the 2014–15 academic year. The results of the project were published by Christopher Krebs et al. in *Campus Climate Survey Validation Study Final Technical Report* (January 2016, http://www.bjs.gov/content/pub/pdf/ccsvsftr.pdf). The researchers note that more than one out of five (20.5%) of female undergraduates had experienced sexual assault since entering college; more than one out of 10 (10.3%) had been sexually assaulted during the 2014–15 school year.

In September 2014 the White House also unveiled the "It's on Us" program, an initiative aimed at increasing awareness of sexual assault at the nation's colleges and universities. In "President Obama Launches the 'It's on Us' Campaign to End Sexual Assault on Campus"

(September 19, 2014, https://www.whitehouse.gov/blog/2014/09/19/president-obama-launches-its-us-campaign-end-sexual-assault-campus), Tanya Somanader includes a list of White House recommendations for college students confronting the problem of sexual violence on campus:

- Talk to your friends honestly and openly about sexual assault.

- Don't just be a bystander—if you see something, intervene in any way you can.

- Trust your gut. If something looks like it might be a bad situation, it probably is.

- Be direct. Ask someone who looks like they may need help if they're ok.

- Get someone to help you if you see something—enlist a friend, RA, bartender, or host to help step in.

- Keep an eye on someone who has had too much to drink.

- If you see someone who is too intoxicated to consent, enlist their friends to help them leave safely.

- Recognize the potential danger of someone who talks about planning to target another person at a party.

- Be aware if someone is deliberately trying to intoxicate, isolate, or corner someone else.

- Get in the way by creating a distraction, drawing attention to the situation, or separating them.

- Understand that if someone does not or cannot consent to sex, it's rape.

- Never blame the victim.

According to Eilperin, as of July 2016 the "It's on Us" campaign had more than 344,400 members, with chapters on 530 campuses nationwide.

Another key development in the movement to end sexual violence on college campuses was in September 2014, when California implemented a law that clarified the legal definition of consensual sex. Bill Chappell reports in "California Enacts 'Yes Means Yes' Law, Defining Sexual Consent" (NPR.org, September 29, 2014) that the new law requires individuals to establish

TABLE 8.12

Percentage of public schools reporting sexual harassment of students by other students, by selected school characteristics, selected years 2003–04 to 2013–14

Year and school characteristic	Happens at least once a week[a] Student sexual harassment of other students
2003–04	4.0
2005–06	3.5
2007–08	3.0
2009–10 All schools	**3.2**
School level[b]	
Primary	1.8
Middle	6.1
High school	3.2
Combined	7.5
Enrollment size	
Less than 300	4.5
300–499	2.4
500–999	2.6
1,000 or more	4.7
Locale	
City	3.6
Suburban	2.6
Town	2.9
Rural	3.6
Percent combined enrollment of black, Hispanic, Asian/Pacific Islander, and American Indian/Alaska Native students	
Less than 5 percent	4.5
5 percent to less than 20 percent	1.8
20 percent to less than 50 percent	2.6
50 percent or more	4.1
Percent of students eligible for free or reduced–price lunch	
0–25	2.6
26–50	3.2
51–75	3.2
76–100	3.9
2013–14[c] All schools	**1.4**
School level[b]	
Primary	‡
Middle	3.4
High school/combined	1.8
Enrollment size	
Less than 300	‡
300–499	1.8
500–999	1.3
1,000 or more	3.8
Locale	
City	2.5
Suburban	1.5
Town	‡
Rural	‡
Percent combined enrollment of black, Hispanic, Asian/Pacific Islander, and American Indian/Alaska Native students	
Less than 5 percent	‡
5 percent to less than 20 percent	‡
20 percent to less than 50 percent	2.2
50 percent or more	1.5

TABLE 8.12

Percentage of public schools reporting sexual harassment of students by other students, by selected school characteristics, selected years 2003–04 to 2013–14 [CONTINUED]

Year and school characteristic	Happens at least once a week[a] Student sexual harassment of other students
Percent of students eligible for free or reduced-price lunch[d]	
0–25	‡
26–50	1.2
51–75	2.2
76–100	1.4

‡Reporting standards not met.
[a]Includes schools that reported the activity happens either at least once a week or daily.
[b]Primary schools are defined as schools in which the lowest grade is not higher than grade 3 and the highest grade is not higher than grade 8. Middle schools are defined as schools in which the lowest grade is not lower than grade 4 and the highest grade is not higher than grade 9. High schools are defined as schools in which the lowest grade is not lower than grade 9 and the highest grade is not higher than grade 12. Combined schools include all other combinations of grades, including K–12 schools. Separate data on high schools and combined schools are not available for 2013–14.
[c]Data for 2013–14 were collected using the Fast Response Survey System, while data for earlier years were collected using the School Survey on Crime and Safety (SSOCS). The 2013–14 survey was designed to allow comparisons with SSOCS data. However, respondents to the 2013–14 survey could choose either to complete the survey on paper (and mail it back) or to complete the survey online, whereas respondents to SSOCS did not have the option of completing the survey online. The 2013–14 survey also relied on a smaller sample. The smaller sample size and change in survey administration may have impacted 2013–14 results.
[d]Because the 2013–14 survey did not collect data on the percentage of students eligible for free or reduced-price lunch, the classification of schools by the percentage of students eligible for free or reduced-price lunch was computed based on data obtained from the Common Core of Data.
Note: Responses were provided by the principal or the person most knowledgeable about crime and safety issues at the school. "At school" was defined to include activities that happen in school buildings, on school grounds, on school buses, and at places that hold school-sponsored events or activities. Respondents were instructed to respond only for those times that were during normal school hours or when school activities or events were in session, unless the survey specified otherwise.

SOURCE: Adapted from Anlan Zhang, Lauren Musu-Gillette, and Barbara A. Oudekerk, "Table 7.1. Percentage of Public Schools Reporting Selected Discipline Problems That Occurred at School, by Frequency and Selected School Characteristics: Selected Years, 1999–2000 through 2013–14," in *Indicators of School Crime and Safety: 2015*, U.S. Department of Education, National Center for Education Statistics, U.S. Department of Justice, Office of Justice Programs, Bureau of Justice Statistics, May 2016, http://nces.ed.gov/pubs2016/2016079.pdf (accessed June 13, 2016)

specific verbal consent before engaging in sexual activities. Furthermore, the law states that affirmative consent cannot be obtained in situations when a person is either sleeping or intoxicated. The law also requires Califor-

nia's colleges and universities to implement more stringent policies relating to sexual assault and domestic violence cases on campus.

Unfortunately, the limits of California's new consent law became evident in June 2016, when the Stanford University student Brock Turner (1995–) was found guilty of three felony counts of raping an unconscious woman in a January 2015 assault. Although prosecutors recommended that Turner receive a minimum six-year prison sentence for the crime, Judge Aaron Persky (1962–) of the Superior Court of California, County of Santa Clara, ordered him to serve only six months in jail. According to Ashley Fantz, in "Outrage over 6-Month Sentence for Brock Turner in Stanford Rape Case" (CNN.com, June 7, 2016), Judge Persky's decision sparked nationwide outrage and soon led to a petition

TABLE 8.13

Forcible and nonforcible sex offenses at degree-granting postsecondary institutions, by type of institution, 2001–13

Control and level of institution and type of incident	Total, in residence halls and at other locations												2013 Total	2013 In residence halls	2013 At other locations
	2001	2002	2003	2004	2005	2006	2007	2008	2009	2010	2011	2012	Total	In residence halls	At other locations
All institutions															
Sex offenses—forcible[a]	2,201	2,327	2,595	2,667	2,674	2,670	2,694	2,639	2,544	2,927	3,375	4,017	4,964	3,627	1,337
Sex offenses—nonforcible[b]	461	261	60	27	42	43	40	35	65	33	46	46	45	20	25
Public 4-year															
Sex offenses—forcible[a]	1,245	1,278	1,358	1,482	1,398	1,400	1,425	1,317	1,214	1,461	1,638	1,972	2,257	1,646	611
Sex offenses—nonforcible[b]	207	113	28	16	25	15	23	12	40	15	17	17	17	9	8
Nonprofit 4-year															
Sex offenses—forcible[a]	820	914	1,048	1,026	1,088	1,080	1,065	1,083	1,102	1,225	1,431	1,741	2,368	1,876	492
Sex offenses—nonforcible[b]	113	81	14	5	6	10	8	16	11	8	13	10	12	4	8
For-profit 4-year															
Sex offenses—forcible[a]	4	4	8	5	4	12	12	9	9	22	26	19	20	14	6
Sex offenses—nonforcible[b]	13	1	2	0	1	0	2	0	1	1	0	3	2	0	2
Public 2-year															
Sex offenses—forcible[a]	118	118	160	142	175	167	181	210	205	210	262	265	304	84	220
Sex offenses—nonforcible[b]	119	61	14	6	10	16	7	7	12	8	16	13	12	5	7
Nonprofit 2-year															
Sex offenses—forcible[a]	2	7	6	3	8	3	9	16	8	7	11	8	4	1	3
Sex offenses—nonforcible[b]	2	2	0	0	0	1	0	0	0	0	0	0	2	2	0
For-profit 2-year															
Sex offenses—forcible[a]	12	6	15	9	1	8	2	4	6	2	7	12	11	6	5
Sex offenses—nonforcible[b]	7	3	2	0	0	1	0	0	1	1	0	3	0	0	0

Number of incidents

[a]Any sexual act directed against another person forcibly and/or against that person's will.
[b]Includes only statutory rape or incest.
Note: Data are for degree-granting institutions, which are institutions that grant associate's or higher degrees and participate in Title IV federal financial aid programs. Some institutions that report Clery data—specifically, non-degree-granting institutions and institutions outside of the 50 states and the District of Columbia—are excluded from this table. Crimes, arrests, and referrals include incidents involving students, staff, and on-campus guests. Excludes off-campus crimes and arrests even if they involve college students or staff. Some data have been revised from previously published figures.

SOURCE: Adapted from Anlan Zhang, Lauren Musu-Gillette, and Barbara A. Oudekerk, "Table 22.1. On-Campus Crimes, Arrests, and Referrals for Disciplinary Action at Degree-Granting Postsecondary Institutions, by Location of Incident, Control and Level of Institution, and Type of Incident: 2001 through 2013," in *Indicators of School Crime and Safety: 2015*, U.S. Department of Education, National Center for Education Statistics, U.S. Department of Justice, Office of Justice Programs, Bureau of Justice Statistics, May 2016, http://nces.ed.gov/pubs2016/2016079.pdf (accessed June 13, 2016)

drive to have him recalled. In the petition "Remove Judge Aaron Persky from the Bench for Decision in Brock Turner Rape Case" (2016, https://www.change.org/p/california-state-house-recall-judge-aaron-persky), Change.org criticizes Judge Persky for being unable to recognize "that the fact that Brock Turner is a white male star athlete at a prestigious university does not entitle him to leniency," while failing "to send the message that sexual assault is against the law regardless of social class, race, gender or other factors."

Following Turner's sentencing, his victim released her impact statement to the general public. Her letter, which describes in detail both the circumstances of the rape and the devastating emotional impact it has had on her life, was republished in news outlets throughout the world. Frank Pallotta reports in "Why Ashleigh Banfield Read Stanford Rape Victim's Letter on CNN" (CNN.com, June 6, 2016) that Ashleigh Banfield (1967–), the host of CNN's *Legal View*, devoted nearly an entire episode of her program to reading the victim's full statement on the air. The victim's words even elicited a direct response from Vice President Joe Biden (1942–), who published an open letter in the aftermath of the case. In the letter, which was reprinted in full by Tom Namako in "Joe Biden Writes an Open Letter to Stanford Survivor" (BuzzFeed.com, June 9, 2016), Biden expresses "furious anger" about the victim's ordeal, asserting that she had been "failed by a culture on our college campuses where one in five women is sexually assaulted—year after year after year." At the same time, Biden reiterates the Obama administration's commitment to ending violence against women. "We will speak out against those who seek to engage in plausible deniability," Biden writes. "We will make lighthouses of ourselves, as you did—and shine." Eilperin notes that in July 2016 the White House announced that high-ranking government officials, including the president and vice president, would cease to visit any colleges or universities that had not taken adequate measures to address the problem of sexual violence on campus.

TABLE 8.14

Forcible and nonforcible sex offenses at degree-granting postsecondary institutions, by type and presence of residence halls, 2001–13

[Number of incidents per 10,000 full-time-equivalent (FTE) students]

| | Number of incidents per 10,000 full-time-equivalent (FTE) students[a] | | | | | | | | | | | | | 2013 | | |
| | Total, institutions with and without residence halls | | | | | | | | | | | | | Institutions with residence halls | Institutions without residence halls |
Control and level of institution and type of incident	2001	2002	2003	2004	2005	2006	2007	2008	2009	2010	2011	2012	Total		
All institutions															
Sex offenses—forcible[b]	1.885	1.896	2.051	2.056	2.058	2.001	1.969	1.898	1.715	1.903	2.223	2.665	3.309	4.646	0.513
Sex offenses—nonforcible[c]	0.395	0.213	0.047	0.021	0.032	0.032	0.029	0.025	0.044	0.021	0.030	0.031	0.030	0.035	0.019
Public 4-year															
Sex offenses—forcible[b]	2.408	2.374	2.452	2.634	2.448	2.409	2.390	2.151	1.892	2.210	2.451	2.941	3.347	3.624	0.500
Sex offenses—nonforcible[c]	0.400	0.210	0.051	0.028	0.044	0.026	0.039	0.020	0.062	0.023	0.025	0.025	0.025	0.026	0.017
Nonprofit 4-year															
Sex offenses—forcible[b]	3.169	3.410	3.790	3.617	3.784	3.694	3.587	3.586	3.557	3.848	4.417	5.275	7.122	7.686	1.061
Sex offenses—nonforcible[c]	0.437	0.302	0.051	0.018	0.021	0.034	0.027	0.053	0.036	0.025	0.040	0.030	0.036	0.036	0.035
For-profit 4-year															
Sex offenses—forcible[b]	0.151	0.121	0.196	0.095	0.082	0.179	0.159	0.162	0.129	0.255	0.350	0.259	0.277	0.961	0.072
Sex offenses—nonforcible[c]	0.492	0.030	0.049	0.000	0.021	0.000	0.026	0.000	0.014	0.012	0.000	0.041	0.028	0.000	0.036
Public 2-year															
Sex offenses—forcible[b]	0.344	0.324	0.435	0.383	0.480	0.454	0.484	0.538	0.483	0.487	0.633	0.662	0.780	1.626	0.570
Sex offenses—nonforcible[c]	0.347	0.167	0.038	0.016	0.027	0.044	0.019	0.018	0.028	0.019	0.039	0.032	0.031	0.090	0.016
Nonprofit 2-year															
Sex offenses—forcible[b]	0.516	1.793	1.638	0.877	2.325	0.983	3.622	5.841	3.041	2.826	3.384	2.599	1.536	2.476	1.113
Sex offenses—nonforcible[c]	0.516	0.512	0.000	0.000	0.000	0.328	0.000	0.000	0.000	0.000	0.000	0.000	0.768	2.476	0.000
For-profit 2-year															
Sex offenses—forcible[b]	0.645	0.309	0.674	0.373	0.042	0.347	0.087	0.149	0.170	0.052	0.204	0.407	0.388	4.700	0.185
Sex offenses—nonforcible[c]	0.376	0.154	0.090	0.000	0.000	0.043	0.000	0.000	0.028	0.026	0.000	0.102	0.000	0.000	0.000

[a]Although crimes, arrests, and referrals include incidents involving students, staff, and campus guests, they are expressed as a ratio to FTE students because comprehensive FTE counts of all these groups are not available.

[b]Any sexual act directed against another person forcibly and/or against that person's will.

[c]Includes only statutory rape or incest.

Note: Data are for degree-granting institutions, which are institutions that grant associate's or higher degrees and participate in Title IV federal financial aid programs. Some institutions that report Clery data—specifically, non-degree-granting institutions and institutions outside of the 50 states and the District of Columbia—are excluded from this table. Crimes, arrests, and referrals include incidents involving students, staff, and on-campus guests. Excludes off-campus crimes and arrests even if they involve college students or staff. Detail may not sum to totals because of rounding. Some data have been revised from previously published figures.

SOURCE: Adapted from Anlan Zhang, Lauren Musu-Gillette, and Barbara A. Oudekerk, "Table 22.2. On-Campus Crimes, Arrests, and Referrals for Disciplinary Action per 10,000 Full-Time Equivalent (FTE) Students at Degree-Granting Postsecondary Institutions, by Whether Institution Has Residence Halls, Control and Level of Institution, and Type of Incident: 2001 through 2013," in *Indicators of School Crime and Safety: 2015*, U.S. Department of Education, National Center for Education Statistics, U.S. Department of Justice, Office of Justice Programs, Bureau of Justice Statistics, May 2016, http://nces.ed.gov/pubs2016/2016079.pdf (accessed June 13, 2016)

Sexual Assault in the Military

Over the years sexual assault has been a pervasive problem in the U.S. armed forces. To confront this issue, the U.S. Department of Defense formed the Sexual Assault Prevention and Response Office (SAPRO; http://www.sapr.mil/) in 2005. In the decade after SAPRO was established, the annual number of sexual assault reports in the military more than doubled, from 2,846 in fiscal year (FY) 2007 to 6,083 in FY 2015. (See Figure 8.8.) Despite this increase, sexual violence among U.S. service members still remains largely unreported. Protect Our Defenders (POD), a national advocacy group dedicated to ending sexual violence in the military, reports in the fact sheet "Facts on United States Military Sexual Violence" (2016, http://protectourdefenders.com/downloads/Military_Sexual_Violence_Fact_Sheet_Final _150710.pdf) that the vast majority of rape and sexual assault cases involving members of the military are never reported, largely out of fear of retaliation from both commanding officers and fellow personnel. According to POD, roughly 86% of military personnel who were victims of sexual assault in 2014 ultimately declined to report the crime.

The U.S. military provides slightly different figures for sexual assault reporting in FY 2014. The Department of Defense notes in *Department of Defense Annual Report on Sexual Assault in the Military: Fiscal Year 2015* (May 2016, http://sapr.mil/public/docs/reports/FY15_Annual/FY15_Annual_Report_on_Sexual_Assault _in_the_Military.pdf) that slightly fewer than a quarter (23%) of the estimated 20,300 sexual assault incidents in the military in FY 2014 were ultimately reported.

FIGURE 8.6

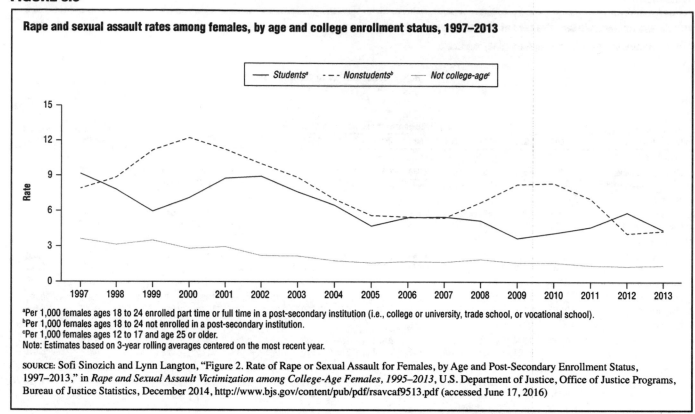

Rape and sexual assault rates among females, by age and college enrollment status, 1997–2013

[Legend: —— Students[a]   - - - Nonstudents[b]   ······· Not college-age[c]]

[a]Per 1,000 females ages 18 to 24 enrolled part time or full time in a post-secondary institution (i.e., college or university, trade school, or vocational school).
[b]Per 1,000 females ages 18 to 24 not enrolled in a post-secondary institution.
[c]Per 1,000 females ages 12 to 17 and age 25 or older.
Note: Estimates based on 3-year rolling averages centered on the most recent year.

SOURCE: Sofi Sinozich and Lynn Langton, "Figure 2. Rate of Rape or Sexual Assault for Females, by Age and Post-Secondary Enrollment Status, 1997–2013," in *Rape and Sexual Assault Victimization among College-Age Females, 1995–2013*, U.S. Department of Justice, Office of Justice Programs, Bureau of Justice Statistics, December 2014, http://www.bjs.gov/content/pub/pdf/rsavcaf9513.pdf (accessed June 17, 2016)

(See Figure 8.9.) As Figure 8.10 reveals, roughly two-thirds (64%) of male service members who were victims of sexual assault in FY 2014 reported that the incident occurred while they were on duty, compared with one-third (33%) of female service members who were sexually assaulted while on duty.

STALKING

Stalking is generally defined as harassment or threatening behavior that involves repeated visual or physical proximity; nonconsensual communication; verbal, written, or implied threats; or a combination of these acts that would cause a reasonable person fear. Stalking is a series of actions that can escalate from legal but annoying acts, such as following or repeatedly phoning a victim, to violent and even fatal actions.

In 2006 the Office on Violence against Women funded the Supplemental Victimization Survey (SVS) as a supplement to the NCVS to explore the extent and nature of stalking in the United States. Shannan Catalano of the BJS indicates in *Stalking Victims in the United States—Revised* (September 2012, http://bjs.ojp.usdoj .gov/content/pub/pdf/svus_rev.pdf) that the survey included 65,270 participants aged 18 years and older who were interviewed during the first six months of 2006 about experiences that had occurred during the previous 12 months. The SVS classified an individual as a stalking victim if he or she had been the recipient

of one of the following seven harassing behaviors on at least two separate occasions:

- Received unwanted phone calls

- Received unsolicited or unwanted letters or e-mails

- Was followed or spied on

- Found the stalker showing up at places without a legitimate reason

- Found the stalker waiting at places for him or her

- Received unwanted items, presents, or flowers

- Had information posted or had rumors spread about him or her on the Internet, in a public place, or by word of mouth

In addition, the victims had to have "feared for their safety or that of a family member as a result of the course of conduct or have experienced additional threatening behaviors that would cause a reasonable person to feel fear." According to Catalano, these criteria were based on federal and state criminal laws that cover stalking. Survey participants who reported experiencing conduct consistent with stalking, but who did not meet the fear criteria, were classified as being victims of harassment, rather than as victims of stalking.

Overall, Catalano estimates that 3.3 million adults aged 18 years and older were stalked during a 12-month period in 2005 to 2006. This represents 1.5% of the adult

FIGURE 8.7

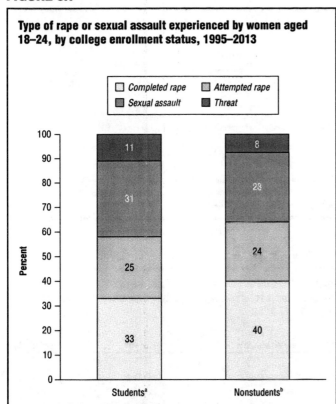

Type of rape or sexual assault experienced by women aged 18–24, by college enrollment status, 1995–2013

Legend:
- ☐ Completed rape
- ▦ Sexual assault
- ▨ Attempted rape
- ■ Threat

Students[a]: Completed rape 33, Sexual assault 25, Attempted rape 31, Threat 11
Nonstudents[b]: Completed rape 40, Sexual assault 24, Attempted rape 23, Threat 8

[a]Includes female victims ages 18 to 24 enrolled part time or full time in a post-secondary institution (i.e., college or university, trade school, or vocational school).
[b]Includes female victims ages 18 to 24 not enrolled in a post-secondary institution.
Note: Excludes a small number of female victims ages 18 to 24 with unknown enrollment status (less than 1%). The average annual population was 5,130,004 for students and 8,614,853 for nonstudents.

SOURCE: Sofi Sinozich and Lynn Langton, "Figure 3. Type of Rape or Sexual Assault Experienced by Female Victims Ages 18 to 24, by Post-Secondary Enrollment Status, 1995–2013," in *Rape and Sexual Assault Victimization among College-Age Females, 1995–2013*, U.S. Department of Justice, Office of Justice Programs, Bureau of Justice Statistics, December 2014, http://www.bjs.gov/content/pub/pdf/rsavcaf9513.pdf (accessed June 17, 2016)

U.S. population. The percentage was higher for females (2.2%) than for males (0.8%) and gradually decreased with age; that is, individuals aged 18 to 19 years had the highest rate, at 2.9%. The percentages decreased with increasing household income, in that people making $7,499 or less annually had the highest rate of 3.3%. On a racial and ethnic basis, the highest 12-month prevalence was among people of two or more races (4.1%). Marital status also played a factor. Divorced or separated individuals (3.3%) and those who had never married (2.4%) had the highest prevalence of stalking.

According to Catalano, the most common stalking behaviors were as follows (the percentages add up to more than 100% because the victims were allowed to name multiple behaviors):

- 66.7% of victims experienced unwanted phone calls and messages
- 36.3% of victims had rumors spread about them
- 34.4% of victims were spied on or followed
- 31.6% of victims experienced a stalker showing up at places where they were
- 30.7% received unwanted letters and e-mails
- 29.3% found a stalker waiting for them
- 12.5% received unwanted presents

Catalano notes that stalking victims were also asked how long the stalking had lasted. The largest share (39.3%) said it had lasted six months or less and 16.9% said the duration was between seven and 11 months. Another 13.4% of victims reported they had been stalked for one year, 9% said two years, 4.6% said three years, and 2.8% said four years. More than one out of 10 (11.1%) victims had been stalked for five or more years.

TABLE 8.15

Average annual incidences of rape or sexual assault among women aged 18–24, by college enrollment status, 1995–2013

	Students[a]		Nonstudents[b]		
	Average annual number	Rate[c]	Average annual number	Rate[d]	Ratio of nonstudent to student rate
Total	31,302	6.1	65,668	7.6	1.2
Completed rape	10,237	2.0	26,369	3.1	1.5
Attempted rape	7,864	1.5	15,792	1.8	1.2
Sexual assault	9,714	1.9	18,260	2.1	1.1
Threat of rape or sexual assault	3,488	0.7	5,247	0.6	0.9

[a]Includes females ages 18 to 24 enrolled part time or full time in a post-secondary institution (college or university, trade school, or vocational school).
[b]Includes females ages 18 to 24 not enrolled in a post-secondary institution.
[c]Per 1,000 female students ages 18 to 24.
[d]Per 1,000 females ages 18 to 24 not enrolled in a post-secondary institution.
Note: Detail may not sum to total due to rounding. Excludes a small number of female victims ages 18 to 24 with unknown enrollment status (less than 1%). The average annual population was 5,130,004 for students and 8,614,853 for nonstudents.

SOURCE: Sofi Sinozich and Lynn Langton, "Table 1. Rape or Sexual Assault Victimization against Females Ages 18 to 24, by Post-Secondary Enrollment Status, 1995–2013," in *Rape and Sexual Assault Victimization among College-Age Females, 1995–2013*, U.S. Department of Justice, Office of Justice Programs, Bureau of Justice Statistics, December 2014, http://www.bjs.gov/content/pub/pdf/rsavcaf9513.pdf (accessed June 17, 2016)

TABLE 8.16

Average annual incidences of rape and sexual assault, by sex and college enrollment status of victim, 1995–2013

Sex of victim	Students[a]			Nonstudents[b]			Ratio of nonstudent to student rate
	Average annual number	Percent of victimizations	Rate[c]	Average annual number	Percent of victimizations	Rate[c]	
Male	6,544	17%	1.4	2,866	4%	0.3	0.2
Female	31,302	83	6.1	65,668	96	7.6	1.2

[a]Includes victims ages 18 to 24 enrolled part time or full time in a post-secondary institution (i.e., college or university, trade school, or vocational school).
[b]Includes victims ages 18 to 24 not enrolled in a post-secondary institution.
[c]Per 1,000 persons ages 18 to 24.
Note: Excludes a small percentage of victims with unknown enrollment status (less than 1%).

SOURCE: Sofi Sinozich and Lynn Langton, "Table 3. Rape and Sexual Assault Victimization, by Sex of Victim and Post-Secondary Enrollment-Status, 1995–2013," in *Rape and Sexual Assault Victimization among College-Age Females, 1995–2013*, U.S. Department of Justice, Office of Justice Programs, Bureau of Justice Statistics, December 2014, http://www.bjs.gov/content/pub/pdf/rsavcaf9513.pdf (accessed June 17, 2016)

TABLE 8.17

Rapes and sexual assaults among women aged 18–24, by location, activity, time of day, and college enrollment status, 1995–2013

	Students[a]	Nonstudents[b]
Location where crime occurred	100%	100%
At or near victim's home[c]	38	50
At or near home of friend/relative/ acquaintance	29	17
Commercial place/parking lot or garage	16	15
School[d]	4	2
Open areas/public transportation/other[e]	13	16
Activity when crime occurred	100%	100%
Traveling to or from other place/shopping or errands/leisure activity away from home	51	29
Sleeping/other activities at home[c]	31	50
Working or traveling to work	10	16
Attending school or traveling to school[d]	5	2
Other/unknown	3	4
Time of day	100%	100%
Daytime (6 a.m.–6 p.m.)	33	35
Night (6 p.m.–6 a.m.)	65	64
Unknown	3	1

[a]Includes female victims ages 18 to 24 enrolled part time or full time in a post-secondary institution (i.e., college or university, trade school, or vocational school).
[b]Includes female victims ages 18 to 24 not enrolled in a post-secondary institution.
[c]In the NCVS, the victim's home is defined as the location of residence at the time of the interview.
[d]Includes schools at any educational level regardless of whether the victim was a student at the location.
[e]Includes locations such as an apartment yard; a park, field, or playground not on school property; a location on the street other than that immediately adjacent to home of the victim, a relative, or friend; in a station or depot for bus or train; on a plane; or in an airport.
NCVS = National Crime Victimization Survey.
Note: Detail may not sum to total due to rounding. Excludes a small percentage of female victims ages 18 to 24 with unknown enrollment status (less than 1%).

SOURCE: Sofi Sinozich and Lynn Langton, "Table 4. Location, Victim Activity, and Time of Day of the Rape/Sexual Assault Victimization among Females Ages 18 to 24, by Post-Secondary Enrollment Status, 1995–2013," in *Rape and Sexual Assault Victimization among College-Age Females, 1995–2013*, U.S. Department of Justice, Office of Justice Programs, Bureau of Justice Statistics, December 2014, http://www.bjs.gov/content/pub/pdf/rsavcaf9513.pdf (accessed June 17, 2016)

TABLE 8.18

Rapes and sexual assaults among women aged 18–24, by victim-offender relationship and college enrollment status of victim, 1995–2013

Victim-offender relationship	Students[a]	Nonstudents[b]
Stranger	22%	20%
Nonstranger	78%	80%
Intimate partner[c]	24	34
Relative	2	1
Well-known/casual acquaintance	50	37

[a]Includes female victims ages 18 to 24 enrolled part time or full time in a post-secondary institution (i.e., college or university, trade school, or vocational school).
[b]Includes female victims ages 18 to 24 not enrolled in a post-secondary institution.
[c]Includes former or current spouse, boyfriend, or girlfriend.
Note: Detail may not sum to total due to rounding. Excludes a small percentage of victimizations in which the victim-offender relationship, number of offenders, or victim enrollment status was unknown.

SOURCE: Sofi Sinozich and Lynn Langton, "Table 6. Victim–Offender Relationship in Rape or Sexual Assault Victimizations against Females Ages 18 to 24, by Post-Secondary Enrollment Status of Victim, 1995–2013," in *Rape and Sexual Assault Victimization among College-Age Females, 1995–2013*, U.S. Department of Justice, Office of Justice Programs, Bureau of Justice Statistics, December 2014, http://www.bjs.gov/content/pub/pdf/rsavcaf9513.pdf (accessed June 17, 2016)

victims identified their stalkers as current or former intimate partners (i.e., spouses, boyfriends, or girlfriends). Another 41.8% of the victims said their stalkers were other known people, including friends, roommates, work or school colleagues, relatives, or other acquaintances. Only 9% of the victims were stalked by strangers. The remaining 21% of the victims either had unknown victim-offender relationships (14.2%) or could not identify a single offender as the stalker (6.8%).

Matthew J. Breiding et al. report more recent findings on stalking in "Prevalence and Characteristics of Sexual Violence, Stalking, and Intimate Partner Violence Victimization—National Intimate Partner and Sexual Violence Survey, United States, 2011" (*Morbidity and Mortality Weekly Report*, vol. 63, no. 8, September 5, 2014). Table 8.21 provides a breakdown of stalking victimization rates, by sex and race and Hispanic origin.

The remaining 2.9% did not know how long the stalking had taken place.

According to Catalano, 69.9% of the stalking victims knew their stalkers. More than a quarter (28.1%) of the

TABLE 8.19

Rapes and sexual assaults among women aged 18–24, by police reporting status, reasons for not reporting incident, and college enrollment status of victim, 1995–2013

	Students[a]	Nonstudents[b]
Reported[c]	20%	32%
Not reported	80%	67%
Reason for not reporting		
Reported to different official	4%	14%
Personal matter	26	23
Not important enough to respondent	12	5
Police would not or could not do anything to help	9	19
Did not want to get offender in trouble with law	10	10
Advised not to report	—	1
Fear of reprisal	20	20
Other reason	31	35

—Less than 0.5%.
[a]Includes female victims ages 18 to 24 enrolled part time or full time in a post-secondary institution (i.e., college or university, trade school, or vocational school).
[b]Includes female victims ages 18 to 24 not enrolled in a post-secondary institution.
[c]Includes only reports to the police, not to other officials or administrators. The NCVS does not collect information on victim reporting to parties other than law enforcement.
Note: Detail may not sum to total due to multiple reasons for not reporting. About 0.4% of student and 0.6% of nonstudent victims did not know or did not report whether the victimization was reported to police.

SOURCE: Sofi Sinozich and Lynn Langton, "Table 8. Rape or Sexual Assault Victimizations against Females Ages 18 to 24 Reported and Not Reported to Police and Reasons for Not Reporting, by Post-Secondary Enrollment Status, 1995–2013," in *Rape and Sexual Assault Victimization among College-Age Females, 1995–2013*, U.S. Department of Justice, Office of Justice Programs, Bureau of Justice Statistics, December 2014, http://www.bjs.gov/content/pub/pdf/rsavcaf9513.pdf (accessed June 17, 2016)

TABLE 8.20

Rates of rape and sexual assault among women aged 18–24, by demographic characteristics and post-secondary enrollment status, 1995–2013

Victim characteristic	Students[a]	Nonstudents[b]	Ratio of nonstudent to student rate
Age			
18–19	6.6	10.4	1.6
20–21	5.8	8.9	1.5
22–24	6.0	5.4	0.9
Race/Hispanic origin			
White[c]	6.7	9.2	1.4
Black[c]	6.4	6.2	1.0
Hispanic	4.5	4.5	1.0
Other[c, d]	3.7	5.9	1.6
Region[e]			
Northeast	5.2	4.1	0.8
Midwest	8.3	11.0	1.3
South	4.7	6.5	1.4
West	5.9	8.0	1.4
Location of residence			
Urban	6.6	8.7	1.3
Suburban	6.0	6.3	1.0
Rural	4.6	8.8	1.9

[a]Per 1,000 females ages 18 to 24 enrolled part time or full time in a post-secondary institution (i.e., college or university, trade school, or vocational school).
[b]Per 1,000 females ages 18 to 24 not enrolled in a post-secondary institution.
[c]Excludes persons of Hispanic or Latino origin.
[d]Includes American Indian, Alaska Native, Asian, Native Hawaiian, and other Pacific Islander, and persons of two or more races.
[e]Includes data from 1996 through 2013 because information about region was not collected prior to 1996.
Note: Detail may not sum to total due to rounding.

SOURCE: Sofi Sinozich and Lynn Langton, "Table 10. Rate of Rape and Sexual Assault against Female Victims Ages 18 to 24, by Demographic Characteristics and Post-Secondary Enrollment Status, 1995–2013," in *Rape and Sexual Assault Victimization among College-Age Females, 1995–2013*, U.S. Department of Justice, Office of Justice Programs, Bureau of Justice Statistics, December 2014, http://www.bjs.gov/content/pub/pdf/rsavcaf9513.pdf (accessed June 17, 2016)

In 2011 more than 18.3 million women reported having been stalked at some point during their lifetime, while nearly 5.1 million reported having been stalked during the previous year. By comparison, approximately 6.5 million men had been victimized by stalking during their lifetime. Among women, American Indian and Alaskan Natives reported the highest rate of lifetime stalking victimizations, with nearly a quarter (24.5%) of all women in that group having been stalked at some point during their lifetime, followed by multiracial women (22.4%), non-Hispanic white women (15.9%), Hispanic women (14.2%), and non-Hispanic African American women (13.9%). Multiracial (9.3%) and non-Hispanic African American (9.1%) men were the most likely to report having been stalked at some point during their lifetime, followed by Hispanic men (8.2%) and non-Hispanic white men (4.7%).

Among lifetime stalking victims in 2011, women were considerably more likely than men to have been stalked by an intimate acquaintance. (See Figure 8.11.) More than half of female lifetime stalking victims were first victimized before the age of 25. (See Figure 8.12.) As Figure 8.13 shows, approximately one out of five male stalking victims were first stalked before the age

of 18 and less than half were first victimized by stalking before the age of 25.

Among women who had experienced stalking at some point during their lifetime, 61.7% reported in 2011 that the perpetrator had either approached the victim or appeared at the same place as the victim when the victim did not expect the perpetrator there. (See Table 8.22.) Approximately 55.3% of female lifetime stalking victims had received unwelcome voice or text messages from the perpetrator, while 54.5% received unwelcome telephone calls or hang ups. Nearly half (49.7%) of female lifetime stalking victims reported that the perpetrator had either followed them from a distance, or else spied on them using a listening device or some other form of surveillance technology. In more than a quarter (26.8%) of lifetime stalking incidents involving women, the perpetrator invaded the victim's property with the purpose of making the victim know the perpetrator had been there. Among male lifetime stalking victims, 58.2% received unwelcome phone calls or hang ups, 56.7%

FIGURE 8.8

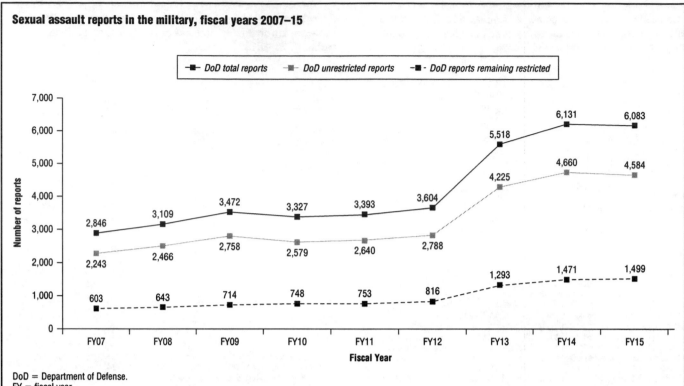

Sexual assault reports in the military, fiscal years 2007–15

- DoD total reports
- DoD unrestricted reports
- DoD reports remaining restricted

DoD = Department of Defense.
FY = fiscal year.

SOURCE: "Sexual Assault Reports," in *Department of Defense Annual Report on Sexual Assault in the Military: Fiscal Year 2015*, U.S. Department of Defense, May 2016, http://sapr.mil/public/docs/reports/FY15_Annual/FY15_Annual_Report_on_Sexual_Assault_in_the_Military.pdf (accessed June 17, 2016)

FIGURE 8.9

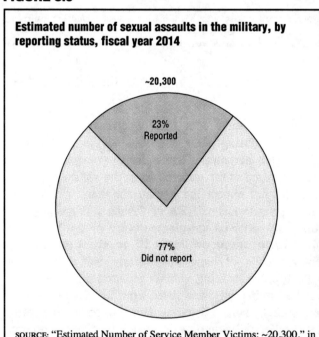

Estimated number of sexual assaults in the military, by reporting status, fiscal year 2014

~20,300

23% Reported

77% Did not report

SOURCE: "Estimated Number of Service Member Victims: ~20,300," in *Department of Defense Annual Report on Sexual Assault in the Military: Fiscal Year 2015*, U.S. Department of Defense, May 2016, http://sapr.mil/public/docs/reports/FY15_Annual/FY15_Annual_Report_on_Sexual_Assault_in_the_Military.pdf (accessed June 17, 2016)

received unwanted voice or electronic messages, 47.7% were either approached by the perpetrator or encountered the perpetrator in a place where the victim did not expect to see the perpetrator, and 32.2% were followed or spied on by the perpetrator.

Anti-stalking Legislation

All 50 states and the District of Columbia have laws that make stalking a crime, but whether it is a felony or a misdemeanor varies by state. In addition, how much fear or distress the victim must experience before the behavior is considered to be stalking varies considerably. In 2000 the National Center for Victims of Crime and the Office on Violence against Women created the Stalking Resource Center. The center maintains the website Criminal Stalking Laws (http://www.victimsofcrime.org/our-programs/stalking-resource-center/stalking-laws/criminal-stalking-laws-by-state), at which visitors can access state stalking laws. For example, according to the Stalking Resource Center (http://www.victimsofcrime.org/our-programs/stalking-resource-center/stalking-laws/criminal-stalking-laws-by-state/california), as of September 2016 California Penal Code Section 646.9 set forth the definition and penalties for stalking as: "Any person who willfully, maliciously, and repeatedly follows or willfully and maliciously harasses another person and who makes a credible threat with the intent to place that person in reasonable fear for his or her safety, or the safety of his or her immediate family, is guilty of the crime of stalking,

punishable by imprisonment in a county jail for not more than one year, or by a fine of not more than one thousand dollars ($1,000), or by both that fine and imprisonment, or by imprisonment in the state prison." There are stricter penalties for perpetrators who are convicted of stalking while subject to restraining orders and under other circumstances.

In 1996 the Interstate Stalking Punishment and Prevention Act, which is part of the National Defense Authorization Act of 1997, made interstate stalking a felony. This federal statute addresses cases that cross state lines. In the past interstate offenses were difficult for state law enforcement agencies to take action against. In 2005 the Violence Against Women Act was renewed, which criminalized stalking by surveillance and expanded the definition of "accountable harm" to include substantial emotional harm to the victim.

Cyberstalking

Cyberstalking (online harassment and threats that can escalate to frightening and even life-threatening offline violence) is a relatively recent phenomenon. Brian H. Spitzberg and Greg Hoobler note in "Cyberstalking and the Technologies of Interpersonal Terrorism" (*New Media and Society*, vol. 4, no. 1, February 2002), a study of college students, that almost one-third of students responded that they had experienced some degree of computer-based harassment and pursuit. The researchers state that "it stands to reason that if there are classes of people who elect, or are driven obsessively, to pursue intimacy with others that these pursuers will seek whatever means are available that might increase their access to the objects of their pursuit, and that people's increasing exposure on and through the computer will make them more accessible as victims."

FIGURE 8.10

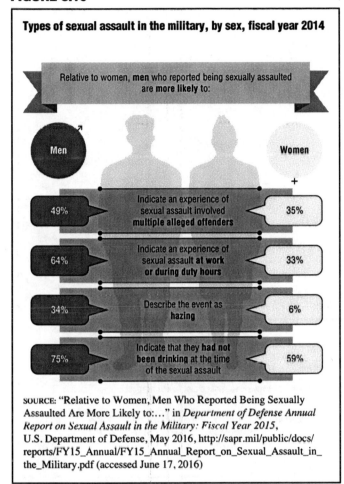

Types of sexual assault in the military, by sex, fiscal year 2014

SOURCE: "Relative to Women, Men Who Reported Being Sexually Assaulted Are More Likely to:..." in *Department of Defense Annual Report on Sexual Assault in the Military: Fiscal Year 2015*, U.S. Department of Defense, May 2016, http://sapr.mil/public/docs/reports/FY15_Annual/FY15_Annual_Report_on_Sexual_Assault_in_the_Military.pdf (accessed June 17, 2016)

TABLE 8.21

Prevalence of stalking victimization, by sex and race and Hispanic origin of victim, lifetime and previous 12 months, 2011

	Women		Men	
	%[a]	Estimated no. of victims[b]	%[a]	Estimated no. of victims[b]
All races/ethnicities (lifetime)	15.2	18,330,000	5.7	6,487,000
White, non-Hispanic	15.9	12,749,000	4.7	3,581,000
Black, non-Hispanic	13.9	2,020,000	9.1	1,159,000
Hispanic	14.2	2,295,000	8.2	1,342,000
American Indian/Alaska Native	24.5	—[c]	—	—
Asian or Pacific Islander	—	—	—	—
Multiracial	22.4	461,000	9.3	192,000
All races/ethnicities (12-month)	4.2	5,094,000	2.1	2,435,000

[a]Percentages are weighted.
[b]Rounded to the nearest thousand.
[c]Estimate is not reported.
Notes: Race/ethnicity was self-identified. The American Indian/Alaska Native designation does not indicate being enrolled or affiliated with a tribe. Persons of Hispanic ethnicity can be of any race or combination of races.

SOURCE: Matthew J. Breiding et al., "Table 4. Prevalence of Stalking Victimization, by Sex and Race/Ethnicity of Victim—National Intimate Partner and Sexual Violence Survey, United States, 2011," in "Prevalence and Characteristics of Sexual Violence, Stalking, and Intimate Partner Violence Victimization—National Intimate Partner and Sexual Violence Survey, United States, 2011," *MMWR*, vol. 63, no. 8, September 5, 2014, http://www.cdc.gov/mmwr/pdf/ss/ss6308.pdf (accessed June 13, 2016)

FIGURE 8.11

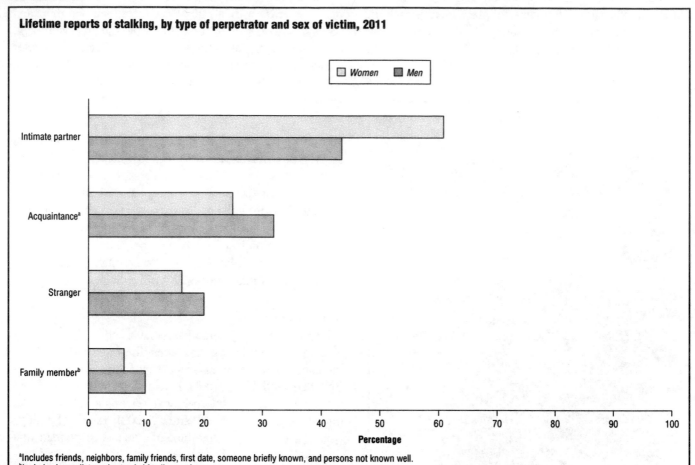

Lifetime reports of stalking, by type of perpetrator and sex of victim, 2011

[Legend: Women, Men]

Percentage

[Categories: Intimate partner, Acquaintance[a], Stranger, Family member[b]]

[a]Includes friends, neighbors, family friends, first date, someone briefly known, and persons not known well.
[b]Includes immediate and extended family members.
Notes: Relationship is based on victims' reports of their relationship at the time the perpetrator first committed any violence against them. Due to the possibility of multiple perpetrators, the combined percentages exceed 100%.

SOURCE: Matthew J. Breiding et al., "Figure 1. Lifetime Reports of Stalking among Female and Male Victims, by Type of Perpetrator—National Intimate Partner and Sexual Violence Survey, United States, 2011," in "Prevalence and Characteristics of Sexual Violence, Stalking, and Intimate Partner Violence Victimization—National Intimate Partner and Sexual Violence Survey, United States, 2011," *MMWR*, vol. 63, no. 8, September 5, 2014, http://www.cdc.gov/mmwr/pdf/ss/ss6308.pdf (accessed June 13, 2016)

In January 2006 a federal anticyberstalking law was signed into law by President George W. Bush (1946–) as part of the reauthorized Violence Against Women Act. It prohibited anyone from using a telephone or telecommunications device (including a computer) "without disclosing his identity and with intent to annoy, abuse, threaten, or harass any person."

Although the extent of the problem is difficult to measure, by 1999 cyberstalking had generated enough concern to warrant the report *Cyberstalking: A New Challenge for Law Enforcement and Industry* (August 1999) by the U.S. attorney general. The attorney general's report cautions that although cyberstalking does not involve physical contact, it should not be considered less dangerous than physical stalking. In *Stalking and Domestic Violence: Report to Congress* (May 2001, http://www.ncjrs.gov/pdffiles1/ojp/186157.pdf), the DOJ compares the similarities and differences between offline and online stalking. Most stalking cases, offline and online,

involve stalking by former intimate partners, although there are cases of stranger stalking in each. Stalking victims, offline and online, are most often women, whereas stalkers are most often men. Most stalkers are motivated by a desire to control the victim.

The DOJ also notes major differences. Cyberstalking is actually easier for the stalker than offline stalking; the online environment lowers barriers to harassment and threats. Offline stalking, for example, requires the perpetrator to be in the same area as the victim, whereas cyberstalkers can be anywhere. In addition, the online environment makes it easy for a cyberstalker to "encourage third parties to harass or threaten a victim." For example, a stalker can impersonate a victim online and post inflammatory messages, causing others to send threatening messages back to the victim.

Cyberstalking is increasingly used by perpetrators of intimate partner violence. According to Cynthia Southworth

FIGURE 8.12

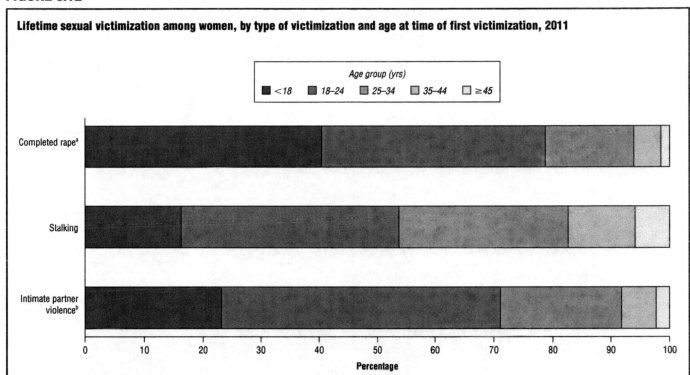

Lifetime sexual victimization among women, by type of victimization and age at time of first victimization, 2011

[a]Includes completed forced penetration and completed alcohol/drug-facilitated penetration but not attempted forced penetration.
[b]Represents the age at time of first experience of intimate partner violence among women who experienced contact sexual violence, physical violence, or stalking by an intimate partner. Includes physical violence, all forms of sexual violence, stalking, psychological aggression, and control of reproductive or sexual health. Contact sexual violence by an intimate partner includes rape, being made to penetrate a perpetrator, sexual coercion, or unwanted sexual contact perpetrated by an intimate partner.

SOURCE: Matthew J. Breiding et al., "Figure 3. Age at the Time of First Victimization among Female Victims, by Type of Victimization—National Intimate Partner and Sexual Violence Survey, United States, 2011," in "Prevalence and Characteristics of Sexual Violence, Stalking, and Intimate Partner Violence Victimization—National Intimate Partner and Sexual Violence Survey, United States, 2011," *MMWR*, vol. 63, no. 8, September 5, 2014, http://www.cdc.gov/mmwr/pdf/ss/ss6308.pdf (accessed June 13, 2016)

et al., in "Intimate Partner Violence, Technology, and Stalking" (*Violence against Women*, vol. 13, no. 8, August 2007), the same technologies that have provided victims of intimate partner violence access to information, resources, and social support have also led to "disinhibited communication, online harassment, and stalking technology." The researchers note that because of technology, stalkers are finding it even easier to monitor the whereabouts and activities of their victims. Among other uses of technology, stalkers can tap telephone lines and intercept cell phone and cordless phone calls, implement caller ID services to locate victims, use global positioning system devices to track victims, install spyware and keystroke logging hardware to track victims' computer use, and employ hidden wireless cameras to spy on victims.

CYBERSTALKING CASES IN THE NEWS. The attorney general's report recounts many serious instances of cyberstalking that attracted attention in the media and among policy makers. The first successful prosecution under California's cyberstalking law was in Los Angeles, where a 50-year-old man stalked a 28-year-old woman who had refused his advances. He posted her name, address, and telephone number online along with messages saying that she wanted to be raped. The Internet posts prompted men to knock on the woman's door, often during the night, in the hopes of fulfilling the fantasy her stalker had posted. In April 1999 the accused pleaded guilty to stalking and solicitation of sexual assault and was sentenced to a six-year prison term.

In July 2002 the CBS News program *48 Hours* investigated a lethal case of cyberstalking that shocked the nation. In 1999 a 20-year-old New Hampshire resident named Amy Boyer was killed by a cyberstalker she had met, but never befriended or dated, years earlier in the eighth grade. Unknown to Boyer, her stalker had apparently obsessed over her for years and had constructed a website that described his stalking of Boyer and his plans to kill her. He used an investigation service to discover where she worked and ambushed her as she left, shooting her and then killing himself. Boyer's death inspired her parents to speak out and champion anticyberstalking laws.

Cyberstalkers sometimes "meet" their victims on social networking sites such as Myspace and Facebook. In one such case reported by Levi Pulkkinen in "Convicted Cyberstalker Back at It, Prosecutors Claim" (SeattlePI.com, August 15, 2010), 23-year-old William Thomas

FIGURE 8.13

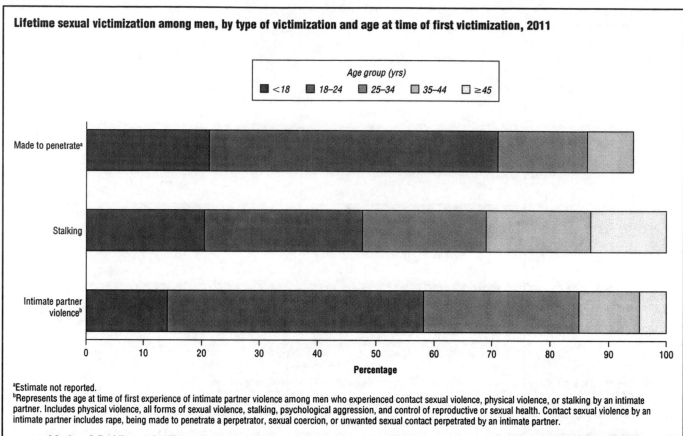

Lifetime sexual victimization among men, by type of victimization and age at time of first victimization, 2011

Age group (yrs)
■ <18   ▨ 18–24   ▨ 25–34   ▨ 35–44   □ ≥45

[Bar chart with categories: Made to penetrate[a], Stalking, Intimate partner violence[b]; x-axis labeled Percentage from 0 to 100]

[a]Estimate not reported.
[b]Represents the age at time of first experience of intimate partner violence among men who experienced contact sexual violence, physical violence, or stalking by an intimate partner. Includes physical violence, all forms of sexual violence, stalking, psychological aggression, and control of reproductive or sexual health. Contact sexual violence by an intimate partner includes rape, being made to penetrate a perpetrator, sexual coercion, or unwanted sexual contact perpetrated by an intimate partner.

SOURCE: Matthew J. Breiding et al., "Figure 4. Age at the Time of First Victimization among Male Victims, by Type of Victimization—National Intimate Partner and Sexual Violence Survey, United States, 2011," in "Prevalence and Characteristics of Sexual Violence, Stalking, and Intimate Partner Violence Victimization—National Intimate Partner and Sexual Violence Survey, United States, 2011," *MMWR*, vol. 63, no. 8, September 5, 2014, http://www.cdc .gov/mmwr/pdf/ss/ss6308.pdf (accessed June 13, 2016)

Pritchard met a 17-year-old girl on Myspace. When he asked her to send him nude photos of herself, she refused. Pritchard soon began sending nude photos of himself to her. He also tried contacting her friends to obtain personal information about her and even went to a job fair that she was attending with her high school classmates. Frustrated by her refusals, he threatened to kill her and then carve his name in her chest. Pritchard was arrested in August 2010. Court records indicate that he had already been convicted twice before of cyberstalking. According to Pulkkinen, in "Cyberstalker Who Terrorized Teen Sentenced" (Seattle-PI.com, March 3, 2011), Prichard was convicted and sentenced to five and a half years in prison.

Because of the global reach of the Internet, cyberstalking is not limited to a nation's physical borders. One notable case of international cyberstalking involved Colin Mak Yew Loong, a Singaporean man accused of harassing several musicians from around the world between 2005 and 2013. One of Mak's victims was the aspiring American opera singer Leandra Ramm (1984–), who developed post-traumatic stress disorder as a result of Mak's actions, forcing her to abandon her career. Although Ramm's initial attempts to press charges against Mak proved difficult due to the complexities of international law, she was eventually able to bring the case before a Singaporean court. Mak was found guilty on a number of charges, including harassment and sending threatening e-mails, and sentenced to three years in jail. Katharine Quarmby notes in "How the Law Is Standing up to Cyberstalking" (Newsweek.com, August 13, 2014) that with the verdict Mak became the first person to be convicted in a case of global cyberstalking.

LAW ENFORCEMENT AND CYBERSTALKING. According to Robert D'Ovidio and James Doyle, in "A Study on Cyberstalking" (*FBI Law Enforcement Bulletin*, vol. 72, no. 3, March 2003), cyberstalking presents some unique law enforcement challenges. Offenders are often able to use the anonymity of online communication to avoid detection and accountability for their actions. Appropriate interventions and recourse are unclear because often the stalker and his victim have never been in physical proximity to one another. Complicating the situation, the identity of the stalker may be difficult to determine. Furthermore, many law enforcement agencies are unprepared to investigate cyberstalking cases because they lack the expertise and training. The attorney general's report

TABLE 8.22

Percentage of stalking victims who experienced particular stalking tactics, lifetime and previous 12 months, by sex, 2011

	Women				Men			
	Lifetime		12-month		Lifetime		12-month	
Stalking tactic	%[a]	Estimated no. of victims[b]	%[a]	Estimated no. of victims[b]	%[a]	Estimated no. of victims[b]	%[a]	Estimated no. of victims[b]
Watched or followed victim from a distance, or spied on victim with a listening device, camera, or global positioning system	49.7	9,109,000	25.9	1,322,000	32.2	2,090,000	—[c]	—
Approached victim or showed up in places (e.g., home, school, or workplace) when victim didn't want them to be there	61.7	11,313,000	33.6	1,709,000	47.7	3,094,000	40.0	975,000
Left strange or threatening items for victim to find	15.0	2,754,000	—	—	14.7	956,000	—	—
Sneaked into victim's car or home and did things to scare victim by letting victim know they had been there	26.8	4,905,000	7.8	396,000	—	—	—	—
Left victim unwanted messages, including text or voice messages	55.3	10,132,000	52.7	2,686,000	56.7	3,681,000	48.7	1,186,000
Made unwanted telephone calls to victim, including hang-ups	54.5	9,987,000	45.4	2,311,000	58.2	3,777,000	58.9	1,434,000
Sent victim unwanted emails, instant messages, or messages through social media websites	14.3	2,618,000	30.0	1,527,000	9.4	607,000	18.1	440,000
Left victim unwanted cards, letters, flowers, or presents when they knew victim didn't want them to do so	24.7	4,524,000	17.8	—	—	—	—	—

[a]Percentages are weighted.
[b]Rounded to the nearest thousand.
[c]Estimate is not reported.

SOURCE: Matthew J. Breiding et al., "Table 5. Proportion of Stalking Victims Who Experienced Individual Stalking Tactics, by Sex of Victim and Time Period—National Intimate Partner and Sexual Violence Survey, United States, 2011," in "Prevalence and Characteristics of Sexual Violence, Stalking, and Intimate Partner Violence Victimization—National Intimate Partner and Sexual Violence Survey, United States, 2011," *MMWR*, vol. 63, no. 8, September 5, 2014, http://www.cdc.gov/mmwr/pdf/ss/ss6308.pdf (accessed June 13, 2016)

finds that some victims had been advised by law enforcement agents to simply "turn off their computers" or to "come back if the cyberstalkers confront or threaten them offline."

Furthermore, some state and local law enforcement agencies are frustrated in their efforts to track down cyberstalkers by the limits of their statutory authority. For example, the Cable Communications Policy Act of 1984 bars the release of cable subscriber information to law enforcement agencies without advance notice to the subscriber and a court order. Because a growing number of Internet users receive services via cable, the act inadvertently grants those wishing to remain anonymous for purposes of cyberstalking some legal protection from investigation. The attorney general's report calls for modifications to the act to include provisions that help law enforcement agents gain access to the identifying information they need while maintaining privacy safeguards for cable customers. Spitzberg and Hoobler note that "it may be ironic that to combat the risks of cyberstalking, law enforcement may need the very tools of electronic surveillance and intrusion that are currently the source of many citizens' fundamental fears of privacy invasion."

CHAPTER 9

DOMESTIC VIOLENCE, LAW ENFORCEMENT, AND COURT RESPONSES TO DOMESTIC VIOLENCE

DOMESTIC VIOLENCE AND LAW ENFORCEMENT

Historically, family disturbance calls were not taken seriously by law enforcement, which reflects society's attitude about domestic violence at the time. For example, during the mid-1960s Detroit, Michigan, police dispatchers were instructed to screen out family disturbance calls unless they suspected "excessive" violence. A 1975 police guide, *The Function of the Police in Crisis Intervention and Conflict Management*, taught officers to avoid making an arrest at all costs and to discourage the victim from pressing charges by emphasizing the consequences of testifying in court, the potential of lost income, and other detrimental aspects of prosecution.

Changes in society's tolerance for domestic violence mean that these approaches to domestic violence no longer enjoy official support (although they may still influence the actions of individual officers). By 2008 every state had moved to authorize probable cause arrests (arrest before the completion of the investigation of the alleged violation or crime) without a warrant in domestic violence cases. (A warrant is a written legal document authorizing a police officer to make a search, seizure, or arrest.) Many police departments have adopted pro-arrest or mandatory arrest policies. Pro-arrest strategies include a range of sanctions from issuing a warning, to mandated treatment, to prison time.

The police are often an abuse victim's initial contact with the judicial system, which makes the response by the police particularly important. The manner in which the police handle a domestic violence complaint will likely color the way the victim views the entire judicial system. Not surprisingly, when the police project the blame for intimate partner violence on victims, the victims may be reluctant to report further abuse.

Reporting Domestic Violence to the Police

Domestic violence incidents come to the attention of the police via reports from the victims themselves, from witnesses to the violence, and from people who learn about the victimization after it occurs. As is explained in Chapter 1, some states require medical personnel to report suspected or known abuse cases involving adults to law enforcement agencies.

The Bureau of Justice Statistics (BJS) is an agency within the U.S. Department of Justice. Since 1972 the BJS has conducted the National Crime Victimization Survey (NCVS), an annual survey that measures the levels of victimization resulting from criminal activity in the United States. It should be noted that only victimizations against people aged 12 years and older are included. As of September 2016, the most recent NCVS data are discussed by Jennifer L. Truman and Lynn Langton of the BJS in *Criminal Victimization, 2014* (August 2015, http://www.bjs.gov/content/pub/pdf/cv14.pdf).

As shown in Table 9.1, less than half (45.6% to 46%) of all violent crime victimizations compiled in the 2005, 2013, and 2014 NCVS surveys were reported by the victims to the police. The reporting rates were higher (53% to 56.9%) for domestic violence victimizations and for the subset of domestic violence victimizations that were intimate partner victimizations (56.9% to 57.9%). The latter are victimizations committed by current or former spouses, boyfriends, or girlfriends. For rape and sexual assault, the overall reporting rate reached 35.1% in 2005, but dropped to 33.6% by 2014. In 2014 the reporting rate for domestic cases involving serious violence (rape, sexual assault, robbery, or aggravated assault) was 60%; for serious intimate partner violence, the reporting rate was 56.7% that year.

Table 9.2 compares violent victimizations reported and not reported to police in terms of victimization rates (number of violent victimizations per 1,000 people aged 12 years and older) for 2005, 2013, and 2014. In 2014 the victimization rate for domestic violence incidents reported to the police was 2.3 victimizations per 1,000

TABLE 9.1

Crime victimizations reported to the police, by crime type, 2005, 2013, and 2014

Type of crime	2005	2013	2014[a]
Violent crime[b]	**45.8%**	**45.6%**	**46.0%**
Rape/sexual assault	35.1	34.8	33.6
Robbery	55.4	68.0	60.9
Assault	44.9	43.4	44.6
Aggravated assault	65.0	64.3	58.4
Simple assault	39.4	38.5	40.0
Domestic violence[c]	53.0	56.9	56.1
Intimate partner violence[d]	56.9	57.0	57.9
Stranger violence	48.1	49.6	48.8
Violent crime involving injury	59.6	55.5	54.9
Serious violent crime[e]	**59.0%**	**61.0%**	**55.8%**
Serious domestic violence[c]	61.4	65.3	60.0
Serious intimate partner violence[d]	57.4	60.4	56.7
Serious stranger violence	53.4	61.9	65.4
Serious violent crime involving weapons	64.0	65.7	57.6
Serious violent crime involving injury	64.5	66.2	61.0
Property crime	**38.7%**	**36.1%**	**37.0%**
Burglary	55.3	57.3	60.0
Motor vehicle theft	81.7	75.5	83.3
Theft	31.5	28.6	29.0

[a]Comparison year.
[b]Excludes homicide because the National Crime Victimization Survey (NCVS) is based on interviews with victims and therefore cannot measure murder.
[c]Includes victimization committed by intimate partners and family members.
[d]Includes victimization committed by current or former spouses, boyfriends, or girlfriends.
[e]In the NCVS, serious violent crime includes rape or sexual assault, robbery, and aggravated assault.

SOURCE: Jennifer L. Truman and Lynn Langton, "Table 6. Percent of Victimizations Reported to Police, by Type of Crime, 2005, 2013, and 2014," in *Criminal Victimization, 2014*, U.S. Department of Justice, Office of Justice Programs, Bureau of Justice Statistics, August 2015, http://www.bjs.gov/content/pub/pdf/cv14.pdf (accessed June 14, 2016)

people aged 12 years and older; the rate for serious domestic violence incidents was 0.9 victimizations per 1,000 people aged 12 years and older. For domestic violence incidents not reported to the police in 2014, the victimization rate was 1.7 victimizations per 1,000 people aged 12 years and older; the rate for serious domestic violence incidents that were not reported was 0.6 per 1,000 people aged 12 years and older.

Table 9.3 presents the reporting data between 2010 and 2014 broken down by victim-offender relationship. The two offender categories involved in domestic violence cases are intimates and other relatives. Overall, NCVS data indicate that more than 1.1 million domestic violence victimizations took place in 2014. The 56.1% that were reported to the police included 367,618 intimate partner victimizations and 255,509 victimizations by other relatives. The 41.7% that were not reported to the police included 243,333 intimate partner victimizations and 219,756 victimizations by other relatives. It should be noted that for another 19,757 victimizations by intimate partners, the survey participants did not know if the victimizations were or were not reported to the police. However, this number made up 1.8% of the total domestic violence victimizations in 2014.

OUTCOME OF POLICE INTERVENTION

During the early 1970s it was legal for the police to make probable cause arrests without a warrant for felonies, but only 14 states permitted it for misdemeanors. Because the crime of simple assault (assault without a weapon that results in minor injuries) and battery is a misdemeanor in most states, family violence victims were forced to initiate their own criminal charges against a batterer. By 2008, however, all states authorized warrantless probable cause misdemeanor arrests in domestic violence cases. Regardless, more than half of the states have added qualifiers, such as visible signs of injury or a report of the violence within eight hours of the incident. Most state codes authorizing warrantless arrests require police to inform victims of their rights, which include the acquisition of protection orders and referral to emergency and shelter facilities and transportation.

Mandatory Arrests

Arrest gained popularity as a tactic after the publication of the first in a series of six studies funded by the National Institute of Justice known as the Spouse Assault Replication Program. All the studies were designed to explain how arrest in domestic violence cases could serve as a deterrent to future violence. In "The Specific Deterrent Effects of Arrest for Domestic Assault" (*American Sociological Review*, vol. 49, April 1984), Lawrence W. Sherman and Richard A. Berk, the authors of the influential first study in the series, found that "the arrest intervention certainly did not make things worse and may well have made things better."

Although Sherman and Berk cautioned about generalizing the results of a small study dealing with a single police department in which few police officers properly followed the test procedure, they concluded that in instances of domestic violence an arrest is advisable except in cases where it would be clearly counterproductive. At the same time, Sherman and Berk recommended allowing the police a certain amount of flexibility when making decisions about individual situations, on the premise that police officers must be permitted to rely on professional judgment based on experience.

Sherman and Berk's study had a tremendous impact on police practices, even though J. David Hirschel, Ira W. Hutchison III, and Charles W. Dean explain in "The Failure of Arrest to Deter Spouse Abuse" (*Journal of Research in Crime and Delinquency*, vol. 29, no. 1, February 1992) that the five other Spouse Assault Replication Program studies found that arrest had little or no effect on domestic violence recurrence. Some police departments have adopted a presumptive arrest policy. This policy means that an arrest should be made unless clear and compelling reasons exist not to arrest. Presumptive arrest provisions forbid officers from basing the

TABLE 9.2

Rate of crime victimizations reported and not reported to the police, by crime type, 2005, 2013, and 2014

Type of crime	Reported to police			Not reported to police		
	2005	2013	2014[a]	2005	2013	2014[a]
Violent crime[b]	**13.0**	**10.6**	**9.2**	**15.0**	**12.2**	**10.5**
Rape/sexual assault	0.3	0.4	0.4	0.6	0.7	0.7
Robbery	1.7	1.7	1.5	1.4	0.8	1.0
Assault	11.0	8.5	7.4	13.1	10.7	8.9
Aggravated assault	3.4	2.4	2.4	1.8	1.3	1.7
Simple assault	7.6	6.1	5.0	11.3	9.5	7.2
Domestic violence[c]	5.8	2.4	2.3	2.4	1.7	1.7
Intimate partner violence[d]	1.9	1.6	1.4	1.4	1.2	0.9
Stranger violence	5.6	3.9	4.0	5.7	3.8	4.1
Violent crime involving injury	4.3	3.4	2.8	2.8	2.6	2.3
Serious violent crime[e]	**5.4**	**4.5**	**4.3**	**3.7**	**2.8**	**3.3**
Serious domestic violence[c]	1.1	1.1	0.9	0.7	0.6	0.6
Serious intimate partner violence[d]	0.7	0.8	0.6	0.5	0.5	0.4
Serious stranger violence	2.4	1.7	2.3	2.1	1.0	1.2
Serious violent crime involving weapons	4.3	2.9	2.8	2.4	1.5	2.0
Serious violent crime involving injury	2.2	1.9	1.6	1.2	0.9	1.0
Property crime	**61.8**	**47.4**	**43.7**	**95.9**	**83.1**	**72.8**
Burglary	16.9	14.8	13.9	13.4	10.9	8.8
Motor vehicle theft	7.0	3.9	3.4	1.5	1.2	0.7
Theft	37.8	28.7	26.4	81.0	71.0	63.3

[a]Comparison year.
[b]Excludes homicide because the National Crime Victimization Survey (NCVS) is based on interviews and therefore cannot measure murder.
[c]Includes victimization committed by intimate partners and family members.
[d]Includes victimization committed by current or former spouses, boyfriends, or girlfriends.
[e]In the NCVS, serious violent crime includes rape or sexual assault, robbery, and aggravated assault.
Note: Victimization rates are per 1,000 persons age 12 or older for violent crime and per 1,000 households for property crime.

SOURCE: Jennifer L. Truman and Lynn Langton, "Table 7. Rates of Victimizations Reported and Not Reported to Police, by Type of Crime, 2005, 2013, and 2014," in *Criminal Victimization, 2014*, U.S. Department of Justice, Office of Justice Programs, Bureau of Justice Statistics, August 2015, http://www.bjs.gov/content/pub/pdf/cv14.pdf (accessed June 14, 2016)

decision to arrest on the victim's preference or on a perception of the victim's willingness to testify or participate in the proceedings. Proponents point out that arresting an offender gives the victim a respite from fear and an opportunity to look for help. Furthermore, they claim it prevents bias in arrests.

By the 1990s as many as one out of three police departments had adopted a mandatory arrest policy in domestic abuse cases. According to David Eitle of Florida International University, in "The Influence of Mandatory Arrest Policies, Police Organizational Characteristics, and Situational Variables on the Probability of Arrest in Domestic Violence Cases" (*Crime and Delinquency*, vol. 51, no. 4, October 2005), mandatory police arrest policies do result in more arrests when the police are called to the scene of a domestic assault. In addition, he notes that these policies reduce somewhat the overrepresentation of African Americans among those being arrested. However, do these arrests reduce violence against women?

Some studies suggest that mandatory arrest policies have positive effects. For example, Jacquelyn C. Campbell et al. explain in "Risk Factors for Femicide in Abusive Relationships: Results from a Multisite Case Control Study" (*American Journal of Public Health*,

vol. 93, no. 7, July 2003) that previous arrest for battering actually decreased women's risk of being subsequently killed by the batterer. According to Christopher D. Maxwell, Joel H. Garner, and Jeffrey A. Fagan, in "The Effects of Arrest on Intimate Partner Violence: New Evidence from the Spouse Assault Replication Program" (July 2001, http://www.ncjrs.gov/pdffiles1/nij/188199.pdf), the arrest of batterers is consistently related to subsequent reduced aggression against their intimate partner.

However, Debra Houry, Sudha Reddy, and Constance Parramore of Emory University suggest in "Characteristics of Victims Coarrested for Intimate Partner Violence" (*Journal of Interpersonal Violence*, vol. 21, no. 11, November 2006) that some battered women's advocates do not support mandatory arrest. They fear that poor and minority families are treated more harshly than middle-class families and that if the police arrive and both spouses are bloodied by the fight, both will be arrested, forcing the children into foster care. In fact, Mary A. Finn and Pamela Bettis of Georgia State University state in "Punitive Action or Gentle Persuasion: Exploring Police Officers' Justifications for Using Dual Arrest in Domestic Violence Cases" (*Violence against Women*, vol. 12, no. 3, March 2006) that "mandatory and preferred arrest policies may be resulting in a backlash for victims who are arrested along with their batterers...."

TABLE 9.3

Violent victimizations, by victim-offender relationship and reporting to police, 2010–14

Crime type	2010	2011	2012	2013	2014
Violent victimization	**4,935,983**	**5,812,523**	**6,842,593**	**6,126,423**	**5,359,570**
Intimates	**773,434**	**850,772**	**810,794**	**748,795**	**634,612**
Yes, reported to the police	511,195	508,254	431,959	426,476	367,618
No, did not report to the police	262,239	337,389	350,758	309,528	243,333
Do not know	—	—	17,243!	2,876!	19,757!
Other relatives	**356,129**	**504,135**	**448,598**	**367,291**	**475,265**
Yes, reported to the police	240,023	297,260	259,793	208,020	255,509
No, did not report to the police	116,106	200,157	186,183	152,081	219,756
Do not know	—	6,718!	—	7,190!	—
Well-known/casual acquaintances	**1,573,294**	**1,779,618**	**2,263,252**	**2,445,099**	**1,709,366**
Yes, reported to the police	547,503	791,548	808,448	921,860	630,013
No, did not report to the police	1,006,180	933,866	1,428,133	1,502,767	1,059,564
Do not know	17,554!	43,066!	26,671!	20,472!	14,697!
Stranger	**1,812,303**	**2,146,307**	**2,710,114**	**2,098,170**	**2,166,129**
Yes, reported to the police	992,012	1,029,016	1,324,977	1,041,039	1,058,006
No, did not report to the police	805,335	1,090,328	1,302,507	1,009,358	1,090,485
Do not know	14,956!	26,962!	46,780	44,993!	14,731!
Do not know relationship	**288,667**	**240,956**	**371,910**	**288,795**	**223,847**
Yes, reported to the police	157,914	134,274	122,224	74,111	98,220
No, did not report to the police	125,271	104,815	246,318	210,748	116,845
Do not know	5,482!	—	3,368!	1,492!	2,864!
Do not know number of offenders	**132,156**	**290,736**	**228,660**	**178,273**	**150,351**
Yes, reported to the police	73,978!	87,181	71,601	122,965	56,613
No, did not report to the police	58,178	126,981	150,711	46,678	80,431
Do not know	—	57,431!	2,154!	5,630!	1,237!

—Estimate is equal to 0 sample cases.
!Interpret data with caution, based on 10 or fewer sample cases or the coefficient of variation is greater than 50%.
Notes: Special tabulations from the NCVS Victimization Analysis Tool (NVAT). (NCVS = National Crime Victimization Survey.) Detail may not sum to total due to rounding and/or missing data.

SOURCE: Number of Violent Victimizations by Victim-Offender Relationship and Reporting to the Police, 2010–2014, in *NCVS Victimization Analysis Tool (NVAT)*, U.S. Department of Justice, Office of Justice Programs, Bureau of Justice Statistics, June 10, 2016, http://www.bjs.gov/index.cfm?ty=nvat (accessed June 14, 2016)

Officers justified arrest of both parties, citing that such was required by law and the desire to force both parties to obtain counseling for their relationship."

Victoria Frye, Mary Haviland, and Valli Rajah examine some of the unintended consequences of the mandatory arrest law in New York City and report their findings in "Dual Arrest and Other Unintended Consequences of Mandatory Arrest in New York City: A Brief Report" (*Journal of Family Violence*, vol. 22, no. 6, August 2007). The researchers find that no arrest remained a significant problem, despite the mandatory arrest legislation, and that the police disproportionately failed to arrest abusers of poor women. At the same time, arrest of the victims (both dual arrests and retaliatory arrests) accounted for 34% of police-related calls to the helpline. In spite of these findings, Frye, Haviland, and Rajah conclude that mandatory arrest laws do have a positive impact on domestic violence. Regardless, they call for further police training and better supervision to reduce the problems of no arrest and victim arrest that result from mandatory arrest laws. Amy M. Zelcer outlines possible alternatives to mandatory arrest laws in "Battling Domestic Violence: Replacing Mandatory Arrest

Laws with a Trifecta of Preferential Arrest, Officer Education, and Batterer Treatment Programs" (*American Criminal Law Review*, vol. 51, no. 2, Spring 2014). Zelcer recommends an integrated approach to police intervention in domestic violence situations, one that grants victims some degree of decision-making power in determining whether an arrest should be made, combined with improved officer training and expanded therapeutic opportunities for abusers.

EMPOWERING VICTIMS. Indeed, innovative programs that team social services with the police have shown some promise in empowering women to report violence to the police. In "The Efficacy of a Police-Advocacy Intervention for Victims of Domestic Violence: 12 Month Follow-Up Data" (*Violence against Women*, vol. 16, no. 4, April 2010), Carla Smith Stover et al. of Yale University evaluate a New Haven, Connecticut, program, Domestic Violence Home Visit Intervention, that provides home visits immediately after a domestic violence incident and for several follow-up visits over the subsequent year. The visits are conducted by a partnership of a police officer who has received specialized training in domestic violence and its effects on children and by a victim advocate who is trained in basic domestic violence issues, crisis intervention, legal issues, and social service responses. Stover et al. find that although the level of domestic violence for both the visited women and the control group were similar, women involved in the program were more likely than women in the control group to call the police to report domestic disputes in the year following the initial incident. Women who received the home visits were also much more likely to use court-based services and mental health services for their children.

PROTECTION ORDERS

An abuse victim in any state may go to court to obtain a protection order. Also referred to as "restraining orders" or "injunctions," civil orders of protection are legally binding court orders that prohibit an individual who has committed an act of domestic violence from further abusing the victim. Although the terms are often used interchangeably, restraining orders usually refer to short-term or temporary sanctions, whereas protection orders have longer duration and may be permanent. These orders generally prohibit harassment, contact, communication, and physical proximity to the victim. Protection orders are common and readily obtained, but they are not always effective.

Petitioners may file for protection orders in circumstances other than violent physical abuse, including sexual assault, marital rape, harassment, emotional abuse, and stalking. Protection orders are valid for varying lengths of time depending on the state. Protection orders give victims an option other than filing a criminal complaint. Issued quickly, usually within 24 hours, they provide safety for the victim by barring or evicting the abuser from the household. Statutes in most states make violating a protection order a matter of criminal contempt, a misdemeanor, or even a felony. However, this judicial protection has little meaning if the police do not maintain records and follow through with arrest should the abuser violate the order.

The "full faith and credit" provision of the Violence against Women Act of 1994 was passed to establish nationwide enforcement of protection orders in courts throughout the country. States, territories, and tribal lands were ordered to honor protection orders issued in other jurisdictions, although the act did not mandate how these orders were to be enforced. According to Christina DeJong and Amanda Burgess-Proctor of Michigan State University, in "A Summary of Personal Protection Order Statutes in the United States" (*Violence against Women*, vol. 12, no. 1, January 2006), most states have amended their domestic violence codes or statutes to reflect this new requirement, although the states vary widely on how easy it is for battered women to get their protection orders enforced. Courts and law enforcement agencies in most states have access to electronic registries of protection orders, both to verify the existence of an order and to assess whether violations have occurred.

Effects of Protection Orders

In "Protection Orders and Intimate Partner Violence: An 18-Month Study of 150 Black, Hispanic, and White Women" (*American Journal of Public Health*, vol. 94, no. 4, April 2004), Judith McFarlane et al. report on their study of the "types and frequencies of intimate partner violence" before and after victims had applied for a two-year protection order against an intimate partner. The researchers interviewed 150 women over an 18-month period to determine whether protection orders diminished violence. Although 44% of the women who had been granted a protection order reported at least one violation of the order, the researchers find significant reductions in physical assaults, stalking, and threats of assault over time among all women who applied for a protection order, even if they had not been granted the order. McFarlane et al. hypothesize that it was not the protection order itself that led to the diminished violence but the contact with the criminal justice system that exposed the battering to public view.

Other researchers have linked a number of positive psychological effects to the use of protection orders in domestic violence cases. Caroline Vaile Wright and Dawn M. Johnson report in "Encouraging Legal Help Seeking for Victims of Intimate Partner Violence: The Therapeutic Effects of the Civil Protection Order" (*Journal of Traumatic Stress*, vol. 25, no. 6, December 2012) that protection orders have been shown to alleviate symptoms of post-traumatic stress disorder and other emotional disorders in residents of shelters for battered women. Jane K. Stoever also notes the psychological benefits of protection orders in "Enjoining Abuse: The Case for Indefinite Domestic Violence Protection Orders" (*Vanderbilt Law Review*, vol. 67, no. 4, May 2014). Citing the prevalence of longer court orders in business disputes and other legal areas involving property, Stoever argues that extending standard protection orders for domestic violence cases would enable victims to achieve greater physical and emotional distance from their abuser.

LANDMARK LEGAL DECISIONS

Before the 1962 landmark case *Self v. Self* (58 Cal. 2d 683), when the California Supreme Court ruled that "one spouse may maintain an action against the other for battering," women had no legal recourse against abusive partners. The judicial system had tended to view wife abuse as a matter to be resolved within the family. Maintaining that "a man's home is his castle," the federal government traditionally had been reluctant to violate the sanctity of the home. Furthermore, many legal authorities persisted in "blaming the victim," maintaining that the wife was, to some degree, responsible for her own beating by somehow inciting her husband to lose his temper. However, even after *Self v. Self*, turning to the judicial system for help was still unlikely to bring assistance to or result in justice for victims of spousal abuse. Jurisdictions throughout the United States continued to ignore the complaints of battered women until the late 1970s.

This section summarizes the outcomes of several landmark cases that not only helped define judicial responsibility but also shaped the policies and practices aimed at protecting the victims of domestic violence.

Baker v. City of New York

Sandra Baker was estranged from her husband. In July 1955 the local domestic relations court issued a protective order directing her husband, who had a history of serious mental illness, "not to strike, molest, threaten, or annoy" his wife. Baker called the police the following October when her husband created a disturbance at the family home. When a police officer arrived, she showed him the court order. The officer told her it was "no good" and "only a piece of paper" and refused to take any action.

Baker went to the domestic relations court and told her story to a probation officer. While making a phone call, she saw her husband in the corridor. She went to the probation officer and told him her husband was in the corridor. She asked if she could wait in his office because she was "afraid to stand in the room with him." The probation officer told her to go to the waiting room. Minutes later, her husband shot and wounded her.

Baker sued the city of New York, claiming that the city owed her more protection than she was given. The New York State Supreme Court Appellate Division, in *Baker v. City of New York* (25 A.D.2d 770 [1966]), agreed that the city of New York failed to fulfill its obligation. The court found that she was "a person recognized by the order of protection as one to whom a special duty was owed ... and peace officers had a duty to supply protection to her." Neither the police officer nor the probation officer had fulfilled this duty, and both were found guilty of negligence. Because the officers were representatives of the city of New York, Baker had the right to sue the city.

Equal Protection

Another option women have used in response to unchecked violence and abuse is to sue the police for failing to intervene, alleging that their constitutional rights to liberty and equal protection under the law were violated by the lack of police response. The equal protection clause of the 14th Amendment provides that no state shall "deny to any person within its jurisdiction the equal protection of the laws." This clause prohibits states from arbitrarily classifying individuals by group membership. If a woman can prove that a police department has a gender-based policy of refusing to arrest men who abuse their wives, she can claim that the policy is based on gender stereotypes and therefore violates the equal protection clause.

THURMAN V. CITY OF TORRINGTON. Between October 1982 and June 1983 Tracey Thurman repeatedly called the Torrington, Connecticut, police to report that her estranged husband was threatening both her life and her child's life. The police ignored her requests for help no matter how often she called or how serious the situation became. At one point her husband attacked her in view of the police and was arrested. Thurman obtained protection and restraining orders against him after this incident. However, when her husband later came to her home and threatened her again, in violation of his probation and the court orders, police refused to intervene.

On June 10, 1983, Thurman's husband came to her home. She called the police. He then stabbed her repeatedly in the chest, neck, and throat. A police officer arrived 25 minutes later but did not arrest her husband, despite the attack. Three more police officers arrived. The husband went into the house and brought out their child and threw him down on his bleeding mother. The officers still did not arrest him. Although Thurman was on the stretcher waiting to be placed in the ambulance, her husband came at her again. Only at that point did the police take him into custody. Thurman later sued the city of Torrington, claiming she was denied equal protection under the law.

In *Thurman v. City of Torrington* (595 F.Supp. 1521 [D. Conn. 1984]), the U.S. District Court for Downstate Connecticut agreed, stating:

> City officials and police officers are under an affirmative duty to preserve law and order, and to protect the personal safety of persons in the community.... This duty applies equally to women whose personal safety is threatened by individuals with whom they have or have had a domestic relationship as well as to all other persons whose personal safety is threatened.... A police officer may not ... "automatically decline to make an arrest simply because the assaulter and his victim are married to each other." ... Such inaction on the part of the officer is a denial of the equal protection of the laws.

There could be no question, the court concluded, that the city of Torrington, through its police department, had "condoned a pattern or practice of affording inadequate protection, or no protection at all, to women who have complained of having been abused by their husbands or others with whom they have had close relations." Therefore, the police had failed in their duty to protect Thurman and deserved to be sued.

In "Maimed Wife Strikes Blow for Justice" (ChicagoTribune.com, May 18, 1986), Dick Polman notes that Thurman was left partially paralyzed by the attack and received a $1.9 million settlement from the local police department.

Due Process

The due process clause of the 14th Amendment provides that no state can "deprive any person of life, liberty, or property, without due process of law; nor deny to any person within its jurisdiction the equal protection of the laws." It does not, however, obligate the state to protect citizens from harm or provide services that would protect them. Rather, a state may create special conditions in which that state has constitutional obligations to particular citizens because of a special relationship between the state and the individual. Abused women have used this argument to claim that being under a protection order puts them in a special relationship.

MACIAS V. HIDE. During the 18 months before Maria Teresa Macias's estranged husband, Avelino Macias, murdered her at her place of work in April 1996, Maria had filed 22 complaints with the Sonoma County Sheriff's Department in California. In the months before her death, Avelino sexually abused Maria, broke into her home, and terrorized and stalked her. Maria's family filed a wrongful death lawsuit against the Sonoma County Sheriff's Department, accusing the department of failing to provide Maria equal protection under the law and of discriminating against her as a Hispanic and a woman.

The U.S. District Court for the Northern District of California dismissed the case because Judge D. Lowell Jensen (1928–) said there was no connection between Maria's murder and how the sheriff's department had responded to her complaints. In *Macias v. Hide* (No. 99-15662 [2000]), the U.S. Court of Appeals for the Ninth Circuit reversed the earlier decision and ruled that the lawsuit could proceed with the discovery phase and pretrial motions. Judge Arthur L. Alarcón (1925–2015) of the U.S. Court of Appeals for the Ninth Circuit conveyed the unanimous opinion of the court when he wrote, "It is well established that 'there is no constitutional right to be protected by the state against being murdered by criminals or madmen.' There is a constitutional right, however, to have police services administered in a nondiscriminatory manner—a right that is violated when a state actor denies such protection to disfavored persons."

After this decision the case proceeded to trial. In June 2002 Sonoma County agreed to pay $1 million to Maria's family to settle the case. The settlement agreement did not include an admission of any wrongdoing by the county. Nevertheless, domestic violence activists lauded the result.

TOWN OF CASTLE ROCK, COLORADO V. GONZALES. The U.S. Supreme Court reaffirmed in 2005 that governments are not required to offer citizens protection from violent abusers. According to the case *Town of Castle Rock, Colorado v. Gonzales* (545 U.S. 748 [2005]), Jessica Gonzales's three children were taken from her home by her estranged husband in violation of a protection order. When she alerted the police and repeatedly asked them for assistance, they made no effort to find the children or to enforce the state's mandatory arrest law. The children were killed later that night. Gonzales sued the town, arguing that by failing to respond to her calls the police had violated her right to due process of law, and the case eventually reached the U.S. Supreme Court. In its review, the court found in June 2005 that "Colorado law has not created a personal entitlement to enforcement of restraining orders" and that the state's law did not really require arrest in all cases, but actually left considerable discretion in the hands of the police. So even though the Castle Rock police made a tragically incorrect decision in this case, they did not do so in violation of Gonzales's due process rights.

KEY DOMESTIC VIOLENCE LEGISLATION

Although appealing to the judicial system for help will not solve all the problems an abused woman faces, the reception a battered woman can expect from the system (police, prosecutors, and courts) improved markedly during the late 20th century. The Violence against Women Act (VAWA), which was signed into law by President Bill Clinton (1946–) in 1994, did much to help. The act simultaneously strengthened prevention and prosecution of violent crimes against women and provided law enforcement officials with the tools they needed to prosecute batterers. Although the system is imperfect, legal authorities became far more likely to view abuse complaints as legitimate and serious than they had in the past.

The Violence against Women Act

As is noted in Chapter 1, the VAWA was originally passed in 1994 and was amended and reauthorized in 2000, 2005, and 2013.

CIVIL RIGHTS ISSUES. The original VAWA included provisions declaring that violent crimes against women motivated by gender violate victims' federal civil rights, giving victims access to federal courts for redress. In 2000 the civil rights section of the act was tested in the U.S. Supreme Court. Christy Brzonkala, an 18-year-old freshman at Virginia Polytechnic Institute and State University, was violently attacked and raped by two men, Antonio Morrison and James Crawford, in September 1994. Brzonkala did not immediately report the rape, and no physical evidence of the rape was preserved.

Two months later she filed a complaint with the school; after learning that the college took limited action against the two men, she withdrew from the school and sued her assailants for damages in federal court.

Brzonkala's case reached the Supreme Court in 2000. Briefs in favor of giving victims of gender-motivated violence access to federal courts were filed by dozens of groups (such as the American Medical Women's Association, the National Association of Human Rights Workers, the National Coalition against Domestic Violence, and the National Women's Health Network) as well as by law scholars and human rights experts. However, in May 2000 the Supreme Court ruled 5–4 in *United States v. Morrison et al.* (529 U.S. 598) that Congress could not enact a law giving victims of gender-motivated violence access to federal civil rights remedies. The majority opinion emphasized that "the Constitution requires a distinction between what is truly national and what is truly local," and it ruled that the violent assault of Brzonkala was local.

In October 2000 Congress responded to the Supreme Court decision by passing new legislation, the Victims of Trafficking and Violence Protection Act. The new legislation included the titles Strengthening Law Enforcement to Reduce Violence against Women, Strengthening Services to Victims of Violence, Limiting the Effects of Violence on Children, and Strengthening Education and Training to Combat Violence against Women. The act allocated $3.3 billion over five years to fund support services for victims of violence and for educational outreach programs on dating violence, rape, and stalking via the Internet. The act also funded new programs for transitional housing and expanded protections for immigrant women. The new act did not mention women's civil rights.

ISSUES AFFECTING IMMIGRANT WOMEN. In "The Facts on Immigrant Women and Domestic Violence" (October 2011, https://www.futureswithoutviolence.org/userfiles/file/Children_and_Families/Immigrant.pdf), Futures without Violence explains that abuse of immigrant women is a problem in the United States. Immigrant women may be at increased risk for various reasons, including a cultural background that teaches them to defer to their husband. Many foreign-born women cannot speak English and do not know their rights in the United States. Others have no resources or support systems to turn to for help. Some of the distinctive ways that battered immigrant women are abused include threats of being reported to the U.S. Citizenship and Immigration Services, being deported, being reported for working "under the table," or withdrawing their petition to legalize their immigration status.

U.S. immigration laws have unintentionally contributed to the problem of abuse among immigrant women.

The Immigration Marriage Fraud Amendment Act was passed in 1986 in an attempt to prevent immigrants from illegally obtaining resident status through a sham marriage to a U.S. citizen. The amendment requires that spouses, usually husbands, petition for conditional resident status for an undocumented mate. Conditional status lasts a minimum of two years, during which time the couple must remain married. If the marriage dissolves, the immigrant loses conditional status and may be deported. As a result, some wives can become prisoners of an abusive husband for as long as the husband controls their conditional resident status. Although the law was amended by the Immigration Act of 1990 to permit a waiver of conditional status if the immigrant could prove battery or extreme cruelty, the initial filing for conditional status was still in the hands of the husband.

Reauthorized in 2005, the VAWA provides a way for immigrant women to petition for residency status for themselves and for their children without their husband's knowledge. In addition, the act provides a way for canceling deportation proceedings against battered immigrant women by waiving deportation and allowing them the opportunity to become lawful permanent residents of the United States. These processes are described by William A. Kandel of the Congressional Research Service in *Immigration Provisions of the Violence against Women Act* (May 15, 2012, http://www.fas.org/sgp/crs/misc/R42477.pdf). Kandel notes, "Noncitizen victims of domestic violence who seek to permanently reside in the United States face a precarious situation because their legal immigration status often depends upon remaining married. In addition, research on domestic violence indicates that foreign nationals married to U.S. citizens or lawful permanent residents (LPR) possess factors that increase their risk of spousal abuse compared to U.S. citizens." According to Kandel, 98,192 VAWA petitions on behalf of immigrant women were processed between 1997 and 2011, and three-fourths of them were approved. These protections for immigrant women who are victims of domestic violence were subsequently extended with the passage of the Violence against Women Reauthorization Act of 2013.

During the first decade of the 21st century new policies and programs for immigrant victims emerged throughout the country, especially in cities with large immigrant populations. To improve the communication between immigrants and the criminal justice system, authorities have made special efforts to reach immigrant victims by hiring multicultural criminal justice staffs and providing informational materials in a variety of languages. Police representatives also attend meetings of immigrant groups, and members of the immigrant community are encouraged to serve as representatives on citizen police committees.

The most effective programs that assist immigrant women acknowledge the multiple pressures these women

TABLE 9.4

Police activities conducted as part of the Violence Against Women Act's Grants to Encourage Arrest Policies and Enforcement of Protection Orders Program, by victimization type, 2011–13

Activity	Sexual assault	Domestic violence/dating violence	Stalking	Total activities
Calls for assistance	9,879	405,462	2,464	417,805
Incident reports	8,709	301,205	2,266	312,180
Cases/incidents investigated	8,220	221,702	2,015	231,937
Arrests	1,892	94,425	594	96,911
Cases referred to prosecutor	2,408	87,886	839	91,133

SOURCE: "Table 9. Law Enforcement Activities in Arrest Program for Sexual Assault, Domestic Violence, Dating Violence, and Stalking Cases for All Four Reporting Periods, by Type of Victimization," in *2014 Biennial Report to Congress on the Effectiveness of Grant Programs under the Violence against Women Act*, U.S. Department of Justice, Office of Violence Against Women, University of Southern Maine Cutler Institute for Health and Public Policy, Muskie School of Public Service, 2014, https://www.justice.gov/ovw/file/450866/download (accessed June 17, 2016)

TABLE 9.5

Case referrals funded by the Violence Against Women Act's Grants to Encourage Arrest Policies and Enforcement of Protection Orders Program, by victimization type and prosecution status, 2011–13

Type of case	Cases referrals received	Cases accepted for prosecution	Percent
All cases	218,485	163,326	75
Domestic violence/dating violence	210,084	156,852	75
Sexual assault	4,845	3,212	66
Stalking	3,556	3,262	92

SOURCE: "Table 10. Cases Received and Accepted by Prosecutors Funded by the Arrest Program for All Four Reporting Periods, by Type of Victimization," in *2014 Biennial Report to Congress on the Effectiveness of Grant Programs under the Violence Against Women Act*, U.S. Department of Justice, Office of Violence Against Women, University of Southern Maine Cutler Institute for Health and Public Policy, Muskie School of Public Service, 2014, https://www.justice.gov/ovw/file/450866/download (accessed June 17, 2016)

TABLE 9.6

Case referrals funded by the Violence Against Women Act's Grants to Encourage Arrest Policies and Enforcement of Protection Orders Program, by victimization type and conviction status, 2011–13

Type of case	Cases disposed of	Dispositions resulting in convictions[a] Number	Percent
All cases	157,086	84,939	54
Domestic violence/dating violence	141,290[b]	74,375[c]	53
Sexual assault	2,841[d]	2,074[e]	73
Stalking	1,511	1,167	77

[a]Convictions, for purposes of this report, include cases of deferred adjudication, which represents 12 percent of all conviction outcomes. Deferred adjudication accounts for 13 percent of all domestic violence/dating violence convictions, 7 percent of all sexual assault convictions, and 2 percent of all stalking convictions.
[b]Includes a total of 251 domestic violence/dating violence homicide cases disposed of.
[c]Includes a total of 229 domestic violence/dating violence homicide cases resulting in conviction.
[d]Includes a total of two sexual assault homicide cases disposed of.
[e]Includes a total of two sexual assault homicide cases resulting in conviction. Deferred adjudication accounts for 7 percent of all sexual assault convictions.

SOURCE: "Table 11. Prosecution of Cases by Prosecutors Funded by the Arrest Program for All Four Reporting Periods, by Type of Victimization," in *2014 Biennial Report to Congress on the Effectiveness of Grant Programs under the Violence Against Women Act*, U.S. Department of Justice, Office of Violence Against Women, University of Southern Maine Cutler Institute for Health and Public Policy, Muskie School of Public Service, 2014, https://www.justice.gov/ovw/file/450866/download (accessed June 17, 2016)

face during their efforts to become oriented and assimilated into American culture and society. Along with cultural shock and language barriers, many immigrant women confront racism, class prejudice, and sexism. Fear of authority and the absence of social networks and support services compound the problem. Finally, recognizing that many women are brought to the United States in circumstances that increase the likelihood of victimization (such as mail-order brides, child care workers, or prostitutes) is an important step in stemming the crisis and addressing the crime of domestic violence. According to Marianne Sullivan et al., in "Participatory Action Research in Practice: A Case Study in Addressing Domestic Violence in Nine Cultural Communities" (*Journal of Interpersonal Violence*, vol. 20, no. 8, August

2005), including battered immigrant women in the development of experimental programs that address battering in their communities is crucial to guarantee the success of those programs.

LAW ENFORCEMENT AND CRIMINAL JUSTICE PROGRAMS. Over the years the VAWA has also funded various programs designed to help coordinate and prioritize the prosecution of crimes involving sexual violence. The Department of Justice, working in conjunction with the Office on Violence against Women and the University of Southern Maine Cutler Institute for Health and Public Policy at the Muskie School of Public Service, examines the impact of these programs in *2014 Biennial Report to Congress on the Effectiveness of Grant Programs under the Violence against Women Act* (2015, https://www.justice.gov/ovw/file/450866/download). One initiative, the Grants to Encourage Arrest Policies and Enforcement of Protection Orders Program (Arrest Program), was developed to "encourage state, local, and tribal governments and state, local, and tribal courts to treat sexual assault, domestic violence, dating violence, and stalking as serious violations of criminal law requiring coordination with nonprofit, nongovernmental victim advocates, and representatives from the criminal justice system." Table 9.4 provides a breakdown of police activities conducted as part of the Arrest Program between 2011 and 2013, while Table 9.5 provides an overview of legal actions resulting from these activities. As Table 9.6 reveals, of the 157,086 Arrest Program cases that

FIGURE 9.1

Police activities conducted as part of the Violence Against Women Act's Rural Sexual Assault, Domestic Violence, Dating Violence, and Stalking Assistance Program, 2011–13

Note: Grantees report only on law enforcement activities that are funded under the rural program and they may receive funds for one or for a number of these activities. Therefore, no relationships can be inferred or comparisons made between activities reported here.

SOURCE: "Figure 15. Law Enforcement Activities in Rural Program for Sexual Assault, Domestic Violence, Dating Violence, and Child Sexual Assault Cases for All Four Reporting Periods," in *2014 Biennial Report to Congress on the Effectiveness of Grant Programs under the Violence Against Women Act*, U.S. Department of Justice, Office of Violence Against Women, University of Southern Maine Cutler Institute for Health and Public Policy, Muskie School of Public Service, 2014, https://www.justice.gov/ovw/file/450866/download (accessed June 20, 2016)

FIGURE 9.2

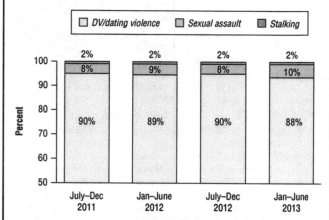

Percentages of victims served by Violence Against Women Act's Grants to Indian Tribal Governments Program, by victimization type, 2011–13

Note: The overall number of victims served represents an unduplicated count; this means that each victim is counted only once by each grantee, regardless of the number of times that victim received services during each reporting period. Because victims can be counted only once, they must be reported under only one primary victimization. It is not uncommon for victims to experience more than one type of victimization (e.g., domestic violence and stalking, or domestic violence and sexual assault), but the reported percentages of sexual assault, domestic violence/ dating violence, stalking, and child sexual abuse victims served do not reflect that fact.

SOURCE: "Figure 17. Provision of Victim Services by Tribal Governments Program Grantees, by Type of Victimization," in *2014 Biennial Report to Congress on the Effectiveness of Grant Programs under the Violence Against Women Act*, U.S. Department of Justice, Office of Violence Against Women, University of Southern Maine Cutler Institute for Health and Public Policy, Muskie School of Public Service, 2014, https://www.justice.gov/ovw/file/450866/download (accessed June 20, 2016)

appeared before a judge between 2011 and 2013, more than half (84,939, or 54%) resulted in a conviction.

Another initiative funded by the VAWA, the Rural Sexual Assault, Domestic Violence, Dating Violence, and Stalking Assistance Program, was formed in recognition that "victims of sexual assault, domestic violence, dating violence, stalking, and child sexual abuse who live in rural communities face unique challenges and barriers to receiving assistance rarely encountered in urban areas." As Figure 9.1 shows, between 2011 and 2013 law enforcement agencies investigated 3,604 cases of sexual violence, over half of which (1,861, or 51.6%) were ultimately referred to prosecutors.

Of the cases investigated as part of the VAWA's Grants to Indian Tribal Governments Program (Tribal Governments Program) between 2011 and 2013, 88% to 90% involved incidents of domestic or dating violence, 8% to 10% involved cases of sexual assault, and 2% involved cases of stalking. (See Figure 9.2.) As Table 9.7 shows, during this span law enforcement filed 4,049 incident reports under the Tribal Governments Program, 3,671 of which involved cases of domestic or dating violence. Between 2011 and 2013, 3,024 victims and 3,487 family members received emergency shelter or

housing assistance through the Tribal Governments Program. (See Table 9.8.)

Domestic Violence Gun Ban

Federal law includes batterers convicted of domestic violence crimes and those with domestic violence protection orders filed against them among the people who are prohibited from owning or carrying guns. Since 1994 all federally licensed gun dealers must run background checks on gun purchasers. The Federal Bureau of Investigation breaks down in *National Instant Criminal Background Check System (NICS) Operations 2014* (2015, https://www.fbi.gov/about-us/cjis/nics/reports/2014-operations-report) the major reasons reported for denying gun purchases between November 30, 1998, and December 31, 2014. Of the 1,166,676 total denials, 112,925 (9.7% of the total) were denied for "misdemeanor crime of domestic violence conviction." Another 47,870 denials (4.1% of the total) were denied for "protection/restraining order for domestic violence."

TABLE 9.7

Police activities conducted as part of the Violence Against Women Act's Grants to Indian Tribal Governments Program, by victimization type, 2011–13

Activity	Sexual assault	Domestic violence/dating violence	Stalking	Total activities
Calls for assistance	317	3,600	24	3,941
Incident reports	356	3,671	22	4,049
Cases/incidents investigated	292	2,937	20	3,249
Arrests	70	1,639	0	1,709
Cases referred to tribal prosecutor	55	1,576	5	1,636

SOURCE: "Table 94. Law Enforcement Activities in Tribal Governments Program Sexual Assault, Domestic Violence, Dating Violence, and Stalking Cases for All Four Reporting Periods, by Type of Victimization," in *2014 Biennial Report to Congress on the Effectiveness of Grant Programs under the Violence Against Women Act*, U.S. Department of Justice, Office of Violence Against Women, University of Southern Maine Cutler Institute for Health and Public Policy, Muskie School of Public Service, 2014, https://www.justice.gov/ovw/file/450866/download (accessed June 20, 2016)

DIFFICULTIES IN THE COURT SYSTEM

An appeal to the U.S. judicial system should be an effective method of obtaining justice. For domestic violence victims, however, this has not always been the case. In the past, ignorance, social prejudices, and uneven attention from the criminal justice system all tended to underestimate the severity and importance of the problem. Over time, society has become significantly less tolerant of domestic violence, and laws in many states criminalize behavior that was previously considered to be acceptable.

Willingness of Victims to Prosecute

One of the most formidable problems in prosecuting abusers is the victim's reluctance to cooperate. Although many abused women have the courage to initiate legal proceedings against their batterer, some are later reluctant to cooperate with the prosecution because of their emotional attachment to their abuser. Other reasons for their reluctance are fear of retaliation by their abuser, mistrust or lack of information about the criminal justice system, or fear of the demands of court appearances. In addition, a victim might choose not to move forward with the prosecution for economic reasons if, for example, the batterer is her husband and the primary income earner for the family. Religious convictions and family influence can also cause victims to drop the charges.

Factors Associated with Prosecutors' Charging Decisions in Domestic Violence Cases

In "Modeling Prosecutors' Charging Decisions in Domestic Violence Cases" (*Crime and Delinquency*, vol. 52, no. 3, July 2006), John L. Worrall, Jay W. Ross, and Eric S. McCord investigate what factors influenced

TABLE 9.8

Victims receiving emergency shelter and/or housing assistance under the Violence Against Women Act's Grants to Indian Tribal Governments Program, 2011–13

Shelter service	July–Dec 2011	Jan–June 2012	July–Dec 2012	Jan–June 2013	Total
Emergency shelter					
Victims	677	520	747	1,080	3,024
Family members	875	657	794	1,161	3,487
Bed nights	26,812	14,242	33,611	40,440	115,105

SOURCE: "Table 93. Victims Receiving Emergency Shelter and/or Transitional Housing Assistance by the Tribal Governments Program: July 2011–June 2013," in *2014 Biennial Report to Congress on the Effectiveness of Grant Programs under the Violence Against Women Act*, U.S. Department of Justice, Office of Violence Against Women, University of Southern Maine Cutler Institute for Health and Public Policy, Muskie School of Public Service, 2014, https://www.justice.gov/ovw/file/450866/download (accessed June 20, 2016)

the decisions of prosecutors to charge a batterer and what factors influenced the decisions of prosecutors to pursue a misdemeanor or a felony charge. They collected data on 245 domestic violence cases that were filed by police officers; examined the impact of characteristics of the victim, the offender, and the offense; and determined how these characteristics influenced the prosecutors' charging decisions.

Worrall, Ross, and McCord find that prosecutors were more likely to charge offenders if they had been arrested or if they had inflicted serious injuries on the victim. The researchers indicate that criminal charges were more likely to be filed against a male batterer than against a female batterer. They also note that if the victim supported prosecution, felony charges were more likely to be filed against the batterer.

Court Case Outcomes

Erica L. Smith and Donald J. Farole Jr. of the BJS analyzed 3,750 intimate partner violence cases in the courts of 16 metropolitan areas to determine their outcomes and reported the results in *Profile of Intimate Partner Violence Cases in Large Urban Counties* (October 2009, http://bjs.ojp.usdoj.gov/content/pub/pdf/pipvcluc.pdf). The researchers find that 84% of these cases involved a female victim and a male defendant. Most defendants were charged with either simple assault (78%) or aggravated assault (12%).

According to Smith and Farole, 56% of all domestic violence cases filed with the courts resulted in conviction. Another 33% of cases were dismissed. Three-quarters (75.3%) of those convicted served a jail sentence, 7.4% went to prison, and 17.3% were put on probation.

Smith and Farole note that certain characteristics of intimate partner violence cases were associated with

Domestic Violence, Law Enforcement, and Court Responses to Domestic Violence different adjudication outcomes. For example, 56.4% of convictions were in cases in which a third party had witnessed the assault. Forty percent of convictions were in cases in which a child was present at the time of the assault. In cases that were dismissed or resulted in acquittal, a child was present only 30.8% of the time. Cases resulting in convictions had a higher incidence of defendant use of alcohol or drugs than did dismissed or acquitted cases (34.7% and 29%, respectively). Certain factors were found to increase the odds of a conviction, including a defendant's formal statement (2 times more likely to result in conviction), the presence of witnesses (1.7 times more likely to result in conviction), a history of abuse (1.7 times more likely to result in conviction), physical evidence had been obtained (1.5 times more likely to result in conviction), and the victim was injured during the incident (1.3 times more likely to result in conviction).

TREATMENT FOR MALE BATTERERS

Rather than serving a prison term, some convicted batterers enter treatment programs. As a requirement of probation, courts may order a batterer into an intervention program. According to Bethany J. Price and Alan Rosenbaum, in "Batterer Intervention Programs: A Report from the Field" (*Violence and Victims*, vol. 24, no. 6, 2009), intervention programs have proliferated because the offenders are typically charged with misdemeanors, which do not justify a prison term; victims usually do not want the offenders jailed; and these programs allow the offenders to continue earning a livelihood. Price and Rosenbaum find in their survey of programs that most of the programs focus on education with a psychotherapeutic component, averaging about 40 hours in length, and often include anger management and alcohol and substance abuse components. Regardless of an intervention program's philosophy or methods, program directors and criminal justice professionals generally monitor offenders' behavior closely. Most batterers enter intervention programs after having been charged by the police with a specific incident of abuse.

The criminal justice system categorizes offenders based on their potential danger, history of substance abuse, psychological problems, and risk of dropout and rearrest. Ideally, interventions focus on the specific type of batterer and the approach that will most effectively produce results, such as linking a substance abuse treatment program with a batterer intervention program. Other program approaches focus on specific sociocultural characteristics, such as poverty, race, ethnicity, and age. Shelly Jackson argues in "Analyzing the Studies" (Shelly Jackson et al., *Batterer Intervention Programs: Where Do We Go from Here?* June 2003, http://www.ncjrs.gov/pdffiles1/nij/195079.pdf) that the effectiveness of batterer intervention programs might improve if the programs were seen "as part of a broader criminal justice and community response to domestic violence that includes arrest, restraining orders, intensive monitoring of batterers, and changes to social norms that may inadvertently tolerate partner violence."

In addition, other researchers have identified specific behavioral issues associated with certain extreme cases of intimate partner violence. In "The Treatment Needs of Substance Abusing Batterers: A Comparison of Men Who Batter Their Female Partners" (*Journal of Family Violence*, vol. 28, no. 2, February 2013), Mark D. Thomas, Larry W. Bennett, and Charles Stoops observe that violent behavior is both more prevalent and more extreme among batterers who struggle with alcohol and drug abuse. The researchers also analyze the connection between substance abuse in batterers and a range of other behavioral issues, including trauma and borderline personality disorder. According to Thomas, Bennett, and Stoops, treatment for batterers struggling with substance abuse must also address the question of chemical dependency to be effective.

Program Dropout Rates

Batterers leave a program either because of successful completion or because they are asked to leave. The reasons for termination include failure to cooperate, nonpayment of fees, revocation of parole or probation, failure to attend group sessions regularly, or violation of program rules. Successful completion of a program means that the offender has attended the required sessions and accomplished the program's objectives. With court-mandated clients a final report is also made to probation officials. To be successful, batterer intervention programs must have the support of the criminal justice system, which includes coordinated efforts between police, prosecutors, judges, victim advocates, and probation officers.

Dropout rates in battering programs are high, even though courts have ordered most clients to attend. Several studies, such as that by Jennifer Rooney and R. Karl Hanson in "Predicting Attrition from Treatment Programs for Abusive Men" (*Journal of Family Violence*, vol. 16, no. 2, June 2001), record varying dropout rates, some finding that as many as 90% of the men who begin short-term treatment programs do not complete them.

High dropout rates in batterer intervention programs make it difficult to evaluate their success. Evaluations based on men who complete these programs focus on a select group of highly motivated men who likely do not reflect the composition of the group when it began. Because a follow-up is not conducted with program dropouts (often the men most likely to continue their violence), research generally fails to accurately indicate the success or failure of a given treatment program. Andrew Day et al. note in "Programs for Men Who Perpetrate Domestic Violence: An Examination of the Issues Underlying the Effectiveness of Intervention Programs" (*Journal of Family Violence*, vol. 24, no. 3, April 2009) that the success of batterer intervention programs in reducing violence is generally much lower than in other established intervention programs. The researchers theorize that batterer intervention programs have difficulty linking theories of causation of domestic violence to intervention strategies and to stages of change in perpetrators; thus, these "program integrity issues" lead to poor outcomes. Day et al. conclude, "There would appear to be a need to further develop intervention approaches for perpetrators of domestic violence, both in terms of greater sophistication in how domestic violence is understood, identifying the needs of treatment participants, and delivering programs in ways that are engaging and motivating for men to change."

Certain characteristics are generally related to dropout rates. In "Batterer Characteristics and Treatment Completion" (*Journal of Interpersonal Violence*, vol. 16, no. 12, December 2001), Bruce Dalton of the University of South Carolina indicates that the level of threat that the batterer perceived from the referral source (e.g., the court) was, surprisingly, not related to program completion. Unemployment was the one characteristic most consistently related to dropping out of treatment. Dalton theorizes that these men had trouble paying for the treatment and a lower investment in the "official social order." Loretta J. Stalans and Magnus Seng of Loyola University Chicago find similar results in "Identifying Subgroups at High Risk of Dropping out of Domestic Batterer Treatment: The Buffering Effects of a High School Education" (*International Journal of Offender Therapy and Comparative Criminology*, vol. 51, no. 2, April 2007). The researchers note that the following groups had a 60% dropout rate or higher: batterers who were aggressive in general, not only in the family setting; high school dropouts who were also ordered into substance abuse treatment; and unemployed offenders who were also ordered into substance abuse treatment.

Recidivism Rates

Recidivism (the tendency to relapse to old ingrained patterns of behavior) is a well-documented problem among people in intimate partner violence treatment programs. In "Predictors of Criminal Recidivism among Male Batterers" (*Psychology Crime and Law*, vol. 10, no. 4, December 2004), R. Karl Hanson and Suzanne Wallace-Capretta examine the risk factors that were associated with the recidivism of 320 male batterers within a five-year follow-up period. Of those men, 25.6%

recidivated with a battering offense. Risk factors included being young, having an unstable lifestyle, being a substance abuser, and having a criminal history. Batterers were not deterred by expectations of social or legal negative consequences. However, maintaining positive relationships with community treatment providers was associated with deterrence of future battering. Rodney Kingsnorth of California State University, Sacramento, notes in "Intimate Partner Violence: Predictors of Recidivism in a Sample of Arrestees" (*Violence against Women*, vol. 12, no. 10, October 2006) that risk factors for recidivism during an 18-month period included use of a weapon, prior arrests (for domestic violence or other offenses), and the presence of a protective order.

According to Matthew T. Huss and Anthony Ralston of Creighton University, in "Do Batterer Subtypes Actually Matter? Treatment Completion, Treatment Response, and Recidivism across a Batterer Typology" (*Criminal Justice and Behavior*, vol. 35, no. 6, June 2008), men who only expressed violent behaviors in the context of their families were much more likely to complete batterer intervention programs than men who were generally violent or antisocial or who had personality disorders. Because of the higher treatment completion rates, these men were less likely to batter again. However, all men who completed treatment reported reductions in violence toward their partner.

In "The Effects of Domestic Violence Batterer Treatment on Domestic Violence Recidivism: The Chesterfield County Experience" (*Criminal Justice and Behavior*, vol. 30, no. 1, February 2003), Jill A. Gordon and Laura J. Moriarty of Virginia Commonwealth University study the effects of batterer treatment on recidivism. The researchers find that attending treatment had no impact on recidivism when comparing the treatment group as a whole with the experimental group. In "Intervention Programs for Perpetrators of Intimate Partner Violence: Conclusions from a Clinical Research Perspective" (*Public Health Reports*, vol. 121, no. 4, July–August 2006), Christopher I. Eckhardt et al. concur in their review of the literature concerning batterer intervention programs and recidivism rates. However, Gordon and Moriarty also indicate that among the treatment group, the more sessions a batterer completed, the less likely he was to batter again. Batterers who completed all sessions were less likely to be rearrested for domestic violence than were batterers who had not completed all sessions.

Still, as Huss and Ralston note, "even small reductions in rates of domestic violence can have a substantial impact in tens of thousands of women's lives." Therefore, research continues into how to identify batterers who are most likely to benefit from batterer intervention programs. According to Marna Miller, Elizabeth Drake, and Mia Nafziger, in *What Works to Reduce Recidivism by Domestic Violence Offenders?* (January 2013, http://www.wsipp.wa.gov/ReportFile/1119/Wsipp_What-Works-to-Reduce-Recidivism-by-Domestic-Violence-Offenders_Full-Report.pdf), a study of five group-based batterer treatment programs proved effective in reducing incidences of domestic violence recidivism by 33%. The researchers note, however, that these programs varied significantly in method and approach, making it difficult to determine which course of treatment ultimately proves most effective.

IMPORTANT NAMES
AND ADDRESSES

ABA Center on Children and the Law
321 N. Clark St.
Chicago, IL 60654
(312) 988-5000
1-800-285-2221
URL: http://www.americanbar.org/groups/
child_law.html

ABA Commission on Domestic & Sexual Violence
321 N. Clark St.
Chicago, IL 60654
(312) 988-5000
URL: http://www.americanbar.org/groups/
domestic_violence.html

ACLU Women's Rights Project
125 Broad St., 18th Floor
New York, NY 10004
(212) 549-2500
URL: https://www.aclu.org/issues/womens-
rights

Bureau of Justice Statistics
U.S. Department of Justice
810 Seventh St. NW
Washington, DC 20531
(202) 307-0765
E-mail: askbjs@usdoj.gov
URL: http://www.bjs.gov/

Center for Women Policy Studies
1776 Massachusetts Ave. NW, Ste. 450
Washington, DC 20036
(202) 872-1770
FAX: (202) 296-8962
E-mail: cwps@centerwomenpolicy.org
URL: http://www.centerwomenpolicy.org/

Centers for Disease Control and Prevention
1600 Clifton Rd.
Atlanta, GA 30329-4027
1-800-232-4636
URL: http://www.cdc.gov/

Child Welfare Information Gateway
Children's Bureau/ACYF
330 C St. SW
Washington, DC 20201
1-800-394-3366
E-mail: info@childwelfare.gov
URL: http://www.childwelfare.gov/

Child Welfare League of America
727 15th St. NW, 12th Floor
Washington, DC 20005
(202) 688-4200
FAX: (202) 833-1689
E-mail: cwla@cwla.org
URL: http://www.cwla.org/

Children's Bureau
Administration for Children and Families
U.S. Department of Health and Human Services
330 C St., SW
Washington, DC 20201
URL: http://www.acf.hhs.gov/programs/cb/

Children's Defense Fund
25 E St. NW
Washington, DC 20001
1-800-233-1200
E-mail: cdfinfo@childrensdefense.org
URL: http://www.childrensdefense.org/

Crimes against Children Research Center
University of New Hampshire
15 Academic Way
125 McConnell Hall
Durham, NH 03824
(603) 862-1888
FAX: (603) 862-1122
E-mail: doreen.cole@unh.edu
URL: http://www.unh.edu/ccrc/

Gunderson National Child Protection Center
Maxwell Hall, Winona State University
Winona, MN 55987

(507) 457-2890
URL: http://www.gundersenhealth.org/ncptc

Institute on Violence, Abuse, and Trauma
10065 Old Grove Rd.
San Diego, CA 92131
(858) 527-1860
FAX: (858) 527-1743
E-mail: ivat@alliant.edu
URL: http://ivatcenters.org/

International Society for the Prevention of Child Abuse and Neglect
13123 E. 16th Ave., Ste. B390
Aurora, CO 80045
(303) 864-5220
FAX: (303) 864-5222
URL: http://www.ispcan.org/

National Center for Missing and Exploited Children
Charles B. Wang International
Children's Bldg.
699 Prince St.
Alexandria, VA 22314-3175
(703) 224-2150
1-800-843-5678
FAX: (703) 224-2122
URL: http://www.missingkids.com/

National Center for Prosecution of Child Abuse
National District Attorneys Association
1400 Crystal Dr., Ste. 330
Alexandria, VA 22202
(703) 549-9222
FAX: (703) 836-3195
URL: http://www.ndaa.org/ncpca.html

National Center for Victims of Crime
2000 M St. NW, Ste. 480
Washington, DC 20036
(202) 467-8700
FAX: (202) 467-8701
URL: http://www.victimsofcrime.org/

National Clearinghouse for the Defense of Battered Women
125 S. Ninth St., Ste. 302
Philadelphia, PA 19107
(215) 351-0010
1-800-903-0111
URL: http://www.ncdbw.org/

National Coalition against Domestic Violence
One Broadway, Ste. B210
Denver, CO 80203
(303) 839-1852
FAX: (303) 831-9251
E-mail: mainoffice@ncadv.org
URL: http://www.ncadv.org/

National Council on Child Abuse and Family Violence
1025 Connecticut Ave. NW, Ste. 1000
Washington, DC 20036
(202) 429-6695
FAX: (202) 521-3479
E-mail: info@nccafv.org
URL: http://www.nccafv.org/

National Domestic Violence Hotline
PO Box 161810
Austin, TX 78716
(512) 453-8117
1-800-799-7233
URL: http://www.thehotline.org/

National Runaway Safeline
3141B N. Lincoln Ave.
Chicago, IL 60657
(773) 880-9860
1-800-786-2929
FAX: (773) 929-5150
URL: http://www.1800runaway.org/

Office for Victims of Crime ITVERP Resource Center
810 Seventh St. NW
Washington, DC 20531
1-800-363-0441
E-mail: ITVERP@usdoj.gov
URL: http://ojp.gov/ovc/

Office of Juvenile Justice and Delinquency Prevention
810 Seventh St. NW
Washington, DC 20531
(202) 307-5911
URL: http://www.ojjdp.gov/

Office on Violence against Women U.S. Department of Justice
145 N St. NE, Ste. 10W.121
Washington, DC 20530
(202) 307-6026
FAX: (202) 305-2589
E-mail: ovw.info@usdoj.gov
URL: http://www.justice.gov/ovw

Prevent Child Abuse America
228 S. Wabash Ave., 10th Floor
Chicago, IL 60604
(312) 663-3520
1-800-244-5373
FAX: (312) 939-8962
E-mail: mailbox@preventchildabuse.org
URL: http://www.preventchildabuse.org/

Protect Our Defenders
20 Park Rd., Ste. E
Burlingame, CA 94010
E-mail: info@protectourdefenders.com
URL: http://www.protectourdefenders.com/

Rape, Abuse, and Incest National Network
1220 L St. NW, Ste. 505
Washington, DC 20005
(202) 544-1034
1-800-656-4673
URL: http://www.rainn.org/

Survivors Network of Those Abused by Priests
PO Box 6416
Chicago, IL 60680-6416
(312) 455-1499
1-877-762-7432
FAX: (312) 455-1498
E-mail: bdorris@snapnetwork.org
URL: http://www.snapnetwork.org/

RESOURCES

The U.S. Department of Health and Human Services (HHS) is a major source of national information about issues related to family violence. The HHS agencies consulted for this book include the Children's Bureau and the Office of Planning, Research, and Evaluation (OPRE) within the Administration for Children and Families and the National Center for Health Statistics and the National Center for Injury Prevention and Control within the Centers for Disease Control and Prevention.

The U.S. Department of Justice compiles and publishes large amounts of data on crime and victimizations. Agencies that provided data include the Bureau of Justice Statistics, the Federal Bureau of Investigation, the National Institute of Justice, and the Office of Juvenile Justice and Delinquency Prevention. The Federal Interagency Forum on Child and Family Statistics is a group of 22 federal government agencies that are involved in research and activities related to children and families. The U.S. Government Accountability Office and the Congressional Research Service are also important sources of information about government programs and policies.

Four studies in the National Incidence Study of Child Abuse and Neglect were conducted by the private research company Westat under contract to the OPRE. Two key resources at educational institutions were the Crimes against Children Research Center at the University of New Hampshire and the National Scientific Council on the Developing Child, a project of the Center on the Developing Child at Harvard University. Criminal law information was obtained from the National Center for Prosecution of Child Abuse, a project of the National District Attorneys Association. In addition, the U.S. Conference of Catholic Bishops was a valuable source of information.

Many journals published useful articles on child maltreatment and domestic violence that were used in the preparation of this book. They include *American Criminal Law Review, Child Abuse and Neglect, Child Maltreatment, Criminal Justice and Behavior, Journal of Adolescent Health, Journal of Child Sexual Abuse, Journal of Clinical Psychology, Journal of Consulting and Clinical Psychology, Journal of the American Academy of Child and Adolescent Psychology, Journal of the American Academy of Psychiatry and the Law, Journal of the American Medical Association, Journal of Family Violence, Journal of Interpersonal Violence, Journal of Perinatal Medicine, Journal of Psychiatric and Mental Health Nursing, Journal of Traumatic Stress, National Institute of Justice Journal, National Survey of Child and Adolescent Well-Being Research Brief, Pediatrics, Proceedings of the National Academy of Sciences, Violence against Women*, and *Violence and Victims*.

INDEX

Page references in italics refer to photographs. References with the letter t following them indicate the presence of a table. The letter f indicates a figure. If more than one table or figure appears on a particular page, the exact item number for the table or figure being referenced is provided.

A

Abelson, Jenn, 76

"Abnormal T2 Relaxation Time in the Cerebellar Vermis of Adults Sexually Abused in Childhood: Potential Role of the Vermis in Stress-Enhanced Risk for Drug Abuse" (Anderson et al.), 80

"About CAPTA: A Legislative History" (Children's Bureau), 7

"About the CDC-Kaiser ACE Study" (CDC), 71

"Abuse Subtypes and Nonsuicidal Self-Injury: Preliminary Evidence of Complex Emotion Regulation Patterns" (Muehlenkamp et al.), 81

Abusers
   victims of domestic violence, reasons for staying, 120, 123, 127–128
   women's response to domestic violence and, 128
   See also Offenders; Perpetrators

ACEs (Adverse Childhood Experiences) Study, 56, 71–72

Achenbach, Thomas, 59–60

Ackerman, Alissa, 77

Acquaintance rape
   college, sexual violence at, 142–146
   date rape, 137–142
   high school students who have ever been forced to have sexual intercourse, by sex, grade, race/Hispanic origin, 138t
   high school students who have ever been forced to have sexual intercourse, by sex, state, metropolitan areas, 139t

high school students who have ever been physically forced to have sexual intercourse, 138f

high school students who have ever been physically forced to have sexual intercourse, by race/Hispanic origin, grade, sex, 137t

military, sexual assault in, 147–148

number of, 136–137

percentage of, 135

rape/sexual assault, average annual incidences of, by sex, college enrollment status of victim, 150(t8.16)

rape/sexual assault, type of, experienced by women aged 18–24, by college enrollment status, 149f

rape/sexual assault among women aged 18–24, by location, activity, time of day, college enrollment status, 150(t8.17)

rape/sexual assault among women aged 18–24, by victim-offender relationship, college enrollment status of victim, 150(t8.18)

rape/sexual assault rates among females, by age, college enrollment status, 148f

ACYF. See Administration on Children, Youth, and Families

ADHD (attention deficit/hyperactivity disorder), 63

Administration for Children and Families, 42

Administration on Children, Youth, and Families (ACYF)
   on behavioral problems in maltreated children, 59–60
   children in foster care, use of psychotropic medications by, 63–64
   on neurobiology in childhood maltreatment, 54, 56
   on six domains of childhood maltreatment, 53–54
   on social/emotional well-being in child welfare system, 64
   on traumatic childhood events, effects of, 59

Adolescents
   arrests of by sex/age/race/ethnicity/home setting, 48(t3.3)
   birth rates among adolescent females, by race/ethnicity, 3f
   birth rates for adolescent females, by age, race, Hispanic origin, 2t
   birth rates for adolescent females, trends in, 2–3
   childhood/youth victimization as risk factor for domestic violence, 116–117
   consensual/nonconsensual sexual activity/pregnancy among in child welfare system, 49f
   effects of child sexual abuse, 79–80
   in foster care, 63
   juvenile delinquency among, 47–48
   sexual abuse, disclosure of, 74–75
   sexual abuse surveys, 72–74
   sexual experience/pregnancy among females aged 11–20, 49t
   sexual predators on Internet and, 78–79
   substance abuse as effect of child sexual abuse, 80
   See also High school students

Adoption and Foster Care Analysis and Reporting System (AFCARS), 36

Adoption and Safe Families Act
   for state performance measurement, 40
   termination of parental rights, 35

Adoption Assistance and Child Welfare Act, 36–37

"Adrian Peterson Controversy: Is It OK to Spank Your Children?" (Fowler), 20

Adverse Childhood Experiences (ACEs) Study, 56, 71–72

Adverse Childhood Experiences (ACEs): What Happens Early Can Change Lives (CDC), 71–72

AFCARS (Adoption and Foster Care Analysis and Reporting System), 36

Fourth National Incidence Study of Child Abuse and Neglect (NIS-4) Report to Congress (Sedlak et al.)
overview of, 31–33
on types of child sexual abuse, 66–67
Fowler, Tara, 20
Francis I, Pope, 77
Fraternities, 140
Fréchette, Sabrina, 20
Freud, Sigmund, 91
Frye, Victoria, 162
Full faith and credit provision, 163
Full Report of the Prevalence, Incidence, and Consequence of Violence against Women (Tjaden & Thoennes), 110–111
The Function of the Police in Crisis Intervention and Conflict Management, 159
Funding
for child abuse prevention, federal, 3
FVPSA funding purposes, 9
from Violence against Women Act, 9, 10
Futures without Violence, 166
FVPSA (Family Violence Prevention and Services Act), 9

G

Gamma hydroxybutyric acid (liquid ecstasy), 142
Garner, Joel H., 161
Gelles, Richard J.
The Book of David: How Preserving Families Can Cost Children's Lives, 37
on substance abuse as risk factor for domestic violence, 115
on women's response to domestic violence, 128
Gender
arrests of adolescents by, 48(t3.3)
of child abuse victims, 22–24, 32
child maltreatment, prevalence of among juvenile offenders by, 72t
child sexual abuse by priests and, 76
of child sexual abuse victims, 67–68, 72, 73
college rape statistics by, 139
disclosure of abuse by, 74
domestic violence, risk factors for, 114–117
domestic violence, theories on causes of, 113–114
domestic violence legislation and, 9–10
equal protection and, 164
high school students who experienced physical dating violence in past year by, sex, 140f
high school students who experienced sexual dating violence in past year by, 142f
high school students who have ever been physically forced to have sexual intercourse by, 137f

high-risk behaviors in female child sexual abuse victims, 79–80
NCVS data on domestic violence, 17
of perpetrators of child maltreatment, 33
of polyvictims, 18
psychological disorders in adolescence and, 61
rape/sexual assault, average annual incidences of, by sex, college enrollment status of victim, 150(t8.16)
of rape/sexual assault victims, 133
rapes/sexual assaults, by victim's sex, race/Hispanic origin, 134(t8.6)
same-sex relationships, violence in, 111
sexual harassment and, 74
stalking victimization, prevalence of, by sex, race/Hispanic origin of victim, lifetime/previous 12 months, 153t
of stalking victims, 149, 151
stalking victims who experienced particular stalking tactics, percentage of, lifetime/previous 12 months, by sex, 157t
victims of child maltreatment by, 27f
Geoghan, John J., 76
Geographical region, rape/sexual assault cases by, 133, 136t
Global Initiative to End All Corporal Punishment of Children, 19
Gonzales, Jessica, 165
Gonzales, Town of Castle Rock, Colorado v., 165
Goodstein, Laurie, 77
Gordon, Jill A., 171
Graham, Geralyn, 39
Graham, *Hearndon v.*, 91
Graham, Kenneth, 91
Graham, Pamela, 39
"Grant Programs" (OVW), 10
Grants to Encourage Arrest Policies and Enforcement of Protection Orders Program (Arrest Program), 167–168
Grants to Indian Tribal Governments Program (Tribal Governments Program), 168
Great Recession, 51
Greene, Sheila, 75
Greenwood, James, 7
Gresham, Frank, 62
Groden, Claire, 142–144
Grounds for Involuntary Termination of Parental Rights (Children's Bureau), 35
Guardians ad litem (guardians at law), 83
Gun ban, 168
Guyer, Melvin J., 92

H

Hall, Nancy K., 80
Halligan, Caitlin, 128
Hamby, Sherry, 17

Hammon v. Indiana, 90
"Handmade Memories: The Robustness of the Gestural Misinformation Effect in Children's Eyewitness Interviews" (Kirk et al.), 88
Hanson, R. Karl, 170–171
Hanson, Rochelle F.
on disclosure of sexual abuse, 74
National Survey of Adolescents, 72–73
Hardy, Greg, 119
Harm Standard
child sexual abuse incidence rates by, 67–68
definition of, 31
for NIS studies, 66
NIS-4 findings on, 44–45
sex/age/race/ethnicity/family characteristics of victims and, 32–33
Harris, Sara, 88
Haviland, Mary, 162
Hazen, Andrea L., 80
Health
effects of domestic violence on, 117–118
medical treatment for victims of domestic violence, 120
NSCAW data on needs, 46
public health, child abuse/domestic violence, 11–16
Health insurance
children with coverage, 15
domestic violence preventive services, 119
Hearndon, Paula, 91
Hearndon v. Graham, 91
Hearsay, 89–90
Helplessness: On Depression, Development, and Death (Seligman), 127
Help-seeking behaviors, 128
Hershkowitz, Irit, 88
HHS. *See* U.S. Department of Health and Human Services
Hide, Macias v., 165
High school students
public schools reporting sexual harassment of students by other students, 145t
rape/sexual assault statistics, 137–138
who experienced dating violence/sexual dating violence, by sex, race/Hispanic origin, grade, 117t
who experienced physical dating violence in past year, by race/Hispanic origin, grade, sex, 140f
who experienced sexual dating violence in past year, by race/Hispanic origin, grade, sex, 142f
who experienced sexual dating violence in past year, by state, 141f
who have ever been forced to have sexual intercourse, by sex, state, metropolitan areas, 139t

*Intimate Partner Violence: Attributes of
Victimization, 1993–2011* (Catalano)
  on female homicide victims in domestic
    violence incidents, 110
  on intimate partner violence, trends in,
    99–100, 102–104
"Intimate Partner Violence: Predictors of
  Recidivism in a Sample of Arrestees"
  (Kingsnorth), 171
"Intimate Partner Violence, PTSD, and
  Adverse Health Outcomes" (Dutton),
  118
"Intimate Partner Violence, Technology,
  and Stalking" (Southworth et al.), 155
Intimate partners
  description of, 96
  female victims of intimate partner
    violence, 102–104
  intimate homicide, 109
  National Intimate Partner and Sexual
    Violence Survey, 104–108
  National Violence against Women
    Survey, 110–111
  violence, rates of, 97
  violence, trends in, 99–100, 102
  violence against, 61–62
Intimate Violence (Gelles & Strauss), 128
Investigations, child maltreatment, 34–35
"It's on Us" program, 144

J

Jackson, Shelly, 170
Jensen, D. Lowell, 165
"Jerry Sandusky Sex Abuse Case Has States
  Re-examining Mandatory Reporter
  Laws" (Associated Press), 78
"Joe Biden Writes an Open Letter to
  Stanford Survivor" (Namako), 146
John Jay College of Criminal Justice of the
  City University of New York, 76–77
Johnson, Dawn M., 163
Jones, Jerry, 119
Jones, Lisa M., 78
Jones, William G., 85
Judicial system
  intervention measures of, 35–36
  rape outcomes, 135–136
Juvenile court system, 35
Juvenile delinquency, 47–48
*Juvenile Justice Bulletin: National Survey of
Children's Exposure to Violence*
(Finkelhor et al.), 73, 74

K

Kahn, Jeffrey H., 61–62
Kaiser Permanente, 71–72
Kandel, William A., 166
Kane, Kathleen, 78
"Kane Preps for Trial of 3 Former Penn
  State Officials" (Erdley), 78

Kansas, repressed memory law in, 92
Karakurt, Gunnur, 118
Katz, Carmit, 88
Kaura, Shelby A., 116
Kempe, C. Henry, 10
Kentucky, high school rape rate of, 137
Ketamine hydrochloride, 142
Kingree, J. B., 115–116
Kingsnorth, Rodney, 171
Kirchgaessner, Stephanie, 77
Kirk, Elizabeth, 88
Kirkpatrick, Dean G., 142
Knox, David, 128
Kovacs, Maria, 63
Krebs, Christopher, 144

L

Langton, Lynn
  *Rape and Sexual Assault Victimization
    among College-Age Females,
    1995–2013*, 138–140
  on victimizations reported to police,
    159–160
  on violent victimizations, 96–97
Lanning, Kenneth V., 87
Lauritsen, Janet L., 74
Law, Bernard, 76
Law, child abuse and
  child maltreatment victims with court
    action, 84(*t*5.1)
  child maltreatment victims with court-
    appointed representatives, 84(*t*5.2)
  child sexual abuse prosecutions, 84–88
  children's legal rights in child protection
    cases, 83–84
  confrontation clause, 88–89
  hearsay, 89–90
  legal protections for children, 92–93
  prosecution of child abusers, difficulties
    in, 84
  statute of limitations/recovered memory,
    90–92
  victims of child sexual assault, by age/
    injury status, 86*t*
  victims of child sexual assault, by age/
    reporting to police, 85*t*
Law enforcement
  court system, difficulties in, 169–170
  crime victimizations reported to police,
    by crime type, 160*t*
  cyberstalking and, 156–157
  domestic violence and, 159
  emergency shelter/housing assistance
    under the VAWA's Grants to Indian
    Tribal Governments Program, victims
    receiving, 169(*t*9.8)
  legal decisions, landmark, 163–165
  legal definitions for rape/stalking, 129
  legislation, key domestic violence,
    165–169

male batterers, treatment for, 170–172
police, reporting domestic violence to,
  159–160
police activities conducted as part of
  VAWA's Grants to Encourage Arrest
  Policies/Enforcement of Protection
  Orders Program, by victimization type,
  167(*t*9.4)
police intervention, outcome of,
  160–163
protection orders, 163
rates of crime victimizations reported/
  not reported to police, by crime type,
  161*t*
VAWA's Grants to Encourage Arrest
  Policies and Enforcement of Protection
  Orders Program, case referrals funded
  by, by victimization type/conviction
  status, 167(*t*9.6)
VAWA's Grants to Encourage Arrest
  Policies and Enforcement of Protection
  Orders Program, case referrals funded
  by, by victimization type/prosecution
  status, 167(*t*9.5)
VAWA's Grants to Indian Tribal
  Governments Program, police activities
  conducted as, by victimization type,
  169(*t*9.7)
VAWA's Indian Tribal Governments
  Program, victims served by, by
  victimization type, 168(*f*9.2)
VAWA's Rural Sexual Assault/
  Domestic Violence/Dating Violence/
  Stalking Assistance Program, police
  activities conducted as, 168(*f*9.1)
violent victimizations by victim-offender
  relationship/reporting to police, 162*t*
See also Police
Laws
  anti-stalking legislation, 152–153
  child abuse legislation, 3, 7–9
  on child sexual abuse, 65
  domestic violence legislation, 9–10,
    165–168
  due process, 165
  equal protection, 164–165
  federal legislation concerned with child
    protection, welfare, adoption, timeline
    of, 8*f*
  legal decisions, landmark, 163–165
  on rape/sexual assault, 143–144
  See also Legislation and international
    treaties
Lawsuits, domestic violence cases, 10
Learned behavior theories, 113
Learned helplessness, 127
Lee, Hee Yun, 128
Lee, Mary, 61–62
Leeners, Brigitte, 80
"Legal and Social Service Responses to
  Child Sexual Abuse: A Primer and
  Discussion of Relevant Research"
  (Wiley), 86

National Longitudinal Survey of Mother-Child Sample, 19

National Scientific Council on the Developing Child (Center on the Developing Child), 57–58

National Survey of Adolescents, 72–73

National Survey of Child and Adolescent Well-Being (NSCAW)
- on behavioral problems in maltreated children, 60
- on caregiver/household placement instability, relational competence, 62
- caregivers represented in, 52*t*
- on child abuse, 29–31
- as child abuse data source, 21
- child service needs reported in NSCAW II, 48(*t*3.4)
- on child sexual abuse, 68
- on children exposed to domestic violence, 104
- on depression in children by placement setting, 63
- on developmental delays/neurological impairments, 54–55
- overview of, 26–29
- parents' need for alcohol/substance abuse treatment reported by NSCAW II, 53*t*
- parents' need for mental health services reported by NSCAW II, 54*t*
- risk factors identified by, 45–48
- risks in home setting reported by, 50*t*, 51*t*

National Survey of Child and Adolescent Well-Being, Child Well-Being Spotlight: Children in Out-of-Home Placements Receive More Psychotropic Medications and Other Mental Health Services Than Children Who Remain In-Home following a Maltreatment Investigation (Stambaugh et al.), 63–64

National Survey of Child and Adolescent Well-Being, Research Brief No. 18: Instability and Early Life Changes among Children in the Child Welfare System (Casanueva et al.), 52–53, 62

National Survey of Children's Exposure to Violence (NatSCEV)
- findings of, 17–18
- sexual victimization findings, 73–74

National Survey of Children's Exposure to Violence (NATSCEV I), Final Report (Finkelhor et al.), 74

National Violence against Women Survey (NVAWS)
- on domestic violence, 110–111
- on rape, 133, 135–136
- rape/sexual assault findings, 133, 135

Native Americans and Alaskan Natives
- emergency shelter/housing assistance under the VAWA's Grants to Indian Tribal Governments Program, victims receiving, 169(*t*9.8)

FVPSA funding purposes, 9

lifetime rape rate, 133

stalking victims, 151

VAWA's Grants to Indian Tribal Governments Program, police activities conducted as, by victimization type, 169(*t*9.7)

VAWA's Indian Tribal Governments Program, victims served by, by victimization type, 168(*f*9.2)

NatSCEV. *See* National Survey of Children's Exposure to Violence

The Nature and Scope of the Problem of Sexual Abuse of Minors by Catholic Priests and Deacons in the United States 1950–2002 (U.S. Conference of Catholic Bishops), 76–77

Nazer, Dena
- on child sexual abuse prosecution, 85
- testimony of children about sexual abuse, 87

NCADV (National Coalition against Domestic Violence), 114

NCANDS. *See* National Child Abuse and Neglect Data System

NCPCA. *See* National Center for Prosecution of Child Abuse

NCVS. *See* National Crime Victimization Survey

NCVS Victimization Analysis Tool, 129

"NCVS Victimization Analysis Tool (NVAT): Definitions" (DJS), 95–96

Neglect, child
- by caregivers as reported in NSCAW II, 56*t*
- definition of, 31
- family structure and, 44
- fatalities due to by age of victim, 59(*f*3.2)
- fatalities due to, by type of maltreatment, 59(*f*3.3)
- incidences of, 30
- perpetrators of, 33
- self-reported, 30–31

Neglect, definition of in state civil laws, 8

"Neighborhood Environment, Racial Position, and Risk of Police-Reported Domestic Violence: A Contextual Analysis" (Pearlman et al.), 114

Neurobiology, 54–58

New Hampshire, cyberstalking case in, 155

New York, high school dating violence in, 138

New York v. Ferber, 92

NFL (National Football League), 118–119

"NFL's Past Penalties for Domestic Violence 'a Different Story'" (Martinez), 118–119

NICHD (National Institute of Child Health and Human Development), 88

NIJ. *See* National Institute of Justice

"Nine Bills Stemming from Earl Bradley Case Become Law" (Delaware), 78

NIS. *See* National Incidence Study of Child Abuse and Neglect

NISVS. *See* National Intimate Partner and Sexual Violence Survey

Noll, Jennie G., 80–81

Nonfamily perpetrators
- of child sexual abuse, 75–78
- disclosure of abuse by victim and, 74
- educators, 75–76
- notorious predators in positions of trust, 77–78
- percentage of child sexual abuse by, 67–68
- priests, 76–77

Nonfatal Domestic Violence, 2003–2012 (Truman & Morgan)
- on domestic violence rates, 97
- on violent victimizations, 16–17

Nonphysical contact, 66

North Carolina, incest loophole, 93

Not Alone: The First Report of the White House Task Force to Protect Students from Sexual Assault (White House Task Force to Protect Students from Sexual Assault), 144

NSCAW. *See* National Survey of Child and Adolescent Well-Being

NSCAW II Baseline Report: Child Well-Being (Casanueva et al.)
- on behavioral problems in maltreated children, 60
- on depression in children by placement setting, 63
- on developmental delays/neurological impairments, 54–55
- on relational competence, 62
- risk factors identified by, 45

NSCAW II Baseline Report: Introduction to NSCAW II (Dolan et al.), 26–27

NSCAW II Baseline Report: Maltreatment (Casanueva et al.), 68

NSCAW II Wave 2 Report: Child Safety (Casanueva et al.)
- on child sexual abuse, 68
- on NSCAW II data, 29–31

NSCAW II Wave 3 Report: Wave 3 Tables (Casanueva et al.)
- on caregiver/household placement instability, relational competence, 62
- on children exposed to domestic violence, 104
- on effects of maltreatment, 45

NVAWS. *See* National Violence against Women Survey

NYTimes.com, 92–93

O

Obama, Barack, 144

O'Connor, Sandra Day, 89

Offenders

rapes/sexual assaults, among women aged 18–24, by victim-offender relationship college enrollment status of victim, 150(*t*8.18)

rapes/sexual assaults, by victim-offender relationship, 131*t*

rapes/sexual assaults, by victim-offender relationship, injury/medical treatment status, 126*t*

rapes/sexual assaults, by victim-offender relationship, race/Hispanic origin, 132*t*

rapes/sexual assaults, by victim-offender relationship, weapon use, 133*t*

rapes/sexual assaults, by victim-offender relationship/victim services status, 123*t*

victim-offender relationships in rape/sexual assault, 129, 131

violent victimizations, by victim-offender relationship, race/Hispanic origin, 130*t*

violent victimizations, by victim-offender relationship, type of victimization, victim services status, 121*t*–122*t*

See also Perpetrators

Office for Victims of Crime, 120

Office of Family Assistance (HHS), 42

Office of Head Start (Administration for Children and Families), 42

Office of Juvenile Justice and Delinquency Prevention (OJJDP)

National Survey of Children's Exposure to Violence, 17–18

NatSCEV project, 73

Office of Planning, Research, and Evaluation (OPRE)

description of, 21

NSCAW II data, 29–30

reporting of, 21

Office on Violence against Women (OVW)

CES Pilot Test, 144

on control motivations, 114

creation of, 9

on grant programs, 10

Stalking Resource Center, 152–153

Supplemental Victimization Survey, on stalking, 148–150

Ohio v. Roberts, 90

"On the Pervasiveness of Event-Specific Alcohol Use, General Substance Use, and Mental Health Problems as Risk Factors for Intimate Partner Violence" (Reingle et al.), 115

Ontario, Canada, child pornography ring in, 92

Original outcome measures

overview of, 40–41

state performance on, 40*t*

"Outrage over 6-Month Sentence for Brock Turner in Stanford Rape Case" (Fantz), 145–146

"Overcoming Sequelae of Childhood Sexual Abuse with Stress Management" (Wilson et al.), 82

OVW. *See* Office on Violence against Women

Owen, Richard, 77

P

Pallotta, Frank, 146

Palm, Cathleen, 7

Palmer, Janay, 118–119

Paltrow, Lynn M., 93

Palusci, Vincent J.

on child sexual abuse prosecution, 85

testimony of children about sexual abuse, reliability of, 87

"Parent Training for Attention Deficit Hyperactivity Disorder (ADHD) in Children Aged 5 to 18 Years" (Cochrane Database of Systematic Reviews), 63

Parental Drug Use as Child Abuse (Children's Bureau), 93

Parenting in America: Outlook, Worries, Aspirations Are Strongly Linked to Financial Situation (Parker, Horowitz, & Rehal), 1–2

Parents

as child sex abuse perpetrators, 67–68

childhood/youth victimization as risk factor for domestic violence, 116

corporal punishment, effects of, 19–20

family structures, changing, 1–3

foster, maltreatment by, 39

foster, of attachment disrupted infants, 62

high-risk behaviors in female child sexual abuse victims, 79–80

in-home mothers' need/referral to/receipt of domestic violence services, by age/race/ethnicity, 105*t*

murder of children, 110

need for alcohol/substance abuse treatment, 53*t*

need for mental health services, 54*t*

parental abuse victims, 17

self-reported violence/aggression/neglect, 30–31

substance-abuse of, 30

testimony of children and, 87

unemployed, risk factor of, 44–45

"Parents' Discipline of Young Children: Results from the National Survey of Early Childhood Health" (Regalado et al.), 19

Park, Eonju, 128

Parker, Kim, 1–2

Parramore, Constance, 161

"Participatory Action Research in Practice: A Case Study in Addressing Domestic Violence in Nine Cultural Communities" (Sullivan et al.), 167

Paterno, Joe, 77–78

"Pathways from Childhood Abuse and Neglect to HIV-Risk Sexual Behavior in Middle Adulthood" (Wilson & Widom), 61

Patient Protection and Affordable Care Act, 42

Pearlman, Deborah N., 114

Pedophiles, 78–79

Peer pressure, 140

PennLive.com, 77–78

Pennsylvania State University (Penn State), 77–78

Perpetrators

in adolescent child sexual abuse survey, 72–73

of child abuse, 26

of child abuse, factors influencing, 45

of child maltreatment, 33

of child maltreatment, by age, 29(*f*2.4)

of child maltreatment, by race/ethnicity, 29(*f*2.5)

of child maltreatment, by relationship to victim, 28(*t*2.6)

of child sexual abuse, 67–68

of cyberstalking, 153–157

date rape drugs used by, 140–142

disclosure of abuse by victim and, 74–75

high-risk behaviors in female child sexual abuse victims, 79–80

nonfamily perpetrators in positions of trust, 75–78

stalking, 148–152

stalking, lifetime reports of, by type of perpetrator, sex of victim, 154*f*

See also Offenders

Persky, Aaron, 145–146

Personal Responsibility and Work Opportunity Reconciliation Act

NSCAW studies authorized by, 26

risk factors identified by NSCAW, 45–48

Personality theories, 113

Peterson, Adrian, 20

Phillips Exeter Academy, 76

Phone calls

as part of stalking behavior, 148, 149

received by stalking victims, 151

Physical abuse

definition of in state civil laws, 7–8

incidences of, 30

Physical assault

as common type of victimization, 17

rates for polyvictims, 18

Physical contact acts, 66

Physical health. *See* Health

Physical violence

domestic, definition of, 105

intimate partner, overview of, 107

among intimate partners, 105–106

Placement instability

psychotropic medications and, 63–64

relational competence and, 62

victim-offender relationships, BJS on, 96

victim-offender relationships in rape/sexual assault, 129, 131

victims of child sexual assault, by age/injury status, 86*t*

victims of child sexual assault, by age/reporting to police, 85*t*

violent victimization, rates of by degree of violence/victim-offender relationship, 97(*t*6.3)

violent victimizations, 96–99

violent victimizations, by crime type, 96*t*

violent victimizations, by degree of violence/victim's sex/victim-offender relationship, 99(*t*6.4)

violent victimizations, by type of violence/weapon use/victim-offender relationship, 101*t*–103*t*

violent victimizations, by victim-offender relationship, 97(*t*6.2)

violent victimizations, by victim-offender relationship, race/Hispanic origin, 130*t*

violent victimizations, by victim-offender relationship/reporting to police, 162*t*

violent victimizations, locations of by victim-offender relationship, 100(*t*6.6)

violent victimizations, rates of among maltreated individuals, 61

See also Domestic violence

Victims of Trafficking and Violence Protection Act

description of, 166

passage of, 9

Violence

cycle of violence theory, 60–61

domestic, maltreatment victims and, 47–48

injury/medical treatment, violent victimizations resulting in by victim-offender relationship/types of injury/treatment status, 99(*t*6.5)

self-reported, 30–31

victim-offender relationship, by sex of victim, 98(*f*6.2)

victim-offender relationship, domestic violence rates, 98(*f*6.1)

violent victimization, rates of by degree of violence/victim-offender relationship, 97(*t*6.3)

violent victimizations, 96–99

violent victimizations, by crime type, 96*t*

violent victimizations, by degree of violence/victim's sex/victim-offender relationship, 99(*t*6.4)

violent victimizations, by type of violence/weapon use/victim-offender relationship, 101*t*–103*t*

violent victimizations, by victim-offender relationship, 97(*t*6.2)

violent victimizations, locations of by victim-offender relationship, 100(*t*6.6)

violent victimizations, rates of among maltreated individuals, 61

See also Domestic violence

"Violence, Abuse, and Crime Exposure in a National Sample of Children and Youth" (Finkelhor et al.), 73

Violence against Women Act (VAWA)

anti-stalking law in reauthorization of, 154

criminalization of stalking, 153

emergency shelter/housing assistance under the Grants to Indian Tribal Governments Program, victims receiving, 169(*t*9.8)

Grants to Encourage Arrest Policies/Enforcement of Protection Orders Program, case referrals funded by, by victimization type/conviction status, 167(*t*9.6)

Grants to Encourage Arrest Policies/Enforcement of Protection Orders Program, case referrals funded by, by victimization type/prosecution status, 167(*t*9.5)

Grants to Encourage Arrest Policies/Enforcement of Protection Orders Program, police activities conducted as part of, 167(*t*9.4)

Grants to Indian Tribal Governments Program, police activities conducted as, by victimization type, 169(*t*9.7)

Indian Tribal Governments Program, victims served by, by victimization type, 168(*f*9.2)

overview of, 9, 165–168

reauthorization of, 9–10

Violence against Women Reauthorization Act, 143–144

Violent Crime against Youth, 1994–2010 (White & Lauritsen), 74

Violent environments

children in, 16

National Crime Victimization Survey on, 16–17

National Survey of Children's Exposure to Violence, 17–18

Virginia Polytechnic Institute and State University, 165–166

Vuchinich, Sam, 80

Vulnerabilities, 123, 127

W

Walker, Lenore E., 127

Wallace-Capretta, Suzanne, 171

Walsh, Wendy A.

on child sexual abuse prosecution, 85–86

on online relationships of adolescents, 79

Walters, Mikel L., 111

Ward, Rose Marie, 81

Warshaw, Carole, 116

Washington, Crawford v., 90

Washington, Davis v., 90

Watkins, Laura E., 117

Waves. *See* Data collections, NSCAW

"'We Don't Have Time for Social Change': Cultural-Compromise and the Battered Woman Syndrome" (Rothenberg), 123

Weapons

domestic violence gun ban, 168

rapes/sexual assaults, by victim-offender relationship, weapon use, 133*t*

use of during rape/sexual assault, 131

used in domestic violence, 99

used in spousal homicides, 109–110

Well-being

children's well-being, national indicators of, 12*t*–14*t*

investigatory data, 30

national survey of, 26–29

NSCAW II data, 29–30

status of U.S. children, 11–16

violence/aggression/neglect, self-reported, 30–31

"What Is Domestic Violence?" (NCADV), 114

"What Is the Link between Corporal Punishment and Child Physical Abuse?" (Fréchette, Romano, & Zoratti), 20

What Works to Reduce Recidivism by Domestic Violence Offenders? (Miller & Drake, & Nafziger), 172

Wheeler v. United States, 86

"When Does a Battered Woman Seek Help from the Police? The Role of Battered Women's Functionality" (Lee, Park, & Lightfoot), 128

"Where Do the Children Go When They Are Taken Away?" (Rosenbloom), 39

"Where Teachers Are Still Allowed to Spank Students" (Anderson), 20

White, Nicole, 74

White House Task Force to Protect Students from Sexual Assault, 144

White v. Illinois, 90

Whites

child population, trends in, 11

child sexual abuse incidence rates, 68

college rape statistics, 140

corporal punishment, effects of, 19

dating violence rates for, 116–117

disclosure of abuse by, 74

high school rape, 137

lifetime rape rate, 133

rape/sexual assault offenders, 131

stalking victims, 151

victims of child sexual abuse, 67

Whiting, Jason, 118